Canadian and Australian Politics in Comparative Perspective

Canadian and Australian Politics in Comparative Perspective

HENRY S. ALBINSKI

New York
OXFORD UNIVERSITY PRESS
London Toronto 1973

With appreciation, to
W. F. D.
C. A. H.
J. D. B. M.
and other colleagues
and to Ethel

Library of Congress Catalogue Card Number: 72–91004
Printed in the United States of America

Preface

As its title suggests, this book deals with Canadian and Australian politics in comparative perspective. In the first place, the perspective is comparative in that the narrative is integrative, moving back and forth and striking comparisons between the two systems. Second, the material is developed within the distinctive, orienting, analytic framework of political process and outcomes. Three major themes which contribute to the process of politics are identified and treated at length. Briefly, these are societal inheritances and outlooks, the atmosphere in which organized politics is conducted, and the way in which authoritative decision-making takes place. Third, the interpretations which are offered are based on a distillation of various types of sources and data, including historical commentaries, social science literature on Canada and Australia, official documents, newspapers and journals of opinion, survey research and electoral data, and the author's own personal impressions gathered from research, observation, and discussions in Australia and Canada.

The author's genuinely felt debt of gratitude incurred in the preparation of this study extends to a great many individuals. Among them are academic, public, and other figures, primarily

Australian and Canadian, but American as well, through whose acquaintance the author's appreciation of Canada and Australia has been sharpened. It is in this sense that the book's dedication refers to colleagues, and more particularly to the men who were heads of departments at universities when the author held visiting appointments—Professor William F. Dawson of the University of of Western Ontario, Professor Colin A. Hughes of the University of Queensland, and Professor J. D. B. Miller of the Australian National University. This book is also dedicated to the author's wife, Dr. Ethel Bisbicos Albinski. Although not a political scientist, her own insights into Canadian and Australian society, her critical reading of the manuscript, and above all her good-humored patience and encouragement deserve a solid vote of thanks. Thanks also for the many kindnesses and material support rendered by the Department of Political Science and the Central Fund for Research of the Pennsylvania State University, and to Mrs. Lucia Swanson and Miss Susan Sorrell for typing contributions well beyond the call of duty.

H. S. A.

University Park, Pennsylvania
February 1972

Contents

I
SOCIETAL CONDITIONS AND PUBLIC VALUES

In Canada and Australia, as in other political systems, the style and consequences of political life are intimately associated with the legacy of political culture, meaning the nature and distribution of politically relevant public outlooks. Such outlooks have, in turn, been shaped by a variety of social, demographic, economic, and historically derived forces.

The first section examines the characteristic features of the Canadian and Australian political cultures—their content, the impulses which have conditioned them, and the implications which they carry for systemic coherence and performance. Our first concern will be with public perceptions of the two systems as legitimate and attractive objects of authority. We will then explore the degree to which the two publics do or do not have reason to express satisfaction with the adequacy of and manner in which material and nonmaterial resources and opportunities have been distributed, both among individuals as such and among variously defined groups. With these considerations in mind, we will then evaluate the extent to which the two societies are willing and able to associate themselves with political life and its implied responsibilities, and their propensity to seek social change or redress through mutually accepted or extrasystemic channels.

1

Value systems: systemic legitimacy, public authority, and national consciousness

National genesis and cultural norms

Circumstances surrounding the foundation of the Canadian and Australian nations suggest certain theories about the development of political attitudes and behavioral patterns in the two societies. Canada and Australia began their modern national experience at fairly proximate points—Canada in 1867, Australia in 1901. Both had been claimed for European powers—Canada for France by Jacques Cartier in 1524, Australia for Britain by James Cook in 1770. At the time of European annexation, populations of native Canadian Indians and Australian Aborigines were already well-established. French colonists began settling in Canada in the early seventeenth century. British settlements eventually appeared in Nova Scotia and Newfoundland. With the French defeat in the Seven Years' War (French and Indian War), French Canada was ceded to Britain in 1763, and with it, its French-Canadian inhabitants. The secession of the thirteen American colonies from Britain prompted European settlement in both Canada and Australia. American loyalists and subsequently British settlers, arrived in Canada. Thus Canada, within the space of a few years, not only came under British jurisdiction, but began its march toward becoming a dominantly English-speaking and English-oriented society, superimposed upon a significant historical French community. Australia took the place of the American colonies as a repository for British convicts, and criminals continued to be transported there until the middle of the nineteenth century. The original convicts were quickly followed by free settlers, who eventually became a majority, while much of the convict element was assimilated into the general population.

This historical background left an indelible stamp on the society and politics of both emerging countries. When they became separate nations, their European populations were about equal. The Canadian population in 1867 was about 3,500,000, and in 1901 Australia's population was 3,700,000. The Australian people were, however, almost entirely of British descent, and had evolved under a common set of British cultural and political traditions. Canada began its national life with a population one-third French, and the remainder British, except for some 6 per cent whose ancestry was neither French nor British. As will be explained, Canada's heterogeneity involved much more than differences of language and manners; the differences touched on basic points of political outlook, style, and expectation. Furthermore, the bicultural partnership in Canada involved the French as a conquered people, and the British as conquerors.

At confederation, Australia was already geographically complete, but Canada only partially completed. To be sure, the Northern Territory, comprising 520,000 of Australia's nearly 3 million square miles, and the Yukon and the Northwest Territories, containing nearly a million and a half of Canada's 3,800,000 square miles, still lack state/provincial status, and authority over them rests with the respective federal governments. But the current complement of six Australian states—New South Wales, Queensland, South Australia, Tasmania, Victoria, and Western Australia—formed part of the original federation of 1901. On the other hand, Canada in 1867 was comprised of only four of the present ten provinces—New Brunswick, Nova Scotia, Ontario, and Quebec. Three other provinces joined shortly thereafter—Manitoba in 1870, British Columbia in 1871, and Prince Edward Island in 1873. But Alberta and Saskatchewan did not acquire provincial status until 1905, and Newfoundland not until 1949. Moreover, several of the provinces underwent substantial boundary changes in the years following their attainment of provincial status.

Although all Australian states had, as colonies, established working political institutions, there had been no comparable experience in 1867 within what were to become Canada's western provinces. Thus, from the standpoint of the inclusiveness and continuity of member political parts, the idea of "nationhood" may therefore be regarded as a more concrete concept for the Australians, at an earlier stage, than for the Canadians. Also, all Australian states, unlike the present Canadian provinces, shared in the building of the country's early political-party formations, developed related political styles, and otherwise were able to encourage a relative uniformity of public expectations.

Neither Canada nor Australia entered nationhood without some prior cooperative efforts among what later became provinces and states. In this sense, the two publics were already to some degree aware of the necessity for some senior authority. This was especially true in Canada. There had been experience with political cooperation, especially between "Canada West" (Ontario) and "Canada East" (Quebec), in the form of a "Province of Canada" since 1840. The presence of both English- and French-speaking groups in the Province of Canada introduced a practice of English and French "double majorities" and dual English-French leadership under a system of representative and ministerially responsible government. It was a cumbersome arrangement, but in the quarter century of its existence it did produce an atmosphere of mutual political effort. The Australian colonies in prefederation times failed to evolve any formal political bonds. For at least fifteen years prior to federation, however, a fairly elaborate scheme of intercolonial cooperation was instituted under the direction of the Federal Council of Australia. Furthermore, there was considerable interchange and cooperation in such nonofficial realms as trade unions and business organizations.

The end product of political union in Canada and Australia was the result of about a decade of deep and widely publicized deliberations, both within what were to become provinces and states, and at conferences among them. Since neither Canadian nor Australian federation was achieved precipitously, the two publics had become adjusted to the prospect of living under a higher national political authority. When the compacts of 1867 and 1901 were confirmed, no major political-party group in either country was irreconcilably opposed to them. Numerous nonpolitical leaders such as prominent religious figures, Protestant and Catholic alike, also favored union.

Despite these various forms of conditioning, the publics themselves did not universally welcome national union, though negative sentiment was far more prominent among the Canadians. Despite some reservations about the need for or terms of federation, no Australian colony chose to remain apart from the new Commonwealth. Advisory popular referendums were conducted in all the colonies, though the Western Australian referendum occurred shortly after the constitutional bill had been approved by the British Crown. Throughout Australia, federation was favored by a 2.5 to 1 margin, and each colony voted affirmatively. Canadian confederation began under less auspicious conditions. There were no popular referendums to test popular opinion. However, Prince Edward Island and Newfoundland, two of the original participants in the discussions of the 1860's refused to associate themselves with the 1867 compact. Nova Scotia and New Brunswick joined, but in the face of considerable resistance from their publics, and only after substantial political maneuvering, including the promise of an intercolonial railway which would connect them with the central portions of Canada. At one point, the pro-confederation New Brunswick colonial government was driven from office in an election fight over the confederation issue. The Maritime provinces were jealous of their political independence. They feared that their economic interests would be neglected and even sacrificed to the cause of western Canadian development. They were also uneasy about being subject to the governance of a greater, united Canada which would be one-third French. When the legislature of the Province of Canada voted on confederation, only 26 of its French-Canadian members were in favor, and 22 were opposed.

Certain common impulses inspired the Canadian and Australian movements for national unification. A comparison of these impulses helps us understand why union was received much more ambivalently in Canada than in Australia. In particular, the comparison illuminates the decidedly lower degree of societal integration which was present in Canada in 1867 than in Australia in 1901.

Canadian and Australian proponents of an overall national authority sought a more efficient basis for conducting economic and administrative business than was possible under the divers colonial governments. They regarded unification as a spur to national development. Especially in Australia they sought to eliminate competing intercolonial practices. Unification was also championed in both countries on grounds of national defense and even survival. Australia was a numerically small community on a huge island-continent. It was part of European society, but thousands of miles removed from traditional European centers; it was situated on the doorstep of a potentially volatile Asia, yet virtually unprotected. The people were genuinely frightened by international colonial rivalries in the Pacific, by Russian ambitions, and eventually by the motives of a militarily potent Japan. At one point, the Queensland colonial government, acting alone, launched an expedition into New Guinea, desperately trying to alert London to the dangers of further German penetration into the eastern portion of the island. The security impulse for Australian federation also had a racial feature. Australians were determined to devise a common and effective migration policy which, by blocking the entry of Asians, would preserve the ideal of a white, western, and wealthy Australia. They had already experienced friction with the Chinese who had come to work the Victorian gold fields, and with Kanaka Pacific islanders, who had been imported for labor on Queensland's sugar fields. Canadians, on the other hand, were not geographically isolated, nor particularly fearful of racial absorption. Their apprehension derived from their location vis-à-vis the United States. In 1775, American colonial troops had crossed into Canada, hoping to enlist French Canadian support against British authority. They found the French unreceptive, however, and were forced to retreat. There had been severe fighting on the Great Lakes during the War of 1812, and American troops had burned York (Toronto). There were innumerable disputes with the United States' government relating to boundaries and economic relations.

The American Civil War was an object-lesson to the Canadians. They saw in it the fruits of an imperfect and contentious union. In 1865 they also viewed the United States as a formidable military power, as a country which resented Britain's solicitude toward the South, and as a muscle-flexing society with certain factions not averse to annexing or otherwise dominating a relatively defenseless Canada. In 1866, various portions of Canada were actually attacked by the Fenians, Irish fanatics who had learned military skills during the Civil War. Canadian confederation was therefore impelled by the conviction of many Canadians, French and English alike, that a national union among them would deter threats of invasion from their neighbor.

Turning now to dissimilar tendencies in the two societies prior to nationhood, by 1901, Australian union had been preceded by a well-developed sense of community. In Canada, the 1867 compact represented a national unity which still awaited a genuine spirit of Canadian community, mainly because of tensions between the English and French subcultures. Therefore, 1867 was regarded by many Canadians as an opportunity to *undertake* construction of a real national identity.

When the Act of Union for the Province of Canada was passed in 1840, French-speaking Canada East had 200,000 more inhabitants than did predominantly English-speaking Canada West. Nonetheless, the two parts were equally represented in the legislature. Within a generation, the West's population had outstripped the East, raising English demands for representation by population. The French agreed to the new national government, but with the stipulation that the political order be federally organized, and French Canada guaranteed autonomy in key areas. A further incentive for the French to accept the confederation was, once again, much less a concern for "Canada" as such, but rather for the preservation of French-Canadian linguistic, religious, and cultural inheritances. Fear of English/Protestant *Canadian* domination was counterbalanced in 1867 by a fear of assimilation into a giant English/Protestant United States. The American population was at that time 40 million, more than ten times greater than Canada's.

Once confederation had been achieved, most English Canadians construed the national undertaking as a bargain struck among various and diverse individuals. French Canadians decidedly did not regard confederation as a democracy of numbers, but as a compact between two conspicuous and distinct cultures, without reference to relative numerical strength. In Australia, although state loyalties remained strong after 1901, nationhood was not inaugurated under a pall of such stubbornly held subcultural allegiances, or divergent views of what the promise of a federated Australia was all about.

Public views of state authority

Popular opinion about the activities of constituted state authority is instructive in two ways. First, it can suggest whether or not the state at large is regarded respectfully, free of suspicions which could otherwise impugn its legitimacy. Second, public opinion can disclose the openly sanctioned parameters of state activism which help to define the workings of the socioeconomic system.

The character and disposition of the groups which settled Australia and Canada have contributed to the evolution of public viewpoints about the state. It should be kept in mind that, whatever other differences there may be between Australians and Canadians, the Australian settlers came from essentially common national and cultural stock, while Canadian society did not. French Canadians regarded themselves as a conquered people and something of an embattled minority, and felt that the state authority which emerged in 1867 was only in a limited sense a matter of their personal choosing. To them the Canada of 1867 was essentially an "English" invention, reflecting perhaps the same British authority that in the eighteenth century had expelled French Acadians from Nova Scotia, and asserted itself over French Canada at large. It was British authority which had attempted a forced assimilation of the French community for a time in the 1830's and 1840's.

The French in Quebec (Québecois) acquired a defensive outlook, which was parochial, and concretely oriented toward French Canadian values. Although this orientation did not lend itself to a strong attachment to Canada at large, it did not preclude respect for authority per se. There was something of a feudal inheritance within the French community, stressing patterns of hierarchical authority and encouraging submission to a detailed regulation of life. The Roman Catholic church in French Canada, before and after confederation, was a powerful and authoritative influence. It focused on "community" as defined by language, religion, and tradition, characteristics associated with Quebec specifically, not with the Canadian national state. The defense of the French-Canadian homeland implied a suspicion of real or imagined Anglo-Saxon, Protestant, and therefore national, intrusions. This French "solitude" within the province of Quebec was hardened by the absence of any supportive loyalty for many of the Québecois. They felt no particular affinity for Britain, for the

United States, or even for France, with which their contacts virtually vanished after the Conquest. For French Canada, the temper of the French Revolution had been unnervingly iconoclastic, and there was resentment against the secularism of the Third Republic, whose founding nearly coincided with Canadian confederation.

Such antinationalistic tendencies were missing among English-speaking Canadians. Their outlook was more expansive, more innovative than the French, and therefore less prejudiced against national authority. In this way English Canadians were more like Australians than Canadians of French extraction, though the comparison is by no means perfect. For instance, there was no Australian counterpart of the American loyalists who ventured into Canada. These loyalists carried a truly strong spirit of allegiance to authority; it was a loyalty to the British Crown, but indirectly to the Crown's government in Canada. Nor, for instance, was there a Canadian counterpart of the Australian convict population. Upon emancipation, these persons looked to Australia as a fresh opportunity for closing out their lives. They were generally without means, and depended upon "government," that is, public authority, to supply land and job opportunities. Members of the British middle class did migrate to Australia, but in general the socioeconomic status of British migrants in Australia was more depressed than the status of those who entered Canada. Migrants came to both countries in search of opportunity. They often encountered a harsh climate, poor land, and difficult terrain. Only official authority could insure security, open and clear lands, establish roads and transport systems, and otherwise provide the funds for development that private enterprise was too weak or timid to handle.

The Canadian and Australian societies could not approach self-regulation; government was the prime regulator. Official power was called upon to prevent settlement from proceeding in haphazard fashion. In Australia the weight of public authority was eventually applied to break up the land holdings of the so-called squatter element. In Canada, western expansion was supervised by militia and police (that is, agents of public authority), which maintained order, dealt with Indians, and served to counteract American influence. Eventually, the Northwest Mounted Police (later the Royal Canadian Mounted Police), a national police organization, oversaw expansion in the west, and provided an official presence in various gold-mining communities such as the Klondike. To this day, the RCMP serves across the country, helping to enforce a common, all-Canadian criminal law code. It frequently assists in the enforcement of provincial laws and supplements local police forces, including those in Ontario and Quebec, where there are all-provincial as well as local forces. Australia has no force equivalent to the RCMP. But from prefederation times to now, police functions have been strictly centralized under colonial/state rather than local control. By comparison with the United States, the Canadian and Australian traditions in legal and/or law-enforcement organizations have long reflected more centralization, and therefore a more apparent tendency toward public authority.

By the time federation had arrived in the two countries, and for a time following, state activity in socioeconomic fields had acquired characteristics broadly congruent with public expectations. In this way, systemic legitimacy was enhanced, easing the development of the two new political systems during their formative years. The absence of a nobility or an established upper class in either country made for more uniform public views about what legitimate authority was, and helped to avert sharp class conflict over permissible state action. But there were important Canadian-Australian distinctions relating to state intervention. In the latter part of the nineteenth century, Canadian state involvement in socioeconomic affairs existed, but it reflected two conditions which differentiated it from Australia: a stronger mercantile-entrepreneurial class, and the French Canadian subculture.

Canada's "National Policy" in this period emphasized economic diversification and improved communications. The state employed such means as erecting tariff barriers to foster native industry, overseeing territorial expansion, and using public funds to assist the construction of interprovincial railways. It was a policy designed not only to raise material standards as such but, particularly, to promote national unity in a geographically strung out and culturally mixed society. The French did not object to this strategy, since the state's intervention did not result in an actual invasion into Quebec's domain. Other, dominantly English-speaking provinces, being more materialistic and achievement-oriented, found a "National Policy" type of state activism stylistically congenial. For both of Canada's cultural communities, therefore, legitimacy bonds tended to be strengthened, and precedents were set for future, more elaborate state action for relieving economic discontent.

In so far as governmental social service measures were concerned, early Australian and Canadian experience also seemed to coincide with popular dispositions. The Australian society was more egalitarian, more working-class conscious, and less able to rely on the exertions of private business classes. In English Canada, Protestant social morality preached that charity was a private thing, while in Quebec the Catholic church was the prime dispenser of public welfare. And so for decades after confederation, state-directed welfare programs in Canada were extremely modest. Australians, however, pressed for, and got, an early and substantial governmental role in social services. Before the colonies had federated in 1901, railways were publicly owned. There were minimum wage laws and legislation governing working conditions. Government regulation of industrial conciliation and arbitration was introduced. In 1900 and 1901, New South Wales and Victoria adopted an old-age pension. Within a dozen years after federation, the Commonwealth government had enacted programs regulating old age and invalid pensions and child allowances to mothers, and put into force a system of basic wage-setting and industrial dispute settlement techniques across the country.

Canadian and Australian attitudes toward public authority have been refined in several other ways. Both systems have developed elaborate bureaucratic forms, and considerable dependence upon them. The elaboration of bureaucratic structures has resulted from the expansion of dual layers of federal and state/provincial enterprises, and from the general multiplication of official concerns in social and economic matters. Primary-industry groups, elaborate business concentrations, and trade unions have become prominent. They have established intricate relationships with federal and state/provincial authorities via agricultural marketing arrangements, tariff boards, state-created mechanisms dealing with labor-management relations, and in other ways. For Australians and Canadians, "authority" has in this sense become both commonplace and necessary.

The Canadian and Australian acceptance of authority has been pragmatically rather than ideologically motivated. There has been little sentiment in either society to glorify the mantle of authority for its own sake, and reform movements have generally sought to employ government as a means toward limited ends rather than consummatory ideals. The lack of reverence for authority has, in Australia, acquired special overtones. The Australian penchant for expecting a constructive governmental role has been coupled with a conviction that governments and their political agents are to be kept strictly accountable. The overgenerous or casual investiture of authority in governments poses dangers of elitism and of superordination to a self-consciously egalitarian society. Such feelings are partially founded in historical experience. For instance, there was an absence of a great patriotic movement, or clashes with or undue reliance upon the state while the Australian community was being molded. Rather, as we have seen, the Australian sense of community was established before nationhood. The Australian ethos was born of individualism in the bush country and transplanted to the cities, evoked by a sense of self-interested solidarity within primary producing and working-class communities.

As part of the syndrome of diffidence toward authority, Australians are sometimes reputed to be contemptuous of rules, and of the enforcers of rules. Canadians, on the other hand, are seldom characterized as fractious or disrespectful of the law and its agents. Actually, by western standards, neither society has a particularly high crime rate, especially in major crime categories. Where Australians appear to be somewhat less law abiding, or at least more independent vis-à-vis the law, is in fairly specialized circumstances. For example, they are at or near the top of the world in number of traffic fatalities per miles traveled, a not surprising statistic to observers of Australian driving habits.

Popular reactions toward the police in Canada appear to be more favorable than they are in Australia, but not dramatically so. A mid-1960's survey in selected Australian states indicated that 64 per cent of the public held the police in great respect; 29 per cent had mixed feelings, and only 2 per cent felt little respect. In 1967, 72 per cent of a nationwide sample expressed great respect, 23 per cent some respect, and only 4 per cent hardly any respect. Canadian data for 1969 showed 76 per cent approving of the way in which the police performed their jobs in the community, while 11 per cent were explicitly opposed. During a separate survey in Toronto, 85 per cent expressed very favorable to moderate feelings toward the police, and only 2 or 3 per cent were unfavorably disposed. In late 1970, when Quebec separatists carried out two kidnappings and a murder, the Canadian federal government imposed the War Measures Act. Troops were posted in various Quebec cities and in Ottawa, and security forces were granted great latitude in arrest and detention. All this was done with little public explanation of how much of a conspiracy to undermine or overthrow constituted authority by the terrorists was actually involved. Yet, various surveys disclosed that over 85 per cent of the Canadian public applauded this extraordinary show of force and authority, and that Quebec residents themselves were almost if not as much as other Canadians disposed to sanction the measures.

In our effort to contrast Canadian and Australian public outlooks toward authority and its agents, data of this sort must be used cautiously. For instance, it cannct be overlooked that the Canadian War Measures Act was imposed in an exceptional, emotionally supercharged atmosphere; acquiescence in the use of forceful methods may have had more to do with fear, or with revenge against Quebec terrorists, than with pliant acceptance of authority. On the Australian side, it may be instructive that the strongest respect for police is found among older and less well-educated people, that is, persons who might be considered the most "unmodern" and most bound by an allegedly traditional cultural antipathy toward the police. Another variable which might affect public perceptions is the nature of the police themselves. The overall educational level of Australian police is lower than among their Canadian counterparts; a substantial number of Australian policemen have not gone beyond the primary grades. If there is adverse feeling toward the Australian police force, it may be more attributable to the qualities of the policemen, rather than to a more diffused dislike for symbols of authority. In any event, it has been contended that conventional Australian views of authority have made a special contribution to upholding public institutions. For instance,

> our profound suspicion of authority and pretentiousness provides some safeguard against the main danger of our time: dictatorship from either the right or the left . . . it is probably harder to imagine a Hitler, a Stalin or even a Perón flourishing here than in any other country on earth, including England itself.*

National identification and nationalism

Conceptions of nationhood are an important dimension of political culture. Nationhood is not a synonym for patriotism as such,

* Russel Ward, *The Australian Legend* (Melbourne: Oxford University Press, 1958), p. 239.

though patriotic feelings may be a part of the concept. Our interest lies in uncovering the manner and extent to which the Canadian and Australian people have become conditioned to displaying a common attachment, pride, and loyalty toward their national communities. Are Canadians and Australians united or divided in their regard for nationhood? Do they construe their countries as proper and legitimate entities, deserving of support, and perhaps even of exertion and sacrifice?

We begin by probing for clues in the ethnic and cultural makeup of the two publics. Other variables being equal, a working generalization is that an ethnically and culturally homogeneous society is apt to carry a more unified, and stronger, sense of nationhood than a heterogeneous one. The homogeneous society fosters a more widely shared set of values, political and otherwise. Moreover, ethnically/culturally heterogeneous societies are more susceptible to intergroup suspicions or rivalries. For instance, if one group jealously guards itself against the real or imaginary domination of others, it tends to disparage the political system, which it holds responsible for its grievances.

Differences between Canadian and Australian ethnic composition have always been striking. Throughout the nineteenth century Australia's population was remarkably uniform. By the time of federation, the country was approximately 97 per cent Anglo-Saxon in origin. There was some Italian and Yugoslavian and a bit of other non-British migration in the 1920's, but there was very little change in the makeup of the population during Australia's first half century. Massive post-World War II migration has been over half non-Anglo-Saxon, resulting in a drop to under 1 in 10 of the population of British extraction.

In Canada, as has been seen, the French population's majority was gradually supplanted, and at confederation the country was one-third French, and about 60 per cent Anglo-Saxon. The French proportion has remained essentially intact. The principal change has come in the steady lowering of the Anglo proportion to a present figure of about 44 per cent, the remainder primarily being of non-French, Continental European derivation. A fraction of each country is of native stock—Indian, Eskimo, and Australian aboriginal. Historically, therefore, both in its formative stages, and for decades afterward, the Australian population was unusually homogeneous, while the Canadian population since shortly after the Conquest has never been so, creating a national mosaic of large numbers of two and later three population components—French, English, and other, or "ethnics" as they are called, all with potentially distinct impressions of the nation, and of their place in it.

Anglo-Canadians, as the numerically largest and economically and politically most powerful group, have not, as a whole had any special reason to dissociate themselves from positive feelings toward Canada. The French, particularly in their ancestral home of Quebec, have had less reason to embrace the notion of nationhood with equal conviction. Not only did they begin as a minority at confederation, and have remained so, but they remember that they were once the paramount group, only to be conquered and then outscored in numbers and wealth by Anglo-Saxons.

The fact that the French have remained at a third of the population since 1867 is in itself remarkable. In the second half of the nineteenth and the first quarter of the twentieth centuries, some 1 million Quebeckers migrated to the United States in search of better conditions. Although there are in the neighborhood of a million and a half persons of French extraction outside Quebec, even in New Brunswick, where they constitute 40 per cent of the population, there has been a noticeable tendency for them to lose their French language, and otherwise to merge with the Anglo community. There has been only the most incidental replenishment of Canada's French population through migration from France itself. Quebec receives a disproportionately small number of migrants who enter Canada from any source; in 1970, under 16 per cent of new arrivals settled in Quebec, compared to nearly 55 per cent who selected Ontario. The great majority of persons who do settle in Quebec, regardless of their origin, tend to assimilate into the English-language community, despite the fact that Quebec is 80 per cent French. Understandably, Quebec has traditionally been more resistant to large-scale migration than has the rest of Canada. In Australia, for non-English-speaking arrivals, wherever they settle, there is only one option open for linguistic and cultural assimilation. The French in Canada have maintained their 1 in 3 ratio by sheer reproductive prowess. But their birth rate, once among the world's highest, has by now actually fallen below the all-Canadian level, exacerbating historically conditioned feelings of minority and inferior status.

These French-Canadian feelings, and correlate perceptions of nationhood, have been reinforced by certain patterns of socialization. Much of Canadian history has been written in terms of the tension, or even conflict, between the two major groups. Generations of French-Canadian children in Quebec have been inculcated with a version of history stressing the plight of the French and the sturdiness of their defense against waves of English-Protestant influence. Outside Quebec, Canadian children have been served a very different ideological diet. Again, no counterpart problem exists in Australia.

Quebec's misgivings about heavy migration by non-French people have had a partial Australian parallel. Australian thinking has historically tended toward insularity. This was brought about by geographic isolation, tense experiences with Asian and Pacific-island workers in the nineteenth century, by a certain narrow-minded pride in the "good society" that was under construction, and by fears that economic standards would be impaired. For decades, this insularity meant the virtually total exclusion of non-Europeans, and only a minor intake of Continental Europeans. Racial prejudice was often openly expressed. There also was prejudice against the small non-Anglo European community, and even some unflattering reaction to the "Poms," recent arrivals from Britain. Still, Australia's racial and ethnic uniformity, in terms of our analysis, avoided the creation of distinctive and potentially antagonistic groups. The vigor with which many Australians held to their pride of being such a homogeneous society probably in itself was a fillip to building a sense of nationhood—identifiably white, western, and reasonably affluent.

The appearance of hundreds of thousands of non-British migrants in Australia after World War II was originally received with some misgivings. The official justifications for the ambitious migration program, were, however, consistent with popular opinions. A larger population was needed for security purposes, and the memory of Japanese advances through Southeast Asia during the war was very vivid. A larger population was needed to insure economic growth, an argument which made sense to people who recalled the dismal years of the depression, only a decade removed. The migrants have come from a variety of countries—Greece, Italy, Yugoslavia, Poland, the Netherlands, and so on. This very mixture has obviated the possibility that Australian society would take form in the Canadian fashion, with two distinctive and numerically significant ethnic groups confronting one another. The "New Australians'" appearance from the late 1940's onward has occurred in a period of strong economic performance and high employment. The migrants have not huddled together in one or two locations, but have spread themselves quite evenly among the several states and the capital cities. A recent change in policy has resulted in the admission of permanent Asian settlers, now numbering several thousand annually. This too has become generally acceptable, in part for the same reasons which apply to non-British white migrants, and in part because the Asian migrants are very carefully screened for their skills, education, linguistic competence, and the like.

Australia's non-Anglo newcomers have not, in any event, become estranged from their adopted country. The dissatisfied can and often do leave, and since the mid-1960's departures by migrants generally have been rising year by year. Many of those who remain look upon Australia as an opportunity for betterment, or an escape from political, social, economic, or other problems they may have experienced at home.

By and large, Canadian "ethnics" have also adopted a positive and approving national outlook. Their roots in Canada reach back several generations. They are in this sense an integral part of Canadian national growth and development, not newcomers upon the scene of an Anglo-based, ready-made community, as applies in Australia. If anything, these people, especially in the Prairie provinces, where they are concentrated and where they greatly outnumber the resident French population, often seem to be more "all-Canadian" spirited than are Canadian Anglos. The ethnics have found a good life in Canada, and feel that the French in Quebec are as they are—a cultural minority, no more, no less. Therefore, they tend to be among Canada's staunchest opponents of concessions to and special treatment for Quebec. Many believe that such capitulations will impair Canada's national viability, and they resent what they perceive to be preferential treatment for the French, unavailable to Ukrainians, Germans, and others.

In Canada, the cultural gaps among different conceptions of nationhood have been increased by additional breakdowns in public socialization. For instance, there is the obstacle of communication. In 1941, 17 per cent of the population was bilingual in English and French; by 1961, the figure has dipped to 12 per cent. Although proportionately more French-origin persons know English than non-French-descended persons know French, various obstacles have reduced French Quebec's understanding of what was happening and what was being said in the nine English-speaking provinces. As of 1970, no French newspaper had resident correspondents outside Quebec, the national capital of Ottawa, or Paris. This included Montreal's *La Presse* which, with a circulation of 220,000, is the largest French-language paper in North America. The English press has done better. In 1970, Toronto's *Globe and Mail,* Canada's most influential English-language paper, in addition to Ontario and foreign cities, had offices in Vancouver, in Montreal, and in Quebec City, and then created an office in Halifax. On the other hand, American news, and even world news filtered through American services, is bombarding Canadians through all the media. Canada's Royal Commission on Bilingualism and Biculturalism (B and B) discovered in the 1960's that there was a wide, and nationally devisive, perceptual gap between English- and French-speaking young people. Sixty-eight per cent of the English felt they had more in common with English-speaking Canadians and *Americans* than with a combination of English- and French-speaking *Canadians;* 41 per cent of the French respondents chose the first category, and 39 per cent the latter.

Australia's relative homogeneity has prevented such problems of selective socialization, and therefore, a split in the society's national perceptual set. Australian survey research has not probed public feelings about divisions among cultural groups and the appropriate distribution of privileges to particular sectors of the country, because such topics are not meaningful there. In Canada, however, this type of opinion research has flourished. Data from 1969 indicate, for example, that 61 per cent of Quebeckers, as opposed to 32 per cent in Ontario and only 24 per cent in the west, believe that a Canadian prime minister should encourage Quebec's claims. In the same year, asked whether Quebec should enjoy a special constitutional status, 20 per cent of Quebec's residents agreed, while only 1 per cent in Ontario and in the west agreed. Canadians in 1967 were asked whether they were interested in the country's centennial celebrations. There was no great enthusiasm at large, but Quebec respondents were by far the most ambivalent: 41 per cent of them could not say. Indeed, for a combination of reasons, including their cultural divisions and

American influences of all kinds, Canadians on the whole are strikingly unsure of what "Canadianism" means to them. A 1970 survey indicated that a quarter of the population interpreted "Canadian nationalism" as meaning a united Canada, less than a quarter as a personal dedication to Canada, and a tenth as independence from foreign control (that is, a negative definition). Some 46 per cent could not at all define what "Canadian nationalism" meant to them. A useful comparative example of how cultural divisions affect national unity can be drawn from Canadian and Australian military history. In the nineteenth century, Australian men were readily enlisted for service with the British in the Sudan and in South Africa during the Boer War. The Canadian government did not authorize troops for the Sudan, partially because it recognized no significant Canadian interest, partially because it did not wish to invite an English-French dispute. Canadian troops were, however, dispatched to South Africa. The decision was made to pacify the English-speaking community, but it offended the French. Both countries entered the two world wars, made impressive manpower investments, and took heavy casualties. The issue of conscription divided both countries, in both wars, and especially during the 1914–18 conflict. The Canadian public was divided along essentially cultural lines—English for conscription, French against. When Australians argued over conscription, the division was considerably more diffused.

Symbolic aspects of nationhood

Symbols are intangible, but they can rally, divide, or leave people indifferent toward images of nation and nationhood. Australian and Canadian symbolic national inspiration will be examined from several, disparate standpoints.

Both Australia and Canada are federal systems, meaning that jurisdiction is divided between central and state/provincial authorities. Both countries are immense, and their small populations are literally stretched from one ocean to another. The two most distant Canadian provincial capitals, Victoria, British Columbia, and St. John's, Newfoundland, are over 4300 road miles apart. Perth, Western Australia, and Brisbane, Queensland, Australia's most widely separated state capitals, are 3200 miles apart. As the crow flies, Perth is closer to Djakarta, Indonesia, than it is to Sydney, while Vancouver is closer to the Soviet Union than it is to Montreal. In Canada, the distinctive English and French subcultures can be interpreted as deterrents to a strong sense of nationhood, because local loyalties are self-perpetuating. The presence of a magnetic federal capital might therefore be a partial counterweight to fissiparous tendencies. Neither Canberra nor Ottawa, however, qualifies as a natural symbol of nationhood.

Historically, Ottawa has a better claim than Canberra as a national seat. Ottawa was the capital of the Province of Canada even before confederation, and has always been Canada's capital. Canberra, however, did not even exist when the Commonwealth of Australia was formed in 1901. Because Sydney and Melbourne were the capitals of the rival states of New South Wales and Victoria, neither would accept the other as the national capital. It was therefore decided to build a new capital. An Australian Capital Territory was carved out of an inland portion of New South Wales (and another fragment, on the coast), and a capital city named Canberra was to be erected there. For years, Melbourne served as an interim capital, until Canberra opened for business in 1927—a generation late. For many years afterward, a number of federal government departments continued to be housed in Melbourne, and the transition is not yet complete. Officials often regarded Canberra posts as exile to a Godforsaken place. The town grew very slowly, had few amenities, and no industry to speak of save government. To this day, Australian federal parliamentarians are more inclined to scatter to their homes across the country when Parliament is out of session than their Canadian counterparts are inclined to depart from Ottawa. National organizations with political interests were slower to establish offices in Canberra than in Ottawa.

Canberra has undergone remarkable changes since the advent of the 1950's. It now houses a distinguished university; a beautification program has made great strides, and there are now some light industries in the area. Tourists pour in. Canberra's population has skyrocketed, and by the beginning of the 1970's, stood at 130,000. By comparison, despite continuing to be a basically government town, Ottawa has always been larger and more diversified. The greater Ottawa area had over half a million people as of the 1970's. Nevertheless, neither city approaches the size or cosmopolitan reputation or financial concentration found in the 2 million-plus population cities of Sydney, Melbourne, Montreal, and Toronto.

Geographically, Canberra lies within the southeast corner of Australia's most densely populated area. But that location makes it very remote from Western Australia and northern Queensland communities, and the city is not easily accessible by most means of transport. Ottawa is more central vis-à-vis Canada at large. It is on the border of the two largest provinces, and is well served by highways and by rail and air transport. Even so, Victoria, British Columbia, is nearly 2800 road miles from Ottawa—several hundred less than separate Perth, on Australia's Indian Ocean coast, from Canberra.

In both national capitals the population is representative of the population mixtures of the two countries. This would seem to matter in Canada especially, with its dual or even tricultural makeup. Ottawa in 1961 was 55.7 per cent English, 37.7 per cent French, and 6 per cent other. Unfortunately, Ottawa has not lived up to the ideal of the capital of a culturally diverse nation. It is barely over 30 per cent bilingual, and most bilinguals are of French origin. Almost all government business has traditionally been conducted in English, and English speakers have held the best jobs. Until recently, most public buildings were marked in English only. In the 1966 phonebook for Ottawa and Hull (the Quebec city directly across the river from Ottawa), the federal government listings were in English only.

In sum, Canberra as a capital has not served as a nationally symbolic point. In a number of respects, Ottawa has enjoyed advantages over Canberra, but Ottawa's potential as a symbol of Canadian nationhood has been undermined. Ironically, as a city on the border of the most important English and French provinces, and with a population fairly representative of national subcultures, for Canada's French Ottawa has failed to fulfill the promise of a truly national and culturally integrating capital.

Constitutions can be another, quite different, source of inspiration to nationalism. Apart from the jurisdictional and procedural particulars which they spell out, constitutions can be symbolically meaningful according to the circumstances of their origins, the ideals they enshrine or the manner in which they become a genuinely respected mantle of high law.

Neither the Canadian nor the Australian constitutions originated in circumstances dramatic enough to weld the people. They were the products of years of tedious deliberations and horse-trading, and not the credos of bold and victorious societies, not declarative charters, but sets of clauses describing marriages of convenience. Their preambles are prosaic and unassuming. Canada's constitution is perhaps more a set of guidelines than a national constitution, and its actual name, the British North America Act (BNA Act) of 1867, strikes no emotional chord. The Australian constitution is at least Australian-labeled—the Constitution of the Commonwealth of Australia. Like the BNA Act, it has a dry, matter of fact quality, and it dwells neither on principles of personal freedom (neither document has a "bill of rights" section), nor on the principles of distributive justice. Since individuals in their private or corporate capacities are hardly mentioned in these constitutions, the potential for symbolic appeal is negligible.

Both Canada and Australia began their national experience before they were juridically sovereign. They were self-governing "dominions" within the British Empire, and did not acquire genuine international personalities until the interwar period. For instance, they were automatically at war in 1914 when Britain declared war. Furthermore, for a period after confederation, legislation passed by the Canadian Parliament was subject to review and disallowance by the British government through the Governor-General, the Crown's representative in Canada. By the time the Commonwealth of Australia was organized in 1901, the practice of discretionary British review of political actions in the dominions had virtually disappeared. During Canada's formative years this power had been exercised, though sparingly; during Australia's formative years, the practice was just about gone. To some degree, therefore, the public image of the Canadian constitution as a symbol of unfettered national status was held back in a way that did not obstruct public images of the Australian constitution.

Well beyond the time when there was any question of complete legal personality and national status, two special factors, absent in Australia, operated in Canada to depress public regard for the constitution as a symbol of nationhood. The first factor involved the final source of judicial appeal for Canadian cases. When the Supreme Court of Canada was organized shortly after confederation, no prohibitions were imposed on the removal of cases on appeal from it to the Judicial Committee of the Privy Council in London, the highest appellate body for cases originating in the various parts of the British Empire. Not until 1949 did Canada abolish appeals to the Privy Council. Until then, the Supreme Court of Canada had largely served as a waystation for cases heading for London, and in a number of instances was bypassed entirely. The Privy Council frequently overruled the Supreme Court's judgments, so that Canadian constitutional law, and therefore the BNA Act itself, were for three quarters of a century crafted by a foreign court staffed by foreigners. The experience of the Australian High Court was noticeably different. Until 1968, certain federally related cases could be appealed to the Privy Council without the High Court's own consent. It is still possible to carry cases arising out of *state* law to the Privy Council. However, in those federal cases which until 1968 did find their way to London, the Privy Council tended to be more supportive of the High Court than it had been of Canadian cases brought on appeal from the Supreme Court. Furthermore, in cases arising out of federal-state relations, an especially critical constitutional area, the High Court had, and retains, the right to deny leave for appeal to the Privy Council, and no such leave has been granted since 1912. In other words, because Australia's constitution has been preeminently interpreted and fleshed out by an Australian based and Australian-staffed court, its potential for commanding respect and inculcating national feelings has been greater than the BNA Act's.

A second feature of constitutional development pertinent to the building of national symbols has been the method of constitutional amendment. Here again, the BNA Act seems to have rendered a lesser service than the Australian constitution. Prior to 1949, any and all amendments to the BNA Act required the concurrence of the British Parliament upon an address from the government of Canada. The problem has not been one of securing such consent, but has been internal to Canada itself. In 1949, portions of the BNA Act were made subject to exclusive Canadian amendment. The entire constitution was not "patriated" in this way because Quebec felt that key provisions relating to provincial and cultural rights might better remain in the ultimate trust of the British Parliament than of the Canadian government itself. Quebec no longer feels this way. However, two major efforts at a complete overhaul of the BNA Act, including removal of all British association with the amending process, have miscarried, because Quebec found certain of the draft provisions unacceptable. One result of these failures to devise a modernized constitution is that Canada continues to operate under a constitution which, technically, is not entirely within its own right to alter, though nearly everyone agrees in principle that this anachronism is a disgrace and should be ended. Widespread feeling that the BNA Act is a horse-and-buggy document, and the extensive efforts which have gone into producing a refurbished constitution, have been public reminders that the existing constitution is not revered higher law. Quebec's veto of the two substitute constitutional drafts has served to underscore how politically and culturally contentious the entire constitutional issue is in the country. In various ways, therefore, the Canadian constitution has failed to develop attributes which might otherwise inspire public confidence or serve as symbols of national pride and unity.

The Australian constitution has not suffered from being an expatriate document. True, many proposed amendments to it, at various stages of political history, have been the object of partisan debate. But the acceptance or rejection of proffered changes has been a piecemeal thing, not springing from a concentrated public debate over whether to scrap the old document and start afresh. When amendments have been brought forward, adversary opinion has not been given the subcultural undertones prevalent in the English-French dialogue in Canada. In the same vein, public referendums, which are prescribed for constitutional amendments in Australia, have not reflected voting patterns suggestive of acute regional differences. Canadian constitutional amendment procedures do not prescribe public referendums, but the country does reflect some regional and ethnic differences in what the constitution is supposed to be. As one of the charter provinces, and the most populous and most prosperous, Ontario has generally not been overly disturbed by the parameters of power available to Ottawa under the BNA Act. The Prairies and the Maritimes have often and heavily relied on central authority for relief of their economic ills, but have felt somewhat left out and cheated, partially because their small populations have precluded great political leverage within the state apparatus. Quebec has tenaciously guarded its cultural heritage, and has been inclined to interpret the BNA Act as a plaything of English centralizers. This was so even when, as after World War II, central power was employed in English-speaking quarters to foster a more equitable distribution of resources among Canada's various regions, provinces and cultural concentrations, Quebec included. Manifestly different conceptions of the constitution's role, and, by implication, of the meaning of Canadian nationhood, were uncovered by a 1965 survey, in which 57 per cent of English speakers but only 24 per cent of French speakers claimed that the federal government, rather than provincial governments, handles the most important problems.

We now look at symbolic contributions to Canadian and Australian nationhood from still another perspective, namely the uses of myths and trappings. Neither country's history has produced events whose legacy is remembered and cherished in ways suitable for an idealization of nationhood. Dominion Day in Canada and Australia Day are public holidays, but neither country has the equivalent of a Fourth of July or Bastille Day which could evoke stirring memories of national accomplishment. Actually, after generations of usage, "Dominion Day" was discarded as a name for Canada's national birthday. It did not sound sufficiently national and distinctively Canadian, so it became "Confederation Day" and "Canada Day." Neither nation has gone through an experience of declaring its independence, overthrowing oppression, or withstanding a Spanish Armada or a siege of Stalingrad. Canada's historical turning point, Wolfe's defeat of Montcalm on the Heights of Abraham and the subsequent cession of the country to Britain, has remained a point of national disunity, not solidarity.

Other myths have to an extent taken hold in the two societies, and some of them have spilled over into personifications of nationhood. Such myths are probably stronger in Australia than in Canada. Whatever its historical accuracy, there arose the myth of an Australian national character, nourished in the nineteenth-century bush country and epitomized by the individualism of the jolly swagman and of mateship. In Canada, there is something, though not very much, of a popular identification with a great "northern adventure" and development. Australian society, as we have seen, was well-formed before nationhood was formalized; there already was a sense of "Australianism." Thus Australian military exploits are treated more as testaments of nobility of personal character, rather than as struggles for national causes. The pertinacity of Australian troops at Gallipoli, in 1915, had nothing to do with defending Australia's sacred shores, and the campaign itself was a strategic failure and a tactical draw. But it helped to spread the myth of the courage and determination of Australians as a people, and indirectly fostered national identification. Canadian military exploits, such as at Vimy Ridge in World War I and Dieppe in World War II, are not celebrated in anything like the sense that the "spirit of ANZAC" is in Australia. Canadians as a people have never been as culturally egotistical or as self-conscious as are Australians. In part, this stems from Canada's own societal diversity. In times of war, French Canadians have fought well and gallantly, and the French Canadian 22nd Regiment has long ranked among the Canadian army's finest units. But the French, in general, have not gone to Canada's wars with the enthusiasm of their English-speaking Canadian neighbors, and two bitter wartime conscription debates polarized Canada on French-English lines.

Neither Australia nor Canada has a set of honored national figures, partially because the national histories have not been congenial to Bismarckian blood-and-iron nation builders, Lincolnesque emancipators, or Leninist revolutionaries. Australians have taken a somewhat jaundiced view of mighty political individualists. Canadian heroic figures, to the extent that they exist, are heroes for the English or for the French, but hardly ever for both. In the late 1830's William Lyon Mackenzie and Joseph Papineau led popular rebellions, but these were, respectively, distinctly English and French rebellions. Later in the century Louis Riel led two revolts in western Canada. He was a hero to the French, but a traitor to the English, who applauded his hanging. Two early Prime Ministers, John A. Macdonald and Wilfrid Laurier, were extremely skillful political compositors. They helped to steer Canada over the rough ground of a developing bicultural society. They are remembered and generally respected. But their achievements were built on traits of patience, compromise, and recovery from disappointment, not charisma. Canadians still cannot, or will not, revere their public figures. In 1970, over half of them were unable to nominate the "greatest living Canadian"; Prime Minister Pierre Trudeau was mentioned by only 14 per cent of the respondents.

Both countries have held to a number of trappings which have reflected British traditions—Australia more than Canada. It is far more Anglo in composition. For generations, security fears prompted by geographic isolation spurred reliance on British protection. British relics and symbols do not aggravate any major sector of the community. Finally, Australians have no compulsive need to develop an indigenous set of symbols to stimulate national identification. In Canada, persons of Anglo derivation represent less than 50 per cent of the population, and their "Britishness" has been diluted by American cross-pressures and by exposure to Canada's non-British subcultures, French and otherwise. The French are either indifferent toward British symbols and trappings, or negatively associate them with the politically dominant English subculture.

Australia retains knighthood and other titles. In 1968, some 60 per cent of the public indicated a preference for an Australian honors system, and another 10 per cent wished to abolish all honors. The Australian Labor party opposes British honors on grounds that they demean Australian nationhood, and urges its members not to accept them. Still, when Labor was in power in the 1940's, it failed to discontinue them, and was persuaded to allow its nominee to the Governor Generalship, himself a former Labor premier of New South Wales, to accept knighthood. British honors are simply not a sore issue in Australia, and in fact are largely immaterial to the Australians' sense of nationhood. Much of the opposition to British honors is actually attributable to the fact that they are generously distributed among conservative politicians, business figures, senior military and naval officers, and other members of what some might regard as an Australian "establishment." But the ranks of Australian knights include the Roman Catholic Sir Norman Cardinal Gilroy, scientists, educators, and other notables not neatly categorizable in establishmentarian terms.

In Canada, British honors were abolished in 1935, and the first steps in that direction had been undertaken some years before. Australians are about evenly divided on whether "God Save the Queen" should continue as the national anthem, or be replaced by an Australian-based anthem. But they strongly favor retaining the Union Jack symbol in their flag, and two-thirds of them, as opposed to 26 per cent who hold decidedly negative views, wish Australia to continue recognizing Charles as their King once Elizabeth's reign ends. Canadian responses in the same year (1970) to questions about the monarchy showed that two-thirds of English speakers wanted Canada to continue as a monarchy. But the national proportion was considerably reduced because only 27 per cent of French speakers were in favor, while 45 per cent of them preferred a republic, and 28 per cent were undecided. The Queen is warmly welcomed wherever she tours in Australia, and in most places she visits in Canada. But her visit several years ago to Quebec City generated strong antiroyalist demonstrations.

In recent years Canadian governments have proceeded to cut back on British symbols. Such symbols have been recognized as an irritant to the French. Perhaps even more persuasively, the country sorely lacks an effective and genuinely transcultural set of its own national symbols. Armed services unification in Canada was effected not only in the interest of efficiency, but to break up English-dominated traditions, especially in the Navy. There now are Canadian Armed Forces; there is no more *Royal* Canadian Navy or *Royal* Canadian Air Force. The old Canadian Red Ensign flag, which bore a Union Jack symbol, was legislated away, and replaced by a culturally neutral Maple Leaf flag. "O Canada" was substituted for "God Save the Queen" as Canada's official anthem. It is somewhat hard on the ear to listen to "O Canada" sung by a mixed English and French assembly, but it is supposed to be easy on Canadian nationalism.

A good deal that is symbolically British remains in Canada. There is still a *Royal* Canadian Mounted Police, official mail goes out "On Her Majesty's Service," and no steps have been taken to institute a republic. If republicanism comes it will almost surely come to Canada before it reaches Australia. But Canadian governments cannot proceed precipitously. Many English-speaking Canadians resent what they regard as Quebec's excessive claims, and what they interpret to be lavish concessions according to it in the name of national unity. Much of the opposition against the abandonment of the Red Ensign flag was tenacious, and some of the most hyperbolic criticisms came from the heavily ethnic Prairies, and by ethnic spokesmen. Hence the ostensible oddity that while Australia appointed its first native-born Governor-General in 1931, not until twenty-one years later was there a native born Governor-General in Canada. A British Governor-General in Canada was in a sense a neutral figure. A Canadian would have been either of English or French descent, and could not have been all things to all men.

Nationhood and foreign influence

Our commentary on symbols has suggested that a society's sense of nationhood can be shaped by influences which are essentially foreign in derivation. Such influences may variously affect public images of nationhood. For instance, if they are obvious and pervasive, they can retard the growth of indigenous loyalties. But they can also serve to break down intercultural barriers which themselves hinder feelings of common nationhood. Foreign influences can weaken intercultural barriers per se, or prompt a fresh sense of common national identity and purpose based on resistance to foreign cultural, economic, or other encroachments. If governments choose, they can try to mobilize an otherwise divided, materially aggrieved, or politically cynical population by aiming their fire against the evils associated with foreign influence.

Although Australian society retains numerous relics of the British heritage, geography has placed Australia thousands of miles away from either European or North American centers of western civilization. Australia is an island continent, and therefore does not share a border with anyone, least of all a neighbor whose cultural or economic influence could be brought to bear from just across a boundary line. Australia's geographically closest culturally related neighbor is New Zealand, a nation with less than a quarter of Australia's population, and 1200 miles removed. Canada's situation is decidedly different. Not only is it not geographically isolated, but it shares a border with the United States. For Canada, the United States is not just another foreign country. The histories of the two nations have been continuously interlocked. They share a common language and a generally common heritage. People, ideas, and trade easily move back and forth. Some 90 per cent of Canadians reside within 200 miles of the United States, and over half live within 50 miles. Montreal, Toronto, and Vancouver, Canada's largest cities, are an hour or two by car from the border.

A review of the nature and extent of American influence provides a basis for assessing still another impact on Australian and Canadian perceptions of nationhood. Canadians far more than Australians are likely to see Americans in their midst. A 1971 survey indicated that Australia ranked as first choice among all countries for Americans who might contemplate migration. Canada, however, is now receiving well over 20,000 American migrants annually, equivalent to the entire American community of 25,000 resident in Australia as of 1971. Nearly 6000 Americans migrated to Australia in 1970–71, but the return rate for Americans has consistently been very high. For various reasons, Americans have become the dominant foreign group on Canadian university faculties, and in some academic departments, at least at English-speaking institutions, they exceed Canadians. Although perhaps 40 per cent of the academics in Australia are foreign, roughly the same proportion as in Canada, the outsiders tend to be predominantly New Zealanders and Britons, rather than Americans.

Through entertainment and communication media, both Canadians and Australians are constantly exposed to material from America, and to material colored by the American life style. Sydney schoolchildren have been found to be considerably more familiar with the American President than with the leader of the opposition in the Australian Parliament. In one Ontario community schoolchildren were far more able to identify the President than the provincial Premier, and in Kingston, Ontario, eighth graders had a better conception of the President's role than that of the Canadian Prime Minister. Neither country has a meaningful commercial film industry, and therefore the vast majority of films shown at cinemas and on television screens are imported, primarily from the United States. Even French-speaking Quebeckers are not exempt, since they can view dubbed American films. Canada and Australia have developed local television industries which excel in some areas, but the bulk of feature shows on television are American. American television material is extremely simple to pick up, and therefore even more extensively viewed in Canada than in Australia. American programs are available to Canadians in two ways. First, about half of the

Canadian population has direct access to American stations. These, of course, are almost entirely lacking in Canadian content, though they do present some commercials bought by Canadian companies. Second, American programs are available through Canadian transmission sources. In a typical week in 1970, the most popular TV presentation on both the public Canadian Broadcasting Corporation and the private CTV network was hockey; the next nine favorites on both networks were almost all American shows.

American journalism is also a formidable influence on Canadians and Australians, though far more so on the former. American newspapers are available on Canadian newsstands, sometimes on the day of publication. In Australia, the only quick and practical access to the American press, outside of libraries, is a facsimile of the *New York Times* Sunday News In Review section, which is available four or five days after American publication. Australians read the Pacific editions of American weeklies such as *Time* and *Newsweek,* but Canadians are literally swamped by American magazine and periodical literature, both because of its inherent appeal, and because of the inadequacy of the local competition. The Canadian edition of *Time* carries a regular section devoted to Canadian news, and a Canadian-oriented *Reader's Digest* is available in French as well as in English. *Time* and the *Reader's Digest* absorb 56 per cent of all magazine advertising revenue laid out in Canada. Between 1960 and 1970, *Time* sales in Canada doubled, reaching 460,000 weekly copies. On a per capita basis, *Time* sells somewhat better in Canada than it does in the United States. A 1970 Canadian Senate committee report disclosed that Canadians were spending more money on American comic books than on the seventeen leading Canadian-owned magazines combined. Australians and Canadians are avid readers, and much of what they read is American material. American educational materials are especially conspicuous in Canada. The Canadian and Australian publishing industries lose business because of American competition, and are to varying degrees propped up by government subsidies.

In the economic field also, Canada and Australia have been subjected to considerable American penetration. In its more obvious manifestation, this is reflected in the numbers of American consumer goods which are available on store shelves. The influence of American consumer tastes upon the two countries has brought an increasing imitation of American styles of living and of material consumption. The economic indices pointing to an American presence are abundantly clear, though again, as in the media area, Canada has been considerably more susceptible than Australia. At the beginning of the 1970's, American investment of all types in Canada exceeded 30 billion American dollars. A substantial majority of all external investment in Canada is American; in Australia, it stands at under 40 per cent, with British investment occupying half of the field. By the close of the 1960's some 450 American firms were operating in Australia —but between 1960 and 1970 the number of Canadian companies newly subjected to American *takeover* was more than twice that amount. Furthermore, the number of major Canadian industries with a very high ratio of either overall foreign, or particularly United States, control is considerably greater than in Australia. Though a much larger portion of Canada's company assets, compared with Australia, are owned by foreigners, American control in both countries is especially conspicuous in such fields as automobiles, mining, and petroleum.

The concentration of American influences has been lamented in various Canadian and Australian quarters, with charges that the two countries are becoming American colonies. But the degree of concern, and of counteraction, has not been nearly as evident in Australia as in Canada. This provides a lesson for our theme of popular approaches to nationhood.

Popular feeling that Canadian life has become overinfluenced by the United States jumped from 27 per cent in 1956 to 53 per cent in 1966. In 1971, Prime Minister Trudeau received a 175,000-signature petition, calling for removal of American influences which were undermining Canada's independent position. By the end of that year, a Committee for an Independent Canada, formed in 1970, was claiming over a quarter of a million members. In 1970, fewer than a quarter of the Australians wished to reduce foreign ownership of local factories, and in the following year only 7 per cent of the population nominated "foreign influence" as the key Australian problem. An obvious reason for higher Canadian disquiet is that while American influences impinge on both countries, on nearly every count the impingement on Canada is far more pervasive. A second reason is that there are some areas in which Australia has simply remained untouched by certain kinds of American-related problems which are manifest in Canada. For example, while Australia's trade union movement is fully domesticated, nearly two-thirds of Canada's organized workers belong to international, American-centered unions. This tie has been controversial, and at times irritating to Canadian locals, which have wanted to employ their own job-betterment strategies. Also, Australia has no territorial disputes with the United States, but Canada does. Concerned about mineral exploitation and pollution dangers in its Arctic territories, Canada has unilaterally extended its territorial water limits from three to twelve miles, and has imposed a shipping safety zone which extends 100 miles from its coastline in the Arctic Ocean-Northwest Passage region. The United States fired off a note of diplomatic protest, but the twin measures breezed through the Canadian House of Commons without a dissenting vote.

Another reason underlying a greater Canadian unease over American influence is that even where there are similar contact points with the United States, the issues are much more aggravating for Canadians. Thus, although there is a substantial American economic stake in both countries, Canada qualitatively as well as quantitatively has more of an American "branch-plant" economic structure than Australia. For years American law prohibited American firms and their foreign affiliates from selling to China. Over 60 per cent of all Canadian exports are bought by the United States, further underlining Canada's economic reliance on America. When in 1971 President Nixon imposed a 10 per cent import surcharge, Canadians panicked. There were countless accusations of unfairness toward Canada, and dire predictions that, despite Canada's high unemployment rate, tens of thousands of additional workers faced layoffs in high labor-content firms which exported manufactured goods to the United States. It was estimated that the American surcharge could cost Canadian firms 200 million dollars, and that many would be bankrupted. These gloomy forecasts proved unfounded, but the climate in which they were bruited about made America appear brutally insensitive toward its best customer.

The American presence in Canadian academia is another Canadian-American irritant which largely is not present in Australia. The large number of Americans on Canadian university faculties has brought imputations that competent Canadians are frequently passed over for appointments in favor of American foreigners. More serious is the allegation that the American invasion of the social science departments, in particular, is exposing an entire generation of students to American values, analyses, and methodologies, while leaving them painfully ignorant of conditions in their own country. It is therefore claimed that in academia as well as in business and industry, Canada has become an American branch plant.

The nature of foreign and defense relations between the United States and Ottawa and Canberra also illustrates the emotion which surrounds Canadian reactions to the country's associations with America. Both Canada and Australia are closely tied to and ultimately dependent for their security on the United States. Neither Canada nor Australia has an entirely carefree foreign policy relationship with Washington, but Australians are more apt to articulate the value of ties with America than are Canadians. Many Australians recall the ominous days of early 1942, when Japan was sweeping down Southeast Asia, into New Guinea, and in Australia's direction. They recall the arrival of General Douglas MacArthur and American troops, and the dashing of any designs Japan might have had on Australia at the Battle of the Coral Sea. There is no equivalent recent experience on which Canadians can draw for special gratitude toward America and Americans. The United States and Canada are partners in NATO, in a greater North American aerospace defense system, and in defense *matériel* production. The United States and Australia are linked through ANZUS and SEATO, and there are various American defense installations on Australian soil, though no military bases as such. Canadians have often sensed that Washington was bossing them around in matters of joint defense concern, and perhaps even regarding them as expendable—a northern buffer for America's own nuclear security. Whatever criticisms of the American connection have been raised in Australia, as over Vietnamese policy, the fact remains that their country's isolated position has convinced Australians of nearly all political stripes that a close working relationship with Washington is desirable, especially as such a relationship is reflected through the intimacy of the ANZUS alliance. The American alliance cannot, at all events, be taken for granted, most Australians would agree.

Finally, there is the rather intangible yet important matter of the general image which America casts in Canada and in Australia. The distasteful features of American life—racial tensions, confrontational politics, blight and poverty, growing crime and drug-consumption rates, errors and embarrassments in foreign policy —are carried into and commented upon in Canadian and Australian homes. But Canadians receive such reports in larger doses, and more graphically, and observe them in special ways, as for instance through the presence of thousands of American war resisters who crossed into Canada. Canadians have always lived in America's shadow, and have been subject to its power and inordinately conditioned by its life styles. Now more than ever they are reasoning that there is much about their pervasively influential neighbor that is unappealing and even objectionable. Familiarity has begun to breed a bit of conceit. Canadians are gradually taking a personal, occasionally supercilious, pride in belonging to an allegedly more level-headed, rational society.

This "discovery" that Canadianism is a prideful thing, and worth defending, has become linked to an evolving Canadian nationalism. It is part of an ongoing *search,* rather than an affirmation of a clear, well-rounded ideal of nationhood. It is elusive, but at least it eschews the notion that a combination of internal ethnic tensions and a floodtide of American influence must produce a faceless Canadian society. In 1970, whatever it might have meant to them, 60 per cent of all Canadians felt that the growing attention to Canadian nationalism was beneficial for the country. All the same, subcultural differences were evident in the survey. English opinion was the most positive and the least undecided, followed by ethnics and finally the French, of whom 49 per cent agreed, 11 per cent disagreed, and 40 per cent were undecided. Presumably, if the rising excitement over Canadian nationalism is to contribute to solidifying national unity, it will need to become less subculturally selective, rather than simply commanding a national majority.

Various officially sponsored nationalistic measures have been undertaken in both Canada and Australia, though the sense of urgency has been expressed more strongly in the former. Both have tightened rules governing "local content" on television—50 per cent for Australia and 60 per cent projected for Canada by 1972. In both countries, British materials (and in Canada, French materials as well) had been included in definitions of local content, but have now been omitted. Both nations already prohibit foreign ownership of television stations. Both nations have accelerated their contributions to local film industries, as well as to the performing arts generally. This has been done to provide an adequate and suitable supply of domestic presentations, to discourage local artistic talent from emigrating, and generally to promote national expression. The Canadian effort to substitute local for American media influence has been more elaborate than the Australian, and more self-consciously aimed at fulfilling the spirit of Canadianization as a national good in its own right. Hence, a plan was developed to curtail the extension of cable television, thereby limiting the reception of American-based programs. However, the scheme was not fully implemented, owing to a public outcry over denial of choice, "choice" meaning preference for American programs. Australia does not, of course, encounter any problems with foreign television reception. Australians who watch the evening news may choose between the Australian Broadcasting Commission and privately owned stations, but they have no access to Walter Cronkite. An Australian listening to a television station signing off invariably hears "God Save the Queen" played, never the "Star Spangled Banner," and he is not confronted by the fluttering Stars and Stripes. Canadian radio has been ordered to play a minimum of 30 per cent local content music, but realism has dictated a very wide definition of what is "Canadian." For instance, a Canadian ensemble singing American rock music qualifies under the terms of "Canadian content." Even sport has been affected by the principle of Canadian content, and with predictably mixed success. The Canadian Football League requires that the teams carry a majority of members representing domestic talent. The remaining players, almost invariably Americans, are, however, among the best, and among the highest paid.

Acceptance of attempts at "nationalization" varies considerably in the two countries. There tends to be approval within the intellectual community but mass resistance to increasing local content in broadcasts. There is approval within that intellectual community for but mass apathy toward a move such as that of the Canada Council, which has tightened rules for awarding research funds to non-Canadian academics teaching in the country. The picture is especially complex regarding moves to counter the Americanization of the Australian and Canadian economies. Attempts at curtailing *Time* and *Reader's Digest* circulation in Canada might pump more breath into the local magazine industry, but the Canadian advertising industry, and Canadian business advertisers themselves, would be adversely affected.

American economic penetration of the two countries has, of course, been debated in specific economic as well as in political/emotional terms. In both countries, accusations have been made that massive foreign investment distorts local economic priorities, inhibits local business initiative, and generates investment expectations which can be quickly overturned by changes in American economic conditions. Foreign investment is said to overdraw on imports for the benefit of foreign-based firms, and curtails indigenous research and development capabilities.

Contrary arguments maintain that foreign investment has diversified what otherwise would have been unsophisticated economies, has allowed for quality and diversification among consumer goods, has aided the tapping of Canada's and Australia's huge reserves of natural resources, has generated employment, and has counteracted trade imbalances. The return on foreign investment has not been excessive, or even much different than that of locally controlled enterprises—about 8 per cent on average for Canada, about 7 per cent for Australia. Many earned dollars are reinvested locally, rather than being expatriated. In Australia, for example, the Ford and Chrysler automaking firms apply dividends toward expansion. The largest firm, General Motors-Holden, remits part of its dividends to the United States, and reinvests some, but it leads the industry in its use of local components, and in vehicle safety research. Canadians save at a higher rate than any other people in the world. But insurance policy and bank saving is not equivalent to investment risk-taking, reinforcing the argument of those who support heavy and continuing doses of external investment.

In both countries, state/provincial premiers of various political complexions have spoken out against an impetuous tampering with foreign firms or investment capital. In Adelaide, South Australia's capital city, about a fifth of the people would be affected if the American-owned automobile industry were removed. Western Australia is riding the crest of a mineral boom, and acknowledges that American and Japanese explorations and development are the key to the state's new prosperity. Saskatchewan and the Canadian Atlantic provinces are inordinately dependent on primary industries, whose fortunes have recently been depressed, and for which redress is often seen in terms of infusions of foreign money. Quebec is committed to a massive socioeconomic renovation, and a reduction in its chronically high unemployment rate, with the result that its premier has actively sought American capital.

Australian and Canadian governments alike have needed to be mindful of the economic assets attributed to American investment, and of the political resistance in various parts of the two countries to any serious dislocation of it. It has been rather easier for Australia to accept foreign investment with relative equanimity. Prime Minister John Gorton, who was generally regarded as something of an Australian nationalist, could remark in 1969 that "The importance to Australia of a strong and continuing inflow of overseas capital has never been questioned by my Government. . . . It confers great benefits on us and it is essential that it should continue." * Recent Canadian prime ministers have not been as sanguine. The American economic presence in Canada is much more visible than in Australia, and its damaging economic and political by-products are defined as larger. There is a spreading popular mood which mirrors unhappiness with the American embrace, and which might be harnessable in a way

* *Commonwealth Parliamentary Debates,* House of Representatives, September 16, 1969, p. 1382.

that will build a positive sense of Canadian nationhood. In 1970, a surprising 46 per cent of the public believed that Canada should buy back majority control in American-held companies, even if a substantial living standard reduction would result.

Public policies in Canberra and Ottawa have reflected the different national tempers toward the foreign economic presence. Both countries prohibit any or all foreign control in enterprises such as banking, broadcasting and civil aviation. The Trudeau government rejected proposals for buying up existing outside investments or damming up all future ones. But in several ways a fairly tough-minded approach has been developing. In some instances the Canadian government has blocked the sale of important Canadian companies to American interests, or has itself bought into the companies concerned. Despite certain guidelines promulgated in 1969, three years later than in Canada, the Australian government has been considerably less interventionist against foreign takeovers of local enterprises. A new Australian Industrial Development Corporation and a Canadian Development Corporation have been created, in part to finance local ventures. But the Canadian instrumentality more explicitly stresses countervailing forces against foreign capital. Legislation has been introduced in Ottawa to remove residual foreign tax advantages, while special tax incentives for domestic firms, and for potential Canadian stock buyers, have been brought forward. Possible takeovers of local firms by foreign interests will henceforth be subjected to very close scrutiny by a special board, and can be disallowed in the national interest.

In Australia, among the relatively small resident American community, approximately 3000 persons are landholders. Some 70 per cent of the upper end of the Northern Territory has been rapidly acquired by Americans on long lease terms, even though Canberra retains discretionary leases for mineral exploitation in the territory at large. In Canada's provinces, a good deal of Crown land has over time been either bought or leased on long term by

Americans. In response, Ontario has decided to end all sales of provincial Crown lands to foreigners, and to accord Canadians preference in leasing it. It has undertaken steps to limit the amount of foreign ownership in firms operating within its borders. But Ontario is already the richest and most developed among Canada's provinces, and the best able to adopt restrictive measures.

In general, then, "nationhood" in Canada has historically been a considerably less developed and publicly admired notion than in Australia. There are signs, however, that one of the factors seriously responsible for retarding a common sense of national identification, namely the weight of American influences, may now actually be contributing to solidifying it.

2

Socioeconomic resource allocation and public satisfaction

General indices of economic strength

The satisfaction of popular expectations and claims strongly affects public confidence in the political system, and helps to temper the climate of political life. Such satisfactions can be both material and nonmaterial. They are predicated not only on whether the system has considerable resources at its disposal, but more particularly on how such resources are in fact distributed —selectively or comprehensively, efficiently or inefficiently, and so on.

Various indices suggest that by comparative, world standards both Canada and Australia are economically advanced and wealthy societies. For instance, so far as urbanization is a sign of complex occupational, producing, and consuming structures, both have achieved impressive levels, though Australia became urbanized considerably earlier, and remains ahead of Canada. During Canada's first census, in 1871, only 20 per cent of the population was urban, but years before federation Australia was already half urban. Canada's major move toward urbanization occurred during the period of 1921 to 1961, when a doubling of total population was accompanied by an increase in urbanization by over 90 per cent. By 1961, compared to Canada's figure of just under 70 per cent, over 80 per cent of Australia's population resided in urban areas, and by 1970 had risen to 88.5 per cent, the world's highest. The Australian urbanization pattern reflects some special characteristics. Not only do most Australians live in cities, but they concentrate in the state capitals. With the exception of Brisbane and Hobart, all state capitals contain well over half of their respective states' populations; in Canada, no capital city houses over half of its province's population.* Despite the fact that Canada's population is nearly three-quarters larger than Australia's, the largest city in either country is Sydney, with a 1970 population of 2,800,000. Although Canada's population has become substantially urban, interprovincial urbanization differences are much wider than are interstate differences in Australia. Every Australian state has for some time contained a decided majority of urban dwellers, but according to 1961 figures, Canada's urbanization ranged from a high of 77 per cent in Ontario to 32 per cent in Prince Edward Island.

The strong urbanization trends in both countries have been associated with important changes which were taking place in the two national economies. In neither country, however, was the *process* of urbanization, socially or politically, particularly unsettling. Neither society was faced with the sorts of disorientations which could have been precipitated by the coupling of rapid industrialization with a sudden swelling of urban centers, or by the mass migration to the cities by uprooted peasant farmers.

Canada and Australia have by now evolved diverse and modern economies. Although over the years agricultural production has risen in scale and value, its relative importance in the two economies has drastically decreased, and so has the proportion of persons employed in it. Agriculture in both nations accounts for

* As of January 1, 1972, with the installation of a "greater Winnipeg" metropolitan entity, the city acquired more than half of Manitoba's population.

less than a tenth of the net value of production, and under 5 per cent of wages and salaries are earned in rural industries. The pastoral industry in Australia, however, despite relative decline, continues to contribute about 10 per cent of the productive value. In both countries the overwhelming net worth of production derives from manufacturing. Both countries have fabulous and diversified stores of natural resources; a 1969 analysis ranked Australia first and Canada second in world terms of mineral industry prospects. About a third of Canada's and slightly less than 20 per cent of Australia's export earnings are now attributable to manufactured products, and Australia's combined manufactured and mineral exports have recently exceeded the value of all primary industry exports, which include wool. The Canadian and Australian work forces reflect the movement toward urban, industrial, technological and service-oriented societies. All forms of primary production employ about a tenth of the work forces, while another quarter is in manufacturing and the remainder in the various services.

As the Canadian and Australian economies have diversified and expanded, both societies have required greater skills as well as the occupational specializations geared to modern economic life. Education in both countries up to the middle secondary grades is very widespread, though short of universal. Beyond that point, although Australia is narrowing the gap, Canada has been keeping its young persons at school longer, provides a probably superior education, produces a higher ratio of university and other tertiary level graduates, and earlier than Australia undertook a systematic program of retraining artisans for modern technological occupations. Canada has become among the world's leaders in the proportion of its Gross National Product invested in education, while Australia's contribution has been middling. In the late 1960's, the approximate Canadian and Australian figures were 8.7 per cent and 4.2 per cent, respectively. For the 1967–69 triennium, the Australian Commonwealth government contributed $3 million (about $3.5 million in equivalent Canadian terms) and the states about another $4 million for university research in various disciplines. The Australian-Canadian data are not fully comparable, but it is noteworthy that in 1969–70 alone, through the Canada Council, the Canadian federal government awarded over $4 million just for social sciences and humanities research.

In the late 1950's, in Canada and Australia, respectively, 46 per cent and 20 per cent of young persons aged 15–19, and 9.3 per cent and 1.9 per cent of persons aged 20–24, were attending educational institutions. Within the following decade, the Australian proportion in each category had doubled, although three-quarters of government school and over two-thirds of Catholic school children were dropping out before completion of all available high school grades. In 1953, the proportion of Australian university students in postgraduate studies was only 3 per cent, but by 1969 it had reached 10 per cent, about the same ratio as in Canada. Canadian university enrollment at the turn of the 1970's was well over 300,000, nearly three times greater than in Australia, even though Canada's population is less than twice as great as Australia's. However, Australian colleges of advanced education, much of whose work is at university level, were expected to enroll 70,000 students by 1972.

The qualitative preparation of Canadians and Australians for contributory roles in modern economies has reflected special national circumstances. The general comparison has favored Canada, although Quebec's educational traditions until very recently were conspicuously restrictive. Australian pretertiary education has been predominantly concerned with orderliness, discipline, and skills, at the expense of breath of outlook or independent thinking. Data from a recent comparative study of British, American, New Zealand, Canadian, and Australian teachers showed that the Australians were foremost in exhibiting authoritarian, conformist, and disciplinarian approaches in their teaching. Australian teachers have also been comparatively undereducated. Data from the late 1960's showed that most primary teachers had only two years of postsecondary training in teachers' colleges, and slightly over half of the secondary teachers had university degrees. Canadian data for the same period, based on most provinces, indicated that 15 per cent of the primary teachers and three-quarters of the secondary teachers held university degrees. Canadian provinces set instructional and other standards, but there is a freedom of local educational experimentation unknown in Australia where, until the first breakthrough occurred in South Australia in 1970, the state education departments imposed rigid statewide controls over what could or could not be done. Earlier decentralization measures in New South Wales and in Queensland had been designed for administrative convenience, not for the devolution of substantive responsibilities. Admission to Canadian universities is determined by various criteria, including scholastic aptitude and achievement tests, high-school rank, and recommendations from school teachers and principals. The Australian admissions system has no doubt been less effective in discovering talent. Universities in the several states have set examinations for high-school students sitting for matriculation. Physical space at universities allowing, all persons who achieved a specified performance level on these tests were admitted. Only very recently, and gradually, have more flexible university admissions criteria begun to appear.

By contrast with either Australia or Canada at large, Quebec's educational situation had for decades been depressed. In 1966, Quebec had the highest Canadian proportion of persons with no more than an elementary education—50 per cent—and the second lowest proportion of university graduates. The Catholic church had been concerned more with maintaining the faith than with enlarging the intellectual horizons of the Quebec French children whose education it effectively regulated. Education was not made compulsory until 1942. Even after that the provincial government failed to enforce compulsory attendance, and there was no provincial Education Ministry until the 1960's. French students proceeding to universities were funneled through Quebec's classical colleges, where they received formal educations unsuited for eventual careers in science, engineering, and the business arts. Since the 1960's, however, Quebec's education has become far more secularized and practical, more conducive to upward mobility, and far more lavishly subsidized than in the past.

The Australian and Canadian educational systems have, whatever their shortcomings, produced considerable scientific establishments. At the beginning of the 1970's, Canada was actually producing more Ph.D.'s in science and engineering per capita than the United States, and it stood third among industrial countries in the number of qualified scientists and engineers it employed in research and development. Australia's projected Ph.D. output in the sciences over the 1970's is predicted to reach 3000, an extremely commendable figure by contrast with earlier periods. The "brain drain" problem which for many years plagued Canada especially has been clearly reversed, and both countries import more scientific personnel than they export. Both Canada and Australia have ranked well on such inventories as the number of quality scientific papers produced, and in various types of discoveries. In the medical area, for instance, insulin was developed in Canada, and the link between thalidomide and physical deformities was established in Australia. There has been a Canadian Nobel Prize in Medicine (for insulin), and another in Chemistry.

A frequent and justified complaint in both countries is that men who hold doctorates in science have an aversion to entering industrial employment, and that industry has an equal aversion to hiring them. The result is that by far the most and the best scientific research is conducted in universities and in governmentally sponsored research centers and laboratories, is more theoretical than applied and, accordingly, "development" gets shortchanged in preference to "research." Although the situation is slowly being rectified, both societies have made embarrassingly low investments in research and development generally. Among the contributing factors have been the lack of a major tradition in this field, governmental parsimony—though noticeably less in Canada than in Australia—and the resistance of numerous foreign-owned companies to duplicate the research that is carried out in America or other home-office countries.

The Canadian and Australian talent pools, and especially the Canadian, have been bolstered by qualified migrants. In many respects, entering migrants have a higher order of skills and professional qualifications than are found among the established work forces. As of 1965, the foreign-born in the Canadian labor force who had completed high school and attended university was 50 per cent higher than among the counterpart native-born group. Among migrants who entered Canada in 1967, an admittedly atypical year, there were three times as many architects, twice as many engineers, and about as many physicians and social workers as were then being graduated annually from Canadian universities. In 1969, 35 per cent of Canada's migrants were classified as professional or managerial. In the two preceding years, such persons entering Australia represented only half of the Canadian proportion, and the ratio of unskilled persons entering Australia was and continues to be far higher than for Canada. All the same, the caliber of Australia's migrant population should not be underestimated. Researchers found that in the period 1961–66, non-British migrants were able to achieve upward occupational mobility at a very respectable rate. According to a 1970 report, migrants comprised a third of Australian hospital staffs, 37 per cent of the professional artistic community, and half of the workers engaged in the flourishing mineral and metals industry. Canada's approach has been especially useful in matching migrants with national requirements. Applicants are admitted under a point system which values such qualities as skills, English- and/or French-language competence, and willingness to settle in areas of high job need. Racial backgrounds are irrelevant, and non-European arrivals have had disproportionately strong professional qualifications. Australia's admission policy has been less systematic, and until very recently hostile to allowing more than a token non-European migrant clientele. These non-Europeans who are admitted are subjected to much closer screening for skills and potential for assimilation than are white migrant applicants.

The tendencies we have cited have become associated with considerable economic vigor and material well-being in Canada and Australia. One calculation made for an early period, 1925–34, placed Canada second and Australia fifth among western nations in terms of real wage living standards. A 1960 international index of real consumption ranked Canada third and Australia fourth. Admittedly, the per capita productivity rates in both nations have not been outstanding, and well behind the 7–10 per cent rates achieved in some European nations and Japan. Canadian per capita output ran at about 3.2 per cent annually in the first half of the 1960's, dipped to 1.8 per cent annually in the second half of that decade, and was 2.4 per cent in 1970. The Australian rate over the 1960's averaged out to about 2.5 per cent per annum, much superior to the 1950's annual rate of 1.5 per cent. Other Australian and Canadian economic indicators have been more attractive. For 1970, in comparable American dollar terms, the Canadian GNP stood at over $80 billion, and the Australian at about $34 billion. Both GNP rates have been rising faster than in the United States, and in 1971 Canada's GNP jumped by 6 per cent in real terms—just about the highest growth among the industrialized nations. Twenty years earlier, in local currencies, the Canadian GNP had stood at $18 billion, and the Australian at only $5 billion.

Also impressive are the countries' performances in the proportion of GNP annually invested in internal development—about a quarter—and a great deal of which is contributed from domestic rather than foreign investment sources. The buoyancy of the two economies is also visible in the foreign trade accounts. In absolute value of goods traded, both countries rate high by world standards, and extremely high on a relative, per capita basis. By total value of trade, Canada ranks sixth and Australia twelfth; in relative terms, Canada stands first. Foreign sales for both now represent a wide variety of agricultural products, minerals, and manufactured goods, which help to insulate them from the vagaries of the international market. The situation with the balance of payments as of the 1970's gives cause for confidence. Canada has shown for several years a favorable balance with its foremost trading partner, the United States, and Australia continued to maintain a good balance with Japan, its principal overseas customer.

Personal measures of socioeconomic resource distribution

The foregoing analysis pointed to considerable Canadian and Australian economic strength. We may predict from this that affluent and optimistic material conditions will promote general public satisfaction, enhance the standing of the two political systems, and lower the incidence and intensity of group conflict. But the data presented so far have dealt mainly with general and essentially impersonal economic indices. It is necessary also to assess the manner in which economic opportunity and disposable wealth are distributed among different sectors of the two populations. Gross indicators of economic performance aside, it will be necessary to check on such factors as unemployment rates, disparities in income levels, poverty, inflationary and taxation pressures, and income differentials measured according to occupational categories, national regions, and population subcultures.

Canadians and Australians maintain an extremely high world

standing according to various tests of personal comfort and well-being, such as per capita possession of automobiles and telephones. But even these sorts of indices conceal differences between the two societies, and certain weaknesses in both. One rather striking, economic discrepancy between the two countries lies in their unemployment rates. Canadians have been nagged by unemployment for some years. Unemployment averaged 5.6 per cent of the work force in 1956, and 7.1 per cent in 1961. The 1970 average was 5.9 per cent, and when the controversial Nixon surcharge was promulgated in the following year, unemployment stood at 6.5 per cent. Australian unemployment rates were high for decades, averaging somewhat under 6 per cent prior to World War I and in excess of 8 per cent in the 1920's. In 1939, well after the depression's crest, the rate was 12 per cent. But since World War II the picture has been extremely favorable. For years the unemployment rate has stood at between 1 per cent and 2 per cent, and at times has even fallen to under 1 per cent. By the close of 1971, it was 1.5 per cent—"high" by prevailing standards and expectations. Very much unlike Canada, therefore, Australia has been among the world frontrunners in full employment.

Australians also have a lower incidence of poverty, in so far as reliable instruments for calculating poverty-line guideposts have been devised in the two countries. The percentage of Canadian families estimated to be living in poverty conditions was 21.2 per cent in 1965 and 18.6 per cent in 1967, and a 1968 estimate placed 29 per cent of all individuals in the poverty group. Suspicions of malingering on the part of persons collecting welfare have been contradicted by hard facts. In 1971, a Canadian Senate committee report made some harsh indictments, asserting that

> The whole welfare system, at all levels, costs Canadians more than six billion dollars a year, yet it has not significantly

> alleviated poverty let alone eliminated it. Welfare rolls have not diminished. The problems grow, costs go up and will, in time, suffocate the taxpayer.*

The Australian data, which are not as thorough as the Canadian, have indicated a poverty rate of 7 per cent or 8 per cent of Australian individuals. There are proportionately more pensioners, invalids, and female heads of households among the Australian than the Canadian poor, because there is no unemployment to speak of among able-bodied Australians.

The results of a nationwide survey announced in 1970 struck a variation on the Australian poverty theme. Rather than dealing with poverty as such, the survey concluded that 30 per cent of Australian families lacked the funds for discretionary spending after basic needs had been met. Included under "basic needs" were certain sums for such expenditures as motor vehicle upkeep and recreation, so "basic needs" were not defined as bare subsistence. Still, the 30 per cent Australian figure was thought to be considerably higher than in the United States. Precise calculations aside, the overall picture in Australia at least suggests that relatively few persons live in poverty and relatively large numbers live in very modest circumstances.

The available data show that Canadian personal income covers a considerably wider spread than in Australia. In Canada, even after adjustments to local cost of living and other conditions have been accounted for, there are proportionately more people who are economically very comfortable or wealthy than in Australia. In Australia, persons defined as occupying lower-income categories receive a greater share of national earnings than the comparable Canadian group. In the late 1950's, for example, 20 per cent of Australia's top earners collected 30 per cent of the national income. In 1964–65, 23 per cent of earned male income was collected by 13.6 per cent of male earners. In Canada, according

* *Poverty in Canada.* Report of the Special Senate Committee on Poverty. (Ottawa: Information Canada, 1971), p. ix.

to 1961 figures, 12 per cent of the earners collected 30 per cent of the nation's income. In addition to smaller Australian wealth concentration among equivalent proportions of upper-income earners, the number of Australians of considerable wealth is low, and Australians in high-paying occupations receive considerably less than their Canadian counterparts. In both countries, physicians and surgeons are the highest paid professions. In 1968, self-employed Canadian doctors realized an average income of over $29,000, while Australian doctors averaged under $13,000, reflecting a 2 to 1 Canadian advantage even after the 18 per cent or so higher value of the Australian dollar is adjusted for. At the opening of the 1970's, top Australian executives in firms with annual turnovers of between 4 and 10 million dollars tended to fall into a $15,000 salary bracket, considerably lower than their North American equivalents. When the focus shifts to lower- and middle-income strata, however, Australians are found to collect a larger slice of national income than Canadians, and rank high in this regard by western standards generally. One recent Sydney survey indicated that some 70 per cent of the city's households earned between $3000 and $9000, highlighting the relatively modest yet highly uniform Australian income structure.

Australia's combination of small numbers of poor people and a clustering of modest-level incomes has been prominently affected by officially constituted wage-setting machinery. Nearly from the beginning of nationhood the great majority of Australian working people have had their wages and working conditions influenced and/or enforced by federal and state quasi-judicial tribunals. Nearly 90 per cent of wage earners are now covered in this way, about half of them through the Commonwealth Arbitration Commission, which handles occupations falling under interstate commerce. Federal wage precedents are closely followed by the state tribunals, and are influential even where collective bargaining agreements determine wage scales.

From 1907 to 1967, the federal commission applied the standard of a "basic," or floor, wage to all covered workers, and subjected it to periodic review and adjustment. The basic wage was originally defined in terms of need, as the "normal needs of the average employee regarded as a human being living in a civilized community." Although the "need" criterion was not abandoned, the commissioners progressively added criteria, such as industry's capacity to pay and national economic conditions at large. Rather quickly the basic wage was exceeded by most workers through a maze of wage increments, or "margins," which were prescribed for worker skills, experience, employment in onerous jobs, and the like. Although the margins awards created differential wage rates, the basic wage rate tended to rise at a faster pace than the size of margins awards. In 1967 the basic wage and margins were consolidated under a "total wage" concept of awards, and increments are now granted to the combined wage package, though a theoretical minimum is retained.

The wage-fixing system does not cover all wage earners, and there is a constitutional prohibition on the setting of nation-wide minimum wages which would cover all earners, regardless of whether or not they fall under the federal tribunal's jurisdiction. Organized labor's request for the inclusion of a company profitability criterion for wage determinations has been rejected. Overall, however, through one source or another, a modest yet living wage has been insured for the overwhelming majority of Australian workers. Margins have differentiated wages, but not greatly. Under existing full-employment conditions, workers have steadily been able to negotiate "overaward" wages with employers, and the federal Commission has been generous in its own awards. The 6 per cent rise in December 1970 represented the largest award ever made in a national case. Hence, apart from protecting the lowest range of wage earners, the system has been operating toward lifting the general material well-being of Australian working people, though without opening conspicuous wage ranges among them.

The size and distribution of gross earnings aside, other factors enter into the calculation of effective net income. One such factor is the level of inflation. Recent indicators leave little to choose between Canada and Australia. Until the middle 1960's, Canadian and Australian prices were impressively stable. Then they began to rise. For several years annual inflationary movement in Canada exceeded 4 per cent, aggravating the country's serious unemployment problem. The 1971 inflationary figure was a reasonably acceptable 3.2 per cent. At all events, while in the 1960's the consumer price index rose by 35 per cent, the median family income improved by 85 per cent. Australian inflationary pressures in the late 1960's ranged from 2.5 per cent to 3.5 per cent, but by the 1970's they had escalated, forced up in part by the disproportionate rise in wages vis-à-vis productivity. Still, while in 1970–71 Australian prices rose by 5.4 per cent, wages rose over 10 per cent.

Another factor coloring net income is taxation. For many years, a distinguishing feature of both countries was the presence of an unreformed tax schedule which created serious inequities. Although the tax treatment of the Canadian middle classes had long been reasonable, the Economic Council of Canada estimated in 1971 that 54 per cent of the income of the country's poor was being diverted into taxes. As part of its drive to assist Canada's disadvantaged, Ottawa in that year enacted major reforms which, without imposing fresh personal income taxation on middle-class earners, eliminated all income taxation for about a million low-income taxpayers as of January 1972. A married person with two dependent children would henceforth carry no income tax obligation until his earnings reached $4000 per annum. At that income scale, his tax burden would then be only about a third of what it had been under the previous system. In Australia, there was no meaningful change in the income tax structure between 1954–55 and 1970. Since general-population income grew substantially over that period, great numbers of previously low-income persons found themselves in the much higher tax brackets which had originally been devised for a small group of middle-class earners. What this produced, apart from the imposition of especially high levies on middle-income earners, was the extraction of tax money from the general public amounting to more than double the growth of incomes in the same period. The system became patently unfair, but in its way it contributed to the leveling tendencies operating upon the income structure at large. In 1969, a married Australian with two dependent children earning $4000 (Australian) paid an income tax of $555. His Canadian counterpart earning $4000 (Canadian) paid $210—this before the 1971 tax revisions. At the $6000 and $10,000 levels the tax payments in 1969 were $1267 and $3129 for Australians versus $663 and $1764 for Canadians. Reforms enacted by Canberra in 1970 provided for a degree of across-the-board tax relief. But the middle class remains substantially taxed (an income-tax surcharge was imposed in 1971), and the low-income group continues to be assessed; persons with income as low as $500 continue to pay personal income taxes.

Some group measures of socioeconomic resource distribution

So far, we have assessed some broad Canadian and Australian economic indicators, poverty, personal wealth, and disposable income. It is also helpful to inquire whether such nationwide economic indices may be masking important occupational, regional, or subcultural differences within each society.

It has already been pointed out that rural work forces in the two countries have been steadily declining both absolutely and relatively, and that the number of farms has been declining as well. On the Canadian Prairies, for instance, between 1941 and 1966 the number of farms shrank from 279,000 to 195,000, while the average farm size was expanding from 400 to 700 acres. Although rural production continues to play an extremely prominent role in the economies of both nations and makes a major contribution to sales in foreign trade, the share of the national wealth produced by the rural sectors has been drastically diminished. Wool accounted for 66 per cent of Australia's overseas earnings in 1950–51; twenty years later, it had fallen to 13 per cent. In both nations, many of those who have remained on the land have experienced setbacks, to the extent that some of them may be regarded as economically depressed in relation to most of the other major occupational categories. At least for those with high aspirational values, rural life in both countries imposes other disadvantages. Rural children continue on the whole to have less education, of poorer quality, than urban youngsters.

The agricultural "problem" in Canada and in Australia is most diverse. Some of it stems from climatic misfortunes, some of it from inefficient production, some of it from overefficient production which has created surpluses and depressed prices, some of it from shifting consumer tastes, some of it from conditions in international trading markets. At bottom lies the realization that there are too many people still living and working on the land.

Not by any means do Canada's 400,000 or Australia's 300,000 farms face comparable difficulties, but general tendencies are discernible. Canadian farm income slipped 10 per cent between 1968 and 1969, while the Australian decline between 1968–69 and 1969–70 was 17 per cent. In 1961, 71 per cent of Canadians making their livelihood from farming earned $2500 or less for their labor and return on their investment, and 25 per cent of the entire group received less than $1600. In 1966, 59 per cent of all Canadian farms had *gross* cash receipts of less than $3750. In the same year, in Ontario, Canada's richest province, 40,000 of the existing 110,000 farms grossed less than $2500. In 1969, while retail sales rose 6 per cent throughout Canada, the dominantly agricultural Prairie provinces suffered by comparison; sales were up only 1.5 per cent in Alberta and Manitoba, and in Saskatchewan, 85 per cent dependent on agriculture, they declined by 2 per cent. There has been a steady increase in the Canadian public's belief that farmers were not receiving a square deal from Ottawa. This sentiment rose from 24 per cent in 1956, to 51 per cent in 1970. The Australian rural crisis manifested itself more slowly. But over the 1950's and 1960's, with farm costs up 180 per cent, agriculture commodity prices had risen only 80 per cent. By the opening of the 1970's, about 15 per cent of Australia's farmers were believed to be earning under $1000 annually. Perhaps 45 per cent of all farm properties in Queensland and Western Australia were undergoing hardship, and up to 25 per cent in other states. For wool, Australia's most celebrated and historically most profitable rural industry, the auction price for 1970–71 was the lowest in a quarter of a century. In a four year period the percentage of wool growers living on marginal earnings had jumped from 20 per cent to 40 per cent. Although many members of Canada's and Australia's rural communities who are experiencing difficulties are not poor by the standard of the value of their land and equipment, such assets are essentially nonconvertible, and their economic plight is nonetheless real. In 1971, Canberra announced emergency grants for the relief of rural unemployment.

Another approach to analyzing resource allocation is to chart it by area. If a nation contains political or geographical units which clearly and persistently lag behind the rest of the nation, or behind one or more especially prosperous units, political division and a depreciation of national allegiance can eventuate. Canadian and Australian areal comparisons can be made by calculating significant economic distinctions among provinces and states. In Canada, it is also possible to identify historically and economically meaningful regions, such as the Atlantic region and the Prairies.

There are various economic distinctions among Australia's states, not the least of which is the relative balance in their economic structure. But by most economic indices which relate to the individual's condition, the Australian states diverge from national norms considerably less than Canada's provinces and regions. Moreover, most of the Canadian differences are firmly established, not recent. Most conspicuously behind national Canadian economic standards are the Atlantic provinces. Quebec and the Prairies have ordinarily stood somewhere in the middle. On almost all scales of economic well-being, there have been two undisputed leaders, Ontario and British Columbia. Regarding unemployment, the overall Australian rate at the close of 1971 was 1.5 per cent, ranging from South Australia's low of 1.29 per cent to New South Wales' high of 1.86 per cent. In April of 1970, Canadian national unemployment stood at 6.7 per cent, with 9.2 per cent out of work in Quebec and 10.8 per cent in the Atlantic region. The Atlantic region also has one of the country's weakest educational records, which bears on employment and career opportunities. Its students leave school sooner, and more often, and its teachers have the poorest training and the lowest pay in Canada. Though 64 per cent of the boys in British Columbia and Saskatchewan stay in school until grades 11 and 12, in New Brunswick only 29 per cent of them do so. Australian school figures also disclose interstate disparities, often reflecting strength in Victoria and weakness in Queensland. But the disparities tend to be minor up to the end of compulsory attendance, ages 15 or 16 years, and then grow at the voluntary high-school levels and in tertiary education.

Not only are the margins between unemployment highs and medians narrower in Australia than in Canada, but the absolutely small number of persons unemployed in Australia has helped to make Australian interstate differences relatively inconsequential. The figures indicate that Sydney and Melbourne residents have a slight advantage over other Australian capital city residents in the margin of discretionary income available to them. So far as data are available, it would seem that Queensland's, and more particularly Brisbane's, incidence of poverty is rather higher than in the rest of the country, but not by much—perhaps on the order of one in ten persons as opposed to one in twelve nationwide. Canada's situation is far different. In 1967, 12 per cent of Ontario's families were classified as living in poverty, but the figure for the Atlantic provinces, 34 per cent, was nearly three times as great. At about this time, two-thirds of the farms in the rural province of Prince Edward Island were classified under poverty status. Personal income indicators reveal much the same national contrasts. In 1968–69, Australian per capita income was at its highest in Victoria ($1773), and at its lowest in South Australia and Tasmania ($1499 and $1435, respectively). The average Australian weekly wage at the close of 1971 was $90.00. The state low was in Tasmania ($82.30) and the high in New South Wales ($92.70). In 1970, the Atlantic per capita share of the national income was less than 70 per cent; per capita earnings were twice as high in British Columbia ($3584) as in Newfoundland ($1784). This has been a persistent trend. For instance, Ontario's personal income as a percentage of the national average was 114 per cent in 1926 and 116 per cent in 1962. Comparable year figures for Prince Edward Island were 57 per cent and 63 per cent.

Although Quebec has not ranked at the bottom of various Canadian economic scales, it has tended to rank unfavorably on such indices as unemployment, per capita income, and rate of migrant intake. Furthermore, Quebec often compares itself to neighboring Ontario, whose population is only slightly larger. Quebec naturally regards itself as the key French-Canadian province, and Ontario the prime example of English Canada. Yet Ontario's prosperity clearly outshines Quebec's, not only in the various categories cited, but on such scales as the attraction of developmental capital. In 1969, when new investment across Canada rose by 12 per cent, it jumped by 21 per cent in Ontario, but achieved only a 3.8 per cent gain in Quebec.

We now turn to subcultural dimensions of socioeconomic resource distribution. If native peoples such as Aborigines, Indians, and Eskimos are not taken into account, Australia lacks any established and significant racial or national subculture among its population, but Canada does not. "Ethnic" Canadians are actually a composite of numerous nationalities. Despite their propensity to be more numerous in western Canada than elsewhere, they do not have an identifiable "homeland" within the country. Although ethnics often retain their national customs and languages, they have undergone considerable assimilation into the English community's language and life style. They are often simply considered as part of "English," as distinct from "French," Canada. Although the B and B Commission investigators found that Canadian ethnics earned lower incomes than Anglo Canadians residing in the same communities, the most distinctive and most culturally self-conscious subcultural group, the French, were materially the most disadvantaged. Canada's French are a substantial one-third of the national population. Although there are numerous French outside Quebec, Quebec itself is 80 per cent French, and a kind of French-Canadian homeland for the country's oldest European community. The Québecois in particular, unlike ethnics, have largely preserved their cultural and linguistic integrity. It is therefore especially important to establish the extent of their socioeconomic inferiority.

One of the more ironic features of the French-Canadian material condition is that it has been worse in Quebec, where the French are numerically dominant, than in parts of Canada where they are a minority. B and B Commission research disclosed that while per capita French salaries were 80 per cent of English salaries, countrywide, they were only 65 per cent as high in Quebec. The data for 1961 average male labor force incomes are most illuminating. In Toronto, English, French, and ethnic annual earnings were $5261, $4168, and $4168, respectively. In Ottawa, they were $5504, $4008, and $4714. In Montreal, the spread was the widest: $5896, $3998, and $4502. In Quebec at large, unilingual French male workers averaged $3107. Bilingual persons of French extraction did better—$4523. But unilingual English were by far the best paid among the three categories, averaging $6049.

Australian and Canadian socioeconomic conditions can also be tested on the basis of opportunity and mobility, so far as these bear on the related themes of education and occupation. Our first task is to strike some nationwide comparisons, and then to examine any observable subcultural variations in either or both societies.

Educational opportunity is a key ingredient in occupational and income potential, especially in societies where service and technical skills are in demand. At the voluntary high-school levels, we have seen that proportionately more Canadian children attend than Australian children. Australia has created a scholarship scheme to encourage young people to attend beyond the mandatory school age, but the program is not striking at the core problem of getting the talented poor to remain at school. Commonwealth funds are being distributed on a competitive rather than a need basis, which means that students in the better, urban, middle-class neighborhood schools reap most of the scholarships. Various kinds of Commonwealth assistance is provided to private schools, as are scholarships to advanced private secondary-school pupils, but again without reference to the financial need of the school or the pupil. One result has been that Australia's non-Catholic, exclusive private schools (mostly denominational Protestant), which charge considerable fees and cater to the well-to-do, have had their elitist role in society reinforced. These schools enroll about 8 per cent of the country's secondary-school pupils, of whom over 80 per cent do a full high-school course, compared to about a quarter of the government-school group, which represents three-quarters of all secondary students. This disparity is then mirrored in university attendance rates and, above all, in membership in the more exclusive socioeconomic and occupational sectors. Canada's explicitly private secondary-school population is only 4 or 5 per cent, and schools catering to children of wealthy parents do not receive the sort of official aid now being disbursed in Australia, but the dominance of their graduates among the nation's elite is very noticeable.

Opportunities for higher education in both countries have reflected a clear bias in favor of children of wealthier and better educated parents, but the differences seem to be narrowing. University fees are not prohibitive, but are hard on low-income families, especially in Australia. Considerable scholarship assistance is available, with 60 per cent of Australia's university students being excused from fees. Canadian data for 1956 showed that 15.2 per cent of university students came from the 3.3 per cent of the nation's families which were then earning at least $10,000 annually, while 19 per cent of university students originated among the 31 per cent of families then earning under $3000. Viewed in another way, 7 per cent of the labor force was, in 1956, defined as professional, and its children accounted for 25 per cent of the university population. The unskilled laboring class representing 20 per cent of the work force, contributed 5 per cent of the students. Australian figures, although compiled three years later, revealed somewhat more severe stratification. The professional class (excluding administrative occupations), representing 7 per cent of the population, accounted for 30 per cent of the university entrants. Some 33 per cent of the male labor force was defined as unskilled or semiskilled, and from this group came 8 per cent of entering university students.

A 1968–69 Canadian survey suggested that university students represented economic backgrounds which, proportionately, were extremely close to the actual income distribution of the work force. This survey was, however, confined to Ontario, and was variously criticized. But it probably was indicative of a substantial growth in higher educational opportunities nationwide.

This has certainly been the trend in Australia. Among entering students in 1969, 50 per cent of the fathers and 62 per cent of the mothers had not even completed secondary school, and only 14 per cent of the fathers and 4 per cent of the mothers had completed university studies. About 12 per cent of the students were from homes where the father's occupation was defined as unskilled, basic service or transport—roughly the same occupational group which had contributed only 8 per cent of university students a decade earlier. The major gains seem to be among students representing lower middle-class families. It is estimated that about half of the Australian young persons who could benefit from some form of higher education are still deprived of it.

Growing educational opportunities in Canada and Australia portend occupational upward mobility, and therefore overall enhancement of personal material conditions for the ambitious and the talented. The available Australian data suggest that, at least into the 1960's, occupational upward mobility was decidedly weak, representing one of the lower manual to nonmanual job-movement tendencies among western nations. But a 1965 survey, which contrasted intergenerational occupational movements with Italy and the United States, spoke favorably of Australian tendencies. Some 44 per cent of nonmanual male Australians had fathers who had been or were in manual occupations, compared to 43 per cent in the United States. Most of Australia's mobility was attributed to free choice of occupation, rather than to forces which were reordering the nation's economic/occupational structure. Inference about Australia's improving mobility rate can therefore be drawn from more than the existence of absolute and proportionate increases in educational levels, or from the proportionately greater number of non-elite sector individuals staying on at high school or availing themselves of college- or university-level education. Structural change in the economy has been accelerating. Heavy migrant intakes have resulted in rapid population growth, helping, together with considerable infusions of foreign investment, to develop economic structures not usually associated with small and essentially static populations. The economy has moved in directions detected earlier in Canada, whose economy has resembled that of the United States. Diversification, technological applications and entrepreneurialism have in turn generated an increased demand for a high order of skills.

Religious affiliation is another dimension along which we may assess group measures of resource allocation. In particular, we will be concerned with whether the Catholic minorities in the two countries have reasonable educational and occupational opportunities, and a share of incomes commensurate with their numbers.

Some 27 per cent of Australians are Catholic, and the proportion has been rising. Beginning in the 1870's, the Australian colonies cut off public assistance to Catholic education, and the situation remained virtually unchanged until the 1960's. The Commonwealth government and the states are now providing direct aid to these schools, as well as scholarships to some of their pupils, but even with governmental assistance, the Catholic schools are feeling severe economic pressures, and spend less than one-half as much per student as do state schools. Catholic education is qualitatively quite uneven, and many of its students are less well qualified to enjoy upward socioeconomic mobility than the average state school student. Even so, the proportion of Catholic-school children completing all of high school is slightly greater than state-school pupils, as is the proportion of Catholic school graduates who enter universities. Current university achievement results disclose no material differences among state, Catholic, or non-Catholic private-school matriculants.

Australian Catholics have traditionally been somewhat less fortunate in occupational opportunities than Protestants, but not across the board, and conditions appear to have become increasingly favorable for them. In the past, there tended to be proportionately more Catholics in the working class, although data from the mid-1960's indicated no particular Catholic-Protestant differences at that occupational level. Catholic schools have, over time, effectively prepared their students for eventual placement in teaching and governmental positions, and the percentage of Catholics in government employment is well above their proportion in the general population. There is little doubt that a combination of undertraining and various degrees of discrimination have kept Catholics below parity in senior- or high-status positions in business, industry, and military and government administration, but in certain professions such as medicine they do seem to enjoy proportional parity. In Australia, as in Canada, the very highest, elite stratum of society, though overwhelmingly Protestant, is almost as impenetrable for the ordinary Protestant as for the ordinary Catholic.

Catholics constitute a much greater proportion of Canada's population (45 per cent) than they do Australia's. Although most Canadian Catholics are of French origin, over a third of them are not. The non-French Catholics have come to enjoy reasonable access to higher economic positions. Their main grievance has been an absence of comprehensive subsidization of parochial education. This has been more of a province-by-province than a national problem. Provincial subsidization ranges from being comprehensive in Quebec, Newfoundland, Saskatchewan, and Alberta, to partial in Ontario, to absent in British Columbia. The overall tendency is toward enlarging the character and extent of provincial underwriting of Catholic schools. Manitoba, for instance, abolished aid to confessional schools in the late nineteenth century, touching off a storm of political controversy. But gradually, by the 1960's, it had moved toward extending some support.

Canada's French minorities outside the province of Quebec have understood their educational concerns in essentially cultural rather than economic terms. The non-Quebec French are surrounded by formidable Anglicization pressures. Provinces other than Quebec have been extremely hesitant to allow much instruction in French in government schools. Not until the 1960's did New Brunswick and Ontario, which house the largest French minorities, introduce tax-supported French high schools, and not until 1970 did Manitoba allow the use of French in public schools which serviced a sufficient number of French-speaking students. Federal funds are now being contributed toward the extension of school instruction in the French language, but the job of protecting the French language is a formidable one. Outside Quebec, the proportion of persons of French descent who can still speak French has been declining over the years; a 1970 Ontario survey revealed that 80 per cent of the province's French high-school students even among themselves commonly conversed in English.

The irony of the situation has been that the French community across Canada, in and outside of Quebec, has enjoyed fewer economic prerogatives than either the Anglos or the ethnics. Nationwide in 1961, the French ratio of the male labor force in professional, technical, and managerial occupations was about 75 per cent lower than for Anglo Canadians. Some 7.5 per cent of the French labor force but only 4.6 per cent of the Anglo group were engaged in "laborer" work. To be French has meant preserving cultural distinctiveness at the cost of material advancement. The B and B Commission found that in the business world, education benefits French Canadians less that it does any other subcultural group. Individual competence does not suffice for upwardly oriented Francophones, since a high-level position for them normally entails cultural assimilation. It was discovered that, outside of Quebec, only 2 per cent of the trained English-speaking personnel were obliged to speak French, and that 97 per cent of the businesses functioned in English exclusively.

The traditional failings of the French educational system in Quebec have already been indicated. But data on occupational opportunities reveal a French inferiority which far exceeds qualitative differences in French-English education. Findings based on 1961 census data showed that Quebec and the Maritimes shared the dubious honor of containing native-born populations whose membership in the top SES (Socio-Economic Status) categories was proportionately lower than that of migrants. In the mid-1960's, in Montreal, the French held only 17 per cent of the management positions, though they comprised 60 per cent of the city's labor force. Outside of Montreal, a labor force 93 per cent French-strong occupied 23 per cent of the management jobs. In Montreal, 10 per cent of the business establishments operated in French only, 30 per cent in English only, and the remainder in both languages. Throughout Quebec, bilingualism was required of 96 per cent of the trained French personnel, but among only half of the Anglophones. Less than a sixth of the value of Quebec's industry was found to be French-owned.

French Canadians have been the victims of job inequality in federal government as well as in private employment, especially, but not exclusively, in ranking positions. In this regard a heavier liability has been imposed on Francophones than on the Catholic subcultural group in Australia. While French-speakers comprised 26 per cent of the private soldiers in the Canadian army in 1959, only 8 per cent of the sergeants and officers of the rank of major and above were French. More recently, a survey published in 1971 disclosed that while 16.2 per cent of the personnel in all the armed services were French, only 10.6 per cent held commissioned ranks. Government employment of civilians has shown much the same trend. In 1965, among Ottawa civil servants in contact with the public and serving in nineteen selected agencies, the greatest number nearly everywhere were persons who spoke English *only*. Then came bilinguals, most of whom were of French stock. One unilingual French speaker was located among the two thousand or so persons surveyed. From 1946 to 1971, the position of French-background persons among "executive" civil servants showed uneven improvement. In 1946, 8.7 per cent of the senior federal civil servants were French. The figure of 15 per cent recorded in 1971 was, however, lower than the 16 per cent which had been reached a decade earlier.

Socioeconomic resource allocation and public values: An interpretation

Our data indicate that Canada and Australia are in many respects affluent, even thriving societies. A plausible conclusion would therefore be that the two publics are generally satisfied with their material lot. This in turn would suggest an enhanced public confidence in the two political systems, and political activity relatively free of abrasive conflicts over issues of socioeconomic resource distribution. But our data have also pointed to certain differences in the makeup of and tendencies in economic conditions within the two countries. Here an effort will be made to evaluate how Canadian and Australian cultural idiosyncrasies predispose public attitudes to the structuring of wealth and opportunity. The organized expressions of socioeconomic viewpoints, such as party and interest-group formations, will be treated later.

Despite their internationally favorable economic ratings, Canada and Australia are not paragons of wealth and abundance for one and all. The Australian standard of living is lower that the Canadian. Compressed wages and stiff tax rates have made real wealth and luxury inaccessible to the vast majority of individuals. Although wealth is easier to acquire in Australia than in Canada, the overall Canadian standard of living is roughly 25 per cent lower than in the United States, with which comparisons are inevitable. Then too, high unemployment and poverty rates have deprived numerous Canadians of even modest circumstances.

However, a case can be made that value systems in both societies have generally worked toward depressing excessively strong wealth or achievement norms. A case can also be made that various mechanisms have made decent living conditions possible for many people, and that the interplay of certain public values has made underaccess to wealth and opportunity palatable.

Neither society is especially noted for cultural tendencies for risk and success. The Canadian ethos in this respect is less striking, and more subtle, than in Australia. Canadian society bears many resemblances to the American society. But its evolution reveals a more subdued approach to individualism, greater natural acceptance of authority, and a greater disposition to compromise, owing to circumstances associated with nation-building and cultural plurality. To the extent that Canadian thinking has moved toward promoting a national personality, it has often counterposed itself against America's blunt, individualistic egalitarianism. Canadian values sponsor a rather more elitist view of society. Part of this reflects the tory influence in early Canadian development. Part of it derives from the influence of an ongoing middle-class presence. A noted Canadian sociologist has remarked that

> The Canadian middle class has maintained its middle class position, not by engaging in the competitive struggle which the larger American continental system invited but by building about itself, in this more restricted, and in terms of physical resources poorer, area of the continent, a very largely bureaucratic system of control. . . . It was upon the support of this middle class, for more than two centuries, that the colonial tie of Canada with the old world depended, and it has been upon its support that had depended very largely, in the years since Confederation, the tie of nation. In a way scarcely true of any other Western nation, the middle class, in Canada, has been the Establishment.*

The point is not only that there has been a distinctive middle-class feature in Canadian life, but that it has generally been benign and publicly acceptable, not resented. In addition, middle-class status, at least in its economic and occupational dimensions,

* S. D. Clark, *The Developing Canadian Community,* 2nd ed. (Toronto: University of Toronto Press, 1968), p. 234.

has not been severely restricted. Certainly by Australian standards, Canadian social institutions allowed for reasonable educational opportunities and occupational mobility.

Furthermore, religious influences upon popular values did not foster strong feelings of aspiration and material acquisition. For one, Catholicism has always enrolled a very large minority of Canada's population. The country was 41 per cent Catholic at confederation, and is about 45 per cent Catholic now. Overall, the Roman Church in Canada has not espoused its own equivalent of a "Protestant ethic" so far as personal industry and achievement in the secular world have been concerned. In Quebec, where Canada's Catholics are concentrated, the Catholic church's influence was especially depreciative of acquisitive values. The church became a tenacious promoter of the cultural, linguistic, and religious properties of a distinctive subculture. Canada at large was visualized as being dominated by centrist, commercial, and Protestant Anglophones, whose values the church strenuously opposed. Instead, through its pervasive role in the province's educational system, health and welfare agencies, and for a time trade unions, the church helped implant parochial and socially conservative values. Respect for church, family, and local culture was man's preeminent duty. The traditional French Canadian syndrome of weak material aspirational values was strengthened by events flowing from the Conquest itself, since much of the cream of the French-speaking business and professional community migrated from Canada. For a considerable time following, much of the Quebec French economy was predicated on rural and small-town enterprise, and employment in the service of an *English* entrepreneurial class. Recent research has pointed to a continuing French-Canadian disinclination to seek better conditions at the expense of pulling up familiar roots and disturbing the obligations engendered by family bonds. Canada has experienced considerable interprovincial movement, especially to the wealthier provinces of Ontario and British Columbia. But Quebec's

French have only half as much interprovincial mobility as do other Canadians. Language barriers and low skills are partly responsible, but so is the Québecois' inbred lack of venturesomeness. French Canadians are not as discriminating as the English in their attribution of prestige to various levels of occupations. The French tend to upgrade jobs to which they might normally aspire, and to downgrade those which they perceive as unattainable. The B and B Commission found that even among Canada's young persons the French were less attached to achievement norms than the English, and that they were more impressed by ascriptive than achievement status.

Frustrations with the existing Canadian economic order were also alleviated by substantial outmigration, especially to the United States. Between 1861 and 1901, nearly 2½ million persons left Canada, creating a net loss of over 600,000 in the immigration-emigration balance. From 1901 to 1941 there was a net gain of over 1 million persons in the in-and-out movement pattern. Still, in the decade of the 1920's, over 900,000 persons departed for the United States alone. As late as the first half of the 1960's, an average of 50,000 Canadians were annually moving to America. By the early 1970's that figure had been cut in half, and as many Americans were moving to Canada as there were Canadians moving south. Nevertheless, the historical tendency of the discontent to move elsewhere is clear. Our interest lies in the fact that the exodus from Canada primarily comprised two types of people. One group represented the severely disadvantaged. The other included ambitious persons who were dissatisfied with opportunities available in Canada. The effect was that Canada lost people who, for different reasons, would have been especially alienated by economic conditions had they remained, with imaginably severe implications for the Canadian political system. Those who left not out of economic privation but to satisfy ambitious goals, had they remained, would have represented an approach to industriousness and economic competitiveness which in their absence is only moderately valued within Canadian society.

Australia's value system was even less disposed toward success/acquisitive norms than Canada's. We have seen that the lower-class origins of Australia's settlers and the special nature of nineteenth-century socioeconomic conditions encouraged an egalitarian popular ethos. The dominant myths became mateship, cooperation in adversity, and leveling. "Success" and "striving" were wrong because they were effected at the expense of others, and could produce undesirable posturing under the guise of leadership and expertise, traits which in themselves were held in suspicion. Ordinary people should be divested of badges of material or status inferiority, according to popular thinking, but there was no special encouragement for aggressive personal advancement into a more respectable or wealthy class.

These viewpoints are variously manifested. The idea of a universal standard of adequate wages and working conditions was strongly endorsed, while wealth and status as such commanded little envy or admiration. Every person was entitled to state-subsidized education, but there was little need for educational frills or advanced education as such. Hence Australia enjoyed free and universal basic education well before federation, but as of 1900 there were only three state-supported secondary schools in the entire country, and for years afterward advanced high-school and university education were acquired by a very small minority of the population. The drive for fair and adequate standards and security of employment for ordinary persons encouraged such organized working-class traits as fear of technological progress. It bred opposition to work incentives such as bonuses, piece work, and profit sharing, which could cause pernicious speedups or the demotion of some individuals into lower job categories. Evening and weekend shopping hours were resisted on grounds that they induced worker exploitation and the reduction of job opportunities for the regular working community. Migrants were often treated with suspicion and even discrimination, largely because they were recognized as a threat to employment opportunities and the routines of work preferred by resident Australians.

The Australian preference for respectable ordinariness over wealth and acquisitiveness has been observable at many levels. When wages were generally low, in the minds of many Australians this was sufficiently countervailed by the income security of a wage floor, and by working-hour reductions; an essentially 44 hour week was declared in 1926, and a 40 hour week in 1948. Australia's geographic isolation prevented the sort of outmigration which Canada's location allowed, but there also was not as much Australian incentive to leave for better and bigger things. Australians also have a lower rate of interstate movement, partially because Australian state economic differences are not as wide as they are among Canada's provinces and partially because Australian levels of aspiration and venturesomeness have been relatively low. The productive value of the Australian worker in the late 1960's remained substantially lower than for the Canadian worker, or as compared with most western industrial nations generally. Australians have found comfort in their own life style. During a 1971 nationwide survey, a "good standard of living" was by far the most frequently mentioned positive Australian feature. Although tax rates are steep, excessive taxation as a disadvantageous aspect of living in Australia was mentioned only one-third as often. In the first half of the twentieth century, Australia converted a greater part of its productivity increases into leisure activity than did comparable industrial societies. Australians invest less than Canadians in insurance, suggesting not only a certain optimism about conditions of life, but also the limited goals which they tend to set for themselves. Similarly, Australians have developed one of the world's highest rates of private home ownership. This has been encouraged by programs of state assistance to home buyers which antedate World War I, and by relatively modest housing costs generally. But home ownership acquired a positive status within the Australian value system, reflecting preference for family-oriented, limited, and readily attainable goals.

Since the postwar years, various socioeconomic changes have taken place. Alongside have come certain alterations in public thinking, though established norms continue to play their part. Survey data suggest that there is now a widespread tendency among Australians to discard a self-image as members of the working class and to think of themselves as members of the middle class. This may mirror the increasing openness and prosperity of Australian society. It also may be associated with a continuing concentration of incomes, but at a higher level than before. Perceptions of occupational status continue to be very uniform across different population sectors. A drive toward a standard 35 hour work week is gaining momentum. Apparently, this is true partially because some workers wish to better themselves materially by finding time for a second job. Also, there seem to be lingering fears of redundancy occasioned by technological changes, and wishes to capitalize on a labor-short market to earn more leisure time without reduction of wages. The unions' traditional aversion to work incentives has been considerably allayed, but one is struck by the rather different moods which characterize established Australian and new migrant approaches to work and earnings. For instance, "New Australians" are heavily represented among the cab drivers. "Old" Australian taxi drivers tend to work fairly standard hours. By comparison, New Australian cabbies seem willing to drive longer hours and are more aggressive in seeking out business. No single explanation is sufficient, but one factor appears to be the most important underlying motive.

If Australian society is acquiring more congenial attitudes toward aspiration and acquisitiveness, then the opportunities for this are also more available, thus preserving congruence between cultural norms and objective conditions. We noticed earlier that there has been a substantial relative as well as absolute increase in upper high-school and college level attendance, and that university students are increasingly drawn from backgrounds of modest income and educational attainment. In a 1967 survey conducted in Sydney and Melbourne, an almost equal distribution of persons of various occupational status by a very large margin selected education as the best means for children to be helped in their future careers. There was also overwhelming optimism about the ability of one's children to improve themselves as well or better in relationship to other children. This reflects, in part, the broadly shared values of a perceived egalitarian society in which only a minute fraction of the public, about 1 per cent, actually regards itself as "upper class," and in which class differentiation is very widely believed to rest on money, not on status, privilege, birth, or education. Data gathered in 1970 did disclose considerable public resistance to the suggestion that the present compulsory school age of 15 or 16 be raised. However, among those expressing the greatest support for this were the higher-income groups, which was understandable, and younger persons generally, implying a change in attitude favoring a more intellectually demanding system.

If Australian cultural values, traditional or recently acquired, have generally complemented existing material conditions and opportunities, the same cannot be said for Canada. The traditional English and French Canadian norms were broadly, but not entirely, acceptive of prevailing socioeconomic conditions. Although the special acculturation of the Québecois blocked serious resistance to the group's inferior economic status and lack of opportunity, the poorest portions of Canada have traditionally been the Maritimes, where French Canada's cultural norms have not been generally applicable. Likewise, the Prairies have for many decades faced highly unpredictable economic conditions. Both the Maritimes and the Prairies have been tied to primary industries. National or subcultural value systems aside, postwar Canada has undergone a relative deprivation which has not been the case in Australia. Poverty rates are considerably higher in

Canada than in Australia, and there is a sizable group of the rural poor. Over the years the plight of Canadian rural people has not only been recognized by those directly affected, but by the general public. Survey data show a noticeable decline in public belief that farmers have been fairly treated by the federal government. By 1970, only 25 per cent felt so, and there were substantial negative majorities in all regions of the country.

The most startling changes in public feelings toward recognized socioeconomic conditions have occurred in Quebec. By the 1960's, industrialization and other forms of economic advancement had come on rapidly. The most dynamic influences operating within the province were now oriented toward democratic, materialistic, and secular values. The Catholic church, the political leadership, and the general public all shared in the transformation. As education became far more available, and more relevant to contemporary society, French Canadians began to catch up with the remainder of Canada. The church's social and ideological hold had slipped. For instance, the use of contraception became widespread, and family limitation popular. A radio program which for years had been the most popular in Quebec—a nightly recitation of the rosary—was discontinued in 1970 after the listening audience had fallen by nearly two-thirds.

All the same, shifts in the elite and to a degree in popular viewpoint were not accompanied by commensurate improvement in French Quebec's opportunity to realize its proportionate share of material gain and opportunity. Although French Canada has historically lagged behind the rest of the country, this lag has now become sharply resented. Being French, or even being bilingual French, has meant economic inferiority vis-à-vis an English-speaking community whose willingness to communicate in French, even in Quebec, has been minimal. In 1961 Canada was 12 per cent bilingual, down from a 17 per cent figure in 1941. It has been found that one-half of French personnel in Quebec feel that a French Canadian who is successful actually becomes more English than French in his makeup. In 1967, 33 per cent of Quebec respondents felt that French Canadians were not being treated well in the federal civil service, and 43 per cent of them believed that they were receiving poor treatment in business. In the Canadian west, by comparison, only 8 per cent ascribed poor treatment to the French in federal employment, and 7 per cent felt there was poor treatment of them in business. In 1971, 73 per cent of all Canadians felt satisfied with their living standards. But in special and potentially systemically disruptive ways, French Canadians have become dissatisfied and restless over their material conditions and access to opportunities, opening a very wide gulf among the nation's regions and subcultural groups. Some of the implications of this phenomenon, such as French and English community perceptions of Quebec separatism and prospects for intersubcultural reconciliation, must be examined.

3

Personal and group rights

Canada and Australia announce themselves as open societies, operating on liberal-democratic principles. Security of person, freedom from capricious authority, and adequate access to impartial justice are assumed to obtain, as are ideals of tolerance and equal opportunity for various classes of individuals. Public satisfaction with political systems is ordinarily enhanced if expected rights and opportunities are matched in practice, and if social and political change is attainable through available procedures. These matters will be discussed in the present chapter under rubrics of civil and political rights, the status of women, religious freedoms, and the position of racial minorities. In the chapter which follows, we shall assess the disposition of the two societies toward accommodation or nonaccommodation in the settlement of differences.

Civil rights

There is almost nothing in the Australian and Canadian constitutions prescribing basic guarantees in the manner of the American bill of rights. The BNA Act makes reference to the protection of certain public rights, specifically, of linguistic and religious groups, but not to private rights between citizens. The Australian constitution is nearly as silent. There is a freedom of religion clause, and a requirement that in federal trials undertaken on indictment, the Commonwealth must proceed by jury trial, but even this can be circumvented if the authorities choose to bypass formal indictment procedures. Among Australian states, only the smallest, Tasmania, has anything in its constitution which carries a "civil rights" feature, and the reference is to religion only. Saskatchewan's bill of rights, enacted in the 1940's, is the only such statement found among Canada's provincial constitutions.

The highest courts in Australia and Canada have had some dealings with civil liberties cases. Their judgments, even when they have tended to uphold civil libertarian principles, have ordinarily been rendered on grounds other than the intrinsic civil rights claims of plaintiffs. Civil liberties may, however, be accorded a new and important reception from the Canadian Supreme Court. In 1960, the Canadian Parliament passed a bill of rights of a sort. It was ordinary legislation, not entrenched in the BNA Act. It was not binding on the provinces. Its stipulations could be neutralized by ordinary legislative exception. This bill made relatively little impact until 1969, when the Supreme Court ruled in favor of an Indian who had been convicted by a lower court of drunkenness in the Northwest Territories, where federal law is applicable. Although the facts of the case were not in dispute, the defendant, one Joseph Drybones, had been convicted under regulations which were more stringent for Indians than for whites. The conviction was overturned on grounds that the bill of rights had an overriding effect on federal law, and the precedent may in future serve to protect Canadians in various circumstances.

Australia not only lacks any type of bill of rights, federal or state, but has lagged behind Canada in instituting codes or oversight procedures. While by 1970 Ontario, Nova Scotia, New Brunswick, and British Columbia had human rights commissions, there were no Australian state counterparts. Alberta and New Brunswick appointed ombudsmen in 1967, Quebec did so in 1969, and Manitoba in 1970. Also in 1970, Ottawa appointed a Commissioner of Official Languages, or "linguistic ombudsman," to oversee the workings of the recently enacted Official Languages Act in various federal agencies, and to process public complaints alleging denials of opportunity for persons to communicate with federal authorities in either French or English. Not until 1970, in Tasmania and South Australia, was Australian state legislation authorizing ombudsmen brought forward. The first ombudsman actually to take office (in 1971) was appointed to oversee a local government in suburban Sydney. Governmentally sponsored legal aid for the poor has generally been weak or nonexistent in both countries. Still, within Canada, Ontario has taken a strong lead in this direction. Manitoba and Nova Scotia followed in 1971, as did the federal government on behalf of the northern territories. In that year, New South Wales supplemented free legal aid for the poor with a contributory policy for middle-income earners, and Canberra undertook certain costs of legal assistance to Aborigines.

The recent movement toward strengthened formal protection broadly coincides with trends in official practices in both countries. Although formal guarantees have their place, the real test of civil liberties ultimately lies in official practice. The major political parties in Canada and Australia have, over time, shared in compiling records tainted with civil rights restriction and encroachment.

Canadian and Australian federal governments have been especially severe toward civil liberties in wartime, when they claimed to perceive serious dangers to national security. They have enjoyed nearly unlimited authority during such emergency periods due to generous judicial interpretations of constitutional defense provisions. In Canada, furthermore, stern action in wartime has been facilitated because of the federal monopoly over the criminal law; in Australia, it is divided among seven jurisdictions, namely the six states and the Commonwealth.

During the two world wars, Canada's War Measures Act and ancillary regulations authorized the suppression of *habeas corpus* writs and allowed restrictions on conventional jury trial proceedings. In World War I, thousands of aliens because they had been born in Germany or the Austro-Hungarian Empire and were for little reason other than that regarded as security risks, were interned in camps. In World War II, over 20,000 persons, for no particular reason other than their Japanese ancestry, were removed from British Columbia and relocated. During World War II printed materials were subject to censorship and, if needed, suppression. The Communist party was outlawed. Personal utterances were carefully monitored. A charge was laid, but later withdrawn, against George Drew, then the leader of the Conservative party in Ontario, for remarks he had made about an official report concerning the deployment of Canadian troops in Hong Kong. The mayor of Montreal, Camilien Houde, was actually imprisoned for advising citizens to disregard national service registration regulations.

During World War I, in Australia, an Unlawful Associations Act made it possible for the government to outlaw organizations which advocated or encouraged the taking or endangering of life or the destruction of property. Membership in or financial contributions to such groups were illegal. Nonnatural-born British subjects were subject to deportation. During the last war, executive orders could dissolve organizations which were considered prejudicial to the efficient prosecution of the war. Numerous organizations were banned, and zealous police went so far as to ransack the homes and libraries of various liberals who were caught up in the dragnet.

The Canadian and Australian governments have even in peacetime retained powerful legal weapons. Some have become virtually dead letters, such as Australia's sedition laws, which are very broadly drawn and impose the burden of proof of innocence upon the accused. In Canada, sedition was charged against participants in the Winnipeg general strike of 1919, and some deportations were ordered. In the 1920's, quantities of radical books and pamphlets were confiscated by Australian customs officials. Federal enactments in the 1920's banned membership in certain organizations, or, in some cases, the printing or distribution of literature on behalf of undesirable organizations. There were also laws which permitted the deportation of persons not born in Australia if they hindered or obstructed interstate or overseas trade or the production of services by federal agencies. Criminal code amendments made illegal the teaching, advocacy, as well as involvement in attempts to bring about, political, industrial, or economic change in Canada by force or intimidation. A person convicted of simply distributing literature of this nature could be imprisoned for up to twenty years. However, only a few prosecutions were undertaken under the 1919 criminal amendments, and the legislation was repealed in 1936.

To this day, the Royal Canadian Mounted Police has access to writs of assistance; they authorize searches which require no court order and are essentially open-ended. Such writs have, however, been used with discretion, and primarily in narcotics and revenue cases. In the autumn of 1970, the War Measures Act was resurrected in a nonwartime situation. Separatist terrorism in Quebec was defined as a "state of apprehended emergency." Normal legal procedures were suspended in the province, and hundreds of persons were rounded up and jailed without recourse to *habeas corpus* privileges, and troops assumed many security duties. They had also been pressed into service during strike eruptions in the 1930's. A Communist sponsored strike shut down coal mining operations during the Australian winter of 1949. Troops were called out to stand by at the mines. When the Communist party was found in contempt of court, Commonwealth and New South Wales security forces raided party headquarters in Sydney and seized records.

Canadian provincial and Australian state governments have not been immune from behavior which has seriously infringed personal liberties. In Canada such action has often taken the form of provincial discretion in the implementation of federal criminal law. Alberta passed laws muzzling the press in the 1930's. Quebec brought forth its celebrated "padlock law," which prohibited the distribution of Communist literature anywhere in the province, and the attorney-general was empowered to padlock for a year any premise where Communist advocacy was suspected. Federal intervention prevented the Alberta regulations from coming into effect, but the padlock law survived for two decades. Even by 1969 a Quebec royal commission was moved to report that the province continued to operate a repressive and vindictive system of justice. It trampled on human rights without cutting down on the causes of crime. Police were often needlessly zealous and penalties were harsh. Between 1961 and 1971, the Australian state of Queensland on three separate occasions declared states of emergency which granted widespread powers to police. The 1961 and 1964 emergencies arose during the industrial difficulties in the mining community of Mt. Isa, and in 1971 the circumstance was anticipated demonstrations against the visit of a South African rugby union team.

Contemporary Canadian and Australian practices reveal more sensitivity and permissiveness than in the past. As has been seen, there is a movement in both countries to adopt statutory protection for citizens. Quebec introduced legislation to compensate victims of crimes, and the ombudsman provided for damages to be paid to numerous persons detained during the 1970 disturbances. In 1971 Canada introduced legislation to outlaw all private wiretaps and electronic eavesdropping; the police were to be required, except in national emergencies, to obtain court authorization. Australian law restricts federal wiretaps to instances of national security and then, except in emergencies, only with the approval of the Commonwealth attorney-general. State governments may not tap without Commonwealth approval. The first state action barring private eavesdropping was sponsored in Victoria in 1969, though the law did not disqualify illegally acquired material from being entered in evidence. In the same year, New South Wales also banned unofficial eavesdropping, but allowed wide powers in this area to state authorities. In 1971, South Australia and Queensland announced their intention to outlaw bugging and other forms of invasion of privacy.

Both nations, and especially Canada, have been making headway toward liberalizing the administration of the law. Canada has abolished capital punishment for a trial period. By the close of 1971, all but one of the Australian states had either abolished or were planning to abolish capital punishment, and the Commonwealth government seemed similarly disposed. In any event, from 1967 to the end of 1971, there were no executions anywhere in Australia. Various Australian states have also been forward-looking in such matters as probation release, open prisons, conjugal visitations, and the treatment of juvenile offenders, though the laws differ drastically from state to state. Major reforms in Canada's criminal law were incorporated into legislation beginning in 1970. They included liberalizing abortion, divorce, and homosexuality laws, a curtailment of police arrest power, liberalized bail, and speedier hearings and trial procedures in the event of arrest. Australia seems a long way from such liberal action, and in recent years has been distracted by problems arising out of its foreign and defense policies. Participation in the Vietnamese conflict and other issues have generated protests and in turn something of a "law-and-order" debate, and have produced stronger penalties in the Commonwealth and in certain state legal codes. Australia's national service legislation has made provision for conscientious objection, but not for alternative forms of service. Still, although the penalties for noncompliance with conscription laws are stiff, there has been a tendency in official circles to avert the eye. Legislation was rushed through to punish persons donating to or collecting on behalf of North Vietnam or the Vietcong, but Canberra was unwilling to precipitate a confrontation with violators.

By now, despite official authority to operate otherwise, both Canada and Australia are almost totally permissive in allowing political materials to enter and circulate within the country. Political pressure has occasionally befallen the CBC and the ABC, as when the former was requested to postpone a television screening of a documentary on Lenin during the 1970 disturbances in Quebec, or when the latter was admonished over material presented on its public affairs programs.

Officials in both countries have not neglected to examine materials for standards of morality. Canada has not exactly been a paragon of permissiveness in this regard. In a recent one-year period, Toronto police seized 72,000 books and charged 30 persons under the obscenity provisions of the criminal code. The Australian situation, though slowly loosening up, continues to reflect severe restrictiveness. The Commonwealth bans large numbers of books from entering the country, and regularly bans or censors imported films. "Love Story," which carried a "PG" rating in the United States (all ages admitted—parental guidance suggested), was edited in several places by Australian censors. "Hair" was performed in Sydney, but barred in Melbourne and Brisbane. Victoria banned Mary McCarthy's *The Group,* even though it had been passed by Commonwealth officials. *Playboy* magazine has had some issues blocked from entering the country, and the state of Queensland banned the sound track to "Hair."

Would it appear that the Canadian and Australian publics have been content with the state of civil liberties in their respective countries? Imputations of civil rights encroachments have occasionally been catapulted into electoral politics. For instance, they did become mixed into the Australian conscription controversy in World War I, and again into Australia's party political debates over dissent and demonstrations relating to foreign and defense policy in the late 1960's. Australian unionists in the 1930's organized pressures against government seizure of radical materials and the intimidation of fringe groups. Popular and political complaints in the 1960's caused Canberra to soften intended amendments to the sedition laws and the penal clauses of the National Service Act. There was grumbling among French Canadians in particular over restrictions in the two world wars, since Quebec was ambivalent about the wars and opposed conscription. There were some sharp reactions among the Canadian trade unions to the draconic laws enacted following the Winnipeg general strike (1919), and to the treatment of organized labor and workers generally during the lean years of the 1930's.

Nonetheless, the civil liberty cause has not really caught the popular imagination in either society. Part of the explanation lies in the fact that some of the most restrictive measures have been instituted in wartime, when many people have been caught up in a nationalist spirit, or otherwise have been willing to countenance special handling of private rights. Part of the reason lies in the only temporary or sporadic resort to, or eventual outright abrogation of, some of the harshest legislation, for instance the post-Winnipeg criminal code amendments. Some of the explanation may also lie in the fact that most of the restrictive measures personally affected only a trifling minority of the two populations; much of it was directed at, and applied against, a minute fringe of radicals who enjoyed little public approval. The ordinary man in his ordinary pursuits was left unmolested. Certain strains in the two political cultures also offer clues. Canadians may expect that the rule of law will prevail, but they are also rather inclined to accept authority, and to respect government and its agents. French Quebec has had less exposure to the canons of "British justice" than the rest of the country, and relatively stronger bonds of authority. In a 1971 survey, 80 per cent of Montreal citizens wished for a restoration of capital punishment, and 85 per cent favored police wiretaps. It can be argued that Australians, with their supposed distaste for authority, should have keenly resented intrusions upon personal rights. But the Australian tradition of fair treatment has inclined more toward protecting class rights than personal rights. Tradition has generally been insensitive to abstractions about freedom and liberty, and perceptibly insular; Australia has been uncomfortable with novel and/or foreign persons and notions. It has stressed instead the rights of people as workers, wage earners, returned servicemen, and the like. In 1967, an absolute majority of Australians favored the whipping of major criminal offenders. In 1970, 55 per cent believed that existing levels of censorship should either be continued or increased.

Growing official concern for personal liberty in the two nations would, however, appear to be in line with a growth in public sensitivity and allowance for relaxed controls over reading and viewing matter. The Canadian Civil Liberties Association and the Council for Civil Liberties in Australia, though they largely appeal to an educated elite, have become persuasive and articulate spokesmen at large. They have provided a worthwhile service in uncovering official neglect or violations of civil liberties, and have served in a publicly educative capacity. In Canada, a rapid shedding of traditionally conservative values has increased the concern of the Québeçois for civil liberties. In Australia, a rather surprising 70 per cent of the public said in 1969 that demonstrations of political dissent carried out in city streets should be allowed. In various surveys dealing with aspects of rights and censorship, the younger Australians, in their twenties, have been clearly more permissive and sensitive on civil liberty issues than older persons, a tendency consonant with their preference for longer compulsory education and other departures from classical Australian thinking.

Representative institutions and the franchise

With few exceptions, contemporary Canadian and Australian elections are based on the principle of universal suffrage. In this sense, classes of individuals cannot complain of discrimination and lack of access to the electoral process which raises or defeats programs, parties, and leaders. Another similarity between the two societies lies in the speed and relative ease with which representative and responsible institutions were established. Beyond that, however, lie important differences in the development of the franchise, and certain lessons about the composition and cultural traits of Canada and Australia.

When convicts were just beginning to be unloaded in Australia, Canada already had representative, that is, elective, political institutions. They were established in Nova Scotia in 1758, in Prince Edward Island in 1773, and in New Brunswick in 1784. The Quebec Act of 1774 which followed the Conquest made no provision for popular institutions in what had been French Canada, and retained considerable influence in the hands of the clergy and the landholding seigneurial class. French Canada had had no previous experience with representative government and had little if any interest in it. The arrangements of the Quebec Act might have been mutually convenient for the British government and the resident French community for some time had there not been an influx of American loyalists into the country. The loyalists and some newly arrived British migrants insisted on popular institutions, and got them in 1791, with separate bodies established for Upper and Lower Canada. Elective bodies were no less desired by Australian settlers. Appointive councils were introduced in the 1820's, but the elective principle was delayed in the mother colony of New South Wales until 1842, by which time there were enough free settlers to outweigh the influence of emancipated convicts.

The Canadian arrangement worked badly. In both Upper and Lower Canada effective influence became concentrated in councils dominated by what were known as "family compacts," narrow groups of mercantile oligarchs, English-speaking even in French (Lower) Canada. The situation got out of hand, and minor rebellions broke out in both Canadas in 1837–38. Both uprisings had strong elements of resentment of the countryside against the cities, and of an urge for a more egalitarian social order against vested interests. But there were subtle differences, distinguishing one as

English and the other as French. The Upper Canadian revolt, led by William Lyon Mackenzie, was aimed at securing genuine democratic self-government. In French Canada, however, the followers of Joseph Papineau were imbued more with a defensive nationalist feeling than with democratic ideology. The rebellions were suppressed, but they prompted events which were to prove enormously significant for Australia as well as Canada. The British government dispatched Lord Durham to Canada, and he found "two races warring in the bosom of a single nation." He recommended that the Canadas be unified under a system of responsible and not simply representative government—in other words, that the Crown's representative generally act upon the advice of his Canadian ministers who, in turn, would be responsible to an elected assembly. Durham was confident and hopeful that the French Canadians would soon be assimilated by the British. This last suggestion proved unworkable and was abandoned, but responsible government in a unified Canada was launched in the 1840's and endured, despite a violent outburst by Montreal's tory business community over the Rebellion Losses Bill, which the legislature had passed and the Governor refused to disallow.

Responsible institutions began in New South Wales and Victoria in 1855. They were hastened by the Canadian precedent, by the preferences of an egalitarian Australian community, and the arrival in Australia of British Chartists and a number of Canadian expatriates who migrated after the defeat of the 1837 rebellion. Ironically, they were also hastened by Australia's version of the family compact, the squatters. These rural elites wished to protect their interests against egalitarian pressures to open up the land. But they often found colonial governors unsympathetic to their cause, and thereby chose to carry out their fight in a representative and even responsible government setting. That was the arena where the squatter issue came to be fought, and the squatter interests were defeated.

To recapitulate: Responsible government appeared in Australia quite effortlessly, but in Canada it was preceded by organized violence. Although there was a conflict between "vested" and "popular" interests in both countries, the Australian conflict was fought out in surroundings which made elected, responsible government a natural and accepted political battleground. Although Australians approached the responsible government issue from different perspectives, their differences were not complicated by the very special kinds of cultural intonations which distinguished the English and French protests in Canada.

These Canadian-Australian cultural and historical peculiarities formed the backdrop against which the suffrage was extended in the two countries. Canada was less egalitarian, more affected by elitist respectability, and by far more distinctively marked by subcultural approaches to representation and popular government. The question of which cultural community would overpower or successfully resist the numerical advantage of another did not arise in Australia.

With confederation, in 1867, the several provincial franchise arrangements were adopted for federal elections. All charter provinces then maintained some form of property qualifications. Resort to provincial franchises in federal elections continued until 1885, at which time, of the seven existing provinces, only British Columbia had virtual universal manhood suffrage, and Ontario had extended its franchise appreciably. The ostensibly "uniform" federal electoral legislation of 1885 in practice proved nonuniform, and failed to remove property qualifications. When in 1898 federal elections returned to provincially-based franchises, five provinces had moved toward essentially manhood suffrage, but Nova Scotia and Quebec retained a limited suffrage. Finally, in 1920, it was settled that federal elections were to be conducted on a common franchise, and universal manhood suffrage was adopted. Plural voting, meaning multiple votes for business and property owners, was abolished in federal elections in 1898. Quebec, in 1920, was the last province to abolish the practice.

In Australia, where open politics and egalitarianism were more pronounced, four of the six colonies adopted universal manhood suffrage between 1856 and 1859, some years before Canada confederated. The 1902 Commonwealth electoral law opted for a universal federal franchise, eighteen years before it happened in Canada. Western Australia, the last Australian state to repeal electoral property qualifications for its popular house, was 56 years ahead of Prince Edward Island, the last Canadian province to do so. Plural voting never obtained in the Australian federal franchise, but for many years it did in Canada, as we have seen. South Australia at no time employed a plural franchise, while the other states abolished theirs by 1907, thirteen years before the practice was finally discontinued in Quebec. Traces of plural voting survive for some municipal elections in both countries. Women's voting rights were also expanded far earlier in Australia than in Canada.

Australia not only was far ahead of Canada in widening the franchise, but it was a world pioneer in making the vote honest and effective. The expression "Australian ballot" refers to the secret ballot, which originated in Victoria and South Australia in 1856 and then quickly spread to the other colonies. At confederation, when provincial franchises and procedures were adopted for federal elections, New Brunswick alone among the charter provinces utilized secret voting. A secret ballot was ordered for federal elections in 1874, but it was amateurish and ineffective. Not until 1888 was a reasonably secret ballot procedure instituted, and even after that some abuses persisted.

Both Canada and Australia have experimented with voting mechanisms which could be construed as serving popular or electoral equity causes. Canada makes frequent use of local referendums, which are normally held apart from federal or provincial elections, thus shielding them from serious partisan and other extraneous coloration. National referendums have no constitutional basis, but there was, for instance, an advisory referendum on the conscription issue in World War II. Australia also used advisory referendums on conscription during World War I. But the referendum is an integral part of the federal constitutional amendment process in Australia, and is also required in the New South Wales and Queensland state constitutions. In the Canadian west, where the popular democratic impulse ran strongest, there has been experimentation with the initiative, referendum, and local recall elections. The single transferable vote was for a time used in Prairie provincial elections, and proportional representation survives in some western municipalities. In Australia, the federal Senate has been elected under proportional representation since 1949, and Tasmanian lower house elections are conducted under a PR system. The adoption of preferential voting for the federal House of Representatives elections in 1918 was inspired as much by maneuvers for political advantage as by a desire for fair play. The system had been introduced as early as 1892 in Queensland, then spread to Western Australia and Victoria before World War I, and after 1918 gradually was adopted for all state lower house elections save in Tasmania. The most radical Australian innovation, which borders on forcing men to be free, has been compulsory voting. First adopted in Queensland in 1915, it became part of Commonwealth law in 1924. Electoral enrollment is compulsory federally and in all states except South Australia. Voting is compulsory for both federal houses, federal referendums, all state popular houses (including for persons who do enroll in South Australia) and in some local elections. Prior to compulsory federal voting, turnout for House elections had varied from 46.9 per cent to 77.7 per cent of the eligible electorate. Now the figure is well over 90 per cent, and Australian man, *malgré lui,* has been emancipated from exercising the option of being a nonvoter.

In respect to upper legislative chambers, however, the Australian penchant for democratizing representation and voting has not sped ahead, except at the level of the Senate, the federal upper house. The Australian Senate has always been popularly elected, while its Canadian counterpart has its members nominated by the government of the day—for life tenure, until a recent change forced retirement at 75. Also, eligibility for Senatorial nomination in Canada includes a property qualification. Below the federal level, it is Canada that moved quickly to remove what some would regard as anachronisms. About half of the provinces originally had second houses, based essentially on nonpopular representation. All such bodies were abolished years ago, except in Quebec, whose appointive house survived until 1969. Australia began its national history with upper houses in all states, carrying them over from colonial practice. Nonpopular councils had appeared earlier than elected assemblies in the Australian colonies, thus carving out an established position for themselves. Furthermore, the very rapid development of representative bodies, responsible government, and universal franchise was understood in some quarters as requiring institutionalized checks through a nonpopular agency should popular government commit excesses. Nomination for life to New South Wales and Queensland legislative councils and election under restricted, business and property franchises for the other colonial councils was an elitist, not a classically egalitarian Australian notion. But the contradiction is only partial. Queensland abolished its second chamber shortly after World War I. The other second houses survive, but by now the Victorian, Tasmanian, and West Australian councils are elected by the same electorate as votes for the lower houses. Among state second houses relying on election, only the South Australian retains an unreformed property franchise. Incoming members of the New South Wales council are now chosen for twelve-year terms through a joint sitting of the incumbent members of both houses of the state parliament. Therefore, in only two states are there second chambers which are removed from direct popular control.

The fact remains that both before and after most of the state second chambers were variously democratized, the public seemed satisfied to retain them, because of their fairly impressive legislative powers. In 1961, a well-entrenched Labor party government in New South Wales, following an altercation with the legislative council, organized a constitutional referendum which proposed the abolition of the council altogether. The measure was convincingly defeated. In the same year, surveys in all five Australian states containing legislative councils, some less reformed than they are now, showed popular majorities opposed to dispensing with them. The explanation of their toleration lies not in public admiration of elitism or privilege, but in the Australian disposition to mistrust and, if possible, to hedge authority—even popularly elected authority. In a peculiarly Australian fashion, therefore, buffering and even unrepresentative institutions have been enlisted in the service of a candidly popular ethos. To this might be added that while the Labor party is in principle opposed to second chambers, it normally does not push its convictions very strenuously. When out of office, it can continue to maintain the sounding board advantage accorded by second chambers, and can use nomination for their seats as patronage for party loyalists. Then, too, with the 1961 New South Wales experience in mind, Labor appreciates the public mood in this matter.

It is difficult to draw workable hypotheses about the relationship between voting age provisions and political culture qualities. At the turn of the 1970's nearly all Canadian provinces had lowered the voting age to 18 or 19, and Ottawa had lowered the age to 18. But there was no particular pattern of allegedly "progressive" political parties standing for age liberalization and "conservative" provincial regimes fighting to maintain a 21 year limit. Nor were there clues based on linguistic or religious distributions among the provinces which moved one way or another on the voting age. As of mid-1971, 21 years remained the legal voting age in three Australian states and in the Commonwealth. But both major federal party groups are pledged to 18 year-old voting, and state legislation authorizing the 18 year-old vote has been undertaken or promised by premiers representing both Labor and non-Labor governments. There is agreement in principle between Canberra and the states if possible to move in tandem toward the federal vote for 18 year olds, since there is some constitutional uncertainty whether a state could unilaterally grant the federal franchise to 18 year olds. Public feeling as of 1970 was almost equally divided between those who explicitly favored an 18 year voting age, and those who opposed it or were undecided. While there was no singularly positive public sentiment, it should be recalled that there was no precedent, state or federal, which at that time could have fostered popular acceptance of the 18 year-old vote.

The rights and status of women

Noticeable manifestations on behalf of insuring the dignity of women in all facets of life have recently become commonplace in western nations. Increasing self-awareness has led to a movement toward removing residual legal disabilities, as well as guaranteeing that equality of status for men and women become a fact in practice and spirit. Like women elsewhere, those in Canada and Australia have experienced inferior status and opportunity, and like women elsewhere, a number of them have become aroused. Canadian-Australian differences in their status and present claims are nonetheless considerable, and point to discernible cultural and historical distinctions in the two national cultures.

In the first place, Canada's extension of female privileges has assumed a predictably more regional/subcultural pattern than in Australia. The few remaining provinces which have not yet adopted equal-pay legislation are in the Atlantic region, which has habitually been the most economically depressed section of Canada. Quebec, long a bastion of conservative thinking and practice, lagged behind in nearly all aspects of female equality. It was the last province (in 1940) to accord women the provincial franchise and parliamentary membership privileges. Until the late 1960's, Quebec women were severely disadvantaged in matters of property, contract, and other areas of self-determination in comparison to their husbands. The traditionally defined social role of Quebec's French women has been confirmed by attitude surveys. The B and B Commission discovered that both men and women in Quebec strongly believed that the home was women's prime responsibility, and that politics was essentially unsuitable for her. Other data indicate that political efficacy among Quebec women is especially low, and that the normal, male-female differential in Canada-wide, political disinterest, is nearly doubled among Quebec women. In the 1965 federal election, 12 per cent fewer Canadian women than men expressed political interest, with the widest gap—22 per cent—being in Quebec. Social and legislative changes in Quebec are beginning to reshape the role and awareness of the province's women, but the reshaping is only gradual. Although the legal and *de facto* status of women has been higher outside Quebec, Quebeckers considerably more than other Canadians felt in 1971 that women *were* being treated as well as men.

Aggregate Canadian-Australian comparisons are also revealing. Canadian women won their principal political rights, both federal and provincial, during and shortly after World War I. These events had been preceded by considerable women's rights agitation. They were stimulated by Canadian women's contributions to the war effort, and coincided with similar reactions in Britain and the United States. In other words, the Canadian process was unexceptional. By comparison, Australia was among the trailblazers in awarding political rights to women. The colony of South Australia extended full female franchise and parliamentary eligibility in 1894. Women were included in all state franchises by 1908, and achieved comprehensive state parliamentary eligibility by 1923. The first Commonwealth electoral law, in 1902, provided women with the federal franchise and eligibility to stand for Parliament. There had been almost no organized female agitation for such rights. It was men who primarily promoted the changes. There was no conspicuous resistance against such concessions. The effort was crowned with success earlier than in most other polities. The reason, at bottom, was that Australian society, compared to the Canadian or to most others, was relatively simple and highly egalitarian, containing a minimum of social stratification or elitist values.

Although Australian women secured political rights quickly and quite effortlessly, the record shows that, if anything, less use has been made of them or practical results produced than in Canada. Though women contested Australian Senate elections a year after they received the federal franchise, no woman was nominated by a major party for either house of the Commonwealth Parliament until 1915, and no woman was elected until 1943. In Canada, the federal franchise was obtained in 1918, and the first woman was elected to the House of Commons in 1921. Between 1921 and 1970, 18 women were elected to the Commons. Although the Australian House of Representatives has always been much less numerous than the House of Commons, it is still a striking fact that after 70 years of operation the House of Representatives should have elected only three women. Five have been elected to the Senate, none before 1943. Two women in each country have been appointed to federal ministries. In Canada, women were elected to provincial legislatures shortly after being granted eligibility. This did not occur in the Australian states until 1959, in South Australia—65 years after women had acquired the legal right to serve. The number of women in Canadian provincial legislatures has also well exceeded their numbers in Australian state legislatures, despite additional opportunities for election accorded to Australians through certain state second houses.

To what degree can the low number of women in politics in both countries be attributable to prejudice foisted upon them by sexist, male-dominated political establishments? We know that in both places women have a lower rate of political interest, and exhibit lower efficacy, than men. We know that women in Canada vote rather less than men, though by now there is only a slight difference, not much beyond 3 per cent. In Australia prior to compulsory voting, the female federal turnout ranged anywhere from 3 per cent to 15 per cent lower than for men, but that was many years ago. In both countries, female legislative candidacies have tended to be proportionately more frequent than female elective successes. Partially, this is because women candidates have, proportionately more than men, contested seats as independents or as minor-party candidates. Partially, it is because the major parties, despite protestations of innocence, have been timid about running women, or have run them in constituencies safely controlled by opposing parties. Australia's first woman judge was not appointed until 1966. In 1969, of 889 judges and magistrates in Canada, 14 were women, and none had ever served on the Supreme Court or on provincial courts of appeal. In the 40 year period, 1930–70, 235 persons were summoned to the appointive Canadian Senate, and only eight of them were women.

Despite the removal of female political liabilities many years ago, various formal discriminations lingered on. In most Canadian provinces and Australian states women do not enjoy equal access to jury duty, and there are provincial/state instances of total female exclusion from jury duty. The criminal codes still contain anomalies, such as the Canadian provision that, in seduction offenses, it had to be demonstrated that the female victim was of previously chaste character. There have also been various official impediments to female equality in employment and earnings, and it is from the economic/occupational sphere that certain lessons about the two societies and their treatment of women can be drawn.

We have seen that World War I was a watershed for the political rights of Canada's women. The grant of suffrage was a partial recognition of the considerable role played by women in the nation's male-scarce mobilization economy. After the war, Canadian women continued to involve themselves in serious and often skilled work. Girls continue to enjoy a somewhat higher rate of high-school completion than boys. Thus they qualify for reasonably good jobs, and are not discouraged from working or competing with men because of any particularly strong social animus, at least in English Canada.

The Australian picture developed quite differently. By the first World War Australian women had been given the franchise. But women's role in the economy had emerged only gradually, and Australia's less industrialized economy did not produce as much reliance on a female labor force as happened in Canada. Indeed, not until World War II were Australian women massively pulled into the economy, a generation later than in Canada. Other factors contributed to keeping the number of working women at a modest level. Australia's historically late stabilization of the sex ratio helped to make the family an especially central and settling force in society. The care and upbringing of children was, and continues to be, very attentively carried out, primarily by the mother. Coupled with strong family ties has been a value system which emphasizes the home more than in English Canada; while the Canadian pattern is for girls to remain in school longer than boys, the opposite is true in Australia. Australians are not known for elaborate and frequent entertaining and evening fraternizing. They tend to stay home evenings and to retire early. Thus the woman who has been at home with children during the day has few opportunities to mix with other company. Then too, Australian society evolved a noticeable masculine-oriented strain. Male-exclusive social activity is far more apparent than in Canada. It is a trait which has not only brought about a somewhat patronizing view of women, but has also stimulated women to become involved in organizations composed of women only.

Australia's economy, in addition to being rather less developed and affluent than Canada's, very early established a number of protections for workers. In practice, this meant the jealous guarding of jobs and wage scales by male workers. Basic wages for men have almost never been matched by women. In 1919, the prescribed federal pay rate for women was 54 per cent of the rate for men. It was often in practice raised beyond that point, and after the second World War its formal setting was up to 75 per cent of the male rate. The rationale was that women did not need as much as men since, overall, their requirements and responsibilities in society were lower than those of men. Organized labor was happy to accept this situation for a considerable time, and was especially fearful of female encroachment into the job world during the depression years. Only recently has organized labor, in a period of secure full employment, championed an equal-pay-for-equal-work principle without tongue in cheek. This principle was originally legislated in Queensland during World War I, but its terms made evasion possible and prevalent. Then came New South Wales in 1958, and then other states. In 1969, the federal Arbitration Commission finally announced a phased equal-pay-for-equal-work dictum. Australian civil services were equally slow in providing for women. Women were not generally recruited into the Commonwealth service until 1949, and not until 1966 were married women allowed to enter or to remain. In 1967, South Australia became the first state to lift bars against women in state employment. Female salary scales in public service continue in many instances to remain lower than for men, even in the armed forces.

With a few exceptions, in the provinces, Canadian official employment, by law or by established practice, rewards women equally, although women have been handicapped in promotional opportunities. There is at least a sprinkling of women in the higher reaches of the federal bureaucracy, and the marriage bar is a foreign notion. In recognition of understood realities, the 1971 federal tax reforms permitted working mothers to write off up to $500 per child and $2000 per family for day care and child-minding expenses. Unemployment insurance benefits are now paid for reasons of maternity. Canadian law and practice have not, however, been fully reconciled. British Columbian legislation was among the first prohibiting unequal pay discrimination, but a 1971 study found it consistently violated, largely because the onus of discriminatory proof was placed on the woman herself.

In both Canada and Australia, women suffer various disabilities and prejudices, especially in employment opportunities. But cultural traditions, the nature of the economy, and legal barriers (or at least lack of legal protections or right to equal treatment) produced particularly confining conditions for Australian women. Data compiled shortly after the second World War did not simply show that Canadian working women had somewhat better wages than their Australian counterparts. Australian women, by international as well as Canadian standards, were shown to be inordinately underrepresented in professional and technical fields. Comparisons such as these suggest why, despite receiving the suffrage and parliamentary eligibility later than in Australia, and with more effort, Canadian women in professional and public life have been personally less restrained, and less gratuitously regarded by men than Australian women. Canadian women were, earlier and more extensively, inducted into occupational, educational, and social dimensions of life. They became more confident, and were more easily accepted by men—again with the exception of Quebec.

Today, with about a third of the work force in each country female, the principle of women as workers is established beyond doubt. Legal obstacles to female equality have nearly vanished in Canada, and have begun to fall in Australia. The principle of unequal pay, long a powerful depressant of women's economic position, is not only breaking down in law, but faces substantial public opposition. Australian young people seem especially free of conventional prejudices. A 1966 survey of persons aged 15–20 showed 82 per cent favoring comparable pay, with boys and girls nearly equal in the extent of their positive sentiment. The political-systemic ramifications of trends in the two nations have not fully crystallized. Canadian women, because they are relatively less inclined to be subdued and inhibited, and because of cues easily available from the United States, have become more feministically truculent than Australian women. Canada's variation on a theme of women's liberation is somewhat more dramatic, more demonstratively expressed, and better organized, at least for the time being. Australian women are now rapidly shaking off their placid, second-class position. More sharply than before they have mobilized behind special-issue causes ranging from consumer protection to opposition to conscription. Above all, they have a larger array of grievances against which to raise their voices than do Canada's women, and in so doing could ripple the political waters. That will surely happen if Germaine Greer, Australia's notable contribution to women's liberation, has her way. But the typical Australian woman seems somewhat reluctant to identify herself with the archetype of Greer's book, *The Female Eunuch.*

Freedom of religious practice

History records that issues touching on religious practice can become the basis of intense political strife. Outwardly the potential for religious tension has always been present in Canada and Australia, since both developed not religious homogeneity, but Protestant majorities living beside sizable Catholic minorities. In Canada, moreover, most Catholics were "different" from the general population in another way, namely their French ancestry and culture, which were foreign and often distasteful to English speakers. For some time, Australian Catholics also were often distinguishable from the rest of society apart from their Catholicism as such. In the 1870's, about half of Australia's Catholics had been born in Ireland. Although the Irish-born Catholic population quickly declined, persons of Irish ancestry continued to dominate Catholic ranks until the influx of Continental European migrants made Australian Catholicism more nationally diverse. Features of Catholic and Protestant involvement in organized politics will be considered elsewhere. Here we are mainly concerned with whether religious bodies have been able to avoid official or popular discrimination in the pursuance of their objectives.

One potentially divisive religious problem, that of an officially established church, has hardly existed in either country. There never was any sort of an established church before or after Australian federation, though in early colonial times bitterness was roused over the Anglican church's virtual monopoly of public grants for education. Public funds were later distributed among various denominations; when the colonies then removed assistance from denominational schools, all denominations were affected. Canada's experience was rather more complex. The Anglican church was at one time established in Nova Scotia and in what is now Ontario, while the Catholic church received special privileges, including the right to exact tithes, under the Quebec Act of 1774. But by the mid-nineteenth century, migration from among British and Continental persons of various religious persuasions had eroded what had anyway been a rather benign Anglican establishment, and the concluding steps toward religious disestablishment were not aggravated by denominational conflict.

Freedom of religious organization and worship has not been markedly threatened either in Australia or in Canada, despite the general absence of constitutionally entrenched religious protections. Australia's federal constitution contains a clause, binding only on Commonwealth authorities, which guarantees the free exercise of religion, and prohibits laws which would establish any religion. Very little case law has developed from this clause. When in the second World War the Jehovah's Witnesses were declared a subversive organization and certain of their facilities were seized, the action was upheld by the High Court. Tasmania, Australia's least populous state, also has entrenched certain formal protections, which prohibit religious disability tests and permit freedom of conscience and practice of religion, but "subject to public order and morality."

In Canada, the BNA Act absorbed earlier Province of Canada

protections for the "free exercise and enjoyment of religious profession and worship, without discrimination or preference," thereby continuing to bind the new provinces of Ontario and Quebec in this way. Saskatchewan's 1947 bill of rights provided for freedom of worship, as did the 1960 federal, nonconstitutionally entrenched bill of rights. In 1970, Ottawa passed what was commonly labeled an "anti-hate bill," which declared it an offense under the criminal code to promote hatred against a group identifiable by color, race, religion, or ethnic origin. Religious minorities in Canada have suffered certain officially imposed disabilities. For a time, male and female members of religious sects which were exempt from military service were federally disenfranchised. There has been provincial harassment in disputes over land use and general law observance on the part of Canada's esoteric religious denominations, such as the Doukhobours in British Columbia and the Amish and Hutterite settlements in Alberta. The Jehovah's Witnesses were proscribed during the second World War. The Witnesses for some time were severely persecuted in Quebec, and the disposition of Witness cases before the Supreme Court in the 1950's began the process of case law dealing with religious subject matter, which has generally been sympathetic toward freedom of religious observance.

Popular religious toleration is much more difficult to measure. Overall, one might expect that Australia's rather insular cultural traits would have produced a greater tendency of intolerance toward the unusual than is found among the people of Canada. Outside the main arena of Protestant-Catholic feelings, however, there seems to be little difference between the two societies. Western Canadians, for instance, have often expressed impatience toward the esoteric religious cults around them. The number of Jewish people in the two countries have not been large, there now being about 80,000 Jews in Australia and a quarter of a million in Canada. They have been prosperous and high-achievement oriented, especially in Montreal, where the Jewish community is substantial. Although Jews have been subjected to a certain amount of anti-Semitic feelings, as a reading of some of the popular press in the late nineteenth century would testify, they have not been the objects of particular derision or discrimination. In Canada, Jewishness has been somewhat overlooked because Jews have tended to identify with the English-speaking middle classes, while in Montreal they have maintained good relations with both language groups. In 1971, David Lewis, a Jew, became national leader of Canada's prominent left/progressive party, the New Democrats, and his son Stephen was elected to NDP provincial leadership in Ontario. In Australia, there have been few Jews, and these have not held many strategic financial positions. The opinion data suggest that the small minority of Australians which continues to harbor anti-Semitic views is composed of undereducated, superstitious, lower class people who are negatively disposed toward ethnic minorities generally. Australian public acceptance of Jews was both cause and effect when a Jew, General Sir John Monash, was appointed to command Australian troops serving abroad in World War I, and when another Jew, Sir Isaac Isaccs, became the first native-born Governor-General.

Protestant-Catholic relations in both countries have undergone serious strains. In Quebec, the cultural defensiveness of the French was hardened by a keen recognition of their Catholicism and their suspicion of English, Protestant Canada. Similarly, French Canadian dependence upon the Roman church made English-speaking Canada more conscious of its own Protestantism. The French Canadian church's admonitions about Protestant evils were matched by hard-bitten, even virulent, Orange and Masonic diatribes against Catholicism. The late nineteenth century gave rise to some extremely scurrilous, anti-Catholic journalism, in which the authoritarian church and the weak-kneed, Protestant politicians who catered to it were denounced. Much of the controversy over French-language schools in Manitoba and Ontario had venomous Protestant-Catholic overtones. The main targets of the Ku Klux Klan in the Prairies during the 1920's were Catholics and migrants.

In Australia, the Irish character of the Catholic church tarnished its public image. Catholic Irishmen were reputed to be anti-British, and therefore irritated Anglophile Protestants. For years Australian Catholics were widely held up as unpatriotic, partially because of certain emotionally charged events. One such was the 1868 attempt on the life of the visiting Prince Alfred, Duke of Edinborough, by a Catholic Irishman. Another was the conspicuous anticonscription and at times anti-British spokesmanship of some members of the Catholic hierarchy following the Easter Rebellion in Ireland. As in Canada the educational policies in Australia exacerbated Catholic-Protestant problems. The removal of aid to denominational schools by the several colonies in the late nineteenth century was interpreted in many Catholic quarters as an open attack upon the Australian Catholic church itself. There was some truth in this; a leader in the antistate-aid movement, New South Wales Premier Sir Henry Parkes, believed and hoped that such measures would spell the defeat of Romanism in Australia.

Protestant-Catholic antipathies in Canada and Australia have not disappeared, but they have receded considerably. Catholics in both countries are socioeconomically somewhat behind the Protestants, but the margin has definitely narrowed in Australia, and Quebec's agitation for a larger slice of the economic loaf is an essentially secular, materialistic, and national movement. Public assistance to Catholic and French schools in Canada is increasing, and since 1963–64 Australian Catholic schools and school children have been receiving a fair amount of federal as well as state assistance. There is now even a Protestant majority in favor of continuing the practice, and persons who have organized themselves politically to end official support to religious schools are essentially motivated by a wish to transfer the savings to undersupported government schools, rather than by outright anti-Catholic sentiment. Australian Catholicism is less Irish than it was in the past, and the idea of a British Australia confronted by seditious Irish Catholics has lost most of its relevance. The recent sectarian troubles in

Northern Ireland have not particularly agitated feelings between the Catholic Irish and non-Irish communities. Despite backsliding here and there, ecumenical feeling among the Christian churches in Australia and Canada is rising. To be sure, the religious variable continues to affect political party and voting behavior in both nations—a subject which will be examined more completely elsewhere. But, since there is not any question of state-imposed liabilities against any of the major Christian denominations, and public religiosity has itself waned, religious freedom and religious acceptance are not issues which induce feelings of grievance and systemic disaffection on the part of any significant religious body.

The status of racial minorities

Canada and Australia are overwhelmingly European in composition. All the types of non-Europeans added together would amount to only between 3–4 per cent of the Canadian population, and under 2 per cent in Australia. The political effect of these non-Europeans is therefore slight, and compared to Europeans, they are generally detached from front-line politics. But they do deserve our attention. Relative to Europeans, their numbers are rising. They are becoming much more politically engaged than in the past. Also, European attitudes and policies toward nonwhite groups are instructive regarding prevailing Canadian and Australian societal values. The discussion will move from nonindigenous non-Europeans, to indigenous peoples, such as Australian Aborigines and Canada's Eskimos, Indians, and to an extent, the Métis, decendants of racially mixed Indian-European unions.

Persons of non-European extraction not native to Australia and Canada include both blacks and Asians, though in both countries the former group is much less numerous. Australia's black population is extremely small—a few hundred at most—and it lacks any group personality of its own. Black migration has not been encouraged, even since non-European admission in general has been liberalized, though certain teacher-deficient states have tried to recruit qualified North American teachers regardless of race. Only one black man has left a visible impression in Australia—the American, Dean Dixon, who for several years conducted Australia's foremost orchestral ensemble, the Sydney Symphony.

Canadian blacks are a historically well-established group, dating back to the seventeenth century. They originally lived as slaves, and then started to arrive as free settlers from about the time of the American Revolution onward. Slavery in Canada died out in the early years of the nineteenth century. A 1971 estimate of their numbers was 100,000, up from 32,000 in 1961, with their two major concentrations being Nova Scotia and Toronto. The Nova Scotian blacks were long overlooked by the rest of Canada. Within the province they enjoyed political and legal equality, but were subject to various discrimination in jobs and through segregated schools. School segregation and Jim Crow housing have by now been virtually swept away, and efforts are underway to raise the blacks' socioeconomic conditions. Nova Scotia's blacks remain worse off than their white neighbors, however. This, given the province's generally depressed condition, classifies them among Canada's most disadvantaged persons. The more politically conscious blacks in Toronto, who are, generally, new arrivals, free from such impositions as school segregation, have nonetheless sensed some racist feeling among whites.

Despite their growing racial awareness, Canadian blacks have not been particularly receptive to black-power blandishments from across the border. They are still less than one-half of 1 per cent of the population. Canada has no modern history of slavery, and for some blacks it was a sanctuary from slave conditions in the United States prior to the Civil War. Nor, unlike American blacks, have the Canadians experienced a constitutional emancipation which for a considerable time was not comprehensively satisfied in practice. Nor have they encountered intolerance on the American scale, though during the first quarter of the present century, there was a sharp antiblack reaction which included some lynchings. Furthermore, Canadian blacks in Nova Scotia, where they did meet some social and economic victimization, were able to gain redress without resort to massive confrontational tactics, and a black lawyer has been elected to the federal Parliament from a white, predominantly working-class constituency in Hamilton, Ontario.

Asians have been resident in Canada and Australia since the nineteenth century, and for many years they faced both public intolerance and legal disabilities. As we saw earlier, the presence of South Sea island laborers in Queensland and the Chinese on the goldfields further south aroused a mixture of economic fears and racial distemper. Although many Asians were deported, Australia's insularity, defensiveness about equitable working conditions for its own white labor force, and paranoia about possible engulfment by Oriental hordes made the exclusionist "white-Australia" policy a foregone conclusion when the Commonwealth of Australia was organized. The first Commonwealth electoral act, passed in 1902, excluded resident Asians and Pacific islanders from the franchise, and similar legislation controlled state ballots in Queensland and Western Australia. The federal authorities removed the electoral ban from Indians in 1925, but not until the early 1960's did all federal and state restrictions on equal Asian citizenship and voting rights disappear. In 1969 Japanese mining officials complained of Western Australian restrictions against Asian mine employment sanctioned by the laws of that state. The incident demonstrated that legal color-bars had not quite been erased.

For decades, Canada's Asians suffered considerable and humiliating treatment. In 1885, Canada's first federal electoral law, like Australia's, excluded Orientals, specifically "Chinese and Mongolians," from the franchise. This was basically a concession to British Columbia, where Orientals were concentrated and often contemptuously regarded by sectors of both the lower and the middle classes. When a uniform federal franchise was again enacted in 1920, it nonetheless barred the vote to per by reason of race *provincially* disqualified. Residual provisions which during the second World War had c certain Japanese were finally removed in 1948. Bri was the worst offender in imposing its own restrictic The Privy Council held in 1903 that British Columbian legislation denying the vote to Asians was a valid exercise of power. This provision remained on the British Columbian statutes until 1945, and not until several years later were all references to race removed in the province. British Columbia at one time tried to exclude the entry of Orientals altogether, and in so doing ran afoul of Ottawa's constitutional dominance in the field of migration. Then the province built up legislation which harassed and discriminated against Orientals in areas of contract, property, and employment, as well as in the franchise. Early in the second World War the federal cabinet decided to evacuate Japanese Canadians from British Columbia to inland detention centers mostly because it feared racist reaction against these people by the British Columbians themselves. To the present, however, apparently for racial reasons, British Columbian law makes voting eligibility contingent on a knowledge of English or French.

For all practical purposes, Asians have by now been freed from legal disabilities in Australia and Canada. Measures such as Canada's "anti-hate bill," provincial human rights commissions, and Australian state actions on the pattern of South Australia's anti-discrimination legislation are finding support. All racial restrictions on Asian migration to Canada were lifted some years ago and, as has been shown, numerous and highly qualified Asians enter the country annually, considerably augmenting the 130,000 Asians found in Canada as of the 1961 census. Despite traditional British Columbian antipathy toward Asians, and the apprehensions generated over the province's Japanese population during World War II, there appears to be a climate of public acceptance of Asians. While Canadian antagonism toward Asians was historically

...tered in British Columbia, Australian suspicions were much more geographically widespread. As late as 1968 there were only about 26,000 Asian citizens or permanent residents across the country but, gradually, public thinking began to change. The geopolitical situation no longer inspired horrific images of Asian hordes sweeping southward, though in 1971 42 per cent of Australians felt that an invasion threat would materialize from somewhere within fifteen years. The constraints of a foreign policy partially aimed at conciliating Asia raised demands for removing the odious color bar in immigration. Full employment relieved fears of cheap Asian competition. The influx of non-British, Continental Europeans relaxed public feelings toward the unknown. Years of easy relations with visiting Asians studying at Australian universities and coming and going on business and other functions further allayed doubts about whether white Australians could successfully mingle with brown or yellow-skinned Asians. The Asian intake is still very small, but it represents a major departure in principle from the earlier exclusionist policy, the pernicious dictation test, stubborn public adherence to the "little Australian" outlook of a "white Australia," and so on. Asians remain a minute community in Australia. The newer migrants from Asia have been thoroughly screened. Their educational, linguistic, and other characteristics enable them to assimilate rather handily. As a group, they have little cause to complain or organize for redress.

The indigenous inhabitants of Canada and Australia have often been referred to as a forgotten people, and for generations this was indeed an apt description. It is less apt now, but generations of neglect cannot be effaced in a few decades, and almost any policy devised to cope with these people is fraught with dilemmas.

When Samuel deChamplain arrived in the early 1600's and founded Quebec City, there were about 200,000 Indians in Canada. When Captain Cook arrived in the late 1700's, there were up to 300,000 Aborigines in Australia. With European settlement, their numbers rapidly declined. Indeed, nearly to the second World War, it was widely believed that pureblood Aborigines would die out, and that those of mixed blood would at some distant point be assimilated into the general population. The native people of both countries had their traditional life styles severely disrupted, particularly in Australia, whose primitive Aborigines were accustomed to a nomadic existence. In both countries, the requirements of European settlement, land use, and occupation generated frictions and disoriented native social organization. White men's diseases took their toll. There was some systematic extermination of Indians in Newfoundland, and considerable persecution of Aborigines, for example, through extermination expeditions in Tasmania and well-water poisoning in various parts of the country.

By the late nineteenth century, something on the order of native "protection" appeared in Canada and Australia. Treaties were signed with various Canadian Indians and reservations set aside for them. The BNA Act gave Ottawa jurisdiction over Indian affairs, but a number of responsibilities were devolved upon the provinces themselves, where the great majority of Indians resided. For most of the post-1867 period, the treatment of Indians was conducted on a capricious basis. The Indian treaties often obligated Ottawa to provide certain amenities such as education, medical assistance, and farm implements, and even annual payments to Indians—often $5 per individual (a chief received more) plus a new suit of cloths every three years. But no direct federal assistance was accorded the Indians until 1912. Before then, Indian bands drew on money accumulated from the sale of reserve lands and other rights, and interest which had accrued therefrom. In Australia, the federal government only had jurisdiction over Northern Territory Aborigines, the remainder being under state care. "Protection" for Aborigines usually meant neglect, and serious discriminatory practices were justified as being in the interest of an adolescent people incapable of fending for themselves.

By the opening of the 1970's, the numbers of native people in both countries were rapidly increasing. Canada had nearly a quarter of a million Indians, defined as "registered" and under official care, and another 200,000 attached to reservations or other protected communities. The great majority were located in the belt of provinces extending from Ontario westward. There were also about 14,000 Eskimos, nearly all in federally controlled Arctic regions. There were at the time about 50,000 pure and another 80,000 halfblood Australian Aborigines, mostly in Queensland, Western Australia, and the Northern Territory.

The numerical recovery of these peoples has run parallel to improved medical and other societal services. It has also been associated with new official policies and a greater effort than in the past to redeem the position of native persons. By 1953, Ottawa had come round to assuming a major commitment for native care and improvement, in and outside of federally controlled territory. While Ottawa continues to fund and oversee Indian affairs, a white paper issued in 1969 argued that special status conditions should eventually be removed. Reserves currently held in trust for Indians would be returned to them. Indians would be eligible for the same provincial services as other persons, and the provinces would assume a wider share of the provision of education and other services for the Indian population. Such policies approach an attempt at social assimilation. Broadly speaking, that is also the objective in Australia. As the result of a 1967 constitutional amendment, Canberra now has the ability to legislate for the welfare of Aborigines located in the states as well as in the Northern Territory, thereby allowing for a reasonably uniform approach.

The attack on native backwardness and underintegration is being carried forth on the socioeconomic and political fronts. It has been recognized that a sickly, undereducated, and socially disorganized people cannot, even if awarded full legal equality, hope to compete and live productively in an advanced European society. Life expectancies have been uniformly lower for native peoples than for the general population. At the end of the 1960's, infant mortality rates were two and a half times greater among Indians and four and a half times greater among Eskimos than among Canadians at large. In Australia, the Aboriginal infant mortality rate was estimated as being anywhere from six to ten times as great as for Australians generally. The spread of education among the natives has been very tardy, particularly at levels required for the development of genuine working and social skills. Partially because of this, native work forces have experienced massive unemployment. In 1966, 40 per cent of Canada's Indians were unemployed and great numbers were on relief, while in 1969 Aboriginal unemployment was three times as severe as among the general Australian population. In Queensland that year, only an estimated 10 per cent of Aborigines reached basic-wage parity with Europeans. Ragged health, idleness, low and insecure employment, and other factors produced socially intemperate behavior. Crime rates among Indians and Aborigines are far higher than among European Canadians and Australians, and a great many arrests and convictions have been for drunkenness. In Western Australia and Saskatchewan, where the Aborigines and Indians constitute about 3 per cent of the respective populations, approximately 30 per cent of all male and 80 per cent of all female prison inmates are natives.

Canadian and Australian authorities are now sponsoring projects designed to upgrade native opportunities. There are federal schemes for encouraging Indian and Aboriginal business ventures. Special funds have been earmarked for native occupational training and advanced educational programs. In Australia, the state and the federal governments have been passing reserve ownership rights to the Aborigines themselves, consistent with Canada's plan to move reserve lands into Indian hands. Aboriginal wages, frequently under European scales, are being raised. These and other assistance projects require money. Spending on natives varies from state to state and province to province. Overall, however, despite considerable spending increases by authorities in both countries, Canada's dollar commitment has been much larger than Australia's. In 1971, *all* state and federal spending directly applicable to Aborigines stood at about $44 million. Five years earlier, the Canadian federal government had allotted $112 million for a five-year program simply to develop the physical facilities of Indian reserves. In 1970, Ottawa and the provinces were spending in the vicinity of $250 million on Indians and Eskimos.

The drive toward expanding native civil and legal equality has taken several forms. One step has been in the area of removing surviving discriminatory regulations and adopting codes designed to insure fair treatment by the general public. In Canada, the *Drybones* decision came at a time when many of the special controls over natives were already being phased out. In Australia, the most severe restrictions on Aborigines living on specially designated lands have been in Western Australia and Queensland, states with the largest concentrations of natives. The Western Australian government has pledged itself to abolish its discriminatory legislation. Under federal pressure, Queensland may do so shortly. It has much to do. For instance, under its 1965 legislation, Aborigines and Torres Strait Islanders living on reserves, and all persons of over 25 per cent Aboriginal blood who might be "declared" to be under public care, could be confined to a reserve, and have their movements and property restricted. They could be incarcerated for such offenses as "carelessness" and "disobedience." In Canada, the anti-hate bill and various provincial human-rights commissions have fixed public requirements of nondiscriminatory treatment of native people. In Australia, South Australia's Prohibition of Discrimination Act, though as yet unique within the country, may prompt similar legislation within other states.

Indigenous people in Canada and Australia, and especially in the former, are also having self-management opportunities arranged for them, on the assumption that this will teach them civic and political skills, increase their sense of pride, and in some instances lead to decisions more sensible than if Europeans alone handled them. Canadian federal and provincial money is being provided for natives, including the often previously neglected nonregistered

Indians and Métis, to develop and operate community action groups. There is a series of regional Indian advisory councils, and a national advisory council as well. South Australia, which has become something of an Australian pioneer in the promotion of civil liberty, originated a land trust scheme for Aborigines governed by a board composed entirely of Aborigines.

These types of aids are supposed to parallel and enhance the meaningfulness of what are by now full franchise rights at the national and subnational levels. The general and traditional pattern in both countries was to deny the franchise to indigenous persons. These people were few in number and could not be expected to make much impact on election results. In addition to a tinge of racial hostility, it was widely felt that social isolation and undereducation had made these people politically naïve and incompetent. Canadian Indians were denied the federal franchise virtually throughout the post-confederation period, until the matter was settled in their favor in 1962, and for a period of time Eskimos were disenfranchised. By the close of the 1960's Quebec, the last holdout, granted Indians the provincial franchise. The Australian situation was somewhat more permissive. Persons from backgrounds half or less Aborigine have always enjoyed federal and state franchise rights. Throughout most of the Commonwealth period, fullblooded Aborigines were deprived of the vote federally and in Queensland and Western Australia. In the early and mid-sixties, these restrictions also fell. The only remaining difference is that these recently enfranchised Aborigines are not, unlike the general population, required to *enroll.* If they choose to enroll, they, too, are subject to compulsory voting regulations. Canberra also exempts full and halfblooded Aborigines from compulsory military service.

Little is known about how many indigenous persons vote, or how they vote, though there is a surmise that voting among them is light, and that in Australia, at least, Aborigine voting is strongly influenced by local personalities and elite views. In Canada, in

1971, in the Northwest Territories, where non-Europeans constitute two-thirds of the population, the European monopoly on territorial council seats was broken. Three years earlier, the first Indian, representing a British Columbian riding (constituency), was elected to the House of Commons. In 1970, in Queensland, the first Aborigine was nominated for an Australian federal Senate seat. He lost, but the following year was appointed to the Senate to fill a vacancy.

Once they develop organization, Indians and Aborigines could become reasonably significant electoral forces, since they tend to be concentrated rather than randomly dispersed across the two nations. In the meantime, the native people are evincing more and more boldness and sense of purpose, sometimes alone, sometimes in conjunction with European sympathizers. Their grievances no longer concern political rights, and there is less and less reason for complaint against discriminatory legislation. What is wanted is far more public investment in native social and economic well-being, and greater respect for cultural heritage. Canada's Indians are somewhat ambivalent about Ottawa's wish to have responsibility for native people transferred to the provinces, since it is the federal government that has become the most progressive and financially generous toward them. Some Indians have also been agitating for a revision of "inequitable" treaties, and "Red Power" in Canada has begun to borrow from Red Power militancy in the United States. There has been some "Black Power" expression among Australia's Aborigines, but it is still very weak. In early 1972, the founding meeting of a Black Panther party was attended by a handful of Aborigines. Absolutely and relatively, the Aborigines are less numerous than Canada's Indians. They have less traditional ancestral identification than Canada's tribes and bands. Comparatively fewer Aborigines than Indians have mingled in European society at large, or have been exposed to socialization processes. Still, their people have produced both a boxer and a female tennis player of world rank, and an artist and a poet of at least Australia-wide renown, distinctions which play on the pride of a race whom the dominant white society long persecuted, or ignored, or for whom it predicted extinction.

Some speculations may be drawn from the Canadian and Australian approaches to native peoples. There is a history of civil and political disability imposition in both countries. Much of this can properly be attributed to sincere feelings, misguided or otherwise, that persons such as Indians and Aborigines were simply grownup children, gullible, uninformed, and disturbingly subject to antisocial behavior. Hence, European stewardship, not equal rights, was believed necessary. For decades, precious little was done to enable native people to improve themselves. Many Europeans, especially in hyperurbanized Australia, seldom laid eyes on natives, who tended to live in rather secluded regions, often in reserved areas. There consequently was little awareness of who or what native people were, and few pangs of conscience were felt. All the same, explicit racial feelings cannot be discounted. Evidence is seen in the hostility encountered by Asians in both countries, and the "white Australia" ingredient in that society's cultural makeup. In Canada, where large numbers of Indians are spread over a number of provinces, there did not seem to be striking differences in official provincial policies. But Australian Aborigines are concentrated in two states, Western Australia and Queensland, and it is there that franchise limitations and the most restrictive controls over them were applied. These two states have also been historically less prosperous than, for instance, New South Wales and Victoria, helping to account for meager service and welfare expenditures, and the perpetuation of the backwardness of their numerous native wards. In 1967 the Australian electorate at large, by a 10 to 1 margin, endorsed a constitutional amendment which made possible the counting of Aborigines in the same way as other persons, and gave Canberra controls over Aborigines domiciled in the states. But the referendum majority was only 8 to 1 in Queensland. A survey in the late 1960's disclosed that Brisbane residents were markedly less tolerant toward Aborigines than Canberra and Melbourne residents. Residents of certain country towns, where contacts with Aborigines were considerably more frequent than in capital cities, Brisbane included, were the least tolerant of all.

Despite certain similarities in the Canadian and Australian treatment of indigenous persons, it is noteworthy that Ottawa undertook a serious commitment to them before Canberra did, and that the sums of money which have lately been earmarked for native development have been far more substantial in Canada. This may be taken as part of the broader and stronger Canadian attitude and policy toward civil liberties and life quality improvement. The Australian public and its officials have long been more insular and culturally self-satisfied, preoccupying themselves with such objectives as wage egalitarianism and racial exclusiveness. We have seen that such traits have of late been visibly weakened, but they have by no means evaporated. There may be a parallel in the foreign-aid effort in the two countries. Although Australia's international position demands more delicate handling of emerging nations, its per capita foreign aid donations, exclusive of assistance to Australian Papua-New Guinea, are measurably lower than Canada's.

4

Political efficacy and conflict resolution

Political trust and efficacy

We have examined Canadian and Australian values from various standpoints. Material in the preceding chapter explored the balance of freedoms and restrictions weighing on individuals and groups, and the opportunities available for political redress. Given the prevailing distribution of cultural norms, perceptions of material and psychic satisfaction, and access to means for effecting desired change, we now ask whether the two societies can be characterized as politically confident, and amenable to resolving differences through agreed, reconciliatory procedures. An important concern, therefore, is with questions of political efficacy—the two publics' perceived competence to influence political outcomes, and their willingness to engage themselves in such efforts. Basically, a reasonably high level of efficacy would imply integrated rather than isolative outlooks. There would be general public optimism, and identification with the purposes and methods of political life. In the last resort, strong public efficacy would suggest a contribution to the legitimacy, and therefore capabilities, of the Canadian and Australian political systems.

We might begin by asking whether Australians and Canadians

regard organized politics as honest, and the practitioners of politics—professional politicians—as basically honest and decent persons. While political corruption has not been absent in either society, neither has it been rampant. At the national level, Canada experienced two major scandals, but one occurred in the nineteenth century, and the other a half a century ago, while Australia has not undergone comparably dramatic exposés. Nor has corruption in the local government been especially prominent in either country. Local politics has never offered the patronage and other prizes often associated with the United States. Local party and organized politics have been traditionally weak, and therefore abuses of the political "machine" variety most likely to be noticed and resented by the citizenry have been absent. Provincial and state politics have carried the heaviest burden of official corruption. These governmental units enjoy substantial powers, and often house entrenched and long-lived political party machines. In Canada, the most notorious contemporary examples have been in Quebec, in the 1930's, 1940's, and 1950's. The provincial Union Nationale (UN) regime of Premier Maurice Duplessis, which gained office in the 1930's on a platform which attacked the wholesale corruption of its predecessors, evolved an intricate machine which flagrantly bought and sold favors of all kinds, and made contractors, sellers, and a host of others beholden to it. Australian state government officials, including ministers, have also been implicated in corrupt practices from time to time, and the general absence of legislation regulating conflict of interest has hardly helped matters. But to locate the most recent serious breach of official probity it is necessary to reach back to the early 1930's, when New South Wales Premier J. T. Lang was found by a royal commission to be implicated in questionable practices in awarding greyhound racing licenses. Then too, although the accusing finger pointed to the very top—the state premier—there was no imputation of wholesale graft, bribery, and intimidation on the scale cultivated by Duplessis in Quebec.

Corruption itself has therefore not been especially prominent. Its most flagrant manifestations are matters of history, not ongoing political practice. Furthermore, when and where it has occurred, there has not necessarily been widespread public indignation, or the buildup of cynical feelings toward politics. The mass of French Canadians did not fulminate against Union Nationale corruption. Duplessis attracted attention away from the negative side of corrupt practices by pursuing a clever strategy of pothole politics and rewards for the faithful. He dwelled on the insular, culturally defensive, and authority-respecting values which had grown up in the province, and usually had the Catholic church and business behind him. Interestingly, ten years after Duplessis' death, and after major reforms in Quebec society, it was found that 43 per cent of the province's French-speaking population approved of the idea that the media ought to be influenced by government. In the case of New South Wales, it should be recalled that Lang was a man who excited fervent popular admiration as well as hostility. Like Duplessis, he was a "loner" in politics, running an essentially autonomous party machine, defying the federal government, and otherwise earning considerable political credit which caused people to overlook improprieties.

Overt political corruption aside, however, we still need to know whether political life in Canada and Australia engenders public trust and respect. The characterizations painted in earlier pages suggest that Canadians would appear to be more trusting and respectful than Australians. In both countries there has been an acceptance of a positive governmental role, but Canadians have been more deferential toward authority than the skeptical and self-assured Australians. The Australian reputation has been one of keeping a tight leash on men in public life, lest they develop delusions of grandeur and separate themselves from popular interests. Hence, when the membership of the Commonwealth Parliament was increased in 1949, only a third of the public approved, presumably because there would now be more, and less controllable, politics. When the nexus referendum was beaten in 1967, the public seemed to be saying again that it wanted no more politicians in Canberra, and that it wished to preserve the full authority of the Senate as a counterweight to any injudicious behavior by governments and their House majorities. The Australian reactions to salary increases for legislators have been more pronouncedly hostile than in Canada; there has been more outspoken support for early retirement from political offices, and a far greater attraction for brief federal and state parliamentary terms.

The Australian notion of elected officials bearing a distinct responsibility to their constituents—accountable to them and available as brokers and fixers for constituents' problems—prompts a comparison with Canada. French Canadian Members of Parliament (MPs) enjoy more personal prestige among their constituents than do their English-speaking colleagues, and in this sense they presumably are unlike Australian parliamentarians. But the French MPs are regarded by their constituents basically not as legislators, but as sources of patronage and personal aid and advice. Therefore, more like Australian MPs, though for different reasons, and unlike English Canadian MPs, the French parliamentarians devote substantial attention to constituency problems. Like the Australian MPs, they tend to leave the capital for home ground as frequently as possible, and to maintain offices at home. In this respect, it is English Canada that seems to stand out as the home of a culture that accepts elected officials not so much as personal and accountable delegates, but as necessary functionaries within a broader, political decision-making system.

Some data seem to indicate a measure of Australian public negativism toward politics and politicians, but the evidence is hardly overpowering, and not generally very different from Canadian findings. Most of the Australian data derive from a late 1960's survey conducted in the Brisbane metropolitan area, but are probably applicable to the country at large. Over 50 per cent of the respondents believed that politicians could not be believed in what they said, or that politicians did not really care what ordinary people thought. Canadian data for roughly the same period indicated that about half of the electorate believed the government of Canada could not be trusted to live up to promises, or to supply credible information. Eight per cent of Australians in the Brisbane survey strongly agreed, and 34 per cent agreed with the proposition that politics was a dirty game. Asked if they would be proud to have a relative enter politics, 6 per cent strongly agreed and 47 per cent agreed. Canadian results from similar surveys have disclosed no more enthusiasm for elected office. In 1965, only a quarter of Canadians said they would like to see a son make politics his career, compared to 13 per cent in 1953, and 15 per cent in 1961. Although the Brisbane survey seemed to buttress some of the conventional wisdom about Australian attitudes, three-quarters of the respondents believed that politicians were on the whole honest, and over half explicitly thought them to be intelligent and hard working. The Australian investigators themselves concluded that "People are not antagonistic toward politicians and other 'things political' as the professional and amateur pundit would suggest." *

Data such as these, while extremely suggestive, should be weighed in context. For instance, although Australian attitudes generally do not reflect the range of regional differences found in Canada, it might be worth mentioning that Queensland state politics have a particularly hackneyed flavor. Then too, at the time that the Brisbane survey was being taken, Australian federal politics were caught up in an exceptionally partisan and recriminatory debate over Vietnam and conscription, with epithets such as "coward" and "traitor" flying about. Until recently Australian politicians as a group have been a very ordinary lot, and much of the political dialogue has been stilted and unedifying. Public

* J. S. Western and P. R. Wilson, "Politics, Politicians, and Parties: Sweet or Sour?" *Politics,* Vol. 5 (November 1970), p. 178.

views of political life may therefore in part have been conditioned by the commodity itself. The ABC broadcasts portions of federal parliamentary proceedings. The regular listening audience is very small. A 1966 survey disclosed that among those who did listen, the number of persons believing that their esteem of politicians had been lowered by hearing the debates was nearly three times greater than those who thought esteem had been enhanced. Respecting Canadian data on political mistrust, it could be significant that the survey cited was carried out in late 1968, only a short time after a succession of wobbly minority governments in Ottawa had come to an end, and that the two major parties had just relieved themselves of leaders whose personal popularity had sunk to an exceptionally low level.

Aside from measures of public regard of politics and politicians, questions of trust and efficacy can also be examined from the standpoint of popular involvement in politics. Do people care enough about politics, and are they sufficiently convinced that popular action can yield results, so that they willingly give of their time, energy, and money?

One of the more obvious indices of public political interest, though not necessarily of political trust, is voting turnout. On the surface, little can be learned on this count from Australian experience, because of compulsory voting. Some Brisbane data show that only 27 per cent of the public pays serious attention to state and federal electoral campaigns, and only 14 per cent follows politics closely between campaigns. In response to the less precise question of "interest" in politics, about half of the Australians in a 1971 nationwide survey said that they were very or quite interested. Still, in Queensland as throughout the rest of Australia, in state and national elections, compulsory voting regularly brings over 90 per cent of the electorate to the polls. Before compulsory federal voting was introduced, no voting turnout pattern had as yet emerged, with participation ranging from a low of 46.9 per cent to a high of 77.7 per cent. Nevertheless, responses to a 1963 Brisbane survey suggested that over three-quarters of the electorate would vote even if compulsion were removed. If true, this would match and even slightly exceed current Canadian federal and provincial turnouts, which are voluntary. By international standards the Canadian figure is, and the hypothetical Australian figure would be, quite respectable. But in themselves such electoral participation statistics are not too helpful analytically. Extremely high voluntary turnout can be more a function of culturally-bred response to civic obligation, than to strongly felt efficacy, or may primarily reflect the intense and even divisive political climate within a society. The Australian willingness to observe high voting turnout, even if compulsion were removed, may be the result of long-time conditioning to the habit of voting which compulsion has instilled; most Australians wish to preserve, not abolish compulsory voting. In Canada, Quebec is a province which, over the past several decades, has registered an above average voting turnout, yet by most measures of interest and political participation Quebeckers score below English Canadians. It is this, nonvoting dimension of political participation that will now be examined for possible clues about political efficacy in the Canadian and Australian societies.

Studies of various political systems have indicated a strong positive correlation between membership in associational groups generally, and high levels of political information, interest, involvement, and feelings of competence—that is, efficacy. These political traits are further strengthened as the number of organizations to which a person belongs increases. The available evidence in Australia on associational participation is based on data collected in Sydney in the late 1950's, another set taken in Melbourne shortly afterward, and a nationwide survey of 1967. The Canadian data are drawn from a nationwide survey conducted in 1968. Under half of the Sydney and national survey respondents and about two-fifths of the Melbourne group had an associational affiliation apart from trade unions. In Canada, the figure was

54 per cent, very high by world standards, and higher than in the United States. The Canadian multiple membership figure of some 36 per cent was again high, even though union affiliation was counted in this datum. The Australian national survey observed just under a quarter of the public carrying plural membership, exclusive of union membership, though the Sydney survey had registered a figure of only about 6 per cent. After correction is made for union membership, Canada seems to emerge slightly higher on a multiple membership scale. Canadians are also somewhat more apt to join political parties, and to make larger financial contributions to party causes than Australians, the differential being on the order of 20 per cent. Such differences may be markedly attributable to Australia's compulsory voting system, which has tended to depress organizational vitality among the country's political parties generally. If notice is taken of the public's activism in political work, then the information on the two nations is similar. One Brisbane-based survey classified 7 per cent of the electorate as carrying out active party work often, and another 13 per cent sometimes. Nationwide Canadian data showed 3–4 per cent highly involved in political campaigns, and 20–25 per cent modestly involved. In 1970, Canadians were asked whether people such as "yourself" had influence over the nation's future, a question closely related to efficacy. Sixty-seven per cent replied that persons such as they had little or no influence; 7 per cent admitted to great influence, and 21 per cent to some influence—the total of "efficacious" persons representing under a third of the electorate.

Some signs therefore imply stronger efficacy among Canadians than among Australians, while other signs are less persuasive. If Canadians do in fact display a higher level of efficacy, the explanation may of course lie in the cultural dispositions which differentiate the Canadian and Australian societies. They may also be a function of social stratification. Data from both countries consistently confirm what is known to be true among various societies: high levels of political interest, associational membership, activism, and the like, are closely related to higher levels of education, occupation, and wealth. Canada is the more educated, and the more openly middle class of the two societies, which in itself may help to account for its suspected higher efficacy rate.

Within Canadian society, however, feelings of political efficacy appear to be unevenly distributed between English and French speakers. The French vote at least as frequently as the English, and contribute about the same proportion of their number to the cadre of political activists. But heavy voting turnout, as has been suggested, may be associated with cultural variables which are not connected to efficacy as such. The inclination of a small minority to become directly engaged in politics tells us nothing about the viewpoints of the vast majority that remains inactive. Proportionately, English Canadians are nearly three times as likely to donate to parties as are the French. The information shows that the French in Quebec, contrasted with all other groups, including Francophones outside Quebec, have decidedly higher refusal rates in answering survey questions. When they are willing to respond, they have the greatest "no opinion" rate. They have a decidedly lower rate of party identification. They are more inclined to stress leaders rather than parties as the basis for electoral choice. In other words, comparisons of Canadian and Australian public efficacy should keep in mind the English-French distinctions which are obscured by aggregate Canadian data. French Canadian society developed parochialism, a lack of salience on national issues, and ascriptive and personalistic values. The causes of the Québeçois traits of underconcern, or low efficacy in national politics at least, have been discussed earlier. Part of the explanation can be attributed to historic feelings that the French have been victimized by English Canada's efforts to assimilate them, deprive them of their birthright, or otherwise to impose a majoritarian dictatorship.

Extra-majoritarian approaches to conflict resolution

The Canadian and Australian political systems have suceeded in avoiding major breakdowns. The two societies have seemed to be reasonably satisfied with conditions of life, have had confidence in established political norms, and have enjoyed access to mechanisms of orderly political change. Despite being fairly well politically aggregated, however, the two nations have by no means been free of antisystemic or violent pressures. The incidence, setting, and results of such departures from orderly and prescribed procedures of redress are important in two ways. Mostly, such evidence can suggest something about the society itself—the societal conditions which inspire resort to protest or violence. In degree, we can also discover something about the political system itself, primarily its ability to adapt and bring about conflict resolution when confronted with crisis. Our focus will be on confrontations inspired by demands for political, cultural, or regionally based redress. Tensions more explicitly arising out of working-class protests can more fruitfully be covered in another context, after there has been an opportunity to deal with trade unionism and working-class politics as such.

Some of Australia's and Canada's more notable experiences with confrontational politics are traceable to the nation-building process in the two societies. In Australia, one particular event stands out—the Eureka Stockade of 1854. Prospectors were incensed by the exorbitant license fees charged them by the unrepresentative, squatter-controlled legislative councils in Victoria and New South Wales. The "diggers" demanded an abolition of the fees and establishment of genuinely popular institutions. There were mass demonstrations, licenses were publicly burned, and the protesters vowed to pay no more fees. A stockade was erected at Eureka, at the town of Ballarat, Victoria. Troops were sent against them, fighting broke out, and twenty-two diggers and six soldiers died. Some of them were brought to trial, but juries refused to convict them, prosecution against others was abandoned, and the licensing system was drastically liberalized. The broader concerns of these landless and politically frustrated persons were also met. Eureka expedited the introduction of responsible government in the colonies, and the ultimate breakup of squatter power. It had been a reaction not of revolutionaries but of men asking for equitable treatment. It was stamped out by force of arms, but was followed by concessions rather than reprisals and repression.

The 1837–38 rebellions in Canada, as we saw earlier, also sought the downfall of a certain form of economic and political privilege, though rather different values inspired the English and French versions of the uprisings. The result of the commotions was Durham's mission, and the installation of responsible government in place of the *de facto* rule of family compact oligarchies. Although there was rioting in Montreal by persons who could not reconcile themselves to the Rebellion Losses Bill, the bill was allowed to go through, providing an extremely important precedent for the realization of responsible government in fact as well as in principle.

For some years after 1867, Canada was still expanding, and attempting to balance its various sectional and subcultural interests. In the Maritimes, and especially in Nova Scotia, where secessionist resolutions were passed in the 1880's, there was widespread feeling that the confederation compact had left the region economically cheated and neglected. Tempers cooled and secessionist sentiment tapered off when Ottawa announced various financial concessions to the Maritimes, and more general prosperity set in. But when contending French-English emotions were aroused in other instances of confrontational politics, no formula of conciliatory policies was able to satisfy the two sides. Louis Riel led the Red River rebellion of 1869–70 and the Northwest rebellion of 1885. Both entailed clashes with security forces. The latter was subdued only after several regiments of militia had been pressed into service, and Riel was executed. Both rebellions occurred in sparsely settled areas which were not yet provinces; the first in Manitoba, the second in what was to be Saskatchewan. Both involved Métis communities, not mainstream English or French or even ethnic populations, and were essentially designed to defend the life style of the Métis against the encroachment of westward-moving Canadian political authority and commercial interests. The rebellions themselves had little importance in and of themselves, except that their defeat cleared the way for more rapid western expansion, an important ingredient in the national design of the governments of the time. Their main effect was indirect, yet deeply divisive, because it rekindled French-English hostility. The English delighted in quelling the rebellions. To them, these were victories on behalf of "national purpose." Many French were appalled. Most of the rebels had French blood. French Quebec identified with them. Francophones interpreted the hanging of Riel, himself of French-Indian derivation, as an affront, while Anglophones and Orangemen, especially, insisted that hanging was only fair justice for a traitor and a scoundrel.

During its twentieth-century period of nationhood, Australia's experience with confrontational politics has centered on problems of regional dissatisfaction. One facet has concerned the long-simmering resentment of persons living in the outlying areas of Queensland and New South Wales. There has been sentiment in the northern portion of the huge state of Queensland that the region's unique economic concerns have been slighted by south Queensland interests, and especially by the capital city of Brisbane, which lies some thousand miles to the south. The northeast portion of New South Wales, basically agricultural and underurbanized, has felt alienated from the great city of Sydney. So-called "new-states" movements developed, asking that the affected regions in the two states be re constituted into separate states. The movement has been especially pronounced in New South Wales. At one point, an informal "constituent assembly" was convened. In 1967, the state finally consented to stage a referendum on the issue. The vote among electors in the area projected for new state status was quite close—168,000 approving and 199,000 disapproving—and would have been much closer had the industrial city of Newcastle, most of whose residents felt little affinity for the movement, been excluded from the advisory referendum. Although new-state sentiment is not dead either in New South Wales or in Queensland, there is no prospect that militants will try to impose any form of "secessionist" solution. At all events, both states have powerful Country parties, which enjoy considerable following in the dissident areas. As of this writing, Country parties are part of government coalitions in both states, and represent the dominant party in Queensland. Thus, spokesmanship and sympathetic state policy for the two regions is reasonably insured.

Western Australia, as a state at large, harbored bitter feelings against "eastern interests" and the federal government during the late 1920's and early 1930's. At the time, it was an economically have-not state, severely underpopulated, and 2000 miles removed from the population centers of the southeast. The distress of the depression years was compounded by complaints against high costs incurred due to steep tariffs and other federal policies which Western Australians believed overlooked their special circumstances. The upshot was a statewide referendum which called for secession from Australia. It passed by a handsome 2 to 1 margin, and a petition requesting that secession be recognized was carried to the British Parliament. The strength of this Western Australian disaffection should not be belittled. But the organizers of the secessionist movement were actually engaged in the shrewd tactic of forcing Canberra's hand. The gambit worked. Later in 1933 the

Commonwealth Grants Commission was established, with responsibility for allocating special funds to needy states. By the late 1960's, fabulous stores of natural resources had been uncovered in Western Australia, and the state's economy flourished. There is still a hangover of western pride and suspicion of the east, but it has little political significance.

In Canada, the main weight of the nineteenth-century secessionist feeling fell in the Maritimes. This region remains poor and underdeveloped by Canadian standards, despite numerous aid programs. Individually or collectively, however, secession is a wholly unfeasible option for the Atlantic provinces, since they would be even weaker if they detached themselves from Canada, and Ottawa's assistance. On the other side of the country, the Prairies have for decades felt themselves victimized by "eastern," that is, Toronto and Montreal, business interests, by unacceptable tariff policies, and by inadequately formulated or financed rural reconstruction programs. We shall examine later what this has implied for party politics. Here we should notice that by the 1960's there was talk in the Prairies about secession from Canada, possibly to go it alone, and conceivably to join the United States. In 1970, informal surveys conducted by two Prairie MPs disclosed a generalized yet widespread separatist mood. No serious secession movement has actually been conducted in the Prairies, and probably will not be, especially if world agricultural market conditions remain steady, and Ottawa devises a proved method for alleviating rural depression. A "Western Canada" party has sprung up. It is not secessionist, but its program reflects the sense of hurt felt among many persons of the Prairies. It is nonetheless noteworthy that in one of the surveys just cited, 79 per cent of the respondents felt that if *Quebec* separated from Canada, so should western Canada. The point is that there is decided separatist sentiment in Quebec, and if it ever matures into an independent Quebec, the Canadian west could be prompted to search for its own way out as well.

Separatist sentiment in contemporary Quebec represents the strongest challenge to national unity ever faced by Canada, or for that matter, by Canada or Australia. In many ways, Quebec has always been different from other Canadian provinces, and hostile to much of its Canadian environment. A separatist resolution was actually debated, but defeated, in the Quebec legislature in 1918, its impetus coming from the conscription controversy. During the second World War, a provincial party, the Bloc Populaire, campaigned on what approached a separatist program, with conscription again serving as the catalyst. By the 1960's, Quebec found itself in the throes of major social and economic changes. Impatient with the "quiet revolution" which was transforming the province, explicitly separatist parties entered the 1966 provincial election, polling 8.7 per cent of the popular vote. In the 1970 election, the separatist Parti Québecois (PQ) earned 23 per cent of the vote.

Quebec separatists are not united on the details of when and how a separatist objective should be achieved. Generally, however, they assert that there are two and essentially noncomplementary personalities in Canada, the English and the French. It is fiction to pretend that there is something like a third, "all-Canadian" personality. Although French Canadians outside Quebec are recognized and commiserated with, Quebec separatists feel that these persons are a lost cause, dispersed over a dominant English-speaking society. Quebec is a compact unit, 80 per cent French, and can and must go its own way to secure its cultural pride and insure socioeconomic development. There is no other self-respecting option; according to René Lévesque, a leading separatist spokesman and head of the PQ,

> More is involved here than simple intellectual certainty. This is a physical fact. To be unable to live as ourselves, as we should live, in our own language and according to our own ways, would be like living without an arm or a leg—or perhaps a heart.
>
> Unless, of course, we agreed to give in little by little, in a

> decline which, as in cases of pernicious anaemia, would cause life to slip slowly away from the patient.
>
> Again, in order not to perceive this, one has to be among the *déracinés,* the uprooted and cut-off.*

The overwhelming majority of separatists activists, including the PQ as such, wish to attain their goal through peaceful political means. They think that violent methods can lead to repression in the province and discredit their movement through charge of guilt by association. Yet violence has come, some of it spectacularly, through the exertions of the small yet unbending Quebec Liberation Front, or FLQ. During the 1960's, FLQ terrorists detonated explosives which resulted in several fatalities. Then, in 1970, as a way of dramatizing their cause, they kidnapped Pierre LaPorte, a provincial minister, and a British diplomat, and executed LaPorte. It was in this climate that Ottawa imposed the War Measures Act, and portions of Quebec for a time resembled an armed camp.

The PQ was embarrassed and revolted by the FLQ's actions, as was the great majority of Quebec's public. Nonetheless, separatist sentiment in the province was neither created nor destroyed by FLQ terrorism. The PQ's performance in the 1970 election was not inconsequential. Persons voting for it, whatever their motive, were aware that the PQ was, first and foremost, a separatist organization. Data collected from the mid-1960's onward nonetheless suggest that the Québeçois commitment to separatism has varied between 8 per cent and 12 per cent, substantially below the PQ's 23 per cent province-wide vote. On the other side, explicit opposition to separatism has ranged between 70–75 per cent. A poll conducted just prior to the 1970 provincial election, and which accurately predicted the PQ vote, discovered that the greatest French Canadian worry was unemployment. Federal-provincial relations, the status of the French language and other central PQ themes were much less salient. The PQ is, however, a movement

* René Lévesque, *An Option for Quebec* (Toronto and Montreal: McClelland and Stewart, 1968), p. 15.

which sharply criticizes the other provincial parties for their inattention to the material dignity of French Canadians, and insists that separation will bring remedy. The PQ is not only French Canadian nationalist, but extremely progressive in socioeconomic areas. Its electoral clientele, like the people who are explicitly separatist by disposition, is decidedly pitched toward the young, the educated, and the middle-class members of French society in Quebec. The party's popularity is especially striking among the young. Separatism among persons in their twenties is twice as prevalent as among people 50 or over. A 1970 survey at Laval University identified 55 per cent of the students as sympathetic toward the PQ. Hence, while separatism remains a distinctly minority view, its adherents are, in effect, an elite group, with skills and influence out of proportion to their numbers.

What of the prospects for a reconciliation between Quebec and Canada which would defuse separatist feeling, and therefore the prospect of a disintegration of Canada in its present form? Opinion data are not infallible barometers of what the public will or will not stand for, but they are suggestive. We know, for instance, that between 1963 and 1970 there was a slight decline in the proportion of Canadians who felt that in the few years preceding, French-English relations had improved. The group believing that relations had worsened jumped markedly, from 27 per cent to 42 per cent. In 1971, only 17 per cent of all Canadians felt that Quebec-Canada relations were better than when Trudeau assumed office more than three years earlier. Twice as many respondents believed that relations had actually worsened.

These data conceal the fact that in 1970 a judgment of worsened French-English relations was offered nearly twice as frequently among persons *outside* Quebec compared to respondents within the province. Non-Quebeckers are also more convinced than Quebeckers themselves that separatism is widespread within the province. Among Quebec residents in 1969, only 25 per cent believed that differences dividing Canada's parts would be solved, and the following year they, much more than persons outside the province, thought that separation by Quebec would be a serious blow to Canada. Taken together, these findings underscore the distance that might have to be traveled to achieve reconciliation. Non-French Canada is the majority group from which important concessions to placate Quebec would need to come. But English Canada widely believes that French-English relations have gone from bad to worse, and that Quebec itself has lost its taste for reconciliation, since it is presumed to be highly separatist. While believing that there has been a breakdown in the French-English dialogue, English Canada seems to be saying that it really does not care very much if Quebec pulls out. Quebeckers have apparently sensed that there is small hope of rapprochement with other parts of Canada, where Quebec's aspirations are thought not to be understood, or are disparaged. Numerous political figures and many parties, in and out of Quebec, are striving to fashion policies capable of overcoming the present estrangement.

II
THE MILIEU OF ORGANIZED POLITICS

The nature and distribution of Australian and Canadian political values, and the forces which have shaped them, have greatly influenced the basis of organized political life. They have affected the orientation and strength of organized interests, and of the two publics' willingness to associate themselves with one or another electoral tendency. Also affected have been the programs and styles of political parties, and party prospects for controlling or influencing the process of public policy decision-making. Ultimately, there has been an effect upon how competing interests have been adjusted and material and psychic resources allocated. Political parties should therefore be regarded as critical mediating agents, linking the public and the decision-making arena. Among other things, they are agents which help determine levels of public satisfaction with policies and the conduct of political business, and ultimately, public regard for the political system at large.

Our treatment of organized politics will fall into two parts. First, we shall examine how and why particular claimant groups and public supporters such as business, labor, the rural sector, and religious denominations have attached themselves to particular parties. Second, we will be concerned with how such variables as voting support, electoral laws and provisions, the institutional setting, and political leadership roles have combined to produce degrees of success or failure for particular Canadian and Australian party formations.

5

Business and professional interests and parties of moderate-conservative persuasion

The conservative temper in party politics

Since the arrival of Canadian and Australian nationhood, political parties of conservative or broadly middle-ground persuasion have either been dominant, or at least equal in influence to other party groups. Canada's two prominent "conservative" parties, the Conservatives (Progressive-Conservative, or PC, since World War II), and the Liberals, reach back to Canadian confederation. One or the other has always controlled the federal government. In fact, no other party has ever been represented in federal ministries. The main Australian conservative party has gone under several labels, Liberal from shortly after federation into the First War, Nationalist during the 1920's, United Australia party during the 1930's, and Liberal from the mid-1940's to the present time. The Liberals and their predecessors have not always been in power nationally. When they have, since the first World War, they have almost invariably shared power with the rural-based Country party (CP). But Australian "Liberals," by whatever name, have been in federal office more often than not. The exceptions have been Australian Labor Party (ALP) ministries for a few months in 1904 and again in 1908–09, from 1910–16, from 1929–31, and during 1941–49.

When they have governed in coalition with the Country party, the Liberals have been the dominant partner. The Canadian and Australian conservative parties have been less successful in dominating provincial/state governments, but prominent nonetheless.

The conservative parties have long enjoyed the support of the business, industrial, and professional communities. The reasons for this can tell us something about the nature and outlook of the two nations' business and professional classes, about the orientations and policy preferences of these parties, and about the general political environment in which Canadian and Australian politics are conducted.

One reason for their business- and professional-class support is that the Canadian and Australian conservative parties have never had a formal alliance with organized labor, whose interests would not ordinarily coincide with those of the higher economic classes. Nor have these parties even had a working relationship with labor, in the sense that American labor has for some years openly favored the Democratic party. Secondly, in both nations, business and industry have traditionally been relatively free from conservative-party interference in practices congenial to their growth and earnings. Australia and Canada began as underpopulated and undercapitalized countries. Their domestic markets were small, and locally produced goods were competitively vulnerable to less expensive foreign goods. Especially in Canada, the economic claims to be a nation of continental proportions were staked out by large-scale, monopolistic enterprise, in such lucrative fields as timber, pulpwood, and furs. In neither country was there a significant tradition of aggressive, liberal capitalism. Hence, to promote the survival and development of local industry, conservative governments have historically allowed considerable latitude for industrial and commercial growth and concentration.

Canada's major business enterprises are wealthier than Australia's, as might be expected. By the close of the 1960's, the 20 leading Canadian companies averaged assets of 792 million

American dollars, while the figure for Australia's top 20 companies was only $265 million. Still, Broken Hill Proprietary, Australia's largest firm, which produces nearly all of the steel used in the country and has various subsidiary enterprises, employs 1 out of 50 of all working Australians. Canada's industrial structure is highly concentrated, with several hundred annual takeovers and mergers having occurred in recent years. Australian industry, more modest in scale than Canada's, is even more concentrated, there being more monopoly and oligopoly than either in Canada or the United States. It has been estimated that a third of Australia's industry is highly concentrated and another third partially concentrated; the four largest firms account for 50 per cent of industrial employment.

Much of the legislative record reflects the objective business-industrial situation. Canada enacted combination legislation as early as 1889, but there was little enforcement, and a most generous interpretation of the legal allowances made on behalf of mergers, monopolies, and the like. Seventy years later, a PC government enacted stronger but still qualified measures, as business lobbies continued to maintain that merger restrictions on native Canadian firms would discourage them from competing with powerful foreign concerns, or from undertaking their own, economical, research and marketing activity. By 1971, a Liberal government was proposing that major company mergers would automatically be subject to review by a new federal agency, and possibly to denial, if the public interest were found to be adversely affected. But the terms for disallowance were to be more stringent against foreign than local takeovers, competitively benefiting Canadian industry. Even if Canadian-sponsored mergers were blocked, the result would not be the stifling of business, but the widening of business competition. Australia's anticombination legislation reaches back to 1906. Based on the American Sherman Antitrust Act, its provisions were strikingly ambiguous. Not only was there little official enthusiasm for enforcement, but prosecutions which were carried to the courts often failed, partially because of certain constitutional inhibitions on the Commonwealth's power to legislate comprehensively in this area. Not until the mid-1960's was fresh legislation enacted. An independent commissioner was to decide if there was evidence of collusion, and a tribunal would then adjudicate the case. But the tribunal was hamstrung by the often contradictory "public-interest" guidelines which were devised to guide it. In 1971 the High Court voided the legislation on constitutional grounds, but intimated that a more meticulously drafted measure would stand the constitutional test.

Canadian and Australian business practices have also enjoyed lenient treatment. Canadian legislation on this subject had existed for some time, but not until 1971, under a Liberal government, was really meaningful legislation introduced, imposing severe penalties on price fixing, market allocation, and other restrictive practices. Australia hesitated for an extraordinarily long time in matters such as these. In 1932, a tentative start was made toward regulating insurance companies. In 1945, under a Labor government, the Commonwealth assumed control over life insurance. Finally, by 1970, a Liberal government proposed to legislate comprehensively over general (nonlife) insurance practices. Until 1971, Australia was quite exceptional among western countries in its lack of legislation regulating retail price fixing. Prices had been kept artificially high, including in a number of key industries, such as pharmaceuticals. This meant higher costs to consumers, and a stifling of progress and innovation in retailing methods. The new legislation was introduced against a background of pressures from trade unions, which had launched a boycott of goods produced by price-fixing companies. But the government had also discovered that, apart from the very largest and most self-contained firms, the business community itself had become receptive to such legislation.

Conservative administrations in both countries have provided business and industrial interests with a wide assortment of financial protections, rewards, and incentives. In Australia particularly, local producers have been screened from foreign competition by impressive tariff barriers. By the outset of the 1970's, the value of tariff protection was estimated to be about $2.7 billion, averaging out to about 46 per cent per industry and, of course, carrying with it predictable consequences of higher consumer prices, depressed competitiveness, and inefficient utilization of labor force. In both countries, business has gained reasonably accommodating tax treatment from conservative parties. There was no capital gains tax in Canada until 1971, when a modest one was imposed, and for practical purpose there still is no such levy in Australia. In the immediate past, company taxes have been lowered somewhat in Canada, and slightly raised in Australia. Overall, however, the rates are hardly confiscatory. The Canadian rate is scheduled to fall to 46 per cent by 1976, and exceptionally low rates apply to *domestically* owned small-profit companies (under $35,000). Under 1970 legislation, Australian company profits exceeding $10,000 are assessed at 47.5 per cent for public (general stock) and 42.5 per cent for private (limited stock) companies. Conservative Canadian and Australian governments have also been extensively involved in industrial subsidies, as in shipbuilding, and in assorted export incentives.

Australian and Canadian business and industrial interests have, by and large, been treated agreeably by conservative parties. But it would be inaccurate to assume that these parties have been purely and simply the political emanations of propertied and privileged interests. It must be remembered that conditions were not propitious in either country for building a competitive, high risk capitalist model. National growth and expansion, pragmatically speaking, meant concessions to capitalists. Pragmatic considerations gave nineteenth-century Conservative subsidies to the private builders of the transcontinental Canadian Pacific Railway and prohibitions on the export of certain raw materials, to stimulate domestic processing industries. Tariff protection in both countries was more than a sinecure to frail, undercapitalized local industry. Despite the higher consumer prices it encouraged, it ensured the survival of relatively diversified industrial structures, and increased employment of the domestic labor force. Canada's nineteenth-century "National Policy" included the erection of tariff walls to protect native industry. It succeeded in avoiding the emasculation of Canadian-*based* industry, but drew in American companies, which created branch plants in Canada rather than attempting to sell across the border, and encouraged United States investment in an expanding, inviting, Canadian economy. Despite the drawbacks of the vast American economic presence, steep tariffs and concessions to local industry contributed substantially to Canada's overall affluence. Much of recent Canadian legislation has been selectively drawn. To protect local ownership and to give expression to Canadian national identity (both of which are strongly espoused by the Canadian *left*), taxation and merger rules are more stringent for foreign than for domestically owned businesses.

By the time of the first World War, high tariffs had virtually become an article of faith in Australia, not just among manufacturers, but among the large and powerful working-class movement. The ALP remains closely committed to tariff protection. Australian conservative governments have been conspicuously lax about imposing and enforcing anticombination laws. But narrow judicial interpretations of federal power in this field have not been helpful, and the Australian public itself has rejected constitutional referendums designed to enlarge the scope of Commonwealth authority.

The conservative tradition in Australia and Canada, whatever else might be said of it, has certainly not been one of rugged free enterprise. Both societies, as we have seen, have from early times leaned heavily on governmental activism. In Australia, the expectation that public authority would exert itself in economic affairs was given a special coating by the radical tradition. Although business generally has little liking for public ownership, in certain spheres public ownership became natural and even necessary in both societies, and aspects of it suited business interests themselves. Canadian public funding and ownership of canals and dams and Australian federal and state funding and ownership of railways are cases in point. Government, not private enterprise, often was the source of needed capital and took the risks inherent in such ventures, and such projects vastly contributed to the ability of business to produce, transport, and sell its products. Similarly, business and industry readily accept the fact that electricity, water supplies, and irrigation works—expensive products but vital to industrial development—are in public hands. Some public ownership projects in Australia were initiated by conservative state governments, others by Labor, but there has been no real temptation among the Liberals to transfer such utilities to private ownership. The federally sponsored Snowy River Hydro-electric project, initiated by the ALP in the late 1940's, was continued and expanded by a Liberal administration. The Victorian Electricity Commission, the oldest and most noteworthy such enterprise among Australia's states, was inaugurated by a conservative government. The creation of Ontario's vast hydroelectric utility by a conservative government was welcomed by Canadian manufacturers in the province, not only because it supplied inexpensive power, but because it helped to avert the entry of privately financed American companies, and Ontario industry's reliance on American coal.

Although Crown, that is, public, lands have often been sold or leased by provincial and state governments, they have also served the purpose of national development and, incidentally, of private developers. Such land control, for instance, made possible the development of an impressive Canadian paper industry, averting straightforward exploitation of timber resources for pulpwood export to the United States. Public ownership and regulation of this kind have complemented various officially sponsored and financed plans, designed to serve the public good while frequently being utilitarian from the standpoint of business and industry. Hence, conservative governments in the two countries have sponsored and underwritten migration, land settlement, housing, central banking institutions, and industrial research programs.

Public ownership in Australia and Canada often stand side by side with private enterprise. The Australian Broadcasting Commission and the Radio Broadcasting Commission (later Canadian Broadcasting Corporation) were created by conservative federal governments. Both public corporations, which include radio and television services, have been retained, though private services operate alongside them. Canada operates both public (Air Canada) and private airlines on domestic as well as international services. The official approach is pragmatic. In 1965, for instance, Ottawa instituted a division of international routes between Air Canada and Canadian Pacific Air, a private carrier, to avoid duplication and losses. Australian interstate air service is shared by the public Trans-Australia Airlines and the private Ansett-Australian Airlines, which fly virtually identical schedules. Overseas services are restricted to the publicly owned Qantas. An Australian Labor government attempted to secure a public monopoly over interstate air services, but was checked by the High Court. It then chose to retain part of the industry in public hands, rather than surrendering all of it to private control. There are occasional complaints of partisanship favoring Ansett-AA, whose owner, Sir Reginald Ansett, an extremely successful businessman, has close contacts with the Liberal party. But the two lines operate essentially as equals, and a succession of Liberal governments has not tried to emasculate TAA, let alone sell it. Nor has Qantas been tampered with. The line enjoys a high reputation, and has generally made profits (on which it pays taxes to Canberra). Australian international air traffic is too light, and too intensely competed for by numerous flag carriers, to justify a second, privately owned Australian line.

In Canada, the Conservative and Liberal parties have shared in bringing various enterprises into the public domain, and neither party has tried to dismantle the efforts of the other. Government holdings in resource and energy enterprises, such as Eldorado

Nuclear, Polymer, and Panarctic Oil, in which Ottawa holds a controlling share, are not political footballs. The picture has been somewhat different in Australia, given the fact that the principal competitor of the Liberals has been a nonconservative party, the ALP. A number of state-government public enterprises such as butcher shops and brickworks were sold by conservative governments during the 1930's. Nationally, Liberal governments sold a whaling station, an engineering works, the public shares in an oil refinery, and other enterprises. Unable to get a suitable price for the publicly operated Australian National Line (interstate shipping), they let the ANL continue, but encouraged private shippers to enter the service. The avowed Liberal purpose in undertaking denationalization was to "get out of business," since much of the public ownership was said to constitute unfair competition, and losses incurred by nationalized enterprises had to be absorbed at public expense. Still, many of the enterprises released to private ownership were only marginally important. The main public holdings, state and federal, have not been disturbed, and there is little agitation in business circles or elsewhere for the Liberals to do so.

Interest articulation among business, industry, and the professions

Australian and Canadian business, industry, and the professions have not, of course, been stoical about public policies which affect their interests. The principal business organizations, such as the Canadian Manufacturers Association, the Chambers of Manufactures of Australia, and the Associated Chambers of Commerce of Australia, were formed almost immediately following nationhood. They have evolved elaborate research and publicity departments, are well financed, and are equipped both for short- and long-term lobbying efforts in the national capitals. Much of their time and effort is expended in the tasks of representing their interests on a host of governmental advisory boards, presenting submissions and testimony, and generally keeping in touch with strategic government departments. The details of these types of contacts will be dealt with later, when policy processes are analyzed. Our emphasis here is more on the kinds of occasions on which such groups have chosen to assert themselves, the sorts of rationales they have put forward, and the general extent to which they have been able to win their case.

One important Canadian-Australian comparison is in regard to the kinds of party alternatives with which groups must realistically contend. In Australia, logic and experience show that business can be expected to complain more when the ALP rather than the Liberal party holds power, despite the fact that Liberal governments have operated a mixed economy, and have promoted various welfare plans. When Liberal governments behave contrary to business-industrial preferences, business will not react so violently as to endanger Liberal tenancy in office. In Canada, the effective choice has been between two rather similar parties, both of which have done good things for business, yet both of which have, over time, shared in launching public ownership projects, extending social services, improving the lot of organized labor, and so on. The Conservative party created the state-owned Canadian National Railway, the telegraph system, shipping lines, and the CBC. More recently, it has assumed a firm stand on a guaranteed annual wage, and on subsidies for home owners who were paying high interest rates. Liberal governments instituted the publicly owned Trans-Canada Airlines (Air Canada), secured holdings in various energy firms, adopted an expensive, nationwide medicare policy, and introduced Canada's first capital gains tax. Hence, Canadian business is not in principle fearful that one rather than the other major party will control the federal government. Its approach is essentially situational—the issue at hand, perceptions of the incumbent prime minister, the general disposition of a particular Liberal or Conservative government.

In Australia, by comparison, there is a strong record of business community activity against Labor party attempts in the 1940's to nationalize the banking system, or to draw up a comprehensive pharmaceutical program. Business reactions to such Labor measures have ranged from alarmist publicity about socialist evils to carefully documented litigation. Many of Labor's nationalization programs in the 1940's in fact floundered because of adverse constitutional rulings, rather than outright legislative defeat. Still, when a Liberal government in 1960–61 imposed economic restraints, Australian business was generally angered, and made its views plainly known. A disgruntled group of Melbourne business figures went so far as to support the ALP during the 1961 election. The election almost brought defeat for the Liberals. Chastened, the Liberals proceeded to remove the most unpopular of the economic restraints. But it should be noted that the Liberals suffered from general electoral unpopularity in 1961, and voter revulsion became a greater Liberal concern, and a goad to an eventual policy shift, than business criticism. Organized business's approach to the recently created Australian Industry Development Corporation was cautious, seeing it as a potentially powerful weapon against big business concerns, should a socialist government direct it someday. Some protections against the misuse of the corporation against large business were incorporated into the legislation, and in the main, business came to regard the agency as a potential vehicle for enhancing the capitalization of various industrial projects. Business interests disapproved of many of the economic policies of John Gorton, Liberal Prime Minister from 1968–71. Not only were they uncertain where he was heading, but they became visibly upset by such measures as increases in corporate taxes, suspension of tax concessions for manufacturing plant and equipment, and reduction in research and development grants. While there was general relief in business circles when Gorton was deposed, organized business had raised no public outcry over its grievances. Its complaints had not, after all, concerned imperatives. Moreover, Liberal party fortunes during the Gorton years had declined, and business was averse to creating scenes.

In Canada, through World War I, business interests were more explicitly pro-Conservative than neutral, due to Conservative sponsorship of the strongly appealing National Policy. But much of the business community, particularly that part of it based in Montreal, energetically but unsuccessfully fought the Conservatives' creation of the public CNR out of various privately owned lines. The break with the Conservatives was made, despite earlier good relations, because the move seemed to be a major step away from private ownership, and it put the CNR in competition with the privately controlled Canadian Pacific. Between the wars, business resisted suggestions, Conservative or Liberal, for governmental regulation of insurance, invoking complex arguments that Ottawa lacked constitutional competence in the field. Yet by 1941 business had reversed its thinking. It had been shaken by failures during the depression, and by the unorthodox financial theories put forward by Alberta's Social Credit government.

After World War II, during Conservative tenancy at Ottawa, the business lobby launched a massive effort to prevent the scrapping of the Canadian-built Avro Arrow aircraft. It proclaimed shrilly that both industrial health and Canadian pride were at stake, and warned that normally Conservative newspapers would be turned against Prime Minister John Diefenbaker if he persisted. However, Diefenbaker was committed, and the lobbying effort failed. Business also trained its guns on Conservative-sponsored anticombine legislation. This time, it followed a more measured and constructive approach. It was able to argue with some credence that the draft legislation would obstruct those native mergers which would otherwise permit Canadian firms to compete with powerful foreign companies, and to operate more viably in general. The result was a compromise version of the bill.

The Trudeau Liberal government instituted the Canada Development Corporation, with the stated purposes of serving as a source of equity capital for new businesses, organizing small company mergers, rationalizing existing combines, and defending against foreign takeovers. As with the more modestly conceived Australian Industry Development Corporation, business had been skeptical, in part because it feared government interference and even the governmental purchase of private company holdings. For years, since the idea was first broached in 1963, business refused to cooperate in constructing such an agency, and pointedly turned its back on supplying a business world figure who might chair it. The Liberals pleaded that if such an agency were not created, foreign domination over Canada's economy would grow stronger, and could precipitate a "socialist reaction." But the Liberals waited, reluctant to proceed without business support, and finally proceeded because, in part, business suspicion had softened.

Australian and Canadian business interests have not been wholly successful in getting their way with governments, and one reason has been that "business" itself has not always held common interests or spokesmanship. Various sectors of the business-industrial community have often provided conflicting advice and pressure, producing compromise or irreconcilable policy outputs. For instance, during the Canadian Liberal administration of Lester Pearson, Finance Minister Walter Gordon introduced a stringent tax on foreign takeovers. A number of manufacturing interests were supportive, but the stock exchange lobby strenuously opposed the measure. It claimed there would be a fall in business confidence and a decline in the helpful economic contributions of American interests, a view shared by many reputable economists and critics of nationalist overreaction. Gordon and the Liberal government retreated.

Recent Australian developments have sharply highlighted intra-business conflict on an issue of central importance, the tariff. We have seen that steep tariffs have been a durable and widely honored feature of Australian economic policy. The Chambers of Manufactures and the Australian Industry Development Association have continued their high tariff campaign, still arguing that tariff reductions would cost jobs and expose small-scale native industry to frightful foreign competition. The Associated Chambers of Commerce, a traditionally low-tariff organization, has recently found new and welcome allies. The mining industry has achieved exceptional importance in the nation's economic development. Its principal spokesman, the Australian Mining Industry Council, attacks high tariffs. It maintains that, with limited manpower but ample foreign capital resources, Australia is foolish to try to manufacture all of its needed commodities at home. The mining industry is not, after all, like manufacturing industries. High tariffs for it simply mean higher costs for its equipment and components. The influential Colonial Sugar Refining Company has branched out into basic minerals, and its once archprotectionist silhouette has been distinctly lowered. Farmers have long been critical of stiff tariffs, but for some years high tariffs did not matter too much, because of government offsets on farm machinery and fertilizers. But there is now something of a price squeeze in Australian agriculture, causing rural interests to take a more severe view of tariff policy. High-tariff thinking in official quarters is weakening, an attitude encouraged by diverse and influential interests, business and otherwise.

The political activity of physicians, a well-paid and well-organized profession in both countries, offers further insight into the opportunities and limitations of interest group behavior. Predictably, physicians have been opposed to suggestions of "socialized medicine," arguing quality of treatment, freedom of choice for the patient, and the independence of the medical profession. The Australian branch of the British Medical Association (later Australian Medical Association) was violently opposed to ALP proposals in the 1940's to institute a noncontributory, comprehensive health plan. Even when a constitutional amendment gave such power to Canberra, short of civil conscription, the profession held back from cooperating, and a medical insurance program was not implemented until the Liberals assumed office. The Liberal program is based on voluntarism, combining private insurance, government donations, and a minor out-of-pocket payment by patients. Since Labor has held out for a comprehensive program which will be funded essentially from general revenue and public demand for more heavily subsidized health care has been increasing, the AMA is willing to live with the present arrangement.

Australian doctors have been made to feel uncomfortable by what they have observed in Canada. In 1962, a left-oriented Co-operative Commonwealth Federation (CCF) government in Saskatchewan submitted a comprehensive and compulsory provincial medical plan. Physicians in the province were so agitated that many of them staged a "doctors' strike." The Liberals, the chief provincial opposition party, did not oppose the plan in principle. But they preferred a voluntary scheme, sharply disputed numerous details of the CCF plan, and some of their members worked closely with striking doctors in organizing letter-writing campaigns, rallies, and the like. The CCF government made some slight concessions, replacement doctors were brought in on an emergency basis to counteract the strike, and the legislation stood. When the Liberals came to office in 1964, they made no move to abolish the medical system, and the physicians themselves were rather quickly mollified. The present program of national public medicare, under which costs are almost wholly borne by federal and provincial insurance, retained patient choice and physician independence. It was opposed by the CMA, but to no avail. At the time of writing, physicians in Manitoba were working to blunt the New Democratic party government's plan to integrate health and social services under a common administrative roof.

The viability of both the Australian and the Canadian national medical care plans depends on uniformly stable, reasonable fees by physicians, and therein lie some clues about medical lobbying. In 1970 Quebec's Liberal government was installing an even more ambitious health plan than generally applied throughout Canada. Quebec's medical specialists were disgusted by the terms, the work load increases, and income reduction they foresaw. Some actually left the province, while others organized a strike. But the forces ranged against them were formidable: an angry public, the mass of general practitioners, and organized labor. Of Quebec's specialists, a very lucratively paid group, 40 per cent happened to be English-speaking, and sensitive French workers denounced them as an arrogant and privileged class. The government offered a few concessions, and enacted legislation imposing fierce fines and prison terms on striking doctors. Lacking allies and facing punitive measures, the specialists capitulated. In the same year, the Liberal government in Canberra produced an upgraded health plan. It originally predicated common fees for common services. The specialist-dominated federal AMA objected; it wanted a higher fee schedule for comparable services performed by specialists. The government acceded. This meant millions more out of the government's pocket, but Canberra wished to insure the profession's cooperation in the overall program. Then the state AMA branches, controlled by general practitioners, rebelled. They claimed that if the changes demanded by the specialists were adopted, patients would flock to specialists even for treatment of minor complaints, since the proposed cost differential would be absorbed by the federal government. It was all quite bewildering. The final solution was something of a compromise. The Liberal government had shown itself to be susceptible to medical lobbying, essentially to protect the integrity of the plan's basic outlines. The lobbying itself disclosed serious rifts among doctors and the professional associations which represented them. Probably more was done to discredit than to enhance the protagonists' image, and possibly their chances for effective political pressure in the future.

Party financial and electoral support among business and higher economic class groups

Since Canadian and Australian business and professional communities have much to gain from sympathetic political parties, they have tried to establish influence through financial donations. In both countries, the bulk of the business contributions finds its way into the hands of the moderate-conservative parties. In both countries, these parties' receipts are in turn heavily dependent on business donations. A very small percentage of the two general publics makes any sort of party donations. Party membership enrollment is small. The legal situation does not, for practical purpose, impose restrictions on who may contribute, or in what amount. The contemporary Australian Liberal party has renounced its pre-1940's dependency on donations from extra-party groups and associations. But its present combined resources from business firms, individual subscribers, and membership dues, are quite sufficient.

Party funding by the business world indicates important Canadian-Australian nuances, reflecting peculiarities in the two business-professional complexes and in the respective party systems. Canadian business is not known to have donated much if anything to the CCF or its successor, the New Democratic party (NDP). Business has not cared for NDP policies, has understandably had little sympathy for a party with intimate trade-union connections, and has known that, at least nationally, the PC and Liberal parties have so far been the only parties with a reasonable prospect for governing. Because these two parties can and do control office, and because there has not been a great deal to choose between them from the business community's standpoint, they both receive business donations. In some degree, donations to the PC party in particular have been influenced by perceptions of the quality and trustworthiness of leaders. Thus, in 1953, the Conservatives, led by the "trusted" George Drew, had about $2.5 million at their disposal, but only about $1 million was available to the party when John Diefenbaker led the party in the 1957 campaign. Ordinarily, however, business firms and a small group of individuals closely associated with particular business concerns have rather systematically hedged their bets—60 per cent of the money going to whichever of the parties occupies power, 40 per cent to the opposition.

In the provinces, the Liberal and PC parties are often electorally frail, and other parties govern. Moreover, there is considerable variety in what provincial PC or Liberal parties represent. Provincially, therefore, party subsidization by business has been very eclectic. For instance, business has been very generous toward the governing Conservative party in Ontario. That party has encouraged industrial growth and development, but has also compiled an enviably progressive record in civil liberties, and education. The Liberal and PC provincial branches in British Columbia are weak. When Social Credit came to office there in the early 1950's, business switched its financial allegiance to that party. Social Credit in British Columbia has in turn been extremely generous toward private enterprise, so much so that its critics have often accused it of following "giveaway" policies. Social Credit in British Columbia has not matched Ontario's progressive social legislation. It should not be overlooked that the NDP is a strong provincial force both in Ontario and in British Columbia, increasing business's motivation to support more "reliable" parties.

Australian business and industry prefer the Liberal to any other party, since the party system does not include two major middle-road formations, and Labor is a major political force, nationally and in the states. All the same, as in Canada, business donations have acquired a pragmatic quality, and parties other than the Liberals have not entirely been left out. Business has on occasion contributed to the Country party, a party of rural interests, but one which in recent years developed a strategy of courting business interests, and attached itself to high-tariff policies. McEwen House, the CP's headquarters in Canberra, was largely financed through industrial contributions. John McEwen for many years was the CP's federal leader, Deputy Prime Minister, Minister for Trade and Industry, and a close friend of industry as well as the CP's rural clientele. Australian business is also known to have made some donations to the Democratic Labor party (DLP). The DLP is strongly anti-Communist and antisocialist. Its present federal parliamentary complement of only five Senators and no House members is deceptive. The party's ability to discipline its electoral followers within the framework of the preferential voting system used in House elections endows it with exceptional leverage over Liberal governments.

Nor have Australian business interests neglected the ALP, though such contributions have been sporadic. Some of these donations have been an acknowledgment that the ALP is a genuine electoral alternative in Australia, particularly in the states. Also, the ALP has in many regards become restrained in its socialist advocacy, and there are instances in which state Labor governments have been as energetic in sponsoring economic development by recruiting business and industry as have Liberal governments. Indeed, some sectors of the business community in one respect prefer Labor to the Liberals, since "Liberals in power" is almost invariably equivalent to Liberals governing in coalition with the rural-based Country party, which enjoys the approbation of only some business elements.

In both Canada and Australia, therefore, there is no single party on which business and industry fully and confidently rely to serve their interests, and no party which is unmistakably committed to free enterprise, distaste for social-service measures, or other outlooks associated with hard-core conservatism. Commercial interests in the two countries have themselves accepted mixed economy programs and various governmental supervision of their activities. When they have intervened to secure a goal, their objectives have—in fact or in rhetoric—often been congruent with the preferences of other sectors of the two communities, even the working class, or with what is alluded to as the national interest. Although, like other interest formations, the two business communities endeavor to further their own goals, their public behavior can at times reflect a high order of social responsibility, and even altruism. Examples of this phenomenon include the banding together of Montreal business interests to promote all-Canadian unity, and the participation of various Australian business concerns in environmental improvement. In Canada, where the acceptance of middle-class authority has been prominent, there has been no frantic outcry against the common practice of the movement of talent between business and governmental/political communities. In Australia, where the egalitarian myth took hold and wealth *per se* commanded little awe, important business figures have very seldom entered politics, and have not been inclined to flaunt their economic status.

These considerations suggest that neither society, electorally or attitudinally, has developed mutually antagonistic economic or occupational political strongholds. Australian data suggest that fewer than a fifth of the public explicitly identifies the Liberals as a party of the middle or upper classes. Opinion surveys seldom if ever disclose a fear of business power as an area of public concern. An analysis of the 1969 House of Representatives election suggested that while over 57 per cent of the managerial and owner group voted Liberal, over 29 per cent supported Labor; unskilled workers went about 54 per cent Labor and 25 per cent Liberal. This diffusion of public sentiment is not recent. In 1947, Liberal and Labor voters had been very closely agreed—over 40 per cent—in perceiving no real difference between the parties. In Canada as of 1968–69, only 18 per cent of the public believed that big business was the single largest threat to the country's future, while 23 per cent nominated government, 34 per cent pointed to big labor, and 28 per cent were unable to say. Data collected less than two years later showed that two-thirds of the public thought that big business would have great influence on Canada's future, and another fifth predicted some influence. In other words, a linkage of these two surveys suggests the presence of a public recognition, with no appreciable fear, of big business. In the 1968 Commons election, Liberals received 51 per cent and the PC 34 per cent of the executive and managerial vote. But this distribution was not at serious variance with overall voting trends. In fact, nonfarming laboring people voted 45 per cent Liberal and 24 per cent Conservative. Over the 1950's and 1960's, Canada's electorate became increasingly convinced that it really did not matter which major party governed in Ottawa; by 1965, 44 per cent held this view. As of 1968–69, the overwhelming majority of Canadians believed that there was no real difference between the major parties. The highest and lowest income/occupational classes shared this view, and almost in the same degree; some 70 per cent of each group were convinced that the parties were much the same.

6

Working classes, organized labor, and reformist parties

Canada and Australia are modern, urban, and industrialized nations. The political behavior of the working classes can be a cardinal factor in determining who governs, and the types of public policies that are followed. Each country contains a party oriented toward progressive programs, and toward the working classes in particular: the Australian Labor party and Canada's New Democratic party. We wish to establish to what extent, and why, the national working classes have chosen to subscribe to these parties, and the manner in which the parties have performed their roles.

The extent and distribution of reformist party electoral strength

The ALP has been conspicuously more successful than the NDP or its progressive/socialist forerunners. The ALP's roots are much more deeply set than those of Canada's left parties. It existed in the various colonies even before federation, and from 1901 onward, operated in all the states and at the federal level. The first time ever that the ALP made a concerted electoral bid, in the 1891 New South Wales election, it captured a quarter of the seats and held the balance of power in the colonial assembly. The NDP in its present form was organized in 1961. Its lineal descendant, the CCF, began in 1932 as an essentially radical-agrarian, rather than industrial working-class, party in the Canadian west. Earlier Canadian socialist parties proved ephemeral, were not truly national in scope, and in certain cases had also, like the CCF, been more agrarian than urban working-class oriented. ALP electoral support has been far more impressive than the CCF/NDP's. Federally, the ALP took 18 per cent of the vote in the first Commonwealth House election, moved to 31 per cent in 1903, and since that time has almost invariably stood at 40–50 per cent. In 1969, it harvested 47 per cent of the vote, about 3.5 per cent more than the *combined* Liberal and Country party (government coalition) vote. The CCF's best national performance was 15.6 per cent, in 1945. The NDP national vote has varied from 14 per cent to 18 per cent. In 1968, it was 17 per cent, placing the party third, behind the Liberals (45.5 per cent) and the PC (31.4 per cent). The CCF/NDP has never governed federally, and has never even achieved the status of the official opposition in the House of Commons. The CCF/NDP has succeeded in capturing provincial office in only two provinces, twice in Saskatchewan, once in Manitoba. In only two other provinces, British Columbia and Ontario, has it ever constituted the official opposition, though a progenitor socialist party in 1912 became the official opposition in the British Columbian legislature. The ALP has governed nationally several times, with one stretch in office extending for eight years (1941–49), and its first, though brief, experience with federal office occurred but three years after the Commonwealth was formed. Within nine years of federation, it had succeeded in assuming federal power with an absolute majority. Over time, Labor has governed in every Australian state at least twice. By one point during the first World War, it occupied office federally and in every state except Victoria. Labor governments in Queensland and Tasmania at one time had a quarter of a century of uninterrupted rule. The

CCF/NDP's longest provincial tenure in Saskatchewan was for twenty years, 1944–64.

The ALP's substantially greater political strength is reflected in its far greater ability to attract the working-class vote than has been possible for the CCF/NDP. In the 1969 Australian House elections, Labor cornered some 60 per cent of the unskilled and semiskilled manual-worker vote, and over 56 per cent of the votes of skilled manual workers. By comparison, in Canada's 1968 federal election, 23 per cent of the electorate defined as "laboring class" voted NDP, and the party captured only 19 per cent of the vote of persons identified as "lower income." Although the NDP's strength is disproportionately urban, in 1968 it managed to win fewer than 12 per cent of the seats in Canada's nine largest cities. In Toronto, English Canada's largest city, the NDP share of the major three-party vote (Liberal, PC, NDP) was only 180,000, placing it third.

The Australian and Canadian left parties do, of course, attract a measure of nonworking-class support. Comparison reveals that the proportion of the NDP electorate which is not working class is considerably higher than the ALP's. Survey data for 1971 showed that the NDP had remarkably uniform backing across occupational categories—9 per cent of the executive/professional group, 11 per cent of the clerical, 12 per cent of the labor, and 10 per cent of agricultural and other categories. If the ALP's share of the nonworking-class vote were as close to its working-class following as is the NDP's nonworking-class support, Labor would be electorally invincible. Still, the ALP in the 1950's garnered a respectable 30 per cent of the middle-class vote, and in 1969 it attracted over 38 per cent of the white-collar and clerical electors. Nearly 27 per cent of the small business owners supported it in 1969, as did nearly 23 per cent of professional persons and over 21 per cent of managers and big business owners.

Working-class persons in both countries do vote for the "middle" or "conservative" parties, though, of course, less so in Australia than in Canada. We have already seen that working-class voters, like the two electorates at large, do not perceive wide differences between and among the Canadian and Australian parties. In Australia, persons of various classes apparently do not rank very differently on scales of radicalism, and a review of survey data indicates a gradual convergence of class opinions on economic questions. The data also disclose that ALP supporters are not intrigued by socialism or socialist policies, and that they are, overall, less enamored of their party's programs than Liberal supporters are of their party programs. Thus the Liberals are hardly a pariah party, either for the working class generally, or for explicit ALP voters. The Australian Liberals are, in fact, a viable voting alternative for working people. In 1969, a relatively poor electoral year for the government coalition, the Liberal and Country parties captured a segment of the working-class vote larger than the ALP's share of the nonworking-class vote.

In Canada, working-class people may perceive numerous resemblances between the two major parties, but electorally they are much more favorably disposed toward the Liberals than toward the Conservatives. When in 1968 the laboring class awarded 23 per cent of its vote to the NDP, 24 per cent of its support went to the Conservatives, and 46 per cent to the Liberals. When electoral data are recomputed according to the direction of voters defecting from one party to another, the tendency is confirmed. A far greater proportion of newly won NDP support flows from former Liberal supporters than PC supporters—16.4 per cent versus 9.7 per cent, respectively, in 1968. Stated somewhat differently, new converts to the PC are much more likely to derive from Liberal than NDP sources, 14.8 per cent versus 2.5 per cent. The Liberal party preference of working people is understandable, given the public's conception of the party system as ranging itself from left (NDP) to right (PC), with the Liberals in the center. In a purely formal sense, it can be argued that Canadian working people need not choose between a "left" party and only one "middle road" or "conservative" party. There is a perceived, comfortable alternative in between.

Bases of progressive political party strength

We have seen that the ALP has realized a far greater working-class electoral advantage than Canada's CCF/NDP. The reasons behind this discrepancy help to explain the balance of power in organized politics and the tone of public policy, and illuminate various cultural and structural features of the two national communities.

There are certain essentially "mechanical" reasons which may help to account for the considerably larger working-class following enjoyed by the ALP. Universal manhood suffrage came more quickly and easily in Australia than in Canada, reinforcing the myth of popular politics and granting ordinary people access to reformist, mass-based parties. Compulsory voting was established some years later Labor had entrenched itself in the nation's political life. The available analytic material indicates that neither Labor nor non-Labor has been particularly assisted by compulsory voting. But it may be useful to point out that working-class persons in various societies are, relatively speaking, less likely to vote voluntarily than middle- and upper-class (and therefore more conservative) electors. One quite simple explanation of ALP superiority over the NDP among workers is that the former is an old, established, and tested party, a "natural" part of the Australian political landscape, while the NDP is behind in all these respects. Also, apart from the quite special and perhaps inapplicable case of the DLP, which in any event is a very recent party, there is no major, "in between" party available for Australian workers. Their effective choice is between Labor and the Liberals, parties separated by a somewhat wider social and programmatic distance than divides Canadian working people and the Liberal party. The Australian Liberals and their forebears have, in fact, often been referred to in negative terms, e.g., as "non-Labor" or as "parties of resistance," characterized more by what they have not been or have been against, than what they have been for.

There are also some societal explanations for differences in ALP and CCF/NDP levels of worker attraction. Canada has been and remains more ethnically heterogeneous than Australia. The populous French Canadian community in Quebec carries an inheritance of traditionalism, domination by a defensive and socially conservative church, and suspicion of centralization attributed to English-speaking planners and reformers. Canada's Continental European migrants, though they normally entered the lower SES categories, were difficult to organize, and frequently entertained quite different perspectives on social reform than did Anglo-Saxons. At the turn of the present century, the Socialist party of Canada was led almost entirely by Anglo-Saxons, while east European settlers gravitated into a competitive Social Democratic party. Australian society, by comparison, was uncommonly homogeneous, and the political mobilization of working people was not handicapped in the manner experienced in Canada.

Australia's consistently higher level of urbanization probably provided further advantage for the ALP's development. Working people were compactly located and easier to marshall for political action than was true in Canada, even though much of the early radical politics in both countries emerged among nonurban workers, such as persons employed in British Columbia's extractive industries, and coal miners and shearers in Australia. Indeed, political radicalism among Australian shearers resulted, in reality, from their being members of a rural proletariat, a situation not replicated in Canada, where there were no great farms or pastoral estates on the Australian pattern. When political discontent surfaced on the Canadian Prairies, it had a decidedly agrarian-populist rather than a "working-class" quality. This was true of nearly all pre-CCF reformist parties in the area, such as the United Farmers of Manitoba, the United Farmers of Alberta, and even the Progressives in Ontario and the west. It also, of course, characterized the CCF in its earlier days.

Differences in cultural values and expectations have also counted. As already explained, nineteenth-century Australian culture acquired an egalitarian bent, and leaned heavily on official authority for the provision of services. Canadian governments in the latter part of the nineteenth century were also called upon to exercise their influence, but with fewer overtones of public ownership and social welfare concerns than in Australia. Canada's more deferential, middle-class culture once again provided fewer natural impulses for a labor/social democratic party alternative, whether broadly or specifically working-class supported.

Another and salient difference continues to be found in the position of the two trade-union movements. Strong and active trade-union organization can be an asset to the electoral fortunes of a reformist party. It can politically arouse and mobilize the working classes. It can publicize and organize such a party, and act as a counterweight to the large-scale donations usually available to conservative parties from business sources. Not surprisingly, union influence in Australia has been far more prominent than in Canada, with important consequences for working-class parties in the two countries.

Unionization in Australia has been consistently higher than in Canada. The proportion of the work force enrolled in unions has recently been declining in Australia and increasing in Canada. This, however, underscores the modest base from which further union growth in Canada can still proceed, and the early and once extraordinarily high level of unionization in Australia, which has receded as the work force has become more technical, professional, and female in composition. As of 1971, 28 per cent of Canada's work force was unionized, a figure achieved in Australia as early as 1911. Australian unionization reached its zenith of over 60 per cent in the 1950's, and by the beginning of the 1970's had fallen off to half of the work force.

Unionism in Australia grew more rapidly than in Canada in part because of the reasons already ascribed to the more rapid development of a major labor/social democratic party—reasons touching on population homogeneity, cultural values, and the structure and location of economic enterprise. An additional and critical stimulant was the appearance of compulsory arbitration arrangements, which placed a premium on unionization. The right of working people to organize and use unions for industrial action was essentially settled before the first World War, having gained acceptance both under law and generally from management itself. Canadian workers, on the contrary, have had a long, uphill struggle. Punitive legislation following the general strike in 1919 in Winnipeg was a reverse for organized labor's cause. Not until 1939 were workers employed in industries under federal jurisdiction accorded collective bargaining privileges, and that legislation did not become fully operative until a few years later. Canada's provinces, which hold labor jurisdiction over three-quarters of the country's organized workers, have frequently assumed antiunion positions, including resort to repressive legislation, strike breaking, and restrictions on collections for political purposes. In the late 1940's, the Union Nationale government in Quebec employed all its resources to smash a strike of asbestos workers. Over a decade later, a Liberal government in Newfoundland outlawed the International Woodworkers' Union and resorted to the RCMP for strike breaking. Over the years, organized labor has chafed at a system of compulsory arbitration, a ban on political collections, and other impositions applied by British Columbia's Social Credit government.

The actual structure of trade unionism has been another factor determining organized labor's influence. Unionization levels are far more uniform among Australian states than among Canada's provinces. British Columbia's unionization level of about 43 per cent, the highest in Canada, lags behind all Australian states. Both countries have an inordinately large number of individual unions—

over 160 in Canada, and just over 300 in Australia. Such organizational dispersion tends to weaken the movements, though in both nations there is a concentration of unionized workers within a small number of large unions. The largest unions, among them Canada's United Steel Workers of America, and the Australian Workers' Union (AWU), a general union, have membership in the neighborhood of 150,000 each. Australia's recently proposed Amalgamated Metal Workers Union, an amalgam of previously separate unions, would enroll 170,000 members. Furthermore, the smaller Australian unions are strengthened by their access to conciliation and arbitration machinery.

Organized labor in Canada has historically been much less coalesced than in Australia. About three-quarters of Australia's unionists belong to organizations affiliated with the Australian Council of Trade Unions (ACTU), which was founded in 1927. The numerically powerful AWU affiliated with the ACTU in 1967. By comparison, Canadian unionism has suffered from disunity bred by a variety of problems. As far back as the nineteenth century, a small, scattered, and inexperienced Canadian working class turned for organizational assistance to the stronger American unions. The result was that the majority of Canadian unions, and unionists, became members of international unions, meaning Canadian locals of parent groups headquartered in America. Over 60 per cent of Canada's unionists are still affiliated in this manner. One of the results of this has been that rules or orders deriving from parent unions have impeded a more natural, Canadian-oriented championship of worker causes. Also, moves toward Canadian labor unity were seriously retarded. For a considerable time, the principal Canadian organization was the Trades and Labor Congress (TLC), patterned on the AFL in the United States. When in the 1930's American labor split and the CIO emerged, much the same happened in Canada, and an industrial union-based Canadian Congress of Labor (CCL) appeared. The two organizations remained apart, often in rival postures, until the

Canadian Labor Congress (CLC) was born in 1956. It now enrolls about the same proportion of Canada's unionists as the ACTU enrolls among Australian workers. In Quebec, an independent, church-dominated, and conservative union evolved in the 1920's. It dissolved in 1960. Its replacement, the Confederation of National Trade Unions (CNTU), has no church connections and is, in fact, militant. Despite its name it is very largely a French-speaking, Quebec union, outside the CLC, and in certain respects competitive with the CLC's provincial arm, the Quebec Federation of Labor.

The temper and style of organized labor

The position and behavior of Canadian and Australian unions have reflected their composition, structure, and cultural legacies. In general, the two organized labor movements have favored progressive and evolutionary rather than radical policies. Such themes as workers' control of industry or the systematic abolition of private enterprise have generally been foreign to them, though it remains to be seen whether some recent radical proposals adumbrated by Quebec's labor organizations will prove acceptable to rank-and-file unionists. At all events, relative national economic well-being, the general absence of reactionary government, and an incrementally oriented political legacy in both societies have contributed to temper union orientation.

Canadian labor was for very long numerically weak, mainly organized along craft lines. It was pervaded by the American Gomperist tradition, following an essentially gradualist and apolitical approach. The movement remains more craft than industry oriented, and the presence of large public service unions contributes a certain bourgeois influence. Australian unionism has long been numerically strong and self-confident. It did not need to struggle long or hard to establish its legitimacy. The arbitration systems sheltered unions and their members, and organized labor's alliance with political Labor was quickly crowned by electoral success. The very large-scale unionization in Australia meant considerable enrollment among the country's white-collar and public-service workers, whose outlook toward industrial action and social change was generally restrained. In more recent times, however, some of the nonindustrial unions, such as the Amalgamated Postal Workers Union, have become more militant. The AWU itself has long been recognized for its moderation.

Radical trade unionism did have some following around the time of the first World War, when the One Big Union in Canada and the International Workers of the World in both nations were prominent. The Wobblies, eager to sabotage the war effort, set fires, and in 1916 produced some excellent banknote forgeries. Both nations have undergone industrial disputes during which violence was present, and one account records 277 Canadian strikes which were marred by violence between 1910 and 1966. But perspective is required in judging such events. The One Big Union and IWW style of unionism passed away. Fatalities associated with labor disputes have been virtually nonexistent. For instance, only one death resulted from the heralded Winnipeg general strike of 1919 which lasted six weeks. In Australia following World War I, there was considerable unrest associated with industrial tension and veteran resettlement. There were outbursts in various cities, but only one death. There was Australian industrial violence in the 1920's and in 1930–31, but very little thereafter during the depression years, and no resort to gunfire or bombing during the 1930's.

The extent and character of industrial stoppages and disputes in the two nations is one index of organized working-class behavior. For decades, until the mid-1950's, Australia registered consistently higher strike rates, as measured by man days lost per working population. In 1926, for instance, the Australian rate was more than twice as great as the Canadian. But from the mid-1950's the picture changed. Although the number of Australian strikes has been much larger than in Canada, the number of working days lost, as a proportion of the labor force, has been substantially higher in Canada. Even with corrections for size of population, it is noteworthy that in 1967 Canada's work stoppages calculated to over 4 million lost working days, versus just over 700,000 in Australia; in 1969, Canada lost 7.3 million working days, and Australia only 1.9 million. While the number of lost working days has been mounting rapidly in both countries, the duration of strikes is far greater in Canada than in Australia. With some exceptions, Australian work stoppages are brief. In the ten year period to 1967, many more than half of all disputes were settled within a day, and three-quarters within two days. It would appear, too, that contemporary Canadian industrial disputes are more apt to generate violence than is the case in Australia.

Throughout much of the first half of the present century, the efforts of Australian organized labor were directed at improved wages and working conditions, not at union recognition as such. There was unemployment in the 1920's as well as in the 1930's, the basic wage was not generous, and there always was pressure for winning wage scales above the margins which were officially authorized. The workers were heavily organized and class consciousness was relatively keen. Canadian workers during this period struggled for recognition and elementary access to collective bargaining, as well as for improved economic conditions. Being underunionized, often confronted by restrictive laws and punitively minded governments, often organizationally fragmented, and not upheld by any political party as Australian labor was by the ALP, the Canadian workers' ability to launch and sustain work stoppages was more limited than in Australia. When major stoppages did occur, however, they tended to be fought over fundamentals.

In recent years, Australian workers have operated within a full employment econcmy, where labor *shortages* have often been severe. Their temptation to institute stoppages has been spurred by an understanding that management is fairly likely to acquiesce. Moreover, although a number of stoppages are attributable to wage demands, over half are not, often, instead, concerning minor points of working conditions. Strikes over wages occur despite the arbitration system in part because in a prosperous economic climate workers often feel they have been slighted by official awards, and think that management will not hold out too long. In fact, Australian organized labor is increasingly skeptical about compulsory arbitration, reasoning that collective bargaining can in many cases produce superior terms. But the Australian arbitration system makes provision for penalties when, in certain circumstances, labor or management has breached the provisions of an officially prescribed settlement. In practice, this has meant the fining of unions which have disregarded the bans on strike action which arbitration commissions occasionally impose. Since strike action has been increasing, penalties have become larger and more severe, leading organized labor to turn its fire on the sanctions system generally. Rising labor disaffection with the prevailing system of industrial relations regulation has, in turn, spawned work stoppages related to that very complaint. It is somewhat ironic that the Australian unions' historical strength may have contributed to a certain complacency.

Union fees are among the lowest in the western world. According to an early 1971 estimate, less than $1 million would be found if all Australian unions pooled their cash reserves. Not only are strike funds therefore low, but so are funds for paying fines imposed against those unions which undertake illegal strikes.

Canada's record of increased labor militancy through strike action is in part a reflection of the increasing numbers of unionized workers, improved organizational unity, Quebec's shift from company unions to militant trade unionism during the period of social awakening in that province, and a sense of confidence gained through recent affiliation with the NDP. As Canadian labor sees it, it needs to focus attention on remaining hostile labor legislation in some provinces, the wage squeeze imposed by the cost of living spiral, and problems derived from persistent unemployment.

The activities of the two labor movements which are not explicitly industrial should also be examined. The Australian movement, traditionally stronger and more assertive, has a more distinguishable political strike tradition. For example, Australian dockworkers and seamen have tried to exert leverage through such means as declaring a "black ban" on Dutch ships during Indonesia's independence efforts, and refusing to service Australian ships carrying munitions to Vietnam. Australian labor has in recent years gone out in protests against a visiting South African rugby team, and against a federal budget which was reputed to have short-changed pensioners. There is little that is comparable among Canada's organized labor movement, though the appearance of political strikes is more likely now than it was in the past. Indeed, both trade union movements have recently begun to expand their interests. The conventional bread-and-butter concerns are being supplemented by pressure and publicity in such areas as native people conditions, the environment, and safety. The ACTU has bought into a department-store business and has approved entry into consumer credit, insurance, and housing finance, with the assistance of the West German and Israeli labor movements.

The two labor movements, in their separate ways, are in a state of change. The extent to which they can expect to make major imprints on public policy depends on at least three factors. The first is organized labor's public image and acceptability. In Australia, where unions are historically very well established and enroll a high percentage of the working force, there is widespread public feeling, even among conservative party supporters, that unions are a "good thing." In 1966, 75 per cent of the electorate felt this way, and only 8 per cent explicitly felt the contrary. The public—unionists included—is cautious in favoring exceptional treatment for unions, such as might be reflected in the rescinding of penal clauses in industrial awards. Canadian organized labor, despite its traditional attachment to pragmatism, has been growing in numbers, unity, and boldness. This is something rather new for

Canada, and in some respects rudely awakening. The survey data do suggest that business/professional and working people alike are willing to accept one another's influence upon government. But more Canadians are apprehensive about labor unions than they are about big business, and the public's esteem of unions actually declined during the 1960's. In 1970, only 54 per cent of the public approved of unions, and 30 per cent disapproved, a decidedly smaller proportion than approves of trade unions in Australia. Among Canadian *working* people themselves, still somewhat unaccustomed to the idea of a powerful union role in society, only 59 per cent approve of unions, and twice as many Canadian unionists believe that laws governing unions are too lenient, as believe they are too strict. French Canadians, despite the recent surge of reform and union militancy in Quebec, continue to be even less enthusiastic about trade unions than are English-speaking Canadians.

A second way to assess the impact of organized labor's policy is to judge the responsiveness of governments. Like business and agricultural interests, labor has access to government through various consultative arrangements. The very size and entrenched position of Australian labor has given it a stronger voice than is true in Canada. For instance, when in 1929 a UAP-Country party government attempted to transfer much of the responsibilities of arbitration to the states, the UAP itself split over the issue, the Bruce-Page government was defeated in Parliament, and at the election which followed was run out of office. When in 1970 organized labor staged a brief shutdown over a 50¢ weekly increase in pension benefits, it was scolded by the Liberal government for applying unfair, extraparliamentary political methods. But these labor protests helped to publicize what already was a widespread public concern over inadequate pension rates, and political realism quickly produced fresh pension increments. Labor's demand for a withdrawal of industrial award penal provisions has been rejected by the L-CP government. But in 1971, when announcing its intention to amend the law relating to industrial relations, and in ways obnoxious to labor, the government did not propose to increase the size of fines, and indicated a reluctance to force collection of unpaid fines which had piled up prior to mid-1970. Organized labor's ability to influence policy is naturally related to which party is in office, and in this regard Australian unions enjoy a considerable advantage. Labor-oriented governments in both countries have been more sympathetic toward working-class interests than have middle-road or conservative governments. For example, when the NDP took office in Saskatchewan in 1971, one of its high priorities was to rescind the outgoing Liberal government's legislation restricting industrial stoppages believed to thwart the public interest. Australian labor has had much more occasion to enjoy close and sympathetic relations with governments, since the ALP has at various times governed nationally, and very frequently in the states, while the CCF/NDP has never ruled in Ottawa, and provincially only in Saskatchewan and Manitoba.

A third measure of organized labor's capacity for political spokesmanship and policy influence lies in the nature of its relations with labor/progressive parties. Although exact figures are unavailable, workers belonging to unions affiliated with the ALP are known to represent several times more of Australia's organized labor force than are affiliated with the NDP in Canada. This disparity is attributable to Canada's smaller incidence of unionization, and to organized labor's traditional hesitation to involve itself directly in partisan politics. The ALP had already become a substantial political force, and had a close working relationship with trade unions, when unionization soared shortly after federation. In Canada, conclusive union-party coalescence did not occur until 1961, when the old CCF gave way to the NDP. In the early twentieth century, union entry into politics was mainly a British Columbian manifestation, and of temporary duration. There also was some feeling in the TLC at one time in favor of political involvement, but efforts in this direction proved insignificant, and by the 1920's the dominant, Gomperist view of staying out of party politics had clearly asserted itself. The CCF's appearance in the early 1930's resulted from a merger of various western farmer and labor parties and the Fabian oriented League for Social Reconstruction. The TLC gave the new CCF no outward support, the CCF itself was determined to remain a basically nonunion party, and most of the party's membership was drawn from among farmers and sectors of the middle class. By 1943 the CCL had endorsed the CCF as its preferred arm for furthering working-class interests, and by the following year about a hundred union locals were affiliated with the CCF. But by the late 1940's the CCF began to lose ground among organized labor. The TLC was continuing to resist political affiliation, pressures from American labor discouraged politicization, and there had been a decline in CCF electoral fortunes. The 1956 merger of the CCL and the TLC into the Canadian Labor Congress foreshadowed the founding of the NDP. Union membership and a sense of confidence in the unions were on the upswing. The CCF had amended its program in a way which closely resembled the gradualist preferences of organized labor. The CCF's severe setback in the 1958 federal election, representing a decline in Commons representation from 25 to 8 seats, actuated a mood of urgency for common, progressive political action, both in CCF and union circles.

Unions affiliated with the NDP are represented on national and provincial party bodies such as policy and leadership selection conferences, but are a minority voice, and the NDP remains a party of essentially individual membership. In Australia, the Labor party in an important sense was created by interested trade union groups, and a pronounced union-party mesh continues to this day. Until recently, organized labor and the state ALP branch in Western Australia were essentially an entity, while the AWU for some time, in actuality, controlled the ALP branch in Queensland. The electoral significance of intimate union-ALP ties will be discussed elsewhere.

Here it is sufficient to point out that the unions are paramount within the party, not only in decision-making organs, but in conducting and financing party business. Without union assistance, the ALP would have very few resources to fall back on. Union-affiliated members form well over 90 per cent of the party's membership, and a similar proportion of ALP funds is supplied by unions. In the late 1960's the ALP's individual membership was somewhat over 40,000, representing only one-third of Liberal and one-half of Country-party enrollment. Australian union collections for party purposes are quite straightforward. In practice, union members are assessed unless they explicitly contract out, a rare and even dangerous step for workers wishing to remain on good terms with the union, and to keep their jobs. In the NDP, only about 40 per cent of the regular party upkeep, though most of federal election campaign money, comes from affiliated unions. Canadian unions are, in any event, more restricted in imposing political fund assessments on their members than are Australia's unions. In British Columbia, for instance, where organized labor is particularly numerous, political donations must be made entirely outside the trade-union framework. In Quebec, the economically reformist and French nationalist CNTU has established political action committees throughout the province, but they remain clear of party connections. The CLC-affiliated Quebec Federation of Labor, in the recent past, provided a modicum of assistance to the NDP. But in 1971, the QFL withdrew its formal backing of the NDP, since the party had withdrawn from Quebec provincial politics. Like the CNTU, the QFL has moved farther to the left, and has taken a more determined view on Quebec's special position, than has the federal NDP. In the 1970 provincial election in Quebec, organized labor's support for the highly progressive but antiseparatist Liberals was basically rhetorical. The only recent and reasonably concerted instance of union-party collaboration in Quebec occurred in the 1970 Montreal municipal election. At that time, the NDP, the

CNTU, the QFL, and the Quebec Teachers Corporation tried to pull together in support of the progressive candidates sponsored by the local Political Action Front.

On many counts, therefore, Australia's political Labor is far more extensively served by trade unions than is Canada's NDP, a party which only with qualification deserves the label of a "labor" party. Nonetheless, the union component of the NDP often makes up in energy and largesse for its relatively modest position within the NDP's membership and organizational organs. It must be allowed that Australia is smaller than Canada, has fewer states than there are Canadian provinces, has fewer federal parliamentary seats to fill, that compulsory voting has removed the party burden of getting out the vote, and that campaign expenditures for parties generally have not reached Canadian levels. But in the 1968 federal election, the NDP spent about $1 million, most of it acquired from unions. In 1971, the ALP federal organization was hoping to raise $300,000 to wage the next election campaign.

We have seen that trade unions occupy a more conspicuous position in Australian politics generally, and within the ALP especially, than they do in Canadian politics, or within the NDP. The *extent* of unionization in particular parts of the two countries does not suggest itself as a viable explanation for determining left-party success; other factors need to be built in. In British Columbia, where unionization is particularly high, the NDP has long been powerful, but has never organized the provincial government. Saskatchewan and Manitoba, where there have been NDP governments, are relatively underunionized. Queensland, Australia's most unionized state, long housed an ALP government, but Labor has been out of power there since 1957. In other states, historically, there seems to have been a tenuous correlation between the unions' *reluctance* to intervene brashly in ALP party affairs and Labor's ability to gain office. Federally, there has been no visible relationship between the level at which unionization has stood at a particular time, and the electoral success of the Labor party. It has been shown that working people generally are proportionately much more disposed to vote for a "labor" party in Australia than they are in Canada. Indeed, the NDP's proportion of the working class vote is not much greater than its share of other groups' votes. As late as 1967, only 24 per cent of electors in *union* families approved of trade-union involvement in politics, while 60 per cent of them explicitly disapproved. In Australia, unskilled workers, both unionized and nonunionized, are much more inclined to favor Labor than are nonmanual workers. There is some evidence that the NDP draws more support from skilled than from unskilled workers, presumably because skilled Canadian workers are, at this stage, more highly unionized and politically socialized, despite the fact that they are not the most economically underprivileged in the work force. While the higher union membership/politicization of skilled workers may help to explain their NDP leanings, the relative lack of unionization among the lowest occupational class does not fully suffice as an explanation of that class's desultory NDP electoral support. To round out the treatment of working-class political behavior, it is useful to sharpen our understanding of ALP and NDP programs in areas especially related to working-class outlooks and interests, and to evaluate such programs vis-à-vis the policy offerings of the more conservative parties.

Working-class reception of progressive party programs

Issues of public ownership have had a very mixed effect on the inclination of the working class to support labor/progressive parties in Australia and Canada. We have seen that public values in the two systems are not instinctively hostile toward the notion of public ownership. On the other hand, the data prominently suggest that both publics, including working-class and trade-union members, are skeptical about elaborate governmental ownership and controls. The party platform of the ALP and the CCF/NDP did at one time and to an extent still does reflect anticapitalist bias and an affinity for state ownership. But such doctrines more often than not have represented a distant ideal, and over time were watered down to the level of an essentially nondoctrinaire, mixed-economy approach.

In Canada, the CCF's charter Regina Manifesto of 1933 denounced capitalism as a "cancer that must be rooted out," and proposed to substitute a socialist economy with "our natural resources and principal means of production . . . owned, controlled and operated by the public." The CCF's Winnipeg Declaration of 1956 affirmed the desirability of public ownership where necessary, recognized the need for private enterprise in "many fields," and pledged the party to encourage both private and public industries. This was the direction of the platform announcing the NDP's program at its birth in 1961. The language of Regina contributed to scaring much of organized labor away from closer ties with the CCF. The language of the Winnipeg document very closely approximated the language of the CLC's own foundation program of 1956, and helped make possible the NDP in its present, labor associated form.

Australian Labor in 1921 proposed the "socialization of industry, production, distribution, and exchange," but a resolution limiting the targets of socialization to industries engaged in "exploitation" was attached. The platform then went through several revisions, all tending to qualify the nationalization objective. The present position reflects the ALP's reconsideration of what is economically necessary and electorally profitable. There is also a realization, based on strict High Court interpretations and an unwillingness of the public to approve remedial constitutional amendments, that conventional public-ownership policies are inappropriate.

The actual record of the two left/progressive parties generally sustains the shifts in platform rhetoric. Many years ago, Labor governments in several Australian states established publicly owned brickyards, butcher shops, bakeries, sawmills, and other enterprises. Such facilities were not designed to replace privately owned enterprises, but to serve as convenient and low-price outlets, and stimulants to lower prices and more efficient methods in the private sector itself. Saskatchewan's CCF government of 1944–64, more out of a wish to improve services and to lower costs than to demonstrate ideological vigor, created such publicly owned facilities as a bus line, a seed cleaning plant, and a shoe factory.

A glance at recent performance shows that this type of inclination toward state ownership has generally ended. Where an emphasis on public ownership persists, it is limited to enterprises that can in a broad sense be interpreted as "public," or it bears little direct connection with orthodox socialism. The NDP government in Manitoba undertook investment in industrial development projects, and bought some shares in private companies which required additional capitalization. The Ontario NDP, an opposition party, has promised to nationalize energy industries and possibly uranium mines. It has promised to become involved in the distribution, but not ownership or retailing, of pharmaceuticals and farm machinery. Like the Manitoba NDP, it has an interest in provincial entry into the insurance field. Australian Labor's historical preference for bringing the banking system under central ownership is gone. Other services or industries, particularly energy and mineral resources, would be affected by government intervention, but through the creation of Commonwealth public corporations operating parallel to private endeavors, or through federal grants to the states to proceed in this manner. Otherwise, the emphasis would be on supervision, not on ownership. During the first year after its most recent accession to office, the South Australian Labor administration limited its "socialism" to proposing government entry into the non-life-insurance field.

Such approaches to public ownership are essentially compatible with public preferences. The middle-ground conservative parties in the two countries, as we have seen, have not themselves been averse to selective public ownership. Also, after a considerable lag, private enterprise itself has begun to fall under the kind of official purview and regulation that reduces the relevance of cries for "people's control" of industry. The Canadian federal Liberals, with whom the NDP primarily competes for the working-class vote, have been promoting shared government ownership in key resource and energy industries, which are particularly susceptible to exploitation and in which the public interest is acutely involved. In any event, both in Canada and in Australia, much of the starch has been taken out of the "socialism" issue in electoral campaigns, thus providing slim advantage to any particular party during the ceremonies associated with wooing the working-class and union voter.

Social service, by contrast, has become a keen public issue in both countries. Various parties openly advertise their achievements and boastfully compare proposals. Social welfare issues have been identified as among the most personally felt and salient topics in the two electorates, particularly in the lower SES strata. In 1971, by far the greatest national problem perceived by the Australian public was the inadequacy of funding for schools and hospitals. Our question is whether NDP and ALP approaches to welfare policy recommend these parties to the electorate, and especially to the lower and laboring classes.

A comprehensive comparison of Canadian and Australian party accomplishments in social welfare is distorted by the continuing absence of the CCF/NDP from national office, and its limited (Saskatchewan and Manitoba) experience with provincial office. The early CCF government in Saskatchewan did in fact establish Canada's first comprehensive health insurance plan. The plan was extremely controversial at the time and—although for various reasons—the CCF lost the election which followed the introduction of the plan. However, the succeeding Liberal government retained the plan's essential framework, and the popularity of the Saskatchewan medicare program grew. The return of the NDP to provincial office in Saskatchewan in 1971 had been preceded by a clear promise to remove certain medical charges previously imposed.

As of the early 1970's, the federal NDP's principal social service proposal was a guaranteed annual income, an understandable proposal in light of Canada's high incidence of poverty and unemployment. In 1971, however, the governing Liberal party unveiled its own income-security plan. It was not a plan for guaranteed annual income as such, but it did provide for quite generous allowances for lower-income families. In recent years, the Liberal legislative record has included comprehensive medicare, elaborate low-income housing, and home-ownership programs, pension and child-benefit supplements, and the maintenance, in conjunction with the provinces, of support to national education, a program which, proportionate to GNP, is one of the world's most expensive. In many regards, the Liberals have done what other Canadian governments, Liberal and Conservative, have been doing over many years—stealing much of the left parties' ideas and using them for their own advantage. Thus in the 1920's, Liberal Prime Minister William Lyon Mackenzie King masterminded the decline and eventual eclipse of the Progressive party by sponsoring various measures dear to progressive and working elements, such as old-age pensions. In the 1930's, the so-called "Bennett New Deal," which provided for unemployment and social insurance, industrial wage minimums, and other reforms, was in large part invalidated by the courts. But it had been brought forward by a Conservative government and a Conservative Prime Minister, R. B. Bennett.

Throughout the provinces, even governments with a conservative reputation have been able to point to certain socially attractive and electorally strategic policies. For instance, British Columbia's Social Credit government has long mixed populism, red-baiting, and welfare reform. It has been antagonistic toward organized labor, but in the 1969 election campaign, as the result of which it improved its electoral standing, it promised new assistance to homeowners and improved old-age pensions and social assistance. In 1970, the government of British Columbia passed sweeping tenant protection legislation. It is this sort of approach that has helped to cut into the working-class vote in a province renowned for its high level of unionization, political militancy, and the relative prominence of the NDP.

For decades Quebec's provincial politics had a conservative bias, and the Duplessis regime was the most socially regressive in all of Canada. Progressive politics of the CCF/NDP variety were ridiculed as the devilish work of Godless collectivists, and the CCF did not even bother to offer candidates in provincial elections. Quebec's working people were French, Catholic, and conservative, and in certain respects remain more conservative than their class counterparts elsewhere in the nation. But recent research has suggested a credible explanation for the frequently disproportionate working-class support of the Union Nationale, and of a conservative party such as Social Credit in the 1962 federal election. Quebec's workers were poorly organized and had an underdeveloped class consciousness. Yet, while they were in these terms "unincorporated," they were restless. Under these circumstances they chose parties such as the UN or Social Credit not because these parties were conservative *qua* conservative, but because they represented an available outlet for a political protest of their own kind, and carried certain populist overtones. Faced with a crisis, unincorporated masses such as those found in Quebec,

> will choose the movement that appears to them most likely to be successful, whether it is conservative or progressive in the eyes of the sophisticated observer. The ideology of the existing movements at that point is of little relevance to them. More particularly, this is true for peasants and farmers, who are often unorganized, but also for the workers, when their organizations are politically very weak.*

Quebec's working people have absorbed much of the spirit of change and reform which has come to the province since Duplessis' death in 1959; and at the same time there emerged a militant

* Maurice Pinard, *The Rise of a Third Party. A Study in Crisis Politics* (Toronto: Prentice-Hall of Canada, 1971), p. 95.

unionism and socially activist governments. Federally, the NDP did quite well in the 1965 election, with 12 per cent of Quebec's popular vote, though the party slipped to 7.5 per cent in 1968. The NDP entered Quebec's 1970 provincial election, did very badly, and subsequently decided to withdraw from the provincial field. But the two parties which attracted the greatest proportion of the urban working-class vote in 1970, the Liberals and the Parti Québecois—especially the latter—were both socially progressive. Once in office, the Liberals continued the already rapid expansion and modernization of the educational program, and instituted the most thorough medicare plan in the nation. The PQ, a separatist party, was attractive to workers because it stood for social progressivism, and because its separatist creed held in part that an independent Quebec could do more to cut down unemployment and otherwise enhance material well-being than was possible while Quebec remained in Canada.

In the first half of the present century, federal Labor in Australia had a clearly stronger record of social reform than did its political opposition. Even before World War I, the party had enacted invalid and old-age pensions and a system of maternity allowances. In the 1920's, a slack period for social reform, the few initiatives taken in the social service field by state governments were essentially of Labor's doing. During and immediately after the second World War, Labor's wish to substantially enlarge social services ran into both constitutional and political impediments, though a successful constitutional referendum did much to settle the question of Canberra's pre-eminence in the field, and Labor's efforts in social legislation were impressive. But nonlabor parties have not been inactive. Before World War I, when the social reform spirit was generally high, they broached a comprehensive, though contributory, social insurance plan, which would have covered sickness, unemployment, and the like, though no legislative action resulted. In the late 1930's, they produced a national health plan, though internal troubles forced them to shelve it. In

1941 it was they, not Labor, who introduced the original federal child allowance plan.

During their lengthy federal domination which began in 1949, the Australian Liberals put into motion a plan for first free, and then partial out-of-pocket pharmaceutical benefits. They installed a health insurance program, which was substantially liberalized in 1970, and developed payments to voluntary organizations operating in such fields as home nursing and marriage guidance. Although Australian conservative parties have consistently preferred social services based on a contributory principle, they have wound up managing a system which, apart from the health program, is essentially funded from general revenues.

Postwar spending in the social services under the Australian Liberals has risen sharply, reflecting the addition and extension of various services. But by western and most certainly Canadian standards, the effort has been modest. As of 1959–60, Canadian social service spending as a percentage of GNP stood at about 9 per cent, while in Australia it was 7.7 per cent. A decade later, cash social service benefits were 9.9 per cent of Canada's GNP, and 5.5 per cent of Australia's. It could be argued that the Australian effort mirrors local conditions, that is, Australians do not require as much state welfare assistance because they enjoy full employment, have a lower poverty rate, and receive numerous social benefits directly from employers. On the other hand, Australia's standard of living is lower than Canada's, and the tax levy is high, even for lower-income groups. Pensioners and other persons not fully and gainfully enrolled in the work force, even if technically not in poverty status, live in extremely frugal circumstances, and have been burdened by the recent onset of inflation. The quality of certain Australian enterprises, such as hospital services, leaves much to be desired.

It is in this context that the ALP has recommended a comprehensive health plan to be administered by the Commonwealth, an end to means test provisions in welfare benefits, and a general upgrading of social benefit payments. It has also proposed the phased adoption of a national dental program. A decade or two earlier, these Labor proposals would have been politically risky. By now, they are widely, though by no means universally, listened to and even welcomed by the electorate, predominantly the lower-income groups. As we have seen, Australians at large now feel that shortages and qualitative deficiencies in the country's social and educational facilities are the country's principal drawbacks. The Liberals have made gains, but not enough to satisfy the critics. Labor advocates major advances, and there may be electoral benefit to be reaped from among working-class persons who presently vote Liberal and even among other classes. The party's historical image, apart from service to organized labor, is that of care and assistance for ordinary people generally—shopkeepers, clerks, even elements employed on the land.

Canada's NDP, by comparison, is unable to score many points off the federal Liberals on social welfare issues, and the Liberals continue to attract a very much greater share of the working-class vote than would seem to befit a conventionally perceived conservative or middle-road party in a political system where a "left" alternative is available. The obstacles which prevent the NDP from scoring an electoral breakthrough at Liberal expense also relate to issues touching on the comfort and protection of the consumer public. To be sure, the NDP is all in favor of clean air, rapid transit, fair advertising, and the like, and Manitoba's NDP government brought in some important consumer-protection legislation. But Ottawa Liberals have not been upstaged. The rigor with which the Trudeau government has moved on the issue of honest labeling, has been impressive. Nor have other parties been negligent. In Conservative-ruled Ontario, for instance, the provincial government abruptly halted construction of a multi-million dollar speedway project in Toronto. Funds were instead diverted into urban rapid transit. Consumer protection, environmental improvement, and similar actions by the state are increasingly felt, and appreciated, on a day-to-day basis by the general population, including ordinary working-class voters and their families.

A more complacent Australian political climate meant a slower start and less achievement in these areas. Nationally, the ALP seems more concerned than the Liberals. In the states, the several governing Labor and non-Labor party groups have reacted variously; South Australia's Labor government and an L-CP governmen in New South Wales both moved quite vigorously with popular consumer protection measures, and New South Wales adopted extremely strict environmental regulations vis-à-vis industry. Sydney now matches New York and Los Angeles in air contamination. Melbourne's Yarra River and Brisbane's Brisbane River were suddenly discovered to be depressingly polluted. Survey data, rather surprisingly, have disclosed that the traditionally penny-wise Australian public seems willing to pay the price of low-pollutant motor fuels. Although it is uncertain how much political capital can be realized from what appears to be a spreading public interest in consumer and environmental concerns, federally, at least, it is Labor, not the Liberals, that has produced the more systematic and creditable set of proposals in these areas.

7

Rural interests and organized politics

We have seen that the rural sector has been losing much of its earlier prominence in the Canadian and Australian economies. Both countries have become heavily urbanized, and have experienced a sharp decline in the proportion of the work force employed in rural industries. Manufacturing has expanded and become more diversified, and has assumed a much greater share of the GNP and of export earnings than was true in the past. These transformations have affected the viewpoints and demands of the rural communities. The rural communities have also responded to problems arising out of a mixture of market shrinkage, low and uncertain prices, and both inefficient and hyperefficient (and therefore overproductive) primary industry undertakings. Rural complaints did not begin recently. Farmers have always been uneasy about the climatic and market vagaries affecting their well-being. Many of them have felt an attachment to the land, and to the values associated with rural life. They have perceived themselves as victims of dominant and even domineering urban financial interests, against which sheer geographic distances have often sharpened rural resentments. Canadian agriculturists, especially in the west, still point to an ogreish "eastern establishment," since nineteen of Canada's twenty largest corporations, and big money and decision-making leverage, are located in Ontario and Quebec, predominantly in Toronto and Montreal. The Australian rural community still notices that, on figures from the mid-1960's, 93 per cent of the assets of the country's 887 largest companies were found in Sydney and Melbourne.

Organized rural interests and rural political parties

Like other occupational groups, rural industry has tried to induce government policies congenial to its interests. The rural communities in both countries are in their own way complex, reflecting distinctions in programmatic objectives, political organization and tactics, and electoral behavior. Canadian agriculture is composed of two broad, covering organizations, the Canadian Federation of Agriculture (CFA), and the National Farmers' Union (NFU). The former affiliates various provincial farm groups, while the latter stresses individual membership. The CFA prefers a soft touch, working closely with civil servants rather than politicians, while the NFU is more explicitly political and militant. The CFA basically stands for large growers, the NFU for smaller farmers. In 1971 the CFA did not join the NFU's threat of a farmers' strike, or the NFU leadership of a farmers' road blockade in Prince Edward Island protesting neglect of small and poor farmers. The Pallisier Triangle Wheat Growers' Association by definition subscribes to a particular rural industry, rather than to farming interests at large. It shares the NFU's sentiments on improved marketing and wheat pooling arrangements. But its membership is drawn from among prosperous farmers who grow a high grade of wheat, who prefer that the Canadian Wheat Board apply differential prices to the wheat it buys from growers, and who therefore are at odds with the NFU's spokesmanship on behalf of the smaller and less efficient wheat farmers. Differences such as these contributed to the decline of the "Farmers' Parliament," devised as a meeting place and debating forum for assorted farmers' organizations, the rural press, certain official and administrative officials, and federal and provincial agriculture ministers and their deputies.

Likewise in Australia, the rural industries have divided themselves into separate, and differently constituted cover organizations. The National Farmers' Union traditionally enrolled commodity associations, while the Australian Primary Producers' Union took on individual membership, and generally covered the smaller rural producers. The recent merger of the two bodies into an Australian Farmers' Federation produced a rather awkward and untidy result. There is also a complex of individual commodity groups, which often is more powerful than the covering organization, and which occasionally generates splits and battles within a given rural industry. Hence, in 1965, the Australian Woolgrowers' and Graziers' Council (AWGC) withdrew from the National Farmers' Union, feeling that it could accomplish its goal more effectively alone. Its goals have not, however, represented the feelings of woolgrowers at large. The AWGC speaks for large-scale woolgrowers, while the competing Australian Wool and Meat Producers' Federation (AWMPF) has stood for smaller and weaker growers. The larger and more prosperous growers have traditionally spoken against controls, the smaller ones for stabilized marketing arrangements. In 1965 a woolgrowers' referendum was held to decide whether a reserve wool-price plan was to be introduced. The AWMPF favored it; the AWGC was opposed, and poured considerable financial resources into the campaign which succeeded in defeating the proposal. Eventually, as the crisis in wool prices became more widespread and acute, growers generally accepted a reserve price plan, and an Australian Wool Commission to operate it within the the auction system. The intra-industry disputes nonetheless had left their mark. The two wool groups had long competed for the right to be recognized as the industry's authoritative spokesman before government bodies. The smaller growers had firmly aligned themselves with the Country party, while a number of AWGC members followed the Liberals. In the 1960's, some large wool-growers formed the nucleus of the Basic Industries Group, or BIG. Disaffected by the Country party's prevailing approach to reserve wool prices, and its high tariff preferences, BIG members insinuated themselves into electoral politics against CP leader John McEwen, and the BIG-McEwen conflict reverberated through Australian politics for some time.

This brings us more explicitly to the politics of Canada's and Australia's rural interests. What stands out is that both nations have, or have had, reasonably successful political parties essentially devoted to farm/rural interests. These parties originated at about the same time, for broadly the same reasons, and at the same level of government. During and just following the first World War, the rural sectors in both countries contained a considerably greater proportion of the population than they now do, and agriculture was much more critical then to the two economies. There was dissatisfaction with the major parties, which in Canada were regarded as urban and either business-conservative in orientation or, in Australia, as urban and business, and organized working-class in orientation. The auguries for agriculture were not favorable, but the standard parties seemed reticent to carry out remedial policies in the form of lower tariffs, easier credit terms, subsidies, and, especially in Canada, lower rail freight rates. Agricultural organization had by that time made rapid strides, and in the two federal systems it was possible to work from state/provincial bases instead of seeking common farmer unity for nationwide political action. It was therefore both desirable and possible to tap the grass-roots support needed to launch parties with rural interests at heart.

In both countries, results came quickly. In 1919, a farmer-labor alliance took office in Ontario. In 1921, the United Farmers of Alberta took control in that province, and Manitoba fell to the United Farmers of Manitoba two years later. In 1921, 64 Progressives, largely from rural seats in the west and Ontario, became the second largest party in the House of Commons. The CCF, born primarily of rural discontent, quickly developed strength in Saskatchewan and British Columbia, and began a twenty-year reign in the former province in 1944. In Alberta, the UFA gave way to Social Credit, a party of evangelical temper, unorthodox economic theories, and a clear appeal to farmers caught in the squeeze of the depression. It came to power in 1935, and was not dislodged from office until 1971. The national CCF was primarily a western rural party in its earlier days, and the same was true of the federal Social Credit.

When during and immediately following World War I Country parties sprang up in the Australian states, much of their backing was from among the strongest rural industries, wheat and wool, but other groups, including small farmers in a variety of rural pursuits, came along. In its first assault on the federal House of Representatives, the Country party returned a dozen MP's, representing five of the six states. Federally, the Country party has never approached the strength required to organize a government, but from 1923 to this day, with only passing exception, it has been a coalition partner whenever non-Labor has governed, supplying the balance needed for a parliamentary majority. Unlike the various agrarian parties in the Canadian provinces, the Country party has never enjoyed an absolute majority in a state parliament. Twice in Victoria—1935–42, and 1950–52—it governed alone, but as a minority government, propped up by the ALP. In Queensland, holding more seats than the Liberals, it has been the senior coalition partner for some years. But with the exception of Tasmania, where it has been moribund for years, the Country party has enjoyed conspicuous influence in state politics, usually as an ally of conservative parties, either in government coalition or as part of a non-Labor opposition, and in South Australia as part of the joint Liberal-Country League. The CP's presence has even been felt where conditions have been special, as at present in Victoria, where it opposes the Liberal administration, but sometimes does common cause with Labor. State second chambers, through a combination of restricted or nonpopular selection and boundary idiosyncrasies, have been traditional centers of country interest strength. Social Credit never caught on in Australia. A Social Credit party contested half of the seats in the 1934 House election, but polled only 4.7 per cent of the national vote, elected no one, and quickly faded.

Canadian and Australian rural parties were therefore developed quickly. The Canadian parties made a rather quicker start than the Country party, but then lost ground, while the CP retained an effective state and federal role. Also, while the CP has been viable nearly across Australia, Canadian agrarian parties drew their strength from a particular national region, the west. They enjoyed only transitory appeal in Ontario, and next to none in Quebec and the Maritimes.

The federal NDP, though a successor to the CCF, has acquired a primarily urban working- and professional-class following. Federal Social Credit was reduced to a corporal's guard in the 1960's, and entirely eliminated from the House of Commons in 1968. A "Western Canadian party" arose in 1971. Planting itself squarely behind such rurally pleasing programs as reduced freight rates and the removal of tariffs on all goods imported into western Canada, it promised an energetic campaign in the next federal election. Its appearance did signify continuing rural discontent, but it also suggested that western farmers had no identifiably agrarian party already available for federal representation.

Saskatchewan's CCF government of 1944–64 started up in a fairly agrarian reform mold, but eventually settled into being a progressive government generally. The province's NDP government of 1971 could not have been elected or received its 55 per cent of the popular vote had it been preoccupied with farmer discontent at the expense of other sectors, although it did display concern for price-squeezed farmers by allowing the temporary forgiveness of certain rural community debts. Manitoba's NDP government, coming into office in 1969, engineered an alliance of ethnics, working-class people in North Winnipeg, and miners, loggers, fishermen, and small farmers in the northern part of the province. The previous PC government had relied on an alliance of grain farmers, cattle ranchers, and business and professional interests in South Winnipeg. British Columbia's potent NDP has almost no farmer support, relying instead on urban workers, extractive industry workers and some professional people. There, the ruling Social Credit government depends a good deal on farmers' votes. But British Columbia's farmers are not like Prairie farmers. Their agriculture is of a different kind. It is smaller in scope, but more varied, less subject to climatic or market vicissitudes, and above all comfortably prosperous. Social Credit in British Columbia also enjoys middle-class and business backing, and even attracts a fair proportion of the working-class vote. Its outlook, like its clientele, is an amalgam. It is strong on law-and-order, anti-unionist, populist, committed to business latitude in provincial development, and proudly British Columbian jingoist. The defeat of Alberta's Social Credit in 1971, after the party had spent thirty-six continuous years in office, was substantially attributable to the party's failure to cultivate the interests and electoral weight of urban Edmonton and Calgary.

Interpretations of Canadian and Australian rural party strength

Several factors help to explain why Canada's agrarian parties declined in strength and programmatic and clientelistic identity, while the Country party in Australia has held on well. In the present context our concern is essentially with the sorts of electoral alternatives which the two rural electorates have had available to them. One factor has been that Canadian agrarian parties, when seeking a national foothold, have confronted great variety in the character, and the requirements, of the nation's farm community. Prairie agriculture, dominated by large grain farms, bears little resemblance to fruit farming in British Columbia, or Prince Edward Island's potato farming. The Canadian rural sector's electoral unity has also been hampered by the country's highly diverse regional, religious, cultural, and political traditions. The flush of agrarian politics in the west starting after the first World War was considerably conditioned by a Protestant social gospel and a commitment to progressivism which not only failed to excite, but in ways offended, other parts of the country, thus handicapping the extension of agrarian politics on the early western model.

Although Australia's rural sector is also diversified, its diversification is not especially localized, at least among the mainland states. Various kinds of rural industries such as grains, wool, meat, and fruitgrowing—even winemaking—are pretty well distributed across the country. Australian agriculture is also more uniform than the Canadian because it is relatively more concentrated in large tracts. There is more tendency to speak of rural "industries" in Australia than in Canada, where large-scale agriculture is essentially a Prairie phenomenon, and even Prairie farms are modest by comparison with Australian rural complexes. An extensive agricultural structure in Australia facilitated generous financial and organizational support for the Country party. Additionally, the CP arose and consolidated itself in a society far more homogeneous than the Canadian. Persons interested in cultivating rural political organization did not need to compete against crosscutting religious, linguistic, and regional pressures.

It is also important to recall the political atmosphere in which the agrarian political movements developed. Canadian farmers built up political strength at a time when trade unionism was insignificant and there were no signs of a "labor" party. The Country party established itself when urbanization was already widespread, organized labor was a large factor, and the ALP was a salient force in Australian politics. The structure of Australian rural industries differed from the Canadian in that the former had, and retains, a substantial "proletarian" component, that is, landless employees, particularly on the sheep stations. The shearers were among the first to unionize and to join with the ALP. One of Australia's earliest major, violent strikes occurred among shearers at Barcaldine, Queensland, in 1891. These circumstances solidified Australia's rural interests. Australian primary producers not only felt they knew what they were for, but had a sharply etched notion of what they opposed and had ample reason to fear, namely a powerful urban working-class party with militant allies in the countryside. To this day, Australian farmers evince some of the strongest anti-trade union, antiwelfare and anticollectivist views. Farm laborers tend to be sympathetic to Labor; 56 per cent of them voted ALP in 1969. But a larger proportion of farmers than even big businessmen and managers votes against the ALP, farmers being less pro-Labor than any other single occupational group. The Country party, we have seen, has in its history almost invariably been allied with Liberals against Labor, federally and in the states, thus sustaining the rural sector's anti-Labor bias. Australian farmers have on the whole preferred to be free of Labor programs, and especially state socialism, but their identification with conservatism, generally, has probably been impelled by a paradoxical element. Existing state ownership at the time of the first World War helped make the Australian farm community more distinctly conservative:

> "socialist" impulses as existed amongst farmers in the United States and Canada were absent in Australia largely because the railways and silos were publicly owned . . . like every other section of the Australian society the farmers have demanded State action but this has always been limited to the immediate interests of the farming community; they want the government to socialize their losses and inefficiencies.*

If Canadian farmers and their families lack a genuinely rural party electoral alternative, for whom do they vote, and why? Since the Country party has survived for over half a century, can we assume that it alone, and distinctively, reflects farm community

* Humphrey McQueen, *The New Britannia. An Argument Concerning the Social Origins of Australian Radicalism and Nationalism* (Ringwood, Victoria: Penguin Books, 1970), p. 173.

interests? There are plausible reasons for farming people to vote for nonagrarian parties even where the rural population constitutes an important part of the scene. The impelling circumstances are more prominent in Canada than in Australia. Australian states are characterized by the coexistence of very large capital cities containing substantial manufacturing and urban-service industries, and rural sectors, stimulating a town-country political cleavage which sustains the Country party. The small island state of Tasmania has the least developed industrial complex, relatively small-scale agricultural properties, and its capital city of Hobart is neither a major commercial center, nor the only important city in the state. It is not surprising that Tasmania's party politics have been Liberal- and Labor-oriented, with both parties catering to rural interests. The Tasmanian Country party has been traditionally weak, ineffective, and was, for a period of time, nonexistent. Canada's Atlantic provinces offer a roughly comparable example. There we find an essentially rural setting, the absence of sprawling, large-scale farm properties, and a lack of powerful urban financial and manufacturing centers. The Liberal and Conservative parties have both, of necessity, relied upon and catered to the rural vote, thus blocking the emergence of viable agrarian parties.

We have already suggested that Quebec's cultural and political traditions inhibited an emulation of the English, Protestant-led, and often collectivist model of western rural parties. Montreal has always been a great financial center, but not a militant working-class center, or the province's capital city. The bulk of agriculture in Quebec has been much smaller in scale than in the west, and the rural community exceptionally bound by conservative family and church ties and marked by low political efficacy. The provincial Union Nationale party had long cultivated this sector of Quebec's electorate, and was able to regain office in Quebec City in 1966 when it exploited the rural and conservative backlash against the provincial Liberal party's efforts at secularizing the schools, raising property and sales taxes for educational and other social programs, and its overall neglect of parish-pump politics. Quebec Social Credit first entered provincial politics in 1970 and, much like the UN, it stressed lower taxes and simpler government, and attacked social forces which it alleged "undermined the public spirit." Nearly 61 per cent of the UN vote and 69 per cent of the Social Credit vote in 1970 was rural, while the Liberals and the PQ, considerably more strongly oriented toward reformist and working- and professional-class preferences, dominated the urban vote, especially in Montreal. Separatist feeling in the province is very largely an urban, working- and intellectual-class phenomenon. It is intimately associated, within the PQ or otherwise, with modern, reformist social and economic programs. In other words, various structural and cultural conditions in Quebec have not been conducive to the mobilization of a rural protest party, while nonexplicitly agrarian parties, especially the UN, have sedulously courted rural votes.

If we look at the two national party systems more broadly, we again discover reasons for the persistence of Country party influence in Australia, and the decline of agrarian parties in Canada. From confederation to World War I, the major Canadian parties had half a century in which to evolve free of serious challenges from a rural or urban working-class party. Whatever their specific programmatic differences, they developed pragmatic styles requiring the patching together of diverse clienteles. The formation of agrarian parties indicated that at least on the Prairies and in parts of Ontario the old-line parties had failed to assuage rural grievances. But, when faced with organized political protest in the rural areas, they made programmatic adjustments in ways reminiscent of American major-party reactions to third-party movements. They did enough borrowing from rural-party programs to turn much of the rural vote back to themselves.

Between the wars Canadian farmers were more inclined to support the Liberals than the Conservatives. Mackenzie King promised, and accomplished, various rural concessions, and the Progressives were gradually absorbed by the Liberals. The Conservative party was avoided by farmers because they perceived its interest to lie in "national" Canadian objectives, identification with eastern money and railway interests, and high tariff policies. Conservative tendencies to take a critical view of the United States were unappealing to the west, which depended on America as a market outlet and as a source of inexpensive commodities.

From the late 1950's onward, however, Prairie farmers have been prominently Conservative. John Diefenbaker, who led the PC in five elections beginning in 1957, was a Saskatchewan populist, openly advertising himself as a candidate for ordinary people. While in office he provided special assistance to agriculture. A Farm Credit Corporation was formed, providing loans for land expansion among low-income farmers. Under ARDA, the Agricultural and Rural Development Agency, Ottawa was authorized to enter into joint projects with the provinces to rehabilitate rural lands and generally to develop the rural economy. Diefenbaker stimulated wheat sales abroad, and took political gambles in selling to the previously untapped Chinese market. In 1958, the PC captured 47 of the 48 Prairie Commons seats, and secured resounding popular majorities in all three provinces. In 1963, although the Liberals won the federal election, the Conservatives again did splendidly in the Prairies. When in 1968 the Liberals won a clear majority in the House, in Saskatchewan and Alberta the PC's ran against the tide. Nationwide, the Conservatives had slightly over 31 per cent of the popular vote, but about 45 per cent of the farm vote. When in 1969 the public was asked whether there was a real difference between the Liberals and the PC's, farmers registered more affirmative replies than any other occupational group. The west, by a nearly 3 to 1 margin, far higher than in any other region of the country, believed that the Conservatives are best suited for the job of disposing of Canadian wheat stocks. The Diefenbaker years are remembered and rewarded, even though Liberal farm policy has become more effective than it was in the 1950's. Under Liberal governments wheat sales were continued, new markets opened, ARDA expanded, a series of expensive, though not always successful grain-stabilization measures introduced. The Canadian farmer benefits from concessional purchase and income tax rates, has access to special credit facilities, and is given marketing assistance and subsidies. Farmers continue to complain, but the major parties are neither insensitive nor inactive.

Even so, the overall impression remains that Canada's rural sector has not exactly been coddled. Much of what has been done for Canadian farmers has been designed to tide them over difficult situations, or to enhance their economic viability or, as with the recent multimillion dollar grain-reconstruction program, to induce them to cut back on wheat planting and turn to more economical crops. Canadian governments have seldom been charged with indulging in lavish agricultural handouts, and by international or rather, western, standards Canada ranks low in the amount of money spent per person employed in agriculture. In 1968, Canada's figure was $350; it was $675 in Germany, $980 in France, $1059 in Britain, and $1287 in the United States.

In Australia, by comparison, there are frequent and often anguished outcries raised against rural favoritism, and the blame is almost invariably traced to Country-party influence. The Country party emerged when Labor was already established, but the conservative party group of the time had only very recently consolidated. Hence, unlike Canada, there was no extended history of an established national two-party system, united to specific interests such as the working class, or well practiced in the art of accommodating various syndicates.

Australia's nonrural parties are not indifferent to primary industries. They have rural policies of their own, and are competitive in seats which are mixed rural and nonrural, and in some cases in rural seats as such. We saw earlier that the Liberals have attracted the support of certain large woolgrowers. While wheat farmers have since 1949 tended to be solidly anti-Labor, graziers and dairy farmers have been somewhat less so. The CP carefully limits itself to contesting rural seats, though among the 26 seats it fought in the 1969 House election, it collected only 44.8 per cent of the vote, versus 42.2 per cent for Labor. The Liberals entered eight of these contests, and in those seats they actually outpointed the Country party, 37 per cent to 31 per cent. All the same, the CP's appearance and early success in rural federal and state seats in itself made Labor and "liberals" less country-oriented than they probably would otherwise have become, and enabled the Country party to embellish the specialized, rural viewpoint which nourished it. Without Country party support, conservative parties have almost never been able to govern alone, meaning that the CP has been able to extract a heavy price for its cooperation. Federally, Liberal fortunes have fluctuated from election to election, but the Country party's representation has been exceptionally steady. Since the House was enlarged in 1949, the CP has always returned between 17 and 21 MP's. Following the 1969 election, although its share of the national vote was only 8.5 per cent, it occupied 30 per cent of the government's House seats, and held a third of the ministerial portfolios. Since it has been able to offer a credible case on behalf of its role in government and influence upon public policy, it has sustained its following among the rural electorate.

During the Bruce-Page coalition government of 1923–29, the establishment of marketing boards, price-stabilization plans, land-tax concessions, and the Australian Loan Council, all demonstrated Country party influence very shortly after its federal appearance. From then onward, when non-Labor governed, the network of rurally supportive measures rose. The central banking system was reconstituted to meet CP preferences, a differential system of prices for exported and domestically consumed commodities was applied to more rural industries, and a host of concessions and subsidies was arranged for the rural sector. Country and Liberal policy preferences have not always coincided, but the CP has usually been able to gain at least part of its desired loaf. In the 1920's, CP influence resulted in a system of road-construction grants to the states which required that at least 40 per cent of the money be spent on minor rural roads. By the 1960's, the minor rural road system was indeed highly developed, but urban traffic was snarled by poor and underfinanced roads and highways. Not until 1969 was the rural road requirement lowered. The double price system has meant that Australian agricultural commodities have been internationally competitive. But the domestic price has been kept artificially high, with Australian consumers sometimes paying several times more than an open price system would have borne. When Britain devalued the pound in 1967, the Country party reluctantly accepted the Liberal view that the Australian dollar should not be devalued, but, as a *quid pro quo,* extracted a promise of increased rural subsidies. When in 1970 the Reserve Bank announced an increase in interest rates designed to curb inflation, the federal government, and essentially CP pressure, succeeded in granting an exemption to primary producers. At the beginning of the 1970's, over two-thirds of the Commonwealth Scientific, Industrial, and Research Organization's budget was directed toward rural industry research. Queensland, a swing state in federal elections, has been especially favorably treated by L-CP governments, primarily in ways which satisfy rural interests, such as heavy sugar subsidies and high wheat quotas at a time when wheat growing cutbacks were being imposed across the states. During various periods CP influence has been partially responsible for poor social welfare performances by nonlabor governments. In Queensland, where it has been the senior state-government coalition partner for some time, the CP has had a particular stake in not enthusiastically supporting programs for Aboriginal advancement. The state's native population is numerous, and Country interests have not been eager to open land rights to Aborigines. Between 1945 and 1970, the general taxpayer had to absorb the $633 million lost by the six state-owned railway systems. Underpopulation, great distances, and other factors were responsible, but so was Country party insistence that freight rates be held at artificially low levels.

Country party leverage has always been dependent on the availability of a supportive rural electorate. But fewer and fewer people live and work on the land, the proportional value of the agricultural and pastoral industries has declined, criticisms of rural-industry pampering have been mounting, and Liberals themselves have been increasingly emboldened to contest CP seats which have begun to lose their basically rural complexions. Particularly under McEwen's leadership, the federal Country party abandoned its historic low-tariff position, and in exchange extracted from the Liberals a variety of concessions to rural dwellers as an offset for the higher prices that steep tariffs implied. His position earned him some enmity among rural interests, such as persons associated with BIG. But he carried his party with him, and squared its tariff policy with the biases of other parties and much of organized labor and industry. McEwen was then better able to court secondary industry interests, and his Trade and Industry portfolio in the federal cabinet provided him with an excellent operational base.

Douglas Anthony, McEwen's successor as CP federal leader and in the Trade and Industry portfolio, assumed his position in 1970, when Australia's "rural crisis" was attracting keen attention. Anthony began to backpedal a bit on high tariffs, just as the high-tariff tradition was falling under close re-examination nationally, particularly among certain business and mining interests. He also shifted some of his ground on rural-assistance programs. McEwen had been instrumental in assembling a lavish package of rural handouts, while Anthony began to speak more of long-term reconstruction of rural industries. If such a program were ever comprehensively and conscientiously implemented, it would mean fewer people in rural pursuits, larger and more efficient properties, and less need for extravagant subsidies. At the time of writing, the reconstruction process had just begun, but has already been criticized for being too timid and misplaced, and much too generous toward certain rural industries. For a time, Commonwealth spending on the rural sector can be expected to climb, regardless of whether genuine reconstruction is effected or not. Rural-industry support rose from 12.9 per cent of all Australian farm income in 1969/70 to a projected 33.9 per cent in 1971/72. Rural "reconstruction" started in Canada before it was undertaken in Australia. It can be argued that Canada's need for reconstruction was more acute, but it should also be pointed out that Canadian rural industries have lacked the kind of powerful, explicitly rurally based friends in high places that the Country party has supplied in Australia. Even as Australian rural reconstruction begins its slow advance, the Country party has reason to believe that the rural community will remain electorally grateful.

8

Religion, churches, and politics

Religious considerations have had noticeable effects upon cultural, socioeconomic, and other public policies within Canada and Australia. Although political parties with explicitly designated denominational interests have been very exceptional, churches and churchmen have often assumed partisan positions, and there has been a distinctive religious component in electoral behavior. Our purpose is to identify the kinds of questions which have attracted religious argument in politics, and to measure the systemically significant results.

The legacy of religion in politics

The present influence of religion upon political life is very much the product of historical legacy—the heritage of cleavage or harmony, trial or victory, cynicism or confidence, withdrawal or involvement—in organized politics by various religious groups. It is reasonable to begin the assessment at the moment of Canadian and Australian nationhood. The minority Catholic populations were urged by their leading spokesmen to accept and cooperate in the building of the two nations. To this extent, nationhood itself did not estrange Catholics from Protestants. But Catholics did develop distinguishable preferences in party politics, largely because of the high congruence between the Catholic confession and national origin groups—the French in Canada and the Irish in Australia.

Long before confederation, the Roman church had been a pervasive social as well as religious force in what later became Quebec province. It was therefore natural for the Quebec church to assume a lively political role after confederation in defense of the traditional values by which it was known. For some years the Conservatives, or "Blues," were favored against the "Rouges," persons associated with the early Liberal party, and suspected for their "liberalism" and anticlericalism. At all events, Macdonald, although himself a Protestant, was popular with the French Canadian church because of his reputation as a supporter of separate, that is, Catholic schools. For over twenty years after confederation, Quebec was strongly Conservative; only once during the first six federal elections did it fail the party, and then only by a slight margin.

In the 1890's, even before Australian federation, Cardinal Moran and most of the church hierarchy aligned themselves behind the Australian Labor party. Moran saw the emerging ALP as the only significant political movement untainted by Protestant bigotry. But the ALP was also a sensible choice because it stood for working mens' interests, and social and economic reform. A large proportion of Australian Catholics were working-class Irish, and the clergy themselves were almost entirely Irish. By the first World War, the ALP was the greatest single Australian party. Much of its electoral clientele as well as a goodly number of its leading figures were by then Irish Catholic.

In both countries, the early patterns of Catholic party preference eventually broke down or took a new turn, for the very reason that much politically active Catholicism in Canada was French, and in Australia it was Irish. In Canada, the Roman church's break with the Conservatives began, paradoxically, during a dispute in which the church was a strong Conservative protagonist. When French-language schools were abolished in Manitoba, the Conservative government in Ottawa was inclined to disallow the measure. Laurier and the Liberals, though sympathetic to French (that is, Catholic) interests in Manitoba, took the view that it would be pernicious to the cause of provincial autonomy if Ottawa intervened, even in the just cause of Manitoba's French-speaking children. The issue intruded itself into the 1896 federal election, and Quebec's bishops went all out for the Conservatives. But French Quebec in this instance followed Laurier, as did much of the province's lower clergy. Pride was felt in the prospect of a French Canadian Prime Minister, and it was reasoned that protection of provincial integrity was, overall, consistent with French, Catholic, and Quebec provincial interests. Among English-speaking Canadians, the Liberals earned credit for resisting "concessions" to Catholic demands. The Liberals won the election. Laurier and a number of other Catholics appealed to Rome in protest against the Quebec hierarchy's intrusive role, and the bishops were ordered henceforth to eschew a direct political role.

Quebec's bishops eventually concluded that their earlier trust in the Conservatives was no longer deserved, and that there were vital issues which demanded their spokesmanship, despite the Vatican's injunction against explicit partisan involvement. Manitoba proceeded to do away with French-language schools. In Ontario, a Conservative government moved to restrict the use of French in its public schools, a step which won the support of many Protestants, and even of English-speaking Catholic churchmen. But restrictions on Ontario's French schools by definition, meant restrictions on Catholic French schools. The Quebec legislature denounced Ontario's action, and Cardinal Louis Bégin of Quebec City and his associates threw their weight behind federal intervention. The Conservative government in Ottawa refused to intervene. Party lines in the Commons became strained and partially broke down on French-English and Catholic-Protestant lines. Again the Pope intervened, admonishing the English and French branches of Canada's Catholic church to avoid intemperance, to search for realistic accommodation in school policy, and above all to strive for Catholic solidarity. However, the Ontario school question was being controverted just as the issue of conscription for military service was inflaming Canadian politics. Quebec's higher clergy had generally supported earlier efforts at raising a voluntary army; but the lower clergy, much closer to the grassroots sentiment, had little use for the war. There was enmity against the French Third Republic for its recent persecution of the church, and no particular devotion to Britain. The recruiting effort was carried out by an Orangeman notoriously hostile to French Canada and to Catholicism generally. When conscription was introduced, even the higher Quebec clergy demurred. Conscription split the country on essentially cultural grounds. Some English-speaking Liberals gravitated into a Unionist government with the ruling Conservatives. Laurier and the remaining Liberals, most of them French, stayed out.

In the 1917 election, the Laurier Liberals were smothered. Of the 82 seats they won, 62 were in Quebec. But for the Conservatives it proved to be a Pyrrhic victory. They won only three Quebec seats, and for decades afterward were utterly ineffectual in the province. The Manitoba and Ontario controversies over schools and military conscription persuaded the Québeçois, and the Roman church within the province, that the Conservatives were an anti-Catholic and anti-French party. Even outside Quebec, many French- and English-speaking Roman Catholics had begun to feel that much of the Conservative party was too Orange for their taste, and disinterested in protecting Catholic education.

In Australia, World War I shook the ALP to its foundations, but with the result of making Labor more, not less, Catholic. As in Canada, the school question continued to trouble the Roman church, but even the Labor party in the several states was unprepared to effect any basic modification in the ingrained practice of denying public funds to parochial institutions. As in Canada, conscription proved religiously divisive. Catholic voluntary enlistment was possibly proportionately higher than among non-Catholics. But in 1916 Labor Prime Minister William Morris Hughes decided that conscription for overseas service could no longer be avoided. While there were numerous nonreligious arguments raised against conscription, religion became entangled because the controversy blew up just as the British were busy suppressing the nationalist rebellion in Ireland. Much of the Australian Roman hierarchy, Irish by origin and sentiment, denounced conscription because it would have forced Australia's Irish youth to fight for a Britain whose hands were soaked with patriotic Irish blood. At the center of the anticonscription movement, unflagging in his mission, stood Dr. Daniel Mannix, the Archbishop of Melbourne. Some Catholic bishops disapproved of his cause, still others of his methods. Not all Catholics, especially from among the middle classes, followed him, and some made appeals that he be silenced. Two national advisory referendums were conducted on the conscription issue. State by state, there was no obvious denominational pattern in the vote, though both referendums lost. The ALP was ripped apart. Hughes and numerous other conscriptionists, federally and in the states, were either driven out of the party or resigned, and a decimated ALP forfeited office federally and in several states. The Catholic campaign had been instrumental in defeating conscription. It had also contributed to the Labor split. All but a few of the elites who had left the party over conscription had been Protestants. The party that remained was now more Catholic than before, both in electoral following and in its leadership. But the ALP was now weaker and, like the Canadian Conservatives, entered a period of political convalescence.

Between the two wars, the religious factor was somewhat more subdued but nonetheless present in Australian and Canadian politics. The religious temper of wartime politics in Australia prompted the brief appearance of explicitly Catholic and pro-educational state aid party movements in New South Wales and Victoria. But Catholics generally remained loyal to the ALP, and the Catholic parties disappeared. A Protestant Labor party made a brief appearance in New South Wales in the 1920's, and in Queensland in the 1930's, perhaps in reaction to the Catholic complexion of the ALP itself in two states where the ALP was at the timc politically vigorous. The Quebec church continued to favor the Liberals federally, but in provincial politics supported parties whose essential values were among the most traditional, for instance the Union Nationale. Quasi-Catholic political movements did nonetheless surface, among them one which played on extremist sympathies in the province and advocated the creation of a semifascist, independent Quebec state of Laurentie. The Quebec church and its communicants at large were certainly not fascist, but there was admiration for Mussolini, especially because of his solicitude for the Vatican and his conclusion of the Lateran agreements, and his adamant anti-Communism. Such tendencies, which acquired a popular as well as hierarchical Catholic following, were reinforced by accounts of depradations against the Catholic church by Republican forces during the Spanish Civil War. The Canadian Liberal government instructed its delegate to the League of Nations to oppose sanctions aimed at Italy for its invasion of Ethiopia. It especially feared the political reverberations in Quebec should Canada appear to be courting war with Italy, and seemingly catering to Soviet policy within the League. Many Australian Catholics also believed that sanctions against Italy might bring war, and therefore suffering for the Papacy. Neither major party group was eager for sanctions. The conservative government was then being led by Joseph Lyons, an apostate ALP man and a

Catholic, while the ALP felt it could not afford any defection to the UAP among its otherwise steady Catholic clientele.

Progressive politics, communism, and the churches

Contemporary Canadian and Australian life has continued to draw on the legacy of religion in politics, though with some notable differences. For one, the national/cultural dimensions of religious politics have been diluted as the makeup of the two religious communities has shifted. The French Canadian birthrate has leveled off, but non-French Catholic migrants have been entering the country in large numbers. Australia's Irish, once the backbone of the nation's Catholic community, have been joined by large numbers of Continental European Catholics. The clergy is now largely Australian-born, and less Irish in origin than in the past. Then too, there has been an overall secularization of public views and behavior both in Canada and in Australia. Although in both societies Catholics continue to attend church much more regularly than do communicants of other Christian denominations, they have shared in the broad trend of declining religiosity. Among both Catholic communities contraception has become common, as have permissive views on legalized abortion. In Quebec, some 2000 men began studies for the priesthood in 1946; by 1970 the number had fallen to about 100. Membership in the Quebec Catholic Action group has declined precipitously, and now attracts mostly women and children.

Another change has been within the Catholic churches themselves. In respect to internal modernization and progressive social outlooks, the Australian hierarchy has moved forward, though sluggishly. With some notable exceptions, the bishops continue to perceive their role in pre-eminently pastoral terms. Australian bishops were among the more conservative spokesmen at Vatican II, and there has not been much philosophical ferment among them. A number of priests joined Catholic laymen in the anti-

Vietnam protest movement, but the bishops discouraged such behavior, and kept a watchful eye on experimental Marxist-Catholic dialogues. The Canadian hierarchy has moved farther and faster. Among the most visible leaders in the modernization/renovation movement have been French Canadians, who have given example to and joined in the excitement generated by Quebec's mood of social change. The Canadian church evolved a plan for Canadian based nominations for bishops, pressed for an extension of decision-making to include priests and laymen in various local Catholic councils, outspokenly urged the acceptance of women into the clergy, and assumed progressive positions on birth control. Prior to the adoption of liberalized federal legislation governing divorce, Ottawa consulted with bishops across the country, and generally received their endorsement. It was a Catholic cleric who headed the special Quebec commission which recommended, in effect, that the Catholic and Protestant confessions should no longer be principally responsible for educational control within the province. Paul Emile Cardinal Léger, Archbishop of Montreal, was one of the foremost liberal protagonists at Vatican II. His successor in Montreal, Archbishop Paul Gregoire, in 1969 launched an experimental program to combat poverty in city slums.

Church attitudes toward the uses of state authority for progressive purposes, and toward the role of the organized working classes, have reflected the quite different sociopolitical conditions in the two nations. They have been bound up not only with the idiosyncrasies of organized religious bodies, but with other variables as well, such as Protestant social politics, the makeup of trade unionism, and Communism.

For a quarter century after World War I, Canada's Catholic hierarchy showed no particular proclivity for socially progressive leadership. The church in Quebec was notoriously conservative, always on the alert to protect the "cultural solitude" of French Canadian society. This outlook was heightened by the appearance of distinctively Protestant political progressivism. Organized Protestant social concern had been rising since before the first World War. In 1907, a Protestant inspired Social Service Council was formed. It promoted welfare activities, and propagandized public officials. The creation of the United Church was more than a union of Protestant churches. The United Church was, and continues to be, extremely forward looking on a range of social and political questions. In the west, the Protestant influence greatly inspired the building of progressive political movements, and

> it is apparent that by 1917 all wings of the social gospel seem to have found a place of such prominence in the farmers' organizations that it might well be termed the religion of the agrarian revolt.*

In the 1930's, the CCF drew heavily on social gospel teachings, and its leader, J. S. Woodsworth, was a minister of religion. Social Credit in Alberta was definitely not socialist. But, like the CCF and the movements of the 1920's, it was colored by religion. It carried a fundamentalist, puritanical appeal, and was headed by the evangelist William "Bible Bill" Aberhart. Such developments were noticed, and resented, by Canada's Catholic church, especially in Quebec, and hierarchical fulminations against the CCF were commonplace. Centralist and ostensibly "materialist" political doctrine was doubly repugnant because of its intimate association with fundamental or at least nonconformist Protestantism. Although Alberta's movement was not socialist, it preached heterodox economic principles, and its brand of Protestantism was peculiarly fundamentalist and anti-Catholic in overtone.

In interwar Australia, the Roman church was attached to rather than alienated from the major progressive, working-class party, the ALP. After the World War I Labor schism, the party was more Catholic in composition than ever. It provided Catholics with opportunities for public service and other forms of respectability, and pursued socially reformist and pro-union programs which

* Richard Allen, *The Social Passion: Religion and Social Reform in Canada 1914–28.* (Toronto: University of Toronto Press, 1971), pp. 200–201.

suited working-class Catholics. The church acquiesced in the ALP's 1921 "socialist objective." It did not wish to stage an open and divisive intervention so soon after the conscription controversy of but a few years earlier, significant qualifications were attached to the socialst plank, and numerous Labor leaders, such as James Scullin, later to become Prime Minister, were trusted by the church.

Eventually, however, it was the very size and strength of the Australian organized labor movement, and its powerful influence within the ALP, that disrupted church-Labor harmony. A massive split was precipitated within the Labor party, fraught with sectarian overtones and raising a jumble of brisk arguments over socialism, Communism, and foreign and defense policies.

The Communist party has always had an insignificant following in Canada and in Australia. Each of the two parties reached a membership peak of somewhat over 20,000 by the close of the second World War, then declined steeply. By the late 1960's, Canada's party enrolled about 3000 persons, Australia's parent Communist party had about 4000, and a Maoist splinter numbered 1000 or less. Only once, in Queensland, has an Australian Communist been elected to state office, and never federally. Canadian Communists have had little better success, though they once elected one of their number to a Quebec federal seat. In the 1968 federal election, Canadian Communist party leader William Kashtan could muster only 250 votes in a Toronto riding. In the 1969 Australian House election, the Communists ran only seven candidates, who collected a grand total of fewer than 5000 votes, or .08 per cent of the national ballot.

All the same, Communists have had more than passing influence in trade union circles. Differences between the two countries have, however, been significant, and they help to explain the reaction of the Catholic church, and the postwar fortunes of progressive parties. By the end of the war, the CCL had about 270,000 members. The Communist controlled unions included some 55,000 persons, and enjoyed influence in other unions with about 63,000 members. On surface, these were impressive figures, though it must be remembered that Canadian unionization at that time, in and outside the CCL, was slight. In Australia, by comparison, of a total work force of 2.1 million, direct Communist control, or influence was estimated to cover trade unions enrolling half a million members. At the beginning of the war, the New South Wales branch of the ALP itself had fallen under Communist influence, and on orders from the federal party it was disbanded and replaced by non-Communist loyalists. The union movement was intimately tied to the ALP, and the extent of Communist trade union infiltration was a grave concern for an ALP which at that time was in power federally, and most certainly for the party's traditional ally, the Catholic church. Communist influence among Canadian workers was condemned by Catholic authorities, especially in Quebec, but in absolute terms the Communist grip over working people in the country was slight. There was no pronounced union-CCF nexus. It is quite true that by the mid-1940's the CCF was the preferred party of about a quarter of the Canadian electorate, and that in 1944 the party captured office in Saskatchewan. Militancy was rising among Quebec workers, and in the 1944 provincial election the Bloc Populaire, a progressive French-nationalist movement, gathered 15 per cent of the vote—but the Bloc quickly dissipated. Still, the CCF was nowhere the political force on the scale of the ALP. Then too, the Canadian Catholic church had never had any special, working relationship with the CCF. Catholic electoral support for the party was slim. Not until 1943, while in the same breath continuing its denunciation of Communism, did the Canadian hierarchy declare that Catholics were as free to vote CCF as they were to vote for the two major parties. In other words, compared to the Australian situation, the Canadian church had less cause to be alarmed over trade-union Communism, or to fear the consequences of Communist influence upon a progressive party through the medium of unions, or leverage within the CCF.

In the late 1940's, CCF people who were prominent in unions played a conspicuous role in reducing Communist influence, especially in Ontario and British Columbia, where it had been strongest. Unions which could not be "reformed" from within were expelled from the CCL. These developments made the Canadian church less apprehensive about Communist influence generally, and about the intentions of the CCF in particular. Any remaining apprehensions about the CCF were further allayed because the party was losing much of its original, Regina Manifesto ginger, and was behaving like an evolutionary, progressive movement; it had moved up to "respectability." The Quebec church in particular was changing and becoming sympathetic toward social reform. Its hold over the tame Quebec labor organizations was weakening, and Quebec labor, in increasing numbers joined the nationally affiliated unions. With a change of leadership, the movement became more socially demanding, and its decline was arrested. The church was influenced by socially progressive ideas emanating from postwar European Christian democracy. It also began to find more and more fault with the Duplessis regime, with which it had previously made common cause in defending traditionalism, opposing union militancy, and rabidly villifying Communism. The Duplessis government had become flagrantly corrupt. It resorted to such imperious, antilabor tactics in the 1949 Asbestos strike that the church spoke up in protest, parish donations were taken to assist the striking workers, and Duplessis and the church openly clashed. Such clashes, over various matters, became more frequent. By the time Duplessis died in 1959, he and his regime had contributed to the liberalization of church opinion through their displays of intemperance and arrogance. Ultraconservatism had discredited itself, while Quebec's climate was becoming more questioning and socially assertive.

During the second World War, a number of Australian Catholic laymen organized themselves to defeat the spread of Communist trade-union influence. In 1943, these Catholic industrial groups were largely subsumed under the Catholic Social Movement, a kind of Catholic Action organization. The "Movement" had its greatest following in Victoria, but assumed national proportions. The Movement was overwhelmingly ALP in composition; in some states, only Labor persons were admitted to its ranks. It enjoyed the approval of the Labor Prime Minister. It also received the moral and financial support of Australia's bishops, though it was understood that the campaign against trade-union Communism was to be directed by laymen. The industrial groups operated with resolve, ingenuity and, of necessity, secrecy. They scored a number of successes, helping to remove or diminish Communist influence within a fairly large sector of the labor movement. As their membership grew, so did their influence within a number of unions, and within the Labor party itself, where they stood for stern anti-Communism at home and abroad. In late 1954, by which time the party had been out of national office for five years, ALP leader Dr. Herbert V. Evatt dropped a political bombshell. He announced that the ALP was in mortal danger of being taken over by a secret sectarian group—the Movement—and that the party would not tolerate such subversion. Then followed furious charges and countercharges between the backers of the Movement and the industrial groups, and of Evatt, who was accused of having raised a false issue, a smokescreen to cover his own shortcomings as a leader.

The upshot was a violent party upheaval. The ALP federal executive disbanded the Victorian state executive, which was dominated by "groupers." At the party's 1955 federal conference, 17 of the 36 delegates walked out in protest against Evatt and the "loyalist" persuasion. The remaining parent party proceeded with a large-scale purge, and outlawed the industrial groups from the party altogether. The Victorian ALP government broke apart, and other state party branches were shaken. Many of those who were expelled or who voluntarily withdrew from the ALP formed their own party, briefly known as the Anti-Communist Labor party, then as the Democratic Labor party, or DLP, which survives to this day. The great majority of those who gravitated to the ACLP-DLP were Catholics, but the remaining ALP still retained a strong Catholic component. Although 15 of the 17 delegates who stalked out of the 1955 conference were Catholics, so were 11 of the 19 who remained, and Catholics continued to be very well represented in the party's federal and state organizations and parliamentary caucuses.

Contemporary religious issues and their electoral effect

The Labor party split was a political bonanza for the L-CP, but a matter of acute concern for the Australian hierarchy. In Victoria, the aging Archbishop of Melbourne, Daniel Mannix, became an indefatigable crusader against the ALP, and an open sympathizer of the DLP. Elsewhere, the situation was mixed, with some members of the hierarchy remaining neutral, or tacitly supporting the parent ALP. The Cardinal himself, Norman Gilroy, Archbishop of Sydney, refused to associate himself with the DLP, reasoning that a flight of conservative Catholics from the ALP could only serve to radicalize the party, and render it electorally impotent. The matter of the church's position vis-à-vis labor politics and the Movement was referred to Rome. Under a compromise decision churchmen could continue to express their views, but the church-Movement connection was severed. The Movement was reconstituted as the National Civic Council. It is a relatively small (about 5000 members), almost exclusively Catholic, social- and political-action group, centered on Victoria. It is organizationally independent of the DLP. But some 80 per cent of its members belong to the DLP, and it and its superbly articulate president, B. A. Santamaria, are a powerful source of ideas and publicity for the party.

The political importance of the Labor split was not, of course, confined to arguments over what role, if any, the Movement people were entitled to play within the party. The entire background of the industrial groups and of the Movement had been tenacious anti-Communism. The people who left the ALP, and who then attached themselves to the DLP, were not simply politically renegade Catholics. The DLP maintained that the country was threatened by Godless and materialistic Communism. There was alleged to be danger from Communism in Asia. There was danger that Communism, through the unions, could affect the gullible ALP. Stripped of many of its former, conservatively inclined members, the ALP committed itself to such policies as the diplomatic recognition of Peking, the dismantling of SEATO's military features, the creation of a nuclear-free zone in the southern hemisphere, withdrawal of Australian troops from Malaysia-Singapore and later Vietnam, and the abolition of conscription, which the L-CP had introduced in 1964. It also continued to be more enamored of public ownership than the DLP. Although Labor eventually jettisoned a number of its more controversial and politically vulnerable policy planks, or eventually saw them adopted by the L-CP (more accommodation with China, withdrawal from Vietnam), the DLP served as an implacable foe of Labor, and a dedicated critic of Communism, appeasement, social permissiveness, and socialism. The L-CP is often chastised by the DLP, especially for not doing enough in defense preparations and welfare programs, but is much preferred to the ALP. As we shall notice in detail later, the L-CP has in part been protected in office because it has received DLP ballot preferences in parliamentary elections.

The Canadian Catholic church, we have seen, has largely accommodated itself to social progressivism. It has not been inclined to denounce "socialism" and local or international Communism. It was a Liberal, not a "socialist" government that cut Canada's 10,000 man NATO troop commitment in half. It formulated a defense policy based on a military establishment of somewhat over 80,000, no greater than Australia's. It defined the role of the Canadian military in largely domestic terms—disaster aid, control of internal disorders, protection of Canada's territorial sovereignty, and so on. It took the initiative in establishing diplomatic relations with Peking. The NDP, which de-emphasizes an international Communist threat somewhat more than the major parties, and which would move somewhat farther toward collectivism at home, no longer raises church hackles as it once did. There are, of course, various situational factors which prevent the contemporary Canadian Catholic church, or Canadian Catholics generally, from heating up over these kinds of questions to the extent of Australian Catholics. Unlike Australia, Canada is not geographically situated on the edge of a volatile region, and has not felt as intimidated by overseas upheavals. It has been preoccupied with French-English relations and the American presence, and has not conducted gouging postwar debates over conscription, participation in the Vietnam conflict, and the like. Nor was there ever a Catholic church association with a major progressive party, characterized by a delicate balance among socialist idealists, Fabian reformers, trade-union functionaries, and socioeconomically progressive but anti-Communist Catholics. There were no aching recriminations of the kind that swept the Australian church and the Catholic community when the ALP broke apart, and nothing comparable to a DLP party to praise, damn, or nervously try to ignore.

But it does not follow that the Canadian church has entirely moved to the political sidelines, or that the Australian church is preoccupied with the rivalry between the two labor parties. Most DLP policies are not, after all, identifiably "Catholic," and despite its composition the DLP disavows the definition of a

"Catholic party." On the other hand, it has been a tireless champion of public assistance to parochial schools. This is a cherished objective of the Catholic church itself, and also happens to be a matter of continuing interest within Canadian religious circles.

We have seen that the issue of "state aid" has a long and stormy tradition in both countries. In Canada, as of 1971, the principle of governmental funding of parochial schools through high school had been established in Quebec, Alberta, Saskatchewan, and Newfoundland, while all other provinces except British Columbia were providing some assistance to Catholic education. Most Canadian Catholic authorities would naturally prefer that comprehensive parochial school funding become universal. Circumstances are not, however, at all alike across the country, and are especially nettlesome for the church in Ontario.

Catholics comprise a third of the population in Canada's largest province, but Ontario also happened to have been the historical site of divisive struggles over educational policy. As required under the BNA Act, the province has supported parochial schools through the eighth grade. In 1964, the Conservative government extended limited aid to grades nine and ten, but none for grades eleven through thirteen. This tapered assistance program was reflected in the school attendance profile. While about half of Ontario's Catholic children were enrolled in parochial schools through the tenth grade, most of them then switched to the public schools and only about 4 per cent were in parochial institutions during the final three years of high school. To many Ontario Catholics, further extension of aid became a matter of simple justice. There already was precedent for exceeding the prescribed grade-level entitled to support, Catholic school costs were inexorably rising, and there was considerable Catholic school attendance loss in unsupported grades. To the PC government, further assistance would have meant a drain on an already strained treasury. Most Ontario Catholics ordinarily did not vote Conservative anyway, and there was a real question whether the party's Protestant supporters would look kindly upon a further diversion of educational funds to Catholic schools. In 1970, the PC government came under heavy Catholic pressure to increase aid. Catholic pickets paraded in front of the hall housing the 1971 PC provincial leadership convention. Later in 1971, Premier William Davis, holding the line on state aid, called an election. Catholic church spokesmen vocally regretted this decision. Though they said that assistance to Catholic schools should not become a political issue, it became one. The two opposition parties, the Liberals and the NDP, both eager for provincial office, campaigned on platforms promising to extend parochial school assistance.

By comparison with Canada, the state-aid issue in Australia has been much more politically pungent. The Roman church never reconciled itself to the nineteenth-century decision to withhold official support from parochial schools. By the 1950's, the financial burdens on Catholic schools had become severe. L-CP governments, state and federal, overwhelmingly Protestant in clientele and leadership, were little interested in disturbing the traditional approach to school funding. In 1953 the ALP conference called for financial aid to *all* forms of education, apparently foreshadowing remedies for parochial school difficulties. But the party split in 1954–55. At its 1957 conference, deprived of its more militantly and consciously Catholic element, bitter against what it felt to be a church-inspired and sectarian DLP, it altered its state-aid policy. Henceforth, it would only countenance competitive scholarships to denominational school children, but no funds for direct use. With the L-CP and the ALP both keeping their distance from Catholic school support, the DLP became the sole and unremitting advocate of state aid, and to that extent, the political patron of the Catholic church and community.

The L-CP looked on. The DLP had brought vast publicity to the cause of parochial-school assistance. The ALP was tied up in knots over it, since proponents of a more permissive position had only succeeded in igniting a caustic and demeaning internal party quarrel. In the 1963 federal House campaign, Sir Robert Menzies' L-CP took a bold step, promising assistance to private-school science facilities. The L-CP swept the election. In 1965, it displaced the Labor government in New South Wales. There the state ALP, desperately eager for an opportunity to offer aid to parochial schools, had been rebuked by the federal party. Not only did the L-CP seem to have scored electorally among Catholics, but its state-aid policies had not outraged Protestants. State aid had always been heavily favored among Catholics. By 1964, it was widely accepted among the various Protestant denominations.

Public assistance to private schools has by now become an accepted policy within Australian politics. Federally, the L-CP gradually enlarged the scope of aid to private institutions, and in 1969 instituted a system of direct grants to all primary- and secondary-school children. By 1971–72, Commonwealth spending on private schools had reached $32 million, $24 million of it for Catholic schools. The Labor party itself, after much agonizing, eventually rescinded its own ban on direct state aid, accepted the federal L-CP's grant programs, and promised further assistance. All Australian states, under both Labor and non-Labor control, provide their own assistance to parochial education, principally through outright grants to pupils. The DLP was delighted with the L-CP's direct aid breakthrough in 1963, and assumed full credit for having forced the issue into public prominence. Though state aid has lost much of its earlier partisanship, the DLP has pressed for increasingly elaborate assistance, and has served as publicist for church complaints that even with existing support, the proportion of Catholic students attending Catholic schools is declining, and many parochial schools are in danger of closing their doors. Even with numerous other priorities, and with economies imposed to offset inflation, late in 1971 the L-CP government in Canberra raised the annual per capita grants to private schools from $35 to $50 for each primary-grade pupil and from $50 to $68 for each secondary-school pupil. There has been a political reaction against the swelling state-aid programs. A Council for the Defense of Government Schools (DOGS) has been formed, and insists that government schools are being starved of funds as federal and state authorities keep raising their private school contributions. The party ran candidates in four states during the 1969 federal election, and in the New South Wales state election of 1971.

Clearly, the state-aid issue in Australia had been elevated to major political importance. Its natural and consistent exponent was the Catholic church itself, with the DLP, in the role of political party conduit, enhancing its own standing among church authorities. Ultimately, all major parties swung into line behind state aid, but sectors of the public were willing to organize politically to refocus attention on how limited public funds should be divided between government and private education. Demands for more and improved education were becoming widespread nationwide, in a society traditionally penurious in its allocation of money for educational purposes.

Both Canada and Australia have experienced the intrusion of religious issues and church expressions into politics. In more recent times, this factor has receded in Canada, but has been kept very much alive in Australia. We need to ask to what extent, and why, the mood of the two national electorates has been affected.

Catholic-Protestant voting distribution in the two countries is easy to establish, and on the surface, conforms to the traditional process by which religious questions have entered politics. Canadian Catholics, and French Canadians even more extensively, prefer the Liberal party, while Protestants prefer the Conservatives. In a 1968 survey, Catholics rated the Liberals high on such indices as competence, coherence, and power, while United Church members were complimentary toward the Conservatives. In Ontario's 1967 provincial election, only 16 per cent of the Catholics voted PC, while 35 per cent chose the Liberals, 10 per cent the NDP, and the remainder abstained. Protestants, on the contrary, voted 34 per cent Conservative, over twice the proportion of Catholics aligned with the party. Ontario's 1971 provincial election, however, suggested that the aid-to-parochial-schools issue was not pervasively influential. Catholic votes hurt the PC in the Windsor area, but apparently not in Toronto. A survey conducted several months before the election revealed that while the vast majority of the province's Catholics favored an extension of school aid, they ranked the issue tenth in order of importance among a list of eleven. Ontario residents at large rated the issue last. Then there is the possibly suggestive case of New Brunswick, a province 40 per cent French and over 50 per cent Catholic. In the 1967 provincial election, only two seats with electorates over 15 per cent French-speaking returned Conservatives, and only three seats less than 30 per cent French-speaking returned Liberals. Calculated another way, only three counties less than half Catholic returned Liberals. During the next New Brunswick election, in 1970, which the Conservatives won, the Liberals still managed to win sweeping majorities in predominantly French regions.

Australian electoral data also seem to conform to predictable Catholic-Protestant patterns. From the second World War to its split, Labor received 70–75 per cent of the Catholic but only some 40 per cent of the Protestant vote. Very rarely did non-Labor parties make a serious dent in Labor's Catholic following. A partial exception occurred in the 1949 federal election, when Archbishop James Duhig of Brisbane was persuaded to denounce Labor Prime Minister Ben Chifley as a socialist, and to advise Queensland's Catholics to oppose the ALP. When Labor split, the proportion of Catholics supporting the ALP dropped to a level of about 50 per cent, nearly the entire group of Catholic defectors from Labor moving to the DLP. The DLP was, and remains, overwhelmingly Catholic in electoral clientele, and Catholic votes account for up to 80 per cent of the party's total support. But during the 1960's the L-CP itself began to increase its share of the Catholic vote; a very solid third of Australian Catholics now vote for the L-CP federally, and the figures have risen in state elections as well.

The religious component in the public political behavior of both countries is, however, more complex than we have heretofore indicated. It is tempting, in view of the more distinctive religious coloration of recent Australian politics, to believe that the religious variable counts for more in Australia than in Canada. There are other factors to consider, however, and we discover that socioeconomic variables disturb the comfortable hypothesis. A partial answer to why Canadian voting preferences reflect religious attachments is that nonreligious attachments are relatively weak. The NDP's clientele is proportionately somewhat more Protestant than Catholic, but the proportionate difference between the party's Protestant and Catholic supporters is decidedly narrower than divides the religious basis of the major party vote. NDP voters have a higher sense of class identification than Liberals or Conservatives, are more apt to subscribe to their party because of their attachment to party programs as such, and their voting is much more associated with socioeconomic factors, such as occupational status and trade-union membership, than with religious affiliation. But trade unionism in Canada is small and recent by Australian standards, class consciousness is incidental, and the NDP is a relatively small party, attracting only a fraction of the working-class vote. When we turn to Liberal and Conservative electors, who constitute the great majority of Canadians, we find that almost no matter how we choose to control for occupational status or ethnicity, Protestants choose the PC, Catholics the Liberals. For example, among Ontarians in the 1968 federal election, 37.5 per cent of the Protestant, British working class voted Conservative, 36.3 per cent Liberal. Of Catholic members of the British working class, 18.6 per cent voted PC, and 62.1 per cent Liberal.

By contrast, we have shown that socioeconomic differentials are substantially more noticeable between the followers of Australia's two major-party groups, Labor and the L-CP. The data do indicate that, regardless of socioeconomic position, Catholics proportionately more than Protestants are likely to support Labor than the L-CP, and vice versa. But socioeconomic factors and party preference do, nonetheless, correlate positively. For instance, in 1967 it was found that 52 per cent of Catholic nonmanual workers preferred the Liberals, but only 34 per cent chose Labor. Some two-thirds of Anglican manual workers preferred the ALP, but only a bit over a third favored the Liberals. Manual workers of nonconformist Protestant background also preferred Labor, though by only a very slight margin.

The DLP clientele is, of course, pre-eminently Catholic. Still, this is not a randomly distributed Catholic vote. For one, the DLP vote has been very uneven among several states. Among the DLP's least electorally productive states have been New South Wales, with the highest proportion of Catholics in the states, and South Australia, with the lowest. The party's most conspicuous success has been in Victoria and in Queensland. In the 1969 federal election, the party, nationally, took 6 per cent of the vote, but won 10.8 per cent in Victoria, and 6.8 per cent in Queensland. States which escaped violent Labor party upheavals when the split was in progress, or where the hierarchy remained neutral, or which have tended to house doctrinally mild ALP branches, produce the lowest DLP turnout. Victoria was the center of the Labor split. The Labor branch there was convulsed, and an ALP government collapsed. Archbishop Mannix of Melbourne spearheaded the long and tenacious battle against the parent ALP. The reconstituted ALP branch became notorious for its militancy. The Queensland ALP split was delayed, but come it did, in 1957. Vincent Gair, ALP Premier before the split and a figure with considerable personal following, became a DLP Senator, and the party's parliamentary leader. The surviving ALP branch eventually became one of the more truculent, particularly when it and its longtime influential and conservative ally, the Australian Workers' Union, parted company for a time.

In other words, Australian Catholics do not vote DLP simply because they are Catholics; local circumstances are decisive. Most Australian Catholics, like Australian Protestants, do not believe that church leaders have a right to tell them how to vote. But, at least according to a 1960 survey, while 88 per cent of the general public took this view, only 71 per cent of Catholics said so, and only 62 per cent of DLP voters. In Victoria, the hierarchy supported the DLP, to the extent that DLP and National Civic Council propaganda was distributed in churches. In New South Wales, it did not. When Labor was pulled from office in New South Wales in 1965, partially because the state ALP branch was unable to win federal-party consent to offer a state-aid package, the lost votes turned to the L-CP, not to the DLP. Within the dozen New South Wales seats it contested in the 1969 federal election, the untried and essentially single-issue DOGS did as well as the far more established DLP.

Also, what little we know about the migrant vote suggests that "New Australian" Catholics from Continental Europe vote DLP in large numbers. Their resentment of Communism appears to be instrumental; the DLP is, of course, uncompromisingly anti-Communist.

The profile of the DLP's Catholic vote indicates that the party is disproportionately supported by upper working- and lower middle-class persons, such as clerks and skilled artisans. A frequent explanation of this phenomenon has been that the DLP serves as a political waystation for upwardly mobile Catholics who feel uncomfortable with the ALP, but still find the L-CP too Protestant, socioeconomically conservative, or otherwise uncongenial. The DLP stresses individual party membership, and de-emphasizes association with unions—related approaches which would appeal to persons who think of themselves as outside the broad mass of working people, and prefer to be treated as individuals, rather than as faceless trade unionists. The DLP's emphasis on state aid would also have special attraction for this group of Catholics. Generous state aid is more than a way for parents with parochial school children to economize. It is also an opportunity for Catholic children to remain in school longer, receive better education, be more competitive for university admission and bursaries, and become more diffused throughout an otherwise Protestant-dominated business and professional world. Such are the aspirations many non-manual, or upwardly mobile, Catholics hold for their children.

In conclusion, we may ask if there are any general tendencies in the play of religious variables among the Australian and Canadian electorates. The degree of religiosity, particular denominational affiliation aside, seems to be an important electoral constraint. The two left-inclined parties, the ALP and the NDP, contain the smallest proportion of religiously active electors. At the other end of the scale, we find that intense religiosity coincides with the supporters of parties most concerned with traditional and/or conservative personal and social values. In Australia, that party is the DLP. In Canada, the trend is reflected within such party movements as Alberta's Social Credit League, the Quebec variant of Social Credit—the Ralliement des Créditistes—and the Union Nationale, renamed Unité-Québec in 1971. In both societies, there are certain public policy issues, such as assistance to parochial schools, which continue to color political dialogue with religious considerations, though there has been a steady decline in religious observance, or religiosity, among Catholics and Protestants. In Australia, this in one sense implies that the traditionally broad Catholic base of the ALP can no longer be taken for granted. As the author of a major Australian religious survey has remarked,

> there is evidence in Australia that it may be increasingly risky to maintain that there is an independent Catholic pro-Australian Labor party tradition, even in the states where the Catholic hierarchy has discouraged the Democratic Labor

> Party. All one can say is that this independent Catholic tradition may be more typical for the non-church-going Catholic than for the church-going one.*

On the other hand, as religiosity weakens among Australians generally, the Labor party could expect to attract increasing numbers of nominal Protestants and even Catholics.

Similarly, the Canadian NDP, with a clientele more nondenominational than any of the country's larger parties, less religiously observant, and in many ways less bound by conservative values, could expect to benefit from the decline in the nation's religiosity. We can already see, for instance, that Quebec's French working class, which is considerably less religious than the French small-town and rural community, is an important source of support for progressive/left parties, such as the Liberals and the provincial PQ, and the federal NDP. Canada's electoral propensities have historically shown a graphic religious bias, but a weak economic-class bias. Here may be a pointer that change is developing on both counts, and that conventional party alignments may in their turn be affected.

* Hans Mol, *Religion in Australia: A Sociological Investigation.* (Melbourne: Nelson, 1971), p. 300.

9

Party organizational and leadership influences upon electoral outcomes

The preceding chapters have stressed the clientelistic basis of party support and programmatic orientation. We now turn to internal party behavior and the role which personality and leadership plays in party fortunes, and ultimately in the formation of public policy.

Organization and decision-making among parties of the left

All major Canadian and Australian parties—NDP, PC, ALP, and the two Liberal parties—outwardly subscribe to the notion that their respective conferences promulgate national-party policy, and all address themselves to the need for effective coordination of party activities. Our interest rests not in the details of party structure, but in those dynamics of party decision-making which reflect themselves in party electoral success.

Predictably, it is within the left/progressive parties, the NDP and the ALP, that conference policy decisions are taken the most seriously. Labor and social democratic parties generally are committed to a particular doctrine of social change, rather than to the politics of cautionary, pragmatic response. More than moderate and conservative parties, their ranks are filled with persons of idealist disposition, who often cannot countenance the subordination of party doctrine, and ostensibly, the democratic decision-making process runs strong. Those who belong to such parties, regardless of their station, are presumed bound to authoritative party decisions. In effect, individuals should not place themselves above the party, and the ideals for which it stands. To the party devotee, such precepts impart qualities of solidarity, purpose, and integrity. To the critic, they often imply rigidities which can spell unrealistic programs, intraparty tensions, and quite possibly electoral disability.

As between the NDP and the ALP, it is the former that has been the more internally tranquil. Compared to the ALP, of course, the CCF/NDP is not only much more recent, and therefore saddled with fewer traditions and nostalgic or bitter memories, but also considerably weaker. It has never been in power federally, or even within reach of it, and has enjoyed only one lengthy tenure of provincial office. It has therefore seldom been confronted by hard choices in the context of how to govern, or how to prepare for the imminent prospect of governing. But there are other reasons for the CCF/NDP's relatively orderly atmosphere. The general cultural and party political mood in Canada has been less affected by egalitarianism, and working-class and reformist inheritances, than has been true in Australia. Despite the strong language of of the Regina Manifesto, the CCF in its formative years adjusted to these constraints, and opted for a nondoctrinal brand of socialism. During its first but lengthy experience with provincial office, certain important precedents were set. There were occasions, especially during the end of the CCF's reign in Saskatchewan and when the controversial medical plan was being bruited about, when the provincial conference advanced certain proposals, such as the lowering of the drinking age and the loosening of religious restrictions on adoptions, which at the time were embarrassing to the government. Still, on several occasions the government found it possible to resist organizational dictation. Overall, party-government relations were smooth, partially because of the organization's own pride in the achievements of the "first socialist government in North America," whose electoral credibility it was loath to undermine.

The organizational makeup of the old CCF and the present NDP has also contributed to relative internal quiescence. National and provincial parliamentary leaders—prospective Prime Ministers and Premiers—are selected at broadly representative party conferences rather than by federal or provincial parliamentary caucuses. This tends to endow the leaders with a certain image of representativeness, and to increase their authority as *party* leaders, not simply parliamentary leaders. There is no particular CCF/NDP animus toward politicians, which a background of violent organization-parliamentary disputes or defections by ranking party figures might otherwise have induced. Politicians are therefore widely represented in party conferences and other organs. Being practicing political persons, stylistically disposed toward an appreciation of politics as the art of the possible, their influence has ordinarily been toward moderation and conciliation.

The trade-union element in the CCF/NDP has also made a difference in the style and direction of the party. The CCF did not begin as a "labor" party, and consciously avoided becoming one later on. When unions began to affiliate with it, the organized labor movement was still small, weak, and generally undisposed toward militancy. These legacies were absorbed into the party when the NDP was formed. The party's federal and provincial conferences, which are the authoritative organizational organs, are so constructed that union representation is in a minority. One advantage of a favorable public image accruing to the NDP from these arrangements is that while the party substantially benefits from financial contributions and campaign work supplied by unions, it can largely sidestep charges that it is dominated and manipulated by special interests of the unions. In Canada, as shown, public aversion to the active presence of organized labor in politics is very much in evidence.

Furthermore, trade-union delegates to party conferences tend toward moderate, nonideological views. This also helps alleviate public anxieties about the NDP's labor ties. It achieves something else as well. In recent years, a strongly socialist and nationalist movement, commonly known as the "Waffle," has sprung up within the NDP. The great majority of Wafflers are individually enrolled NDP members, not trade unionists or trade-union officials. So far, they are a minority within the party at large, a minority at conferences and in other party structures, and almost totally unrepresented in parliamentary caucuses. NDP politicians are generally eager to neutralize what they feel to be unsound and electorally counterproductive Waffle views, and the restraining influence of trade unions is in this sense very welcome. When David Lewis was elected NDP federal leader in 1971, the union component at the convention was overwhelmingly for him, but the nonunion, nonparliamentary group was split between him and his principal rival, a Waffler. Only in British Columbia has there been a major reversal of form. There, the historically powerful and militant union movement has been agitating for more forcefulness in the party, including extraparliamentary action of various kinds. Provincial NDP leader David Barrett refused to accept this line, and his position was strengthened by the fact that of the twenty-person party executive, only six were unionists. While British Columbia's vigorous trade unionism helped forge the NDP into a meaningful electoral force, labor's radicalism has also served to frighten many people in the province, and has led them to accept a conservative, antiunion Social Credit government.

Although the NDP has been able to avert schism and even major internal rancor, not so the ALP. The Australian labor movement and the ALP grew up together, unions became an integral and dominant part of the party's federal and state organization, and a substantial proportion of the party's vote was delivered by unionists. At the present time, all state ALP conferences except Queensland's are heavily dominated by union delegates. Until 1967, the party's federal conference was composed of only thirty-six persons, six from each state, who were selected by state party organizations, and ordinarily contained a majority of trade unionists. In 1967, the federal conference was enlarged to include the leaders and deputy leaders from the two federal houses, as well as state parliamentary leaders. The addition of parliamentary leaders to the federal conference was a striking innovation in Labor circles. There have been numerous examples of conflict between the organizational and parliamentary sections of the party, and the incidence of such conflict only increased the resolve of the organizational wing to insure its supremacy. Such tensions were if anything hardened by the stakes involved. Unlike the NDP, the ALP has several times been in control federally, and otherwise the official federal opposition, and has governed at least twice in every Australian state.

The party has undergone three major national splits, two of them while it was in office, and the third when it seemingly was recovering enough to retrieve federal power. During the World War I split, the party organization opposed conscription, while a number of prominent parliamentarians, federal and state, supported it. The ALP government broke up over the issue. Prime Minister Hughes was repudiated by his own party, he and a number of other recalcitrant parliamentarians crossed the parliamentary aisle, and Hughes became Prime Minister of a non-Labor, Nationalist government. Between the 1914 and 1917 House elections, Labor strength dropped from 42 to 22 seats, and the party lost 7 per cent of its popular vote. In reaction to the "sellout" of Hughes and other former Labor politicians, various steps were taken in the states to curtail the presence of parliamentarians on organizational bodies.

During the depression the governing federal Labor party was again torn apart. New South Wales Premier J. T. Lang broke with the national party over what remedies to apply to the economic crisis. A number of federal parliamentarians supported him, voted against the ALP ministry in Canberra, and brought it down. Among those who voted against their own party was Joseph Lyons, an ALP minister; like Hughes, he subsequently gravitated to the other side, and became Prime Minister of a non-Labor government. The federal ALP national executive disbanded the Lang dominated New South Wales party branch, and substituted a loyalist group. In the 1931 federal election, two "Labor" parties existed—regular Labor, and "Lang Labor." The split and its recriminations cost the ALP dearly. Between 1929 and 1931, the parent party's House representation declined from 40 to 14. In New South Wales, where it had previously held 18 federal seats, it won only 3 seats in 1931, while 4 seats were won by the schismatic group. As of 1930, Labor had held office federally and in five states. A year later, it had a foothold in only one state. It gradually rebuilt in the 1930's, only to have the national executive again take action against the New South Wales branch, this time because the state party had become tainted with Communism.

When the ALP governed nationally from 1941 to 1949, it averted a split, but its internal life was hardly uneventful. Only after elaborate argument and maneuvering was Prime Minister John Curtin, a widely respected leader, able to extract from the conference a grudging compromise, allowing conscription of men for overseas service—up to the Equator. His successor in office, J. B. Chifley, kept the party peace by dint of rare qualities of understanding;

> Chifley thoroughly appreciated that the Government must be determined to govern—and disconcertingly, sometimes

> bluntly, said so. But the Labor Party *myth* had become part of his very being and he instinctively knew when and how far substantial concessions—and how far merely ritual obeisances—must be made to the general membership.*

Just as Labor seemed to be recovering from its 1949 loss of federal office, it was rocked by another split, which was to give rise to the DLP. The L-CP government called a snap election in 1955 to capitalize on Labor's misfortunes, and it succeeded. Between the 1954 and 1955 elections, Labor dropped nearly 6 per cent in popular vote, and from 57 to 47 in House representation. As we have seen, the party split reverberated across the states. Victoria's ALP government crashed almost immediately. After the Queensland Labor government broke apart in 1957, the former Premier transferred his party allegiance and eventually became Senate DLP leader.

The point of this narrative is that Labor in Australia has been plagued by internal schisms, and that the party organization has on several key occasions felt betrayed by the defection of numerous, sometimes ranking party politicians. It has therefore been inclined to maintain close surveillance over the behavior of lower party organs, and over federal and state parliamentarians. The issues which have caused breakdown in the party have not only involved the unions so far as unions have been a prominent part of the ALP's organization, but in a more direct sense as well. For instance, the World War I conscription controversy became tangled in various union outcries over issues such as incomes, profiteering, and conditions in Ireland, as well as the merits of conscription as such. The 1954–55 split was the result of the "Movement" having secured a beachhead in the unions, and through these unions, in the party itself. Even when there has been no internal convulsion, party problems have usually become union problems, and vice versa. Lang's influence upon New South Wales politics was eventually broken when his tactics menaced the position of the unions. For

* L. F. Crisp, *Ben Chifley* (Melbourne: Longmans, 1961), p. 237.

decades the ALP in Queensland lived quite happily and prosperously in a working alliance with the AWU. After the split, when for a time the AWU dissociated itself from the Labor party, the void was filled by the Queensland Trades Hall unions, whose more militant approach affected the state branch of the ALP.

In Victoria, with numerous moderates gone from the party after the split, radical and vehemently anti-DLP trade unions acquired considerable influence over the ALP branch. This reversed the trend that had been built up by the time the industrial groups had reached the zenith of their influence. By 1970, although union strength in the Victorian ALP conference was estimated at 65 per cent, it was 77 per cent in New South Wales. But the New South Wales unions were, by comparison, very moderate, and closely attached to the similarly moderate parliamentary wing of the state party. Eventually, to appease critics of the unduly left complexion of the Victorian party and the right orientation of the New South Wales party, the federal executive ordered both state party branches reconstituted. This was done on the rationale of correcting undue "outside influence." These directives were resented by entrenched union interests in both states. But even after reconstitution, in 1971, the Victorian party became only slightly less left, while the New South Wales party moved a few paces leftward.

As previously explained, union association has proved beneficial to the ALP from many standpoints. It should also be noted that while most Canadians disapprove of the idea of unions in politics, the vast majority of Australians, non-Labor voters included, do not. In general, unlike organized labor's role within the NDP, union influence upon the ALP has had a leftist thrust, though there have been notable exceptions. Generally too, there has been an inverse relationship between party control by nonparliamentarians and ALP electoral success. When the party split in the mid-1950's, it took a precipitate turn to the left, and became vigilant about forces and personalities which might wish to place themselves above the party. These developments compounded the party's electoral vulnerability. In the 1960's, as we saw, the federal party organization stood against state aid, and enjoined the New South Wales state party from breaching that injunction. Public reaction to the cutting debate within the party over the issue carried beyond the substance of the question of whether state aid was advisable. The party's federal organization made itself look stubborn and perverse. The New South Wales party, which at the time governed the state, seemed a victim of the federal organization's dictation. The federal parliamentary leader, Arthur Calwell, who had tried to compose the internecine problems, emerged as a rather pathetic figure. Later, when Calwell found his position eroding, he associated himself, under the mantle of a party "loyalist," with the ALP organization, and became a member of the intransigent Victorian state-party executive. When his critics assailed him, they had to contend with hard-line organizational forces. When Gough Whitlam succeeded Calwell in 1967, he tried to instill more flexibility into the party's platform, and fought a running battle with the organizational forces, which on several occasions openly worked to trap and humiliate him.

As Labor heaved and huffed, the L-CP and the DLP gleefully pommeled the ALP. Labor was not a party fit to govern, they claimed, since an ALP government could not be its own master. The party was shackled to sinister and radical "outside" influences, and the conference decisions which bound it were taken by thirty-six self-serving "faceless men." Calwell was treated not as a leader, but as a captive of the party manipulators. Whitlam was personally no captive, but his struggles with the party organization were said to reveal the divided, noncredible qualities of the ALP. It was within the organization where, after all, final authority rested, not with politicians but with irresponsible outsiders. Such imputations often were caricatures of the actual situation. But even after the 1967 decision to seat parliamentary figures in conference (and on the federal executive), and some of the party rancor had quieted down, the impression of Labor as representing a dangerous rabble was not completely dispelled.

Organization and decision-making among moderate/conservative parties

The middle ground parties in Canada and Australia would on the surface seem to have devised organizational and decision-making features conducive to portraying themselves as orderly, sensible, and responsible. Their organizations are free of explicitly affiliated groups such as labor unions and therefore from charges that they are locked into and subservient to special interests. They claim to be reasonably open and representative at levels where general party policy is promulgated. The Canadian Liberals and Conservatives seem to fit this characterization particularly well, since their party conventions are giant enterprises which include hosts of federal and provincial parliamentarians, organization people, party youth groups, and so on. Although importance is attached to policy drafted at conventions, especially within the Canadian parties, no effort is made to conceal the ultimate primacy of parliamentary groups, and of parliamentary leaders in particular. Hence, the moderate/conservative parties can have it both ways—guidance by broadly representative, higher party organs, and discretion for practicing politicians and party leaders.

In light of the authority enjoyed by leaders of these parties, the process of their selection becomes significant. The Australian Liberals select their national leader by a simple procedure; he is elected by the caucus of all sitting federal House and Senate members. While this definitionally fails to open the selection process to other sectors of the party, it is no different from ALP and Country party procedure. Since a Liberal leader, whether as Prime Minister or as leader of the opposition, is understood to be a stronger figure vis-à-vis his party generally than his Canadian or

PC counterparts, limitation of his election to federal parliamentarians is not really politically disadvantageous.

The selection of the Australian Liberal leader does, however, introduce some special difficulties, as illustrated by the early 1968 selection of John Gorton following the drowning of Prime Minister Harold Holt. Although the Liberal caucus alone voted for a new leader, who in the circumstances would become Prime Minister, the Liberals were, as usual, governing in coalition with the Country party. As it happened, CP leader John McEwen flatly declared that he would not serve under William McMahon, one of the more likely Liberal prospects for the leadership, and therefore McMahon was excluded from consideration. It is also believed that one of the factors obstructing the selection of Paul Hasluck was that a number of his own Liberal colleagues believed that as Prime Minister he would be too soft on McEwen, and on the CP generally. Gorton emerged as a suitable candidate. But much of his support came from among Liberal members of the Senate, where Gorton had served for years. Although upon his selection as leader Gorton resigned from the Senate and stood for and was elected to Holt's vacant House seat, he nonetheless was unfamiliar with the customs of the House.

Major national party leaders in Canada do not face problems of accommodating coalition partners. Also, the Canadian Senate, a nonelective chamber, has less status than the Australian, and the prospect of a Senator's sudden rise to leadership, and then hastily finding a Commons seat, does not exist. What can and has happened in Canada, however, is the introduction of a new leader from outside the federal Parliament altogether, who seeks a Commons seat only after his selection as leader. This occurrence is much more likely than in Australia if for no other reason than because the Liberal and PC leadership conventions which select leaders are composed of such a diversity of delegates. The 1967 PC convention selected Premier Robert Stanfield of Nova Scotia, while the runner-up was Manitoba's Premier Duff Roblin. The convention was composed of all PC federal MP's and Senators, former candidates and members of the various provincial legislatures, five delegates from each federal riding, members of the PC party executive, 50 members of PC student groups, and numerous at-large delegates selected by provincial PC party associations. In any event, although both major Canadian parties moved to convention selection of leaders some years ago—the Liberals in 1919, the Conservatives in 1927—only in fairly recent times, especially among the Liberals, have leadership conventions become truly open, and representative, requiring intensive preconvention electioneering and financial outlays by the leadership hopefuls. These conventions now resemble American presidential nominating conventions.

There has been some criticism that the conventions have become expensive extravaganzas, highly dependent on the image-building techniques associated with the medium-is-the-message notion of one of Canada's better known sons, Marshall McLuhan. Nonetheless, given Canada's national diversity, a "nationally" elected party leader, who has sought and won broadly constituted party support, is provided with an authority, especially in Parliament, which he might otherwise lack. Collaterally,

> The open party convention contributes an influential nationalizing influence to the Canadian political system. Regionalism and localism are endemic to almost all important aspects of Canadian life and many of our political institutions and procedures reinforce these territorially based particularisms. . . . The national leadership convention, on the other hand, has had an important though inevitably sporadic integrative effect.*

The discussion of middle-party leadership selection in Australia and Canada has presumed a situation in which a vacancy has arisen in the ordinary course of events, such as the death or retirement of

* D. V. Smiley, "The National Party Leadership Convention in Canada: A Preliminary Analysis," *Canadian Journal of Political Science*, Vol. 1, December 1968, p. 397.

the preceding party leader. What mechanisms are available to review the records of leaders, or to institute proceedings to depose them? Here again we find that similarities are greater among various parties within a single country than among comparable parties in the two countries. In theory, Australian parliamentary Liberals, in a manner similar to the powers of an ALP caucus, can force a leadership "spill" just about any time enough momentum is generated. Naturally, such actions are not taken lightly, but they are not unknown. Serious losses for the Liberal party in the 1969 House election, compounded by various grievances against Gorton personally, resulted in a challenge to his leadership late that year. The bid failed, but was repeated early in 1971, following continuing dissatisfaction with Gorton. The precipitant factor was an accusation by a senior Minister that he had personally been let down by the Prime Minister. This time the effort succeeded, and Gorton was replaced by McMahon. By then, McEwen had retired from Parliament.

The Canadian picture is more complex. Essentially, the Liberals, PC, and NDP all have by now instituted, through convention methods, procedures for reviewing leadership. The NDP national leader is open to review every other year. The Liberal leader's position may be reviewed, but only at the first general meeting following an election. The 1967 Conservative convention which chose Stanfield was, in a sense, a review meeting, in that the incumbent leader, former Prime Minister John Diefenbaker, had his name placed in nomination. But he had grown old and testy, had forfeited much of his previous party support, and stood no serious chance of regaining the leadership at the convention. In 1969, the Conservatives regularized review procedures. With the party out of office, leadership review would be done in the Liberal manner, except if the party had improved its Commons popular vote by 20 per cent or more. With the party in power, a leadership convention could not act unless the leader had first been repudiated by the PC parliamentary caucus.

Once again, therefore, we find that the Canadian parties resort to a broader, more "legitimate" process in dealing with leaders than is true in Australia. The Australian method is swifter and neater, and can result in a change of leadership at any time, even when a party controls the government. For understandable internal and electoral considerations, the Canadian PC and Liberal parties have virtually prevented the possibility of dislodging an incumbent prime minister. Two options were open to the Australian Liberals in handling the situation with Gorton. One was to depose Gorton, a man who had lost party backing at the risk of the same accusations of intraparty knife-play that the Liberals had for years been fond of hurling at Labor. The other option was to avoid a party battle over the leadership, and therefore Labor's sardonic reaction, at the risk of entering the next election with the party's cracks barely papered over, and conducting a campaign under a man believed to be an electoral liability.

Leadership influence and the personality factor in electoral outcomes

We have suggested that leaders of the middle parties in Canada and Australia derive a measure of special authority from the method of their selection, and are not subject to haphazard removal. These traits of the leader's office strengthen his hand in imposing his policy preferences upon the party. Likewise, despite the presence of policy drafting bodies, these particular parties, unlike the NDP and the ALP, do not have the kind of ethos, or unmistakeable internal rules, which demand that their leaders observe officially announced programs. At all events, the leader is by definition an incumbent or an aspiring Prime Minister, and therefore the person most responsible for party fortunes. His ability to promulgate policies also carries the advantage of timeliness. Official, convention-drafted programs appear only periodically, and cannot hope to anticipate all contingencies. Finally, it must be remembered that a policy statement is not written in a vacuum. A leader's own preferences and his stature in the party minimize the chances for superimposition of policies repugnant to the leader and his senior parliamentary colleagues.

There have been numerous instances, past and recent, when party leaders have chosen to overlook or even contradict official party policy. In 1970, Prime Minister Pierre Trudeau pointedly refused to implement two conference resolutions of the Liberal party, one favoring a guaranteed national income, the other the creation of a board to oversee the administration of the Public Order Act. Trudeau's explanation was, quite simply, that while he took such party resolutions seriously, he insisted that the final judgment rest with him and his government. These remarks produced some long faces in the Liberal party, but no major clamor of the kind that might well have erupted in a party of the left. In Australia, Gorton followed a distinctively centralist approach. He was rather impatient with pleas for scrupulous respect of state privileges, and his fiscal policies particularly were denounced as having the effect of depriving the states of indispensable revenues. Gorton proceeded on his way despite the Liberal party's historical attachment to and frequent expositions on the virtues of viable federalism. The offended state premiers—at the time, five Liberals and one Country party man—resorted to various tactics, including summoning special premiers' conferences to devise common front strategies, and working through the federal council, the Liberal party's highest organizational body. When all was said and done, they still fell far short of getting their way with Gorton.

In a fashion, Gorton won the battle, but lost the war. Therein lies the fact that leadership influence, even when cloaked by prime-ministerial incumbency, is circumscribed. During the first World War, in the midst of the conscription debate, Sir Wilfrid Laurier was unable to prevent the defection of a majority of his English-speaking Liberal MP's into a coalition under the Conservative Sir

Robert Borden. In 1963, Prime Minister John Diefenbaker's minority Conservative government was defeated on the floor, after a period of open criticism of Diefenbaker's defense policy by some of his ranking ministers, and the resignation of their portfolios. In interwar Australia, Prime Minister Stanley Bruce precipitated an irreparable split within his Nationalist party over industrial arbitration and conciliation policy, and Prime Minister Robert Menzies later experienced great difficulties with his UAP over health policies and other matters, and failed to consolidate his personal sway over the party. Gorton's running battle with state premiers was only a part of the dissatisfaction in the party over his leadership. He was accused of arrogance, of ratifying controversial policy statements without clearing them with ranking ministers, of contradicting himself, of failing to supply effective electoral leadership, of questionable judgment in the conduct of his personal life, and of a stubborn attitude toward the states, which were governed not by the ALP, but by his own Liberals. This mixture of complaints prompted the two challenges to his leadership, and eventually brought his downfall.

The Gorton episode opens the related question of the ability of Australian and Canadian federal leaders to deal effectively with premiers, or to influence electoral outcomes in the states and provinces. Some preliminary points should be made. First, Australian states and Canadian provinces are not simply administrative subdivisions within the two nations. They carry substantial individuality, as well as significant independent powers. Second, the middle-ground parties in particular are substantially decentralized, often evincing real differences of style, emphasis and program, state by state and province by province. Third, state and provincial premiers are often very powerful political figures in their own right, perhaps with extremely lengthy tenure of office, and not beholden to a federal party or its leader.

It is commonplace for premiers to differ sharply with prime

ministers of the same party, and even to regard them as electoral liabilities. For years, Victorian Premier Sir Henry Bolte pardoned his Liberal government's inadequate social services by accusing the Liberal government in Canberra of being unfair and penurious in its treatment of his state, and he more than once threatened or undertook legal action to force Canberra's hand. In the 1969 federal election, New South Wales Premier Robin Askin simply refused to make any meaningful effort to help Gorton and the federal Liberals in his state until a few days before balloting took place. In the 1970 South Australian state election, the ALP opposition gladly invited Whitlam to appear and to campaign in the state, but the Liberal Premier kept Gorton at arm's length, regarding him as unpopular generally and unsympathetic to South Australia's requirements in particular. During the Second War Liberal Prime Minister Mackenzie King of Canada wished to forestall the adoption of conscription as long as possible, recognizing how nationally divisive the subject was. But Ontario's Liberal Premier Mitchell Hepburn was an ardent conscriptionist, and the provincial legislature endorsed a resolution censuring the Ottawa government for its lax war effort. Conservative Ontario Premier John Robarts was icy cold toward Diefenbaker and the federal PC's, though Quebec's Premier Daniel Johnson, who was on close terms with Robarts, employed his Union Nationale to assist the federal Conservatives electorally. When Stanfield replaced Diefenbaker and led the Conservatives in the 1968 election, both Robarts and Johnson tried to boost the federal PC, but both were conspicuously unable to deliver a Conservative vote. Stanfield, on his part, had campaigned vigorously for the Conservatives in the Maritimes during the 1965 election, Diefenbaker's last as PC leader, and is believed to have helped the Conservative cause. When in 1970 an election arrived in Nova Scotia, a province in which Stanfield had once served as a notably successful Premier, the provincial Conservatives refused to allow him, now PC federal leader, to become involved in the campaign, since they were reluctant to associate themselves with him or the federal party.

Leadership images and electoral outcomes

We have a general picture that Canadian and Australian conservative party leaders ordinarily enjoy considerable programmatic discretion, but that they may expect a very mixed influence, among state/provincial leaders and their parties. But do party leaders have an important effect upon the direction in which the public casts its vote? Broadly speaking, our preliminary judgment would be that the leadership variable counts for more in Canada than in Australia. Canada's parties are more diffused than Australia's. There is more shifting of electoral loyalties in Canada than in Australia, suggesting that the Canadian vote is susceptible to forces other than partisan party habit. The correlation between class and occupation, and party support, is more explicit in Australia, which leadership considerations would have difficulty in overcoming. Finally, it is a plausible explanation that the vote in Canada, more than in Australia, is colored by leadership images because the Canadian vote is more influenced at another level of political personalities, namely candidates. The Canadian data disclose that, at least until the late 1960's, rural western voters were strongly affected by their candidate preferences. In Ontario, moreover, one survey has suggested that candidate preference is the single most influential factor accounting for party switching, both federally and provincially. Other research in Ontario indicated that, federally at least, the impact of the local candidate is worth just under 10 per cent of the vote, and that uncommitted voters are primarily affected in this way. Australian research gives little credence to meaningful candidate influence, though the DLP vote in Queensland is probably affected by Senator Vincent Gair's personal following of many years' standing, and personality voting has been common in Tasmania's intimate political setting. If candidate influence can roughly be measured by the success of independent candidates, then again Australia ranks lower. In the nine House of Representatives elections between 1949 and 1969, only one or two independents were elected. In the eight Canadian Commons elections, in about the same period, for a chamber slightly more than twice the size of the Australian, either twelve or seventeen independents were elected, depending on definition.

Some Canadian data do suggest that leadership images influence voter choice. Ontario research has indicated that both federally and provincially, but more so federally, party leadership images are powerful conditioners of persons who switch their party vote from one election to another, though individual candidate personality is an even stronger influence. Another survey of three Ontario federal ridings concluded that over a quarter of the voters felt their perception of party leaders to be the critical factor in shaping their vote. The extremely successful 1971 Conservative electoral campaign in Ontario was pitched to exploit the personality of the incumbent premier, William Davis, and polls showed that he was far more popular than the Liberal and NDP leaders.

In an effort to make the Canadian analysis more concrete, it may be useful to turn to the 1968 federal election, in which many commentators felt the Liberals gained a healthy victory because of "Trudeaumania"—the excitement generated by the new Prime Minister, Pierre Trudeau. Trudeau's modish, candid, and intellectually quick manner, his effortless fluency in both English and French, his refreshing lack of standard political jargon, seemed to captivate his audiences. In Ontario, 160,000 volunteers toiled for the Liberal cause, twice the number of formally enrolled Liberal party members in the province. At the close of the campaign, Trudeau enjoyed overwhelming personal endorsement, and by far the single most frequent reason given by the surveyed public was his attractive image. On the eve of the election, the polls gave Trudeau an almost 2 to 1 edge over PC leader Robert Stanfield as the man with the best potential for being Prime Minister. Both were Harvard men, but that was about where the similarity ended. Trudeau was the brilliant swinger from cosmopolitan Montreal, while Stanfield was the sincere yet depressingly stolid Nova Scotian. When the election results were in, the Liberal popular vote advantage over the PC was noticeably close to the earlier popularity margin by which Trudeau had beaten Stanfield. Liberals had 14 per cent more of the electorate than the Conservatives; Trudeau had 18 per cent more personal popular support than Stanfield.

There were also some signs that Trudeaumania had not actually carried the election for the Liberals. For instance, more careful analysis reveals that Trudeaumania was most intense among established Liberal voters, and therefore immaterial to their vote. Although young people voted proportionately more Liberal than the nation at large, the oldest groups were proportionately less Liberal than the national average. A comparison of the election of 1965, when Lester Pearson—once dubbed "M. Personne" (Mr. Nobody) in Quebec—was still leading the Liberals, and the election of 1968, shows no startling shifts in the major party popular vote. The Liberals improved their total by slightly better than 5 per cent, but the NDP vote dropped by only 1 per cent, and the PC vote actually rose by 1 per cent. Three years after the 1968 election, although the Liberals remained well ahead of the Conservatives in the opinion polls, Stanfield was rated much higher than Trudeau on such traits as the amount of personal public trust he commanded, his sympathy for ordinary people, his demeanor, and as an individual people would want for a friend. The public was apparently still willing to vote Liberal, but seemingly was unwilling to buy a used car from the Liberal Prime Minister, who was as trendy as ever.

One account of the Trudeau-Liberal linkup in 1968 points out that the Liberals' improvement was not nationwide. Their vote was actually seriously reduced in three of the four Atlantic provinces, and in the fourth and smallest, Prince Edward Island, it rose almost imperceptibly. In the rest of the country, large Liberal gains were localized—in metropolitan Winnipeg, in the provinces of British Columbia and Alberta, and in Quebec's English-speaking ridings. In Winnipeg, local conditions, referring in part to disillusionment with the provincial PC government, were alleged to be largely responsible. The British Columbia and Alberta Liberal gains were scored almost entirely at the expense of the fading national Social Credit party, which collapsed in that election. The British Columbia and Alberta votes went Liberal because Trudeau, despite being a French Canadian, was a committed federalist, and had stood up to Quebec extremists, an appealing position in two of the most anti-French provinces in the land. Likewise, in Quebec, English speakers flocked to the Liberals, "on the touching faith that Trudeau could put down their French-speaking neighbours." In sum, this analysis concludes,

> Trudeaumania is nothing less than a massive right wing swing to the Liberal party. Is it too much to hope that we will have heard the last of the nonsense which finds Trudeau "radical" or "progressive" and which sees the Canadian electorate as having opted for the "just society"? *

However readily one wishes to accept this argument, the impression remains that "leadership image" is, at least, an extremely complex variable in Canadian electoral behavior.

We have suggested that leaders' images seem less important for electoral outcomes in Australia than they are in Canada. Our hard Australian data on this subject are fragmentary. Allowance must, in any event, be made for unusual cases such as in New South Wales some years ago, where there were few neutral feelings about Lang. He was either despised or, in the phrase of the day, "greater than Lenin." Recent Australian politics also pose a special complication to any neat generalizations. Since the mid-1950's the ALP has been tied up in intricate internal quarrels which have

* G. David Sheps, "The Nature of Trudeaumania," *Canadian Dimension,* September-October 1968, p. 6.

consistently been exploited by the government parties and by the DLP. Evatt, Calwell, and Whitlam have all behaved, and have been the object of partisan criticism, in ways that prevent convenient separation of their personal electoral influence from public perceptions of the party's credibility generally.

Some examination of the 1966 and 1969 federal elections may, however, offer some clues about the influence of leadership images. In early 1966, several months before the election, comparisons were already being struck between Calwell, the ALP leader, and Whitlam, his heir apparent. Calwell was an old line politician who, as 1966 wore on, assumed a dogmatic posture on conscription and the Australian troop commitment in Vietnam, and resorted to a haranguing style. Whitlam was stylistically attractive and younger, of a much more independent turn of mind on policy, and unhappy with the composition and rigidities of the party's higher organizational organs. Shortly before the election itself, among non-ALP voters who said that they might shift their existing allegiance to Labor—the key, target group of voters—Whitlam was preferred over Calwell by a 4 to 1 margin. In 1967, once the election had been fought and decisively lost by Labor and Whitlam had succeeded to the leadership, he was the overwhelming favorite for the position among voters of all partisan affiliations.

Whitlam then proceeded to secure his own standing, in and out of the ALP. He personally intervened in by-elections in which Labor candidates came to poll surprisingly well. Diligently, and with a measure of success, he worked to broaden the ALP's federal conference and executive composition. By the time of the 1969 House election, two of the closest students of Australian political opinion were moved to write that

> An impressive and favorably perceived leader is an incalculably important asset for a party. It is likely that Mr. Whitlam still has this standing in the electorate at large.*

* Don Aitkin and Michael Kahan, in *Australian* (Sydney), October 23, 1969.

ɪtators on the 1969 election generally agree that leader-
nages had an effect on the vote, which swung sharply away ɪ the government and toward Labor. Over the months preced- g the election, Gorton's popularity began to slide, and Whitlam's to rise, closely following shifts in the public popularity enjoyed by the L-CP and the ALP. By the time of the election, 46 per cent of the public explicitly approved of Whitlam, and only 26 per cent disapproved. Whitlam's standing was proportionately far higher among L-CP voters than was Gorton's among Labor supporters. Furthermore, it can be hypothesized that because the electoral swing in 1969 was greatest in Liberal held seats, next largest in CP seats, and smallest in Labor seats, public antipathy toward Gorton was particularly pronounced among previous Liberal voters, who were now induced to vote Labor.

It would also appear that the Country party derives a measure of its strength from the qualities of its leaders. The CP has had a tradition of especially powerful and sagacious federal leaders—Sir Earle Page, Sir Arthur Fadden, Sir John McEwen—all of whom distinguished themselves by their personal hold over their party, and their resourcefulness in winning concessions for the party clientele.

All told, then, as in Canada, leadership perceptions seem to intrude upon Australian electoral judgments, though confident measurement remains out of reach.

10

Electoral mechanics and electoral outcomes

The mechanical features which distinguish the electoral process themselves contribute to electoral outcomes. Such will be the emphasis of the present chapter, as we move across various categories of provisions which govern voting and representation. At the end, as a summation to this entire section of the book, we will attempt an overview of Canadian and Australian political party systems.

Some miscellaneous electoral provisions and their partisan effects: finances, voluntary and compulsory voting, and the ballot

Money counts, in politics as elsewhere. In Canada and Australia, big money is ostensibly not a requisite for being a candidate for elective office, or being able to absorb defeat. In order to deter frivolous candidates, both countries require a deposit from anyone whose name appears on the ballot, but the amounts are very modest. An Australian House of Representatives candidate lays out \$100, and Australian Senate and Canadian Commons candidates \$200. Australian candidates forfeit their deposit only if they fail to gain 20 per cent of the winning candidate's primary vote. Canadians forfeit theirs if their vote falls under half of the winning candidate's total. The "deterrent" objective of these regulations has been minimal. Neither new and untried parties, nor independent candidates with no reasonable chance of success, are really blocked by the required deposit sums. What does happen, of course, is that the major parties are scarcely affected by deposit losses, while smaller parties and independent candidates are far more affected. In Canada's 1968 election, for instance, deposits were forfeited by eight Liberals, 88 Conservatives, and 185 NDP candidates. Australia's more lenient House deposit law makes deposits virtually meaningless for the major parties, though the DLP tends to lose most of its deposits outside Victoria, its strongest state.

Once a person becomes a parliamentary candidate, the law in both countries turns a virtually deaf ear to the sources or amounts of money spent in conducting the campaign. One effect of this permissiveness is that wealthy parties can do far more to groom and advertise themselves and their candidates than poorer parties, or poor candidates. In both countries, the conservative parties, with their business support, are far better prepared to mount elaborate campaigns than the NDP or the ALP, despite the union funds and volunteer workers available to the parties of the left. Canadian campaigns have become immensely expensive. If the ALP had to lose $37,000 in deposits—even in Canadian currency—as the NDP did in 1968, it would be financially staggered, since this sum would amount to anywhere from a seventh to a tenth of the campaign budget planned by the ALP in 1971 for the following year's House election. Despite its million-dollar war chest, in 1968, the NDP was a pauper compared to the two main parties. When the 1971 Ontario *provincial* campaign opened, the NDP hoped to spend just over $600,000—believed to be one-third what the Liberals would spend, and one-seventh of the Conservative party's resources. No amount of envelope licking and house solicitations by volunteer labor can erase a conservative party's dollar advantage in an age of television and air travel expenses. Two Canadian provinces, Quebec and Nova Scotia, have recently adopted systems of public financing for political parties. Australian party expenses are reduced because of compulsory voting. Even so, in both nations, multiplying expenses can lead to undesirable dependence on interested contributors, and create structural electoral handicaps for parties of the left.

Apart from the advantages or disadvantages conferred on them by financial aspects of electoral law, political parties may be helped or harmed by provisions governing the vote itself. For instance, we may inquire whether Canada's voluntary and Australia's compulsory voting systems make a real difference to one party group or another. Voluntary voting is generally disadvantageous to parties of the left, whose potential electoral clientele is disproportionately composed of persons of low socioeconomic status, low political interest and competence, and proportionately low electoral turnout. Among the western world's labor/social-democratic parties the Canadian NDP is, however, somewhat unusual. Its voting support profile reflects a relatively even distribution among SES categories, rather than being severely skewed toward the urban working class. We can therefore surmise that electoral voluntarism in Canada has not been especially prejudicial to the left. Australia's system has compelled the typical ALP working-class voter to march to the polls. But it has also compelled voting by women, who as a group are electorally more conservative (and more Liberal- and Country-party disposed) than men.

Although Australian compulsory voting has only fractionally increased the incidence of spoiled or "informal" ballots cast for the House of Representatives, such spoilage is more common in Australia than in Canadian Commons elections, about 3 per cent versus 1 per cent, respectively, of the total votes cast. Spoiled ballots cast for the Australian Senate, which since 1949 has been elected under a complicated system of proportional representation, can approach 10 per cent of all ballots cast. In other words, as we move from the most simple to the most intricate electoral systems —House of Commons, House of Representatives, Australian Senate—informal voting rises perceptibly. This phenomenon would appear to favor the Canadian NDP, and to harm Australian Labor, which must operate under the more complicated balloting methods. The Australian data show that the least informed and least politically competent persons, of whom proportionately more are found within ALP than L-CP clienteles, are the most apt to vote "informally."

It is also tempting to attach a slight ALP disadvantage to the manner in which candidates are listed on ballot papers. In Commons, House of Representatives, and Senate elections held through the 1960's, candidates were listed in alphabetical order, and without party labels. In 1970, changes in Canadian law allowed candidate identification for parties contesting a minimum of 75 ridings. In any event, there was no evidence that Canadian candidates who stood at the top of an alphabetically listed, party unidentified ballot had previously earned any advantage. In Australia, they did. The descriptively named "donkey vote," marking votes straight from top to bottom, was once believed to represent up to 3 per cent of the votes cast in Australian elections, but by now has probably lessened. If candidates of the several parties are randomly distributed on the ballot, no one party draws an advantage. But the DLP has been especially determined to exploit the donkey vote by selecting House candidates bearing surnames beginning with letters in the early part of the alphabet. In the 1969 election, DLP candidates held top of the ballot positions in 46 per cent of the seats contested by the party. The DLP's primary electoral leverage lies not so much in gathering first preferences for itself, as in being able to insure that its supporters cast their second preferences for L-CP rather than ALP candidates. The alphabet game can backfire if a DLP candidate tops the ballot and a Labor candidate is in second position, since the donkey vote would earn Labor the second preference. The ideal situation is in marginal seats, in which the DLP obtains first-ballot position, directly ahead of an L-CP candidate. The DLP is able to nominate alphabetically appropriate candidates because the major parties select their candidates long before the DLP does.

Electoral systems

Both in Canada and in Australia, the electoral systems themselves have significantly affected party representation in legislative bodies. To that extent, they have affected the decisions of who governs, who may expect to exercise an influence over governance, or expect to be handicapped in achieving political office.

Canada's first-past-the-post, or simple majority system, employed for Commons elections, is the most straightforward of the major electoral systems employed in the two countries. There were several two-member Commons seats in the present century, and two survived until 1966, when single member ridings became the universal rule. Some multimember seats survive in the provinces. The simple majority system has carried important implications, both for parties and for the operation of governmental institutions. Smaller parties with diffused national following have suffered severe representational prejudice, since election by plurality provides no payoff for respectable voting achievement per se, only for the ability to garner more votes than anyone else, seat by seat. We find that parties with diffused electoral support have averted serious underrepresentation in only two Commons elections since World War I. After the 1968 election, for example, the NDP's share of the national popular vote was almost twice as great as the proportion of the Commons seats it held. When, however, a minor party limits its Commons competition to those provinces where it has built up a real following, the tables can be turned on the major party groups. The best example of this is in the Prairies, the seat of many of Canada's protest-party movements. In the fourteen federal elections held between 1925 and 1968, the Liberals and Conservatives together invariably captured over half of the national popular vote, but in three of those elections their combined seat total was less than 50 per cent. In effect, the two main parties divided the traditional vote, enabling the locally strong third party, or parties, to pick up the pieces.

A second consequence of plurality voting has been the overrepresentation of *governing* parties. In 1935, the Liberals held over 70 per cent of the Commons seats on the basis of a 45 per cent popular vote. In 1957, the PC's organized a minority government with 39 per cent of the popular vote, and another minority government in 1962 on the basis of having earned just over 37 per cent of the vote. This governing-party overrepresentation has, through time, been obtained not only at the expense of small parties, but very often at the expense of whichever of the two major parties has happened to be in opposition.

If the Liberals and the Conservatives deserve to be regarded as Canada's mainstream parties, then the electoral system has protected the "vital center" of the nation's politics from serious encroachment from outlying political movements, of whatever persuasion. The NDP was a latecomer to Canada's politics, and has only very recently mounted truly nationwide electoral efforts. Its attempts at gaining representation roughly equivalent to popular support have been frustrated by the electoral system. This has reduced the party's national influence. It has also made an indirect contribution to protecting PC representation in recent years, since the NDP competes far more for the Liberal than for the Conservative vote.

Plurality voting has also measurably enhanced Canadian governmental stability in the face of what has nearly become a multiparty system. Although there have been several minority governments at Ottawa since the first World War, there would have been more such governments, or coalition governments would have been required, had parties with the second, third, and fourth largest popular vote acquired representation nearly equivalent to their electoral strength. But electoral strength does not distribute itself evenly across the nation. One party or another has tended to be dominant in some region for a long period of years, and weak in another. Such imbalances of strength have been exaggerated by an electoral system which severely penalizes weakness. Roughly from the first World War to the late 1940's, the Conservatives were overrepresented in Ontario, and the Liberals were underrepresented. With almost unfailing regularity since World War I, the Liberals have been overrepresented in Quebec. Such imbalances have accentuated Canada's established sectional and cultural distinctions, and have denied adequate intersectional and intercultural influences upon the major parties. The Conservative parliamentary party has tended to be overly English, the Liberal party overly French. In the 1960's, in addition to being overly English, the Conservative parliamentary party became disproportionately populated by MPs from Canada's more marginal areas, the Prairies and the Maritimes.

Preferential voting was for a time applied in Canada's western provinces, but no more, and our interest in the system lies in its impact on Australia, where it is used for the federal House and in every state except Tasmania. Preferential voting was first introduced federally in 1919 at the instigation of the burgeoning Country party, after some application of the system in the states. The theory was that with a third serious party appearing in some electorates, the splitting of the non-Labor vote would, under first-past-the-post, permit Labor candidates to win with modest simple majorities. The addition of preferential voting would negate this prospect, assuming the Country and Nationalist parties agreed to urge their respective followers to exchange second preferences, and that these second preferences would in fact hold firm. The CP's thesis was quickly vindicated, as preference distribution in three-cornered contests almost invariably brought victory to one or the other of the non-Labor parties.

Preferential voting eventually became less critical for the CP, but has remained valuable. In most federal seats which the CP contests, the Liberals stay out, and the fight is essentially between the CP and the ALP, with perhaps the DLP thrown in. But CP-Liberal relations are often cool, Liberals are eager to contest more rural or semirural seats than they have in the past, and three-cornered campaigning is becoming more common. The CP resents such intrusions. Even if preferences are effectively exchanged and Labor is denied victory, there is always the chance that the Liberals, not the CP, will be the eventual winners. In the 1969 federal election, Liberal candidates appeared in 8 of the 26 seats contested by the Country party. In those 8 seats, the Liberal popular vote total was 37 per cent, versus only 31 per cent for the CP. In 1966, in the interest of coalition-government harmony, Prime Minister Holt personally intervened to dissuade the Liberals from entering seats held by incumbent CP ministers. In 1971, Prime Minister McMahon also tried to discourage Liberal candidacies in the Country party's Victorian seats. In the same year, the Queensland state Liberal and CP parties, partners in a CP-led coalition government, entered into a formal agreement, obligating each party to refrain from entering seats currently occupied by the other party.

When three-cornered fights have occurred, the mutual exchange of CP and Liberal preferences has tended to stand up well, on an average of over 80 per cent federally. But the picture is not all that simple. When local CP-Liberal relations are especially embittered, the leakage of preferences can become so extensive that a Labor candidate can hope to win. In Victorian state politics, Liberal-CP relations are very bad, and the CP is not part of the Liberal government. In the 1970 Victorian state election, the CP was so unhappy with the Liberals that it advised its supporters to cast second preferences for Labor candidates—even though Labor was advising its electors to award their second preferences to the Liberals. Then too, the CP is able to continue its practice of running more than one of *its own* party candidates per seat in some state elections only because preference exchange is available.

Preferential voting has ordinarily tended to buffer party splits, but it did not forestall Labor's convulsion of the mid-1950's. The DLP has exploited preferential voting skillfully, but not in the manner for which the system had been designed. Although the DLP contests 80 per cent to 90 per cent of the federal House seats, its only lower-house success has been the election of a single member to the Queensland state parliament. What keeps the DLP going in federal House and various state elections is its ability to direct its supporters' second preferences away from Labor, and to the government parties. In Victoria, well over 80 per cent of DLP second preferences are reliably non-Labor; in other states, somewhat less so.

With the DLP's advent, the number of federal seats which have been decided on preferences has increased, reaching as high as a third. In the five elections between 1958 and 1969, 115 of the seats decided on preference were won by the government parties, and only 28 were won by the ALP. During these five elections, in 40 seats where preferences were distributed, the originally leading candidate—who under a Canadian type, simple-majority system would have been declared the winner—actually was defeated. In all but three of these seats DLP preferences made the difference. An extreme situation occurred during the 1966 election, in a Victorian seat. The incumbent ALP candidate received 47 per cent of the vote on the first count, against 29 per cent for his Liberal opponent, but the Liberal won on preferences.

In 1961 and 1969, even with the DLP putting up candidates, Labor substantially outpolled the government parties, and would have assumed national office had DLP preferences not been brought into play. In 1969, in the 31 seats where there was a DLP candidate and in which the outcome was based on preference distribution, 84.9 per cent of the DLP second preferences went to the L-CP. In 12 of those seats, the originally leading candidate was defeated, and the seat went to the government. The ALP came out of the election 7 seats behind the L-CP. It is no exaggeration to say that the DLP's manipulation of the preferential voting system has profoundly affected Australian politics, and no wonder that the ALP favors a return to first-past-the-post.

It is also understandable that new movements such as the Australia party (a group of middle-class progressives), the DOGS, and the Pensioner Power Association became electorally active both federally and in the states. Such groups realize that their chances of actually electing someone are extremely remote. They do feel that their sheer electoral presence will publicize their cause. But, taking a hint from the DLP, they hope to influence representational outcomes by urging their followers to cast second preferences for those major-party candidates who appear most sympathetic to their programs. Some of the new party candidates poll fairly well. By and large, the second preferences of these parties are directed to the ALP. It is therefore conceivable that in selected state and federal seats this new-party application of second preferences could partially neutralize the effect of second preferences directed to the L-CP by DLP voters.

We come now to the proportional representation system of election. Although the system is used for the lower house of the Tasmanian legislature, our concentration will be on its use in the Australian federal Senate.

The Australian states enjoy equal senatorial representation—six each until 1949, ten thereafter. Senators hold six-year terms, and half of each state's senatorial seats are subject to election every third year. The Senate was elected under a simple majority system until 1919, preferential voting until 1949, and since then has operated under proportional representation. Until the advent of proportional representation, the election of Senators in what corresponded to at-large state elections created incredible distortions. At one time, the Senate's party composition was 35 non-Labor Senators and a single Labor Senator. At another time, there were only three non-Labor Senators. Labor and non-Labor electoral strength is not markedly different state by state. The institution of Senate proportional representation has therefore meant that state senatorial delegations have become quite evenly balanced. The Senate at large has acquired a close party balance, comparable to that in Tasmania's Legislative Assembly. Proportional representation has also given a few independents a chance to gain Senate seats, and has provided the DLP with its only federal legislative representation, with a high of five Senators as of 1970–71.

The political impact of proportional representation on Senate representation has been twofold. In the 1960's, the combination of nearly equal ALP and government representation, and the presence of independent and DLP Senators spelled a loss of L-CP Senate control. This enhanced the Senate's bargaining power and forced concessions from the ministry. Second, Senate proportional representation has been a godsend to the DLP. Its Senate foothold and forum, its ability to juggle the balance of power in the Senate, and therefore affect the outcome of certain public policies, have tremendously enhanced the DLP's visibility, and its credibility as a meaningful political force. Given its standing in the Senate, the DLP can properly claim that its national role is not purely captious and negative, that is, intended to deny Labor control over the House of Representatives, and therefore over the ministry. Here the impact of voting systems upon electoral results comes into particularly sharp relief. Proportional representation has enabled the DLP to establish itself in the Senate. Its Senate status has considerably shored up its national credibility. This credibility has helped it maintain a voter following sufficiently large and committed to the allocation of second preferences in House elections to continue federal Labor's consignment to the political wilderness. It is a plausible conjecture that, had proportional representation not been adopted for the *Senate,* sometime in the 1960's the Australian Labor party might have won a *House* majority, and governed Australia.

Electoral boundary distribution

Like electoral methods, the composition of electoral districts has significantly influenced electoral outcomes. In the idealized version of "one man, one vote," the weight of any person's vote is the same as that of any other person, regardless of the constituency in which a voter may be resident. Some political systems approximate this ideal more than others. Although it depends whether we address ourselves to the federal or to state/provincial levels, an overview suggests that both Australia and Canada have considerably departed from the notion. Such departures have affected the representational status of parties, of their ability to become governing parties, and ultimately the content of public policy.

Electoral boundary equity, or nonequity, may result from several factors, of which constitutional provisions are one. Australia's federal constitution stipulates that the House of Representatives shall be composed of members chosen by the people, and that the number of members chosen in the several states "shall be in proportion to the respective numbers of their people." This is not an arithmetically absolute requirement for equal numbers of voters, or residents, per House district, and a special constitutional clause explicitly provided for a minimum of Tasmanian seats, in actuality awarding the state more representation than its population would ordinarily justify. All the same, the constitution does set a mandate on behalf of approximate population numbers in House electorates. The BNA Act was silent on matters of population balance among federal ridings. It did, however, set out a formula dividing ridings among the provinces, and which provoked outcries of inequitous representation, first from one region of Canada, then from another. Another clause in the BNA Act guaranteed that the territorial integrity of 12, later 17, *provincial* parliamentary seats in a certain portion of Quebec. These seats could not be disturbed until and unless the sitting members themselves consented. The original purpose of these provisions was to protect the representation of what was then an English-speaking community in the area. In time these districts became underpopulated, and French-speaking. In effect they became rotten boroughs. Not only were the entrenched districts themselves untouchable, but their continuation retarded comprehensive redistricting in the province. Not until 1970 did the 17 sitting members acquiesce in the disestablishment of their seats, thereby permitting long overdue and province-wide redistricting.

The weight of votes can also be affected by the extent to which federal, state, or provincial legislatures choose to impose some kind of self-denying ordinance upon themselves respecting the redistricting process itself. Four Canadian provinces, two of Australia's states, the Australian federal government from its beginning, and the Canadian federal government as of legislation enacted in 1964 but not operational until the 1968 election, have essentially vested the task of electoral districting in outside commissions, rather than in the parliaments themselves. It is perfectly true that these legislative bodies, which are if nothing else political, can and do set down guidelines for the commissions to observe. These guidelines usually mirror the expected political advantage of the governing parties, and the independence of boundary commissions' judgments from final parliamentary review varies. But the redistricting process in these national or state/provincial jurisdictions is at least one major step removed from overt legislative manipulation of electoral boundaries.

Demographic trends themselves may also affect the degree to which a one man, one vote principle is satisfied. For instance, even if a boundary redistribution has been carried out with careful attention to the relatively equal numbers of electors across various districts, by the time the next redistribution occurs, whether sooner or later, population movements may already have created serious imbalances, and have distorted electoral results. At the time of Canada's 1952 federal redistribution, the population of ridings varied from 6000 to 54,000. Into the 1960's, with no fresh redistribution applied, the range was between 12,000 and 267,000. Both in Canada and in Australia, there is a trend of movement from the land to the cities, static or declining populations in urban center cores, and a proliferation of suburban living. Of course, inaction on redistricting may in itself be a calculated policy, designed to perpetuate the constituency imbalances which those in power regard as politically desirable. It may also be that the peculiarities of the electoral districts themselves, originally instituted for some other purpose, create windfalls whose effect is to award more electoral weight to one category of electors than to another. Dual or multimember provincial seats still exist in some Canadian provinces, primarily in the Atlantic region. Under a first-past-the-post arrangement electors tend to vote for candidates representing the same party. In New Brunswick, for one, this resulted in the submergence of urban electors and interests, and a rural domination of the legislature.

Apart from explicitly partisan advantages, there are some understandable reasons why some electoral districts might deliberately be made more populous than others. Both Canada and Australia are territorially huge, as are some of the provinces and states. As it is, the size of Australian federal districts varies from a few square miles in major cities, to 900,000 square miles in a Western Australian district. The argument is that for reasons of candidate exposure, voter access to polling stations, preservation of a district's economic and community identity, and perhaps special electoral weight for a numerically small but economically significant sector, such as primary industry, deviations from the one man, one vote principle should be allowed. Indeed, it should not be automatically assumed that the general public, city dwellers included, necessarily resents electoral boundary favoritism. Australia is nearly 90 per cent urban. But a 1968 survey showed that only 45 per cent of the public was opposed to rurally weighted federal electorates, while 35 per cent favored the practice, and 20 per cent had no opinion. Persons residing in the capital cities were only slightly less disposed than others to accept this principle.

We should now examine the actual effects of electoral boundary construction in the two nations. At the federal level, population parity has been much more closely observed in Australia than in Canada. The Australian guidelines have always permitted a 20 per cent deviation up or down from the parity quota, but very few seats have actually reflected a difference of this magnitude. Well over 80 per cent of the seats have over time fallen within a 10 per cent deviation. At the point of the six redistributions carried out prior to the 1969 election, the median deviation, nationwide, was only about 7.5 per cent. The 1969 election was conducted following a redistribution under which the several state boundary commissions continued to operate under a 20 per cent deviation guidepost, but were now, under law, instructed (rather than simply permitted) to make allowances for special constituency features, and whose effect was to favor rural areas. The result was a greater advantage to rural areas, but still not startlingly so, with the rural vote now being worth some 9 per cent more than the urban.

The population spread among Canadian federal ridings has been consistently great. Before the most recent distribution of 1966, based on the 1964 legislation, among the various provinces there were 25 seats with fewer than 40,000 people, and 36 with more than 100,000, three of which contained over 200,000 persons. The 1966 redistribution was the first to be carried out by commissions rather than by Parliament itself, and the first which set legislatively enacted guidelines for computing how much spread, under a specified rationale, was allowed among constituencies. The legislation required the commissions to take into account such factors as community of interests and the territorial size of ridings, and it permitted a 25 per cent up or down deviation from the quota norm. This produced a far more equitable distribution than Canada had known in the past, but one which was still more unbalanced than Australia's. Slightly over 10 per cent of all Canadian ridings departed from the norm by over 20 per cent, and fewer than half were within 10 per cent of the quota.

What kind of partisan advantage has resulted from federal constituency arrangements in Australia and Canada? Although federal constituency variation has been more pronounced in Canada, no single party in either country has been the perennial beneficiary. Neither the Liberals nor the Conservatives in Canada can be considered as a consistently urban or rural party, and even in particular phases of political history both have had some foothold in both town and country. Instead, the trend has been for party domination in national regions. In recent political experience, however, there has been a noticeable PC decline in the cities, and a Liberal and NDP concentration there. After the 1963 election, for instance, Conservatives occupied 74 rural seats, and the Liberals 55, but Liberals controlled 74 urban seats, to the Conservatives' 19. The redistribution which applied to the 1968 election clearly benefited the Liberals, the party in power, and to an extent the NDP, since a number of rural seats had been eliminated and a number of urban seats added, primarily in suburban areas.

The Australian situation must be assessed in terms of the special role played by the Country party. Although both the Liberals and the ALP hold some federal rural seats, they are primarily city parties. The CP, with a few historical exceptions, has offered candidates only in rural or semirural areas, and its representation has therefore been limited to nonurban seats. Although the total number of federal rural seats has declined over the decades, the CP still does not contest all such seats. Where it does so it competes from a position of strength, and usually without the complicating factor of a Liberal candidacy. The result has been that CP House representation has over time varied considerably less than has Liberal or ALP representation. Since 1949, when the House was enlarged, CP strength has never fallen below 17, nor exceeded 21. In 1969, the party contested 26 seats, of which it captured 20, an infinitely better won-lost percentage than either the Liberals or Labor could ever hope to achieve. In 1969, with only 8.6 per cent of the national vote, the CP controlled 16 per cent of the House seats, over 14 per cent of the combined House and Senate seats, and nearly 27 per cent of the seats in the ministry which was constructed following the election. As the rural population shrinks, the Country party is of course interested in avoiding the liquidation of as many of the rural seats it contests as possible, and in maximizing the rural seat weightage. In the 1960's, it caused something of a government crisis and insisted that new legislation require, not simply allow, the boundary commissions to be mindful of local conditions within the parameters of the 20 per cent weightage tolerance. Still, despite its federal parliamentary overrepresentation, the CP often finds its demands for weightage concessions to rural seats resisted by its Liberal coalition partners, and by the ALP. Even if it cannot extract rural weightage guidelines as favorable as those available in Canada, in one important sense the Country party's survival, and its national political influence, are predicated on another factor—the party's ability to continue fighting and winning selected rural and semirural seats, and to apply leverage as a kind of parliamentary party-cum-pressure group. Were the Liberals to launch a full-scale effort to contest CP seats, and if preference exchange were to break down, the party's position would be desperate.

Overall, imbalances in state/provincial electoral districts have been quite striking in both countries. While various parties have attempted to maximize electoral advantage through manipulation of electoral boundaries, the most conspicuous instances of maldistribution have been fostered by individual parties or party coalitions most dependent on rural support, and the general result has been the strengthening of conservative parliamentary forces.

In recent decades, among the most drastically maldistributed Canadian provinces have been British Columbia, Alberta, and

Quebec, whose governments have tended toward conservative and rurally supported party control—Social Credit in the first two, the Union Nationale in Quebec. At one point in the 1960's, it was possible for a mere 27 per cent of the voters to elect a majority in the British Columbian legislature. In Alberta, over half of the legislative districts—all nonurban—contained less than 30 per cent of the population. As of Quebec's 1970 election, the population of legislative districts ranged from 6600 to 75,000. Montreal, with nearly half of the province's population, was entitled to only 32 of the 108 seats. Despite the nonurban bias of Quebec's districts, the Liberals won the 1970 election. One unintended, but in some quarters welcome, impact of the maldistribution was the magnification of the disparity between the popular vote of the separatist and largely Montreal-based PQ, and its representation. While the party won nearly a quarter of the vote, it gained only 7 seats.

In the Australian states, much of the prorural boundary bias has been wrought by non-Labor parties, especially where Country party influence has been felt. A common stratagem has been to divide a state into urban, rural, and sometimes small-city regions. Different population quotas are then assigned to the seats within each region, with discrimination against urban dwellers. The 1936 South Australian redistribution, for instance, provided for a 2 to 1 weighting favoring nonmetropolitan seats. The Liberal-Country League held office for 30 years afterward, although in some elections during that period Labor's popular vote was up to 15 per cent greater than the government's. Queensland has been a fascinating laboratory in which to study the politics of electoral distribution. For years Labor governed the state, and its success was in no small measure attributable to the ingenuity of boundary manipulations. Here, Labor's heaviest electoral strength does not lie in Brisbane, the state's capital and largest city, but in a number of the smaller cities and in some distant nonurban portions of the state. Labor's 1949 redistribution divided Queensland into four electoral zones. The metropolitan (Brisbane) zone was most severely discriminated against. In the most favorably treated zone, the western, an elector's vote was worth 2.4 times as much as that of a Brisbane elector's. When an L-CP government assumed office after the state's Labor party had split, another, this time anti-Labor redistribution was effected. Country party strength in the new coalition government was reflected in the new, 1958 boundary arrangements. Queensland was divided into three zones. The greatest electoral quota advantage was awarded to the country zone, where the CP was dominant. Then followed Brisbane, where the Liberals were strong. Least favored was the "provincial" city zone, where Labor usually prevailed. In the 1969 election, the CP won 25 seats on the basis of 22 per cent of the popular vote, while the ALP could secure only 31 seats from its 40 per cent share of the vote. While L-CP-devised quotas are not as severe as Labor's had been, it has been estimated that Labor must now reach 54–55 per cent of the popular vote if it hopes to attain an absolute majority in the state parliament, an extremely difficult goal. In the meantime, while Labor is kept out of Queensland state office, the coalition parties argue bitterly between themselves over their relative entitlements under one electoral distribution formula or another.

Some broad party patterns

We have examined electoral outcomes from various standpoints, such as the types of clienteles which attach themselves to parties, the role of leadership, and electoral laws and boundary distribution. A concluding overview of the general disposition of the two political party systems may now help to draw the discussion into sharper perspective.

We have already noticed that since the first World War, at the federal level, Canadian political party life has been rather more diversified than the Australian. Like Australian Labor, and the Liberals and their predecessors, Canada's two major parties have always been first or second in popular vote, even though the

Progressives carried more seats in 1921 than did the Conservatives. Likewise, in this period there has never been a Canadian government other than Liberal or Conservative, or an Australian government other than Labor, or which represented Liberal and Country party partnership, almost invariably in coalition form. But then the differences emerge. Even with the CP excluded from the calculation, Labor and the Liberals and their predecessors have normally gathered well over 80 per cent of the Australian popular vote. In Canada, by contrast, "minor" parties, among which for immediate purpose we include the CCF/NDP, have from 1921 onward gained a quarter of the vote half a dozen times, reached a high mark of 32 per cent in 1945, and have been responsible for the frequency of minority governments, representing nearly half of all governments from 1921 onward.

Counting all post-World War I federal lower-house elections, we further discover that the major party vote has been considerably more volatile in Canada than in Australia. The Canadian Liberals have ranged from a low of 33.6 per cent to a high of 51.5 per cent, while the Conservatives have varied from a low of 27.4 per cent to a high of 53.6 per cent, a margin of nearly 1 to 2. The coming and going of various Australian moderate/conservative parties such as the Nationalists, the UAP and the Liberals, plus the special factor of the Country party, makes it difficult to speak confidently of *a* "non-Labor" party in this period. If we look at the party-political constant, the ALP, we discover an extraordinary uniformity in popular vote, whether Labor has been in or out of office. Twenty House elections were conducted from 1919–69, inclusive. On just one occasion was the party able to reach 50 per cent of the popular vote. On seventeen other occasions its vote was somewhere between 40 and 50 per cent. On the remaining two occasions, 1931 and 1934, Labor was bedeviled by a split. But if the regular and Lang Labor popular votes are added, Labor at large won over 37 per cent of the vote in 1931 and 41 per cent in 1934.

Internal splitting has been a far more serious problem for the major Australian parties—the ALP, the Nationalists, and the UAP—than for the main Canadian parties. This may point to an Australian party weakness in dealing with crisis situations. All save one post-World War I Australian "realigning" federal elections, in which there has been a shift of government, have been preceded by the breakup of the previous governing party. In Canada not one of the five realigning elections including the one in 1921, has been the postlude to the breakup of the incumbent party. In other words, the replacement of an Australian government seems to be more dependent on an internal party explosion than would be expected in Canada. The Canadian federal electorate is not only more capricious in its long-term support for any given party, but will more readily move from one party to another without prompting from a party upheaval.

The matter of relative electoral constancy in Canada and Australia requires more elaboration. First, we might consider seeming exception to the thesis that Australian electors of different persuasions are more uniformly distributed and constant than Canadian electors. The Australian electorate's response to constitutional amendment referendums has shown little disposition for nationwide uniformity. Of the 26 proposals voted upon from 1906 to 1967, only four have been rejected in all states. In only one instance have five states been in favor, and in only three cases have five been opposed. In other words, most referendums have shown a very mixed reception to amendment among the several states. In nearly half of the referendums (12 of 26), the states have been evenly divided, three for and three against. But so many elements have impinged on the referendum campaigns that it would be dangerous to conclude that Australian electors are very fluid. The referendum campaigns have had stirred into them, inter alia, national party politics, state party politics, and popular perceptions of the issue at hand.

By broad calculation, it can be inferred that while nearly three-quarters of the Australian House seats are safe for one party or another, perhaps between a quarter and a third of Canadian Commons seats are genuinely safe. Since the early 1950's, an average of only ten Australian House seats per election—about 8 per cent—have changed party hands. The 1961 Australian election brought a strong drift toward Labor, the 1966 election a strong drift to the L-CP, and the 1963 election a modest drift to the government parties. Yet, in all three elections combined, only one seat actually went against the national trend at the time. A glance at the levels of uniformity in the nationwide electoral patterns again corroborates the thesis that Australia's electoral consistency exceeds Canada's. In Australia's 1969 House election, the nationwide electoral swing to Labor was 7.2 per cent. In five of the six states and the two federal territories, the swing was between 6.1 per cent and 11.7 per cent. In Tasmania it was only 1.1 per cent, but the ALP already had exceptionally high popular support there upon entering the election. In every state the L-CP vote declined, and so did the DLP's.

Between the 1965 and 1968 elections, the Canadian Liberals improved their national vote by 5.3 per cent. In three provinces, however, their vote declined. In the remaining seven provinces the range of improvement varied from 0.8 per cent in Prince Edward Island, to 13.3 per cent in Alberta. The PC vote rose in four provinces, dropped in four, and remained essentially unchanged in the remaining two. As previously noted, Quebec has, with very few exceptions, been firm Liberal territory, while until recently Ontario was a Conservative stronghold. These are by far the country's two largest provinces, presently entitled to 162 of the 264 Commons seats. Strong performances in these two provinces by separate parties, or third-party intrusions which have prevented a sweep of either province by a major party, have militated against the formation of majority governments.

Expectedly, the data show that constancy to a particular party is far more deeply rooted among Australians than among Canadians. Fewer than 10 per cent of Australians follow separate voting habits in state as opposed to federal elections, far fewer than in Canada. There are several reasons. Both countries have traditions of very long-lived state/provincial governments of one party or another, led by powerful and popular Premiers. But there is, overall, rather more resemblance between Australian federal and state parties of the same label, than between similarly labeled Canadian federal and provincial parties. Canadian provincial-federal political relations tend to be more stormy and, because of more acutely pressing regional and cultural factors, more complex than is true of Australian federal-state relations. Canada has fathered more, and more powerful, local parties than Australia. Therefore, when voting provincially, Canadians have been able to choose among locally well-grounded parties which may have failed to make much if any impression federally—the Union Nationale, the United Farmers of Manitoba, the British Columbia version of Social Credit, and so on.

Since the first World War, nearly all Canadian provinces have at one time or another been governed by "third" parties. No Australian state has been so affected, if we discount the breakaway Lang Labor and, as seems fitting, the Country party is not regarded, for governing purposes, as a "third" party, given its predilection to cooperate with the Liberals against Labor. Only in Victoria, where the CP and the Liberals have not been friendly, has an exclusively CP government ever been organized, and then on a minority basis.

The principal Canadian holdouts against third-party success have been the Maritime provinces. They entered confederation very early, and grew up with and helped to shape the original party system. They also have been part of the Canadian region which most protected its original culture of groups from foreign migration. This homogeneity may well have helped maintain two-party stability. We know, for instance, that the regions with the highest incidence of third-party development, British Columbia and the Prairies, tended through most of the present century to house the highest proportions of foreign-born persons. In Australia, cultural homogeneity was preserved across the country until the past few years, and even now Continental European migrants are a small proportion of the population. Canadian third parties have achieved a breakthrough, not only where there have been certain predisposing grievances, but also a nonviable two party system. When an effective opposition alternative was absent, the third party filled it. Very seldom in Australian politics has there not been a reasonably viable alternative to whichever political force was in office, despite extended periods of government by one party or coalition.

III
THE SOURCES AND PROCESSES OF PUBLIC POLICY

The first section of this book was devoted to the nature and distribution of Canadian and Australian public political values. The second section traced the manner in which Canadians and Australians have organized themselves and behaved politically, and reference was made to the content of policy outputs for which various party groups have been responsible. We now focus on the institutional environment—the structures, processes, and elites whose interaction shapes public policy.

We will deal first with the authoritative seats of policy-making—ministries, heads of government, and legislative bodies. Attention will then turn to bureaucratic establishments and public participatory organs, two informal yet highly significant sources of input to the policy process. Finally, there will be an assessment of how power is actually divided among levels of governing authority, and the kinds of opportunities for or hindrances to creative policymaking which have arisen within the Canadian and Australian federal settings. In other words, we will be concerned with the distribution, the uses, and the users of power relative to policymaking.

11

Ministries and ministers

Parliamentary, cabinet and prime ministerial, or—in the instance of provinces and states—premiership roles interlock, and form the design and process by which much of public policy is developed and authoritatively enacted. Legislatures themselves are the formal sources of the bulk of policy enactments. In point of fact, however, principal responsibility for choosing and shaping policy priorities lies elsewhere, conspicuously in the hands of ministries (cabinets) and heads of government. Parliamentary majorities provide the basis for the formation and maintenance of governments, and for the elevation of party leaders to the rank of first minister. We shall see that parliaments are not purely reflexive institutions in which party majorities simply ratify cabinet and prime ministerial decisions, or in which nongovernmental parties oppose in frustration. But, in the main, cabinet government and prime ministerial leadership are the hallmarks of Canadian and Australian political life. This is true both in the provinces and the states, and nationally, the level to which we will be devoting most of our analysis.

Sources of ministerial recruitment

Confident, sure-handed cabinet governance is assisted by the nature of the cabinet institution itself. Ministers ordinarily are selected from among the more senior, experienced and respected party men. Ministers can draw not only on their personal political capital, but on the information and advice provided them by the civil servants within the departments they supervise. Ministries in Ottawa and Canberra organize themselves into smaller, subject-matter oriented committees, thereby smoothing the policy-planning process. Both the Australian and the Canadian federal ministries have expanded to well over twenty members, which for some purposes of intimate consultation and high echelon decisions is too many. But since 1956 Australian practice has been to split the ministry into an "inner cabinet" of strategic and ranking ministers, and a remaining outer ministry. Canadian practice has informally moved toward the notion of an internal cabinet circle, in the form of a committee on priorities and planning, without actually segregating the federal ministry.

The functioning of Australian and Canadian cabinet government is considerably affected by such constraints as how ministers are appointed, who gets appointed, and the types of responsibilities which are apportioned among them. In both countries there are deviations from the otherwise familiar practice that a prime minister will personally select his ministerial colleagues from among well-established parliamentary figures. In Australia, the state and federal Labor parliamentary caucuses, some state and the federal Country party caucuses, and the Victorian and Queensland Liberal caucuses, determine by ballot those individuals who will occupy ministerial seats when the party occupies office. Once the roster of names has been decided, the party leader—Prime Minister, Premier or, in the instance of the Country party, usually the second ranking minister in a coalition—assigns persons to particular portfolios. Thus, although the leader may have some influence over who will serve with him, the choice is made collectively by the parliamentary party.

The system seems to have produced mixed results. Overall, it can be said to strengthen governing parliamentary party trust of those who have been selected as ministers. The cabinet, or at least part of it, is of the parliamentary party's own choosing and, to a degree, representative of the wings found within caucus, enabling the cabinet itself to operate with enhanced self-confidence. But what this procedure can also produce is the presence of cabinet personalities who, by temperament or political conviction, are distasteful to the Prime Minister or Premier, or to the majority of his ministerial associates, thus opening the cabinet to otherwise possibly avoidable friction and even breaches of cabinet solidarity. An Australian Liberal Prime Minister or Premier of a coalition government finds himself working with persons who not only are not of his own party, but with persons whom neither he nor often his Country party chief lieutenant personally selected. The Liberals and the CP have, however, been parties with a strong tradition of deference to leadership. This not only enables the leader to enjoy a measure of veto power over who is selected to serve under him, but facilitates the imposition of his will over his colleagues once the government is organized. Since the intraparty standing of ALP leaders is often weaker than among non-Labor parties, Labor governments, state and federal, have frequently been embarrassed by personality conflicts and dissensions partially traceable to the caucus method of ministerial selection. In the main, therefore, caucus selection of ministers has probably weakened policy decisiveness and cabinet solidarity in Australia.

Canada's use of special means of ministerial recruitment has been of a different nature. It has been a practice essentially of the Liberal party, has focused on the federal level, and has been purely informal, rather than bound by party rules. Nonetheless, it has drawn considerable attention and some criticism. In effect, beginning with Prime Minister Mackenzie King during the interwar years, the Liberals when in power have tended to co-opt previously nonpolitical people. Such persons have entered the higher stratum of politics laterally, rather than by working their way up. They have often been found safe Commons seats and quickly appointed to ministerial positions. The practice may be traced to the inordinately high turnover in Commons personnel—some 35 to 40 per cent after each recent election, on the average—which reduces the number of worthy and veteran parliamentarians on whom cabinet membership can be bestowed. It may also be traced to the essentially elitist basis of the major Canadian parties, their respect for middle-class talent, and to the network of connections enjoyed with business and other nonpolitical sectors of the community.

At all events, such co-option has sometimes been deplored for putting political novices where they did not belong, and undermining the sense of cabinet solidarity that lengthy political apprenticeship otherwise helps to engender.

> Canadian cabinets have been consistently "enriched" by members brought in because of their prestige or skill acquired in business, the legal profession, or even the public service. The "depoliticization" of the party leadership, particularly among the Liberals, has removed from the most vital area of political decision-making the necessary political skill required for a creative functioning of the political system.*

Such condemnations must be taken seriously. Retrospect does, however, indicate that Canadian federal cabinets have occasionally, in the best sense of the word, been "enriched" by co-option. In 1965, three unusual French Canadians, not one of them a professional politician, were persuaded to seek election as Liberals. They were Jean Marchand, president of the CNTU, Gérald Pelletier, former editor of *La Presse,* and Pierre Trudeau, then a law professor at the University of Montreal. All were elected and all were appointed to ministerial positions. All represented the new, dynamic conception of French Canada within the larger framework of Canadian nationhood. This "new guard" was able to in-

* John Meisel, "Canadian Parties and Politics," in Richard H. Leach, ed., *Contemporary Canada* (Durham: Duke University Press for the Duke University Commonwealth-Studies Center, 1967), pp. 140–41.

fluence and control the Quebec Liberal parliamentary caucus, and to establish influence with Prime Minister Pearson. By 1968, Trudeau had been elected Liberal leader, and became Prime Minister.

Ministerial backgrounds and cabinet performance

Apart from special modes of ministerial recruitment, a government's effectiveness may also be influenced by various dimensions of cabinet personnel composition. The composition of Canadian and Australian cabinets has by no means reflected the occupational and educational distributions within the societies at large. By comparison with other political systems this is unexceptional, but certain variations stand out. As might be expected, the recruitment of working-class parliamentary candidates by Canadian PC's and Liberals, and Australian Liberals and the Country party has been minimal. Opportunities for working-class persons to sit in and influence cabinets composed of these parties have therefore been exceedingly small. Estimates vary but five or six federal ministers of labor background since Canadian confederation would be close to the mark. A different perspective emerges in Australia. There, the ALP has regularly, though now decreasingly, recruited working-class persons for parliamentary office, and has elevated them to ministerial position. We find that in the first half-century after federation, 35 of 176 occupationally identifiable federal ministers had been manual workers, largely because Labor had governed on several occasions. A sample of 101 state and federal Labor ministers from 1901–61 disclosed that 48 of them had previously served as trade-union officials. The newly elected West Australian government of 1971 was most unusual in counting only one trade-union official within the cabinet group of twelve. Among the major Australian and Canadian parties only the ALP has been "labor" in organization and orientation, only it has to any extent placed working and trade-union persons in ministerially responsible positions, and not surprisingly the most explicit public policy supporting the working class and trade unions has come about under Australian Labor governments.

The Country party represents a somewhat less dramatic instance of specialized interest representation. All major Australian and Canadian parties have nominated and elected a number of candidates with rural backgrounds. But the proportion of federal ministers from a rural background appears to have been about three times as great in Australia as in Canada since the two national systems started functioning. Although Australia has consistently been more urban than Canada, rural industries have occupied a larger share of the Australian than of the Canadian economy. Rural electoral weighting has been more pronounced in Canadian than in Australian federal parliamentary seats. However, Canada's propensity for the regionalization of party electoral strength has meant that governing parties have had little rural talent on which to draw for cabinet membership. At one time, Progressive, CCF, and Social Credit success in the largely agricultural west was responsible. In the 1960's, Liberal governments were built on an essentially urban vote, while the out-of-office Conservatives dominated in rural seats. Pearson's 1966 cabinet of 27 included only one person with a farm background; four years later, Trudeau's cabinet of 28 had no minister qualified in this way. While the Country party's appearance in Australia did not signal the beginning of rural cabinet representation, it strengthened and maintained it, and measurably contributed to the adoption of numerous public policies congenial to primary producers. It does not follow that those cabinets, especially Canadian, which have operated with sparse representation from the rural community, have necessarily discriminated against the rural sector, or have been naïve about rural problems, though some element of this cannot be discounted. The electoral rebelliousness of Canadian farmers who have complained about the power of eastern urban and financial interests has probably been compounded by the sight of governments in Ottawa stacked with ministers with little if any personal appreciation of rural problems.

Another facet of cabinet composition worth exploring is the incidence of lawyers. Strong legal representation in cabinets is to be expected for various reasons. The law is a common stepping stone for entry into politics generally, especially in Canada, where, now, 35–40 per cent of all MP's are lawyers. Neither in Canada nor Australia, unlike the situation in Britain, is there a tradition of an educated "leisure class" taking up politics or, with notable exceptions, of intellectuals becoming much absorbed in party politics. Ministers are, after all, concerned with formulating and applying complex laws. Federalism in both countries adds an element of legal complexity to the whole environment of the public policy process. Comparatively, the law has gained a stronger foothold in Canadian than in Australian cabinets. Whereas about a quarter of all Australian national ministers have been lawyers, the ratio has been about twice as high in Canada. Of Australia's 18 Prime Ministers, 8 have been lawyers; of Canada's 15 Prime Ministers, 11 have come from the law. The presence of ALP unionists and Country party farmers and graziers has depressed the Australian ratio of professional/legal ministers. But even Australian Liberals have not matched the main Canadian parties in lawyer representation in ministries. The Canadian PC and Liberal parties have closely resembled one another in the types of people they have attracted to Parliament, and to their cabinets. Canadian society, being more middle class, elitist, and conservative, produced an alternation of party governments whose likeness was reflected in their conspicuous legal background content. The law as a profession stresses deliberate, routinized approaches, and has an ethos more oriented toward conservation and preservation than toward innovations. Until very recently, at least, this was much more the style of Canadian than Australian public tastes, and of the broad tone of public policy.

The religious affiliation of ministers is still another dimension on which to evaluate cabinet performance. In both nations, all the major parties have at one time or another contributed Catholic ministers, and indeed Prime Ministers. In each country's modern political history, however, Catholics have been overrepresented among *one* major party's parliamentary and cabinet members, and Catholics have been clearly underrepresented within *one* party or party group in each country. Particularly after the first World War, as we have seen, the ALP's parliamentary arm became disproportionately Catholic, and remained so even after the 1955 split. State cabinets often were over half Catholic, and the Scullin governments and that of Chifley in 1946 were nearly two-thirds Catholic. Ranking Catholics in the Australian Liberal party have, by contrast, been extremely scarce. The Catholic, Joseph Lyons, UAP Prime Minister in the 1930's, was something of a fluke, in that he was an ALP renegade and became Prime Minister at a time of considerable non-Labor party fluidity. The appointment of a young Sydney Catholic as Attorney-General in a recent Liberal government was much commented upon.

The proportion of Catholics in ALP and Liberal parliamentary ranks, and therefore their availability for ministerial office, has not varied appreciably according to shifts in each party's electoral success. In Canada, however, the electoral drift has made a difference. In the first place, the PC's put up and elect a higher proportion of Protestant candidates than the Liberals, and the Liberals field and elect a higher proportion of Catholics. During the 1968 federal election, for instance, 84 per cent of the PC but only 60 per cent of the Liberal candidates were known to be Protestants. The regime of the only Catholic Conservative Prime Minister, Sir John Thompson, reaches back to the early 1890's. Almost without interruption since the first World War, Catholic Quebec has given the Liberals far more votes and seats than it has the Conservatives. This has meant that the smaller the Liberal parliamentary delegation, the more Catholic it has been. After the party's 1958 electoral debacle, the Liberal parliamentary group was about two-thirds Catholic. Within ten years the party's Commons delegation had more than tripled, allowing Trudeau to form a government backed by a comfortable majority, but Catholics still represented at least 55 per cent of the Liberal caucus. Thus, on those rare occasions since World War I when Conservatives have governed, the pool of Catholics available for ministerial office has been small and short on experience. Conversely, especially when Liberals have governed with tenuous majorities or on the basis of minority government, the available pool of Catholics has been exceptionally large.

In electoral support, parliamentary representation, and cabinet membership, the ALP and the Canadian Liberals can therefore be regarded as the principal "Catholic" major party groups within their respective countries. But the experience of the past several decades does not bear out a conclusion that, federally, the ALP and Canada's Liberals have given exceptional aid and comfort to identifiably Catholic causes. It is true that for decades Australian Catholics found the ALP congenial, in part because the party welcomed and rewarded them politically, while nonlabor did not. But it was Menzies, a Protestant Prime Minister of an overwhelmingly Protestant L-CP government who broke the ice on the delicate state-aid issue, while Labor's policy lagged behind. It was the Catholic, Trudeau, first as Justice Minister and then as Prime Minister in Liberal governments, who pressed for criminal-code liberalization in such areas as divorce and abortion. It was he who in 1970 was able to impose upon skeptical cabinet colleagues, many of them Catholics, a decision to grant federal assistance to family planning and population control programs not only to developing nations, but within Canada itself.

So far, our discussion has suggested that the personnel composition of Australian and Canadian cabinets may produce some differences in the styles and policy outputs of particular governing parties, or shape certain public images of parties, or both. One remaining dimension of cabinet representation, namely the state/provincial distribution of ministers, is among the most significant in the process of cabinet building and performance. The federal structure of the two nations has produced provinces and states which enjoy considerable constitutional autonomy, emanate self-pride, and have a keen sense of their own special social and economic requirements. The states and provinces have produced powerful party machines and political leaders, which often display an almost imperious political independence from the federal party of the same name; not only formal political authority, but party organization and politics are decentralized in the two nations. There has therefore been a firm tradition in both places that federal cabinets should not only include representation from among all states and provinces, but that the representation should as closely as possible correspond to the relative size and importance of the states and the provinces. It is a maxim that has been observed even when caucus has balloted to choose persons for inclusion in federal ALP cabinets.

The task of producing a satisfactory representational balance has in some respects been easier in Australia, and in other respects in Canada. Balance has been easier to strike in Australia because there are only six states for which to find representation, as opposed to Canada's ten provinces. Canada's electoral behavior has tended to produce parliamentary delegations with very distinctive regional/provincial profiles. Even when a party wins an election quite convincingly, as the Liberals did in 1968, it tends to win heavily in some regions and provinces, and to perform poorly elsewhere. The result often is a desperate search for ministers to represent the governing party's electorally deficient areas. In 1921, for example, the Liberals organized the government, but had been totally shut out in Alberta. After a furious scramble, a solution was found by awarding a ministry to an Albertan who was able to win a vacant Quebec seat at a by-election. Yet the available, regionally distributed manpower is often in extremely short supply, and its fitness for high office questionable. The semblance of cross-sectional representation is therefore often bought at the price of ineffective cabinet members, whose underperformance depreciates their value as spokesmen for their particular provinces.

A variation on this theme arises when a party traditionally weak in some Canadian province stages a major electoral comeback, organizes the government, and needs to fill the appropriate provincial "quota" from among a large number of inexperienced MP's. The PC's faced such a situation in the 1950's. In 1953, in a losing cause, the party won four of Quebec's 75 seats. In 1957, Diefenbaker managed to form a minority government, but his party's Quebec representation rose to nine only. In 1958, the Conservatives broke Quebec open, winning 50 of the 75 seats. Diefenbaker had a vast number of Quebec persons from which to choose his cabinet, but it was an uncommonly inexperienced and undistinguished lot. The subsequent decline of the party's popularity in Quebec was in no small part attributable to Diefenbaker's inability to employ his Quebec ministers in much-needed political bridge building in the province. Then too, Canadian cultural/regional heterogeneity has imposed its own modalities on cabinet construction. To have an appropriate number of Quebec, or French, ministers is not enough. There must be representation for English-speaking Quebec; there must be French Quebec representation both from within and outside of Montreal; there should be a few French Canadian ministers from provinces other than Quebec; there should be some "ethnic" representation as well.

Attention is also paid to the origins of Canadian party leaders themselves. The Conservatives, a primarily English-speaking party, have never had a French Canadian leader, but have not been averse to selecting leaders from the west or the Maritimes. Diefenbaker's Saskatchewan origins and populist style probably helped his party electorally in 1957 and 1958, not only on the Prairies, but elsewhere, including Quebec, since he was removed from the English, Ontario establishment stereotype of the Conservative party. The Liberals, on the other hand, have turned to Ontario and Quebec for their leaders. What has been especially notable about the Liberals has been the alternation between English and French leaders, both the result and partially the cause of Liberal successes in Quebec. All three French leaders whom the party has selected—Wilfrid Laurier, Louis St. Laurent, and Pierre Trudeau—have become Prime Ministers. A mid-1960's survey among MP's predictably showed that English-speaking PC's had very little attraction for the principle of English-French leadership rotation. English Liberals were about evenly divided, but French MP's were enthusiastic. A sample study of delegates to the 1968 Liberal leadership conference indicated that only a minority believed the convention of alternating leaders was necessary, but almost twice as many French as English delegates (45 per cent vs. 24 per cent) favored it. The point is that French Canada, and French political elites, seem to take the prospect of a French Canadian Liberal leader seriously, and even an objectively justified breach in the party's tradition could cause unfavorable electoral reactions.

Based on the record, however, such reactions would probably be minimized by the attitude of succeeding English-speaking Liberal leaders/Prime Ministers. The most successful English Canadian Prime Ministers have provided themselves with able, loyal and influential French Canadian lieutenants. The Conservative Macdonald had such an ally in Sir George Cartier. In the twentieth century, Conservative Prime Ministers and for some time the Liberal Pearson failed to find effective French lieutenants, and they and their party suffered for it. Diefenbaker in particular, after leading his party in 1958 to a resounding success in Quebec, quickly alienated the French. He failed to groom an effective French lieutenant, relegating his French ministers to inconsequential roles, and had no real channels into French Canadian thinking. Mackenzie King's success in Quebec was closely related to his prominent French aides, Ernest Lapointe and, later, Louis St. Laurent.

At the 1967 PC leadership convention, each candidate took pains to offer some remarks in French, and each had a seconding speech made for him by a Quebecker. The incumbent PC leader, Robert Stanfield, has felt obliged to undertake a French language immersion course. Needless to say, all three French Liberal leaders were perfectly bilingual, as much at home in English as in French surroundings, and frequently willing to talk firmly to their own people—as when Trudeau once insisted, in colloquial English, that Quebec's Union Nationale Premier was "off his rocker."

The construction of Australian cabinets carries its own exasperations. Granted that Australian voting patterns do not tend to produce impressive strength for a government party or party group in some states, and a virtual shutout in others; granted too, it is easier to satisfy the representation claims of six than of ten provinces, and for Australia to avoid the wrenching problems faced by Canada's subcultural distinctions; but the Australian House of Representatives, from which most ministers are drawn, has always had considerably fewer members than the House of Commons. Until 1949, the Australian House numbered about 75, and since 1949 has held just over 120—still less than half of Canada's lower chamber. This has made it exceedingly difficult to uncover competent cabinet prospects from the smaller states in particular. The Canadian corrective of finding seats in one province for prospective ministers from another province, while not unknown in Australia, has had less currency. Also, although Australian cabinet building does not need to account for subcultural demands, it must take special care to avoid impressions that one or the other of the two largest states is somehow hogging the cabinet show. A major criticism of the Menzies UAP government in the late 1930's was that it was too Victorian—too Victorian vis-à-vis the country at large, and too Victorian vis-à-vis New South Wales, the largest state and Victoria's perennial rival. The first three postwar Liberal Prime Ministers were Victorians, and they had to proceed with much finesse lest they revive the impression that Liberal govern-

ˌent was of, for, and by Victorians. The problem was complicated by the fact that after the ALP split, the government parties tended to be proportionately much stronger in Victoria than in New South Wales.

Australian federal cabinets face two compositional problems which have no Canadian counterpart—the inclusion of Senators, and of two parties. More will be said about second chambers in a later context. What matters here is that the Australian Senate has traditionally enjoyed a higher status than its Canadian counterpart. It has been an elected body, while the Canadian body has been appointive, until very recently for life tenure. The Australian Senate has been explicitly a party-political chamber, and has wielded a greater influence in national politics. The upshot has been that Canadian cabinets have included only one Senator, or even none, while Senators have comprised up to 20 per cent of Australia's cabinets—five of twenty-six ministers at last count. The Australian practice of Senatorial cabinet membership has enlarged the pool of parliamentarians available for satisfying state representational criteria and, to an extent, of talent, though Senators have tended to be shunted into the outer ministry.

By long understanding, the Country party is entitled to a quarter of the seats in the ministry at large. This recently has meant six of twenty-six seats, but when after the 1969 election Liberal losses brought about a higher ratio of CP MP's within the combined government party group, an additional CP minister was added. Such automatic CP cabinet representation implies direct cabinet spokesmanship for primary industry interests. Apart from shutting out deserving Liberals from ministerial positions, it complicates the task of state balancing in non-Labor governments. The CP caucus itself elects the personalities who will serve in L-CP governments, and a Liberal Prime Minister must then refocus the state representational picture accordingly.

The allocation of cabinet portfolios in Canada and Australia has, in addition to the above considerations, followed certain patterns of matching people of particular backgrounds with particular responsibilities. There is no Australian tradition of reserving certain ministries for persons from specific states, mostly because the states are not all that different in economic structure or population composition. In Canada, provincial and regional dissimilarities have had an effect. Westerners have been favored for Interior/Mines and Resources, Maritimers for the Marine and Fisheries ministry. The economic and financially related ministries have generally gone to Ontarians. Quebec has frequently held the Justice portfolio, partially because a justice minister benefits from understanding the civil code system employed in Quebec. Quebeckers have also disproportionately held the Works and postal portfolios, in part because of the patronage available for dispensation to a province where concrete favors have counted for much. It can be argued that Quebec French Canadians have until very recently suffered some discrimination in portfolio awards. But it is also unfortunately true that the quality of Quebec ministers has sometimes not been of high order, or that their sometimes imperfect English has handicapped them in their dealings with cabinet colleagues, interest groups, or the bureaucrats, or that in fact the senior, English-dominated bureaucracy was inclined to snub them. Thus, although several French Canadians have become Prime Ministers and Quebec has had adequate representation and spokesmanship in cabinets, their absence from key ministries has limited their impact in certain major policy areas.

The Country party's position in Australian federal cabinets has been decidedly different. CP leaders have not been Prime Ministers, except on a brief and interim basis, but they have normally held the title of Deputy Prime Minister. More importantly, CP ministers have held strategic economic portfolios. For many years CP leaders Page and Fadden controlled the Treasury, the central economic ministry. More recently the Treasury has been in Liberal hands, but other key positions have been in the Country party's domain. In the thirteen-person inner cabinet of the McMahon ministry organized in 1971, the three CP portfolios were Trade and Industry, Primary Industry, and Shipping and Transport. The titles of the CP controlled ministries do not in themselves fully convey their importance. Urban centers with glaring road and highway needs have had to contend with CP Shipping and Transport ministers whose priorities have been rural roads. In 1957, when McEwen negotiated a trade agreement with Japan, his own Department of Trade and Industry assumed a dominant voice in Australian-Japanese relations generally. Not until 1971, after McEwen's retirement, was this anomaly removed, and responsibility for relations with Japan shifted to the Department of Foreign Affairs.

The presence of the CP in coalition governments has made Liberal dominated government possible. But the personal authority of the CP leader, the number and character of CP cabinet portfolios, and the fact that CP ministers feel as much responsible to their own party as to joint cabinet decisions, have made for uneasy relations within non-Labor governments. In many instances when vital CP policy interests are at stake, the Liberals are inclined to yield. Decisions in cabinet usually are taken on a consensus basis, not by counting of votes which could range Liberal majorities against CP minorities. The personalities of Liberal prime ministers are naturally important in determining the smoothness with which coalition governments are managed. Before the second World War Menzies had very poor relations with Page and the CP; at one point, the CP withdrew from the government, contributing to events which eventually returned Labor to office. When Menzies regained power in 1949, he made greater efforts to accommodate and conciliate his Country party allies.

The Prime Ministerial office

The prime ministership in the Canadian and Australian political systems is an office of pre-eminent importance. The incumbent of that office is the leader of his party, a figure whose personal image can influence electoral choices, the chief coordinator of government departments and other agencies, and the dominant force within cabinets. His personal sway as the head of government has in recent years been enhanced in both countries through his utilization of personal staffs and other mechanisms. This has not happened simply because Prime Ministers have thirsted for added political power. It has come about because Prime Ministers have felt the need for sources of information independent of the bureaucracy and the numerous ministerial colleagues who surround them, and because of a need to assume tighter control over the vast administrative complex. Relatedly, although they ordinarily trust and even admire their cabinet associates, Prime Ministers have sought the advice of intimates, or of a specialized staff of officials.

The tendency has become more widespread in Canada than in Australia, particularly under Trudeau. The Canadian Prime Minister has two offices working directly under him, the Prime Minister's Office, which is his personal political arm, and the Privy Council Office, which is his agency for overseeing the federal administration. Not only have the staffs of these offices been greatly enlarged, but so have their responsibilities. The Prime Minister can now avail himself of more opportunities for independent, highly professionalized, nonline departmental counsel, with staffs which broadly replicate the subject matter of standard ministries. He has persons and committees who can troubleshoot with considerable latitude, and much more emphasis than before has been placed on intermediate and long-term policy planning. Within the Prime Minister's Office, Trudeau created a set of regional desks, largely to keep in closer touch with Liberal party matters throughout Canada.

Trudeau's approach did not receive a universal welcome. Some of his ministers, as well as senior civil servants, complained about the breakdown of established and, they believed, sensible channels of communication and decision-making. Trudeau's Transport Minister resigned in 1969, charging that a task force report on housing, carefully prepared under his supervision, had been downgraded by the Prime Minister. In the same year, a comprehensive review of Canada's NATO ties was ordered. The Liberal caucus, a parliamentary committee report, and the reports of an interdepartmental civil service task force all argued that the existing level of troop commitment should be maintained. Cabinet itself was divided, though both the External Affairs and the Defense ministers leaned toward preserving the status quo. Two other briefs were placed in Trudeau's hands—one from the president of the Privy Council, the other from the Prime Minister's personal staff. It was the last report, advising a reduction of Canada's NATO troop strength by half, which was adopted by Trudeau, and became policy.

Australian Prime Ministers have long relied on the Prime Minister's Department, both for housekeeping purposes and for the initiation of fresh ideas. The department's influence was raised by a succession of powerful secretaries and, as in Canada, the presence of subject matter branches in miniature. In 1968 Gorton split the department in two, concentrating policy and advisory functions in one, and relegating administrative and housekeeping tasks to the other. In 1971, McMahon undertook further revisions, creating a Department of the Prime Minister and Cabinet, and a Department of the Vice-President of the Executive Council—very roughly equivalent to the Canadian Prime Minister's and Privy Council offices, respectively, and confirming the tendency toward independent channels of information and advice, and the streamlining of control over the administration. Overpersonalized prime ministerial decision-making can rebound, as Gorton discovered. One of his most publicized procedural errors was committed in 1969. Gorton allowed a highly controversial foreign policy statement to be hammered out by the cozy threesome of the Minister for External Affairs, the Secretary of the External Affairs Department (as it was then known), and himself. Cabinet had no chance to study the document before its presentation, the Defense Minister was upset, McEwen was upset, and after all had been said and done the policy statement proved to be politically embarrassing.

12

Parliaments, parliamentarians, and the policy process

Parliamentary influence on public policy can be approached from two general directions. The first is the degree to which parliamentary majorities can maintain the solidarity needed to underwrite measures submitted by cabinets. The second is the degree to which parliamentarians, whether of government or of opposition parties, are sufficiently inclined and organized to make some contribution to the finished product of policy, to keep governments alert and responsive, or to perform a broad, educative role. In this regard, we will need to review the roles of both lower and upper legislative chambers, and of parliamentary committees.

Parliamentary party cohesion and policy outcomes

Australian and Canadian federal governments have on occasion been defeated on the parliamentary floor, but in most such instances the adverse vote has been on a relatively minor issue, or has been quickly reversed. When their survival has been at stake, they have almost invariably won. This has been the record despite the absence of a neat two party system in either country, the Australian parties' inclination toward schism, and the frequency of minority governments in Canada. Since the crystallization of the party system at the close of World War I, Australian governments have resigned three times due to loss of parliamentary confidence, in 1929, in 1931, and in 1941. Governments in Ottawa have lost only twice, in 1926 and in 1963. The two Canadian defeats both befell minority governments. The 1929 and 1931 Australian defeats were, to be sure, attributable to a breakup within governing parties, but the margins of defeat in the House of Representatives were only one and five, respectively. The 1941 defeat, by three votes, resulted from the defection of independent members who had previously supported the government. Stated another way, only twice in modern Australian experience and never in Canada has a federal party, or coalition, when governing with an absolute majority, ever faced a breach of its followers' discipline sufficient to force it out of office.

Various institutional and party-political explanations underlie this record of stability. In general terms, it should be remembered that the parliamentary form of government itself inhibits careless or undisciplined voting. Breaches of governing party discipline at minimum imply grave political embarrassment to the ruling party, and can bring its overturn from office and the substitution of an opposition party, with or without benefit of a fresh election. The individual parliamentarian stands to lose much if he votes disloyally. If he and his fellow insubordinates cause a government to crash, a new election could bring their own personal defeat, and perhaps political eclipse. Whether or not a parliamentarian's voting deviation contributes to the defeat of cabinet-sponsored legislation or policy, and a possible government resignation, such behavior may occasion various sanctions against him. He may become ostracized by his party associates. He may forfeit opportunity for future promotion to ministerial position. He may find that his ability to perform favors and services for his constituents is impeded. He may discover that the party refuses to supply him with customary organizational and financial resources should he seek re-election. Or, he may be expelled from his party's caucus, or from the party at large, or denied his party's renomination. These, among other more situational constraints, have served to maintain a high level of orthodoxy and parliamentary voting in Canada and Australia.

Generally speaking, the narrower the parliamentary majority, the less likely is indiscipline to appear, since the government then cannot afford to sacrifice even a few votes without jeopardizing its desired legislation, or its life. From this standpoint, both Canada and Australia have undergone circumstances which have placed a premium on majority party solidarity. Canada has gone through a number of minority governments, both Liberal and Conservative, situations which dictated intense discipline among government supporters. The Australian experience with minority government has been more rare. However, for half a century the House of Representatives was an exceptionally small body, and even after its enlargement in 1949 it still was numerically modest, with no more than 125 seats during the post-1949 period. In a very small chamber, majorities can become razor thin. In the 1961 election, the L-CP government was returned with a majority of two, and in 1969 with a majority of seven. Under such conditions discipline counts for a great deal. It should be added that many Australian state and Canadian provincial parliaments are themselves diminutive. Prince Edward Island has 32 members, Tasmania 35, Newfoundland 42, and so on. Only the more populous subnational units have parliaments on a scale of seats which permits governments to operate with reasonable margins of safety. Ontario's provincial parliament, Canada's largest, has 117 members; the New South Wales state parliament, Australia's largest, has 94. The prospect of majority party defections is reduced in small parliaments in still another way. In the smaller state and provincial parliaments, ministers may comprise a third to half of the ruling parliamentary majority. Since ministers are considerably less apt to defect than are backbenchers, the likelihood of majority party defection decreases.

Coalitions are ordinarily more susceptible to dissension and instability than are one-party governments, simply because within them two or more political orientations are attempting to coexist. Coalitions have been relatively rare in the Canadian provinces and, with one very special exception during the first World War, unknown in Ottawa. They have been standard fare in Australia even after the party system gelled, with Liberal-Country party governments the rule in the states and federally when Labor has been out of office. We have already seen that these two non-Labor parties are in fact quite distinctive, and that relations between them have often been strained. Still, apart from a few instances, such as their peculiarly deep hostility in Victorian state politics and a few years of undisguised coolness federally in the 1930's, they have managed to coexist, and to avoid a breakup when in power. One solidifying factor has been that their mutual hostility toward Labor has outweighed their own differences. Another has been that neither the CP nor the Liberals can, in most states or federally, expect to form a majority government alone. Since the ALP is a sworn opponent of coalitions, the CP cannot expect to strike an alliance with Labor should it have cause to abandon the Liberals. More specifically, it is customary, at least in Canberra, for a set of policy undertakings to be drawn up before a new L-CP government goes into action, thus reducing the prospects of misunderstanding later on. Indeed, when the CP joined the Menzies ministry in 1940, it was understood that CP ministers, and the party, be exempt from supporting the establishment of an automobile industry, a measure favored by Menzies' UAP. Since both in the states and federally CP leaders are traditionally strong figures and command loyalty from party parliamentarians, CP defection from measures sponsored by coalition cabinets is further minimized.

Parties of the left are in special ways vulnerable to breaches of parliamentary discipline. For one thing, they embody a set of reformist ideals which are less expendable to compromise and expediency than are the less doctrinaire outlooks of moderate/conservative parties. There are, for example, data indicating that NDP federal parliamentarians—despite not being Wafflers—had stronger ideological motives for entering Parliament than did Liberal or PC members. The point is that idealist/ideological supporters of a left government would take particular umbrage at cabinet efforts to produce window dressing reform measures. Conversely, left/socialist parties are quite emphatically expected to adhere to officially authorized policies, and to stand by the movement's traditions of solidarity. There is a very long ALP tradition of a "pledge" signed by party members of state and federal parliamentary caucuses that they will vote according to caucus majority decisions (which in turn are presumed to reflect standing party policy), their private conscience notwithstanding. Such prescriptions can serve to drive restless parliamentarians straight out of the party, since there is little allowance for selective heterodoxy. This is what happened when Labor governments fell apart during World War I and during the Depression; ministers and backbenchers alike fundamentally disagreed with caucus and felt they had no option but to leave the parent party entirely. Tact and sensitivity are critically important traits for left party government leaders if they intend to keep their followers united and peaceful. By and large, Saskatchewan Premier T. C. Douglas and ALP Prime Ministers Chifley and Curtin had such qualities in abundance, and applied them successfully.

There is less ideological spirit among the moderate/conservative parties—the two Liberal parties and the Canadian Conservatives. For instance, a 1966 study of Liberal backbenchers in the Australian federal party failed to uncover any distinctive ideological wings, and showed that consensus among them was both present and valued for itself. Breaches of parliamentary discipline have, however, occurred among the Australian and Canadian moderate parties, just as they have appeared, and will continue to do so, among all parties. The Bruce-Page government fell in Canberra in 1929 when several Nationalist party supporters deserted their own government. More commonly, the outcome of parliamentary indiscipline has been considerably less dramatic. In 1969, for instance, a number of Canadian Liberal backbenchers representing metropolitan ridings were sharply critical of the Trudeau government's urban policy. One Liberal resigned from the party altogether, and only a minority of Toronto Liberals bothered to appear for a vote in the Commons, but the government's safety was never in doubt. As previously suggested, the parliamentary system itself serves to inhibit lax discipline.

But when divisive French-English issues are at stake, Canadian parliamentary discipline, on both the government and the opposition side, has a decided tendency to break down. Here, in its parliamentary manifestation, is evidence of the pervasive political import of Canada's uneasy cultural dualism. Being part of a national minority, and one with a sense of historical injury, French Canadian parliamentarians are the ones whose votes are most inclined to separate from their party, and from the government, when a fundamental issue arises. Surveys of federal parliamentarians have shown that French Canadians much more than English Canadians have a self-perceived obligation to play out a political role based on their cultural identity. Also, in a hypothetical situation necessitating a choice between party loyalty and constituents' wishes, the French are considerably more disposed to opt for their electors. The more sensitive Prime Ministers have, by tactics of delay, conciliation, and compromise, been able to keep the English and French wings of their parties reasonably united. Nonetheless, Prime Ministers of various temperaments have found some issues too brittle, and have been unable to forestall parliamentary defections. During the second World War, Prime Minister Mackenzie King temporized as long as he possibly could to avoid shipping conscripts overseas. When pressures from English Canada and the military itself became oppressive, he did so. His government easily survived a vote of confidence, since the Conservative opposition favored the step, but 34 of Quebec's Liberals voted against him. In 1946, a parliamentary committee recommended the adoption of a new and distinctive Canadian flag design, but with the Union Jack emblem retained. A delegation of French Canadian Liberals met with King, and advised him they would resign from the party if the government moved to adopt such a flag. The issue of a distinctive Canadian flag was not revived until the 1960's, by Pearson's government—which allowed a free vote to its Liberal followers, and eventually refused to make the parliamentary vote a matter of government confidence. Opposition leader Diefenbaker and many of his PC supporters felt that the final flag design, divested of all British or French symbols, was a betrayal of Canada's heritage. But the knot of French Canadian Conservatives openly broke with the party leader. In 1969, the Trudeau Liberal government had little difficulty in marshaling its forces to support its Official Languages Bill, which enshrined English and French as equal languages. But the PC party, dominantly English, voted 41 in favor and 17 against, with 14 abstentions. Sixteen of the 17 defectors, led by ex-PC leader Diefenbaker, were from the Prairies, traditionally the most anti-French portion of the country.

Parliamentary second chambers and government programs

So far, our attention has been fixed on the ability of governments to extract loyalty and policy endorsement from lower chambers. By long tradition, derived from British practice, Canadian and Australian ministries have been responsible only to the lower houses, and it is there that their survival or destruction has been officially determined. But both national parliaments are bicameral, Quebec had a second chamber until the late 1960's, and five of Australia's states continue to operate bicameral parliaments. Since, for practical purpose, legislative enactments in Canadian and Australian bicameral settings require the consent of both houses, it is necessary to examine to what extent, and why, second houses have tation than is true in House elections. The Canadian Senate, reflecting the less egalitarian biases in the nation's cultural and political makeup, has never, in any sense, been "representative." Its members are appointed by the government of the day until the age of 75, a retirement age set in 1965. The overwhelming tendency for both Liberal and Conservative Prime Ministers has been to confine senatorial appointments to persons of their own party. Appointments have usually been a form of patronage for party donors, for retired, electorally unsuccessful, or burned out federal or provincial politicians. In announcing eight appointments to Senate vacancies in 1970, Trudeau registered some break with tradition. In addition to picking some Liberal loyalists, he nominated persons with creative professional careers in such areas as the trade-union movement and academia. He also selected a former Social Credit premier of Alberta, and a Quebec woman identified with women's rights movements and the CCF/NDP. Even so, then as before, the Canadian Senate retained its essential character. There now was one Social Crediter and an NDP follower, but the Liberal contingent enjoyed a 3 to 1 majority in the chamber. Liberal governments have appointed Liberals, Conservative governments Conservatives. Since from the first World War the Liberals have governed far more years than the Conservatives, they have had far more opportunities to fill Senate vacancies, and therefore to create what from 1942 became a continuous and, gradually, an inordinately lopsided Senate Liberal majority.

Cabinet legislative programs have not been seriously threatened by rejection or emasculation when party majorities in the two houses of the Canadian and Australian parliaments have been congruent. In Australia, the constraints of party discipline cover elected Senators as well as House members. Senators have a vested interest in avoiding political embarrassment for governments of their own party. Holding elective office, they must be sensitive to such sanctions as caucus or party expulsion, being pegged so far down the party senatorial list under the proportional representation system that they have no chance of re-election, or being denied renomination altogether. About 20 per cent of government ministers normally are taken from the Senate. The incentive for ministerial appointment therefore helps to fortify discipline, as does the very presence of several government ministers within the Senate chamber itself. As a Senate committee itself noted in 1950, seldom do progovernment Senate majorities overlook their partisan interests, rising up as independently minded critics of the House, or as staunch defenders of state interests. One can merely say that exceptions prove the rule. One such exception occurred in 1939, when the Menzies government passed a gold-tax bill in the House. There was a slight government majority in the Senate at the time. Western Australian senators objected that the measure would retard the expansion of the gold mining industry in their state. All three Western Australian ALP senators voted against the bill, and were joined by two government senators. The third government senator, a minister, did vote in favor, but the bill was defeated. Canada's senators, irremovable except by reaching the age limit, harbor no apprehensions about losing out on nominations and election. Also, since recent cabinets have included no more than one senator, there is no patronage motive to keep senators on steady, disciplined behavior. No effort at strict party line enforcement is made, and formal floor divisions are few. Amendments, sometimes significant, have been insisted upon by the Canadian Senate when party majorities in the two parliamentary chambers have been complementary, though outward rejection of government bills in such circumstances is nearly unheard of. For instance, of the 282 bills considered by the Senate when during 1930–35 there were Conservative majorities in both chambers, only two were rejected; of the 773 bills considered by the Senate from 1942 to 1957, when the Liberals controlled both chambers, no bill was refused by the Senate. The presently overwhelming Liberal majority in the Senate means that deviation by even a fair number of senators from the prescribed government line can hardly affect the outcome, and the essentials of cabinet policy survive Senate handling.

When the party composition of ruling ministries and senatorial party majorities differ, a different set of relationships can be expected. In theory, contemporary Canadian Conservative governments are helpless before the Senate, because it overflows with Liberals, and enjoys vast constitutional authority. Furthermore, the available deadlock breaking procedure outlined in the BNA Act is de facto a dead letter. In the event of a House-Senate deadlock, the government may enlarge the Senate, but only by four, or by eight, additional senators. Such an increment of Conservatives is far too slight to overcome an inflated, opposite-party majority. In all of Canada's history, this device of "miniswamping" has never been invoked. But theory and practice have not been the same. Canada's Senate, as a body, has for a very considerable time been acutely conscious of its anomalous status in an otherwise popularly representative and responsible political system. One constraint has been the practical view that stubborn and recurrent partisanship could hasten the Senate's abolition, or basic reconstruction. Were this to happen, senators would lose their sinecures, and governments the opportunity to reward the party faithful. Also, the Senate's numerous though unspectacular contributions to policy shaping would be endangered. Blatant partisanship is not, at all events, the style of the secure and often elderly men, and a few women, who gather in the ornate Senate chamber. The incidence of amendments to government bills by Senate majorities unlike those in the House has been much the same as when House-Senate majorities have been congruent. There has been a higher incidence of outward rejection under noncongruent than under congruent majorities, but only slightly so. In 1961, in a rare exhibition of closely drawn party-line voting, the Liberal-dominated Senate resisted two bills which were sponsored by a Conservative government then basking in a nearly 4 to 1 Commons majority. This acutely disturbed Diefenbaker and raised a fascinating controversy over constitutional propriety, particularly since one of the bills dealt with revenues. True, the Senate was unyielding, and rolled out some quite old fashioned constitutional arguments about its prerogative to oppose. But its opposition to both measures was not really an attack upon a government's right to enact its basic legislative program, but a rebuff to the serious procedural improprieties contained in the legislation itself.

In Australia, by comparison, with a Senate much more confident of its representative character and with party lines closely observed, there have been major confrontations when governments have faced hostile Senate majorities. When a Labor government officiated during the early years of the Depression, the non-Labor Senate repeatedly scuttled bills, either by outward rejection or, more frequently, by insisting upon amendments which were unacceptable to the government. It also prevented the government from staging a constitutional amendment referendum. Ironically, the amendment's intention was to allow future constitutional amendments to pass if absolute majorities of both Houses concurred; the referendum procedure would have been scrapped. The double dissolution mechanism for breaking deadlocks can be construed in different ways. The procedure has been invoked twice, by a labor government in 1914, and by an L-CP government in 1951. Both times the disputed legislation was of quite basic importance (respectively, preference for unionists in Commonwealth employment, and a banking bill), indicating that on those occasions the Senate had the fortitude to confront the government. Both times the ensuing election produced complementary House and Senate majorities. Nongovernment Senate majorities are mindful that a double dissolution in Australian federal politics is no piece of rarified theory. The real prospect of losing a specially called election can in itself deter a nongovernment controlled Senate from overstepping itself although, of course, a government unsure of its own public popularity may wish to avoid a head-on clash with a hostile Senate, and the march toward a double dissolution.

The absence of either an L-CP or a Labor Senate majority in recent years has produced a situation in which the DLP and a few independents have been able to compel shifts in government policy, but have stopped short of forcing a deadlock, and precipitating a double dissolution which would be inconvenient to both the DLP and the government parties. Apart from exercising an important review and oversight function, the DLP senators have brought about policy alterations. On one occasion, they pushed the government into legislating stringent penalties for the collection of funds for the Vietcong or North Vietnam. On another occasion, they teamed up with Labor to force withdrawal of some highly distasteful methods of dealing with draft resisters. In 1970, DLP and ALP senators combined to defeat five related government bills dealing with receipts tax collection. A second negative Senate action on these measures could have elicited a constitutionally defined deadlock. Labor was at that time electorally very self-confident. It did not suit either the government or the DLP to risk simultaneous House and Senate elections. An L-CP–DLP deal was worked out; the government reintroduced the five bills, but in different form and not as part of the budget proper. The bills lost again in the Senate, as expected, but the double dissolution prospect had been conveniently skirted.

The fitness of parliaments as scrutinizers and refiners of policy

Canadian and Australian governments can usually depend on being able to enact their chosen legislative programs. Even so, the public policy role of the two national parliaments cannot simplistically be characterized as the rubberstamping of government legislation by parliamentary majorities, or as the futile efforts of oppositions to defeat it. Parliamentarians, whether or not of the government party, engage in a variety of functions. These include policy criticism and refinement, identification of and research on matters of public concern which may in time be translated into public policy, compelling the government to explain and justify itself in open view, and sensitizing the public to the relative merits and respective alternatives offered by various parties.

We may first inquire whether Canadian and Australian parliamentarians are personally well equipped to carry out roles of criticism and policy refinement. Canada's electoral politics are more fluid than Australia's, and there are proportionately more marginal lower house seats. With lower chamber membership turnover greater in Ottawa than in Canberra, Australian parliamentarians, enjoying greater electoral security, compile more continuous experience. Australian and Canadian senators both tend toward long service and experience. The former are elected for six year terms, and are electorally protected if their names appear high on their party's proportional representation list. Canadian senators, despite the common practice of appointment in middle age or beyond, long held life tenure, and now may stay on until age 75. When Australian House personnel are grouped together, they represent a wider spectrum of occupational backgrounds than Canadian parliamentarians. Australian parliamentarians represent a better balance of working-class, artisan, small and medium business, rural industry, and professional origins than the middle-upper and middle class Canadian parliamentary contingent which also stresses legal training. Other facts being equal, this would suggest a more varied and informed set of inputs available to the Australian Parliament for purpose of criticism, exposition, and policy refinement.

On the other hand, a larger proportion of Canadian Commons than Australian House and Senate members is recruited from among individuals with prior provincial/state or local elective office. The Canadian Senate, despite its reputation as a repository of political cronies, has always had a remarkable number of politically educated persons, among them former provincial and federal parliamentarians and even ministers. Finally, although Australian parliamentarians may boast a wider spread of backgrounds, Canadian parliamentarians have, as a group, been consistently better educated. The Australian Parliament's membership among both major party groups is becoming increasingly educated. There are now several Ph.D.'s and a number of medical doctors, for example. Nonetheless, compared with the House of Commons members, of whom two-thirds and above have undergone tertiary education, the Australian record has been slim. In 1940, for example, only 10 of 75 House and one of 36 Senate members were university graduates. As of 1967, university degrees were held by about a quarter of the House and a fifth of the Senate membership. It should also be noted that a disproportionate number of Australia's university trained parliamentarians have been drawn into ministerial positions, further depleting the supply of educated backbenchers.

Their occupational and educational backgrounds apart, however, private (that is, nonministerial) members on both sides of legislative chambers, in both countries, are greatly disadvantaged in discharging their various roles because cabinets have infinitely more access to information. Only in the past few years have Australian and Canadian parliamentarians been accorded reasonable facilities for compiling material. There is now a legislative reference service attached to the parliamentary library in Canberra. Although it is widely used, its staff and resources are modest. The Trudeau government, however, authorized a special staff of 70 to serve parliamentarians and parliamentary committees, as well as authorizing fairly handsome sums of money for research use by nongovernment party leaders, and for Liberal backbenchers themselves.

The meaningfulness and impact of parliamentarians' work also depends on the extent to which they are able to organize themselves, whether their party does or does not serve in government.

All Australian and Canadian parliamentary parties are organized into caucuses. The two main Canadian parties, and especially the Liberals, have established regional and provincial caucuses as well. To a degree, this arrangement provides for a sharper articulation and enhancement of regional/provincial spokesmanship within party circles, and in Parliament at large. The Liberal Quebec caucus has long exerted an influence on Liberal governments.

Among the major parties in the two systems, the ALP has had the most influential caucus. It is organized into subject matter committees and, of course, is the principal parliamentary source for setting party policy. The comparison with the two Liberal parties is striking. Partially because of years in government and a succession of powerful Prime Ministers, ending with the ill-starred John Gorton, Australian Liberal backbenchers remained weakly organized and tepid in influence over government policy. In 1971, with sentiment for a change running high, McMahon promised that the party's backbenchers could strengthen their committee structure, would be encouraged to study the operation of government departments, and would henceforth have prospective cabinet legislation presented to them for review and comment before it was formally introduced in Parliament. This arrangement had previously been used with considerable success by the Victorian state Liberal party, and on a more limited basis by New South Wales and Queensland Liberals. The Canadian Liberals also made changes, in 1969–70, to resuscitate an otherwise flabby caucus. As in Australia, the Liberal government promised to submit outlines of legislation before, rather than after, final cabinet consideration. Caucus committees were to be encouraged, and the caucus chairman would henceforth be elected by caucus itself, rather than being nominated by the party leader.

Another perspective on parliamentarians' potential for performing useful and informed roles is the organization and style of parliamentary business. By and large, the cards have been stacked against oppositions, and against private members generally. The

Speaker, as the presiding officer of the two lower chambers, enjoys substantial authority in determining how debates are conducted. Speakers' rulings can determine whether nonministers, and the opposition in particular, will have ample and fair opportunity to be heard, and to force the government to account for its behavior. In both systems, until very recently, speakers combined partisan positions with their duties as parliamentary umpires. They were party men, elected to their office by the parliamentary majority. Their rulings were frequently subject to challenge by oppositions, and during elections they fought their seats under a party label against competing party candidates. In Australia, no particular effort has been made to nominate speakers known for their subdued sense partisanship. Within certain limits, speakers are tacitly expected to assist the government and the party in power. When a government crisis broke in 1929, the presiding Speaker was instructed to cast his vote with the government on a vital division. His refusal caused him to be denounced in his own electorate, and he was defeated in the ensuing election.

In 1956, the Canadian Liberal government was intent on pushing a controversial natural gas pipeline bill through the Commons. In the chair was a Speaker of French extraction, Canadian practice being that the position should alternate between French and English persons. The Speaker promised the opposition parties time to deal with a special issue that had grown out of the Commons debate. Then, under pressure from the government, which wished to expedite the bill, the Speaker reversed himself. Pandemonium broke loose in the already charged atmosphere of the House. Imputations of dictatorial partiality were leveled against the Speaker, and a motion of censure was raised against him. The Speaker then wrote an indiscreet letter to a newspaper, charging his parliamentary critics with having falsified the facts for their own political ends. The opposition returned to the attack, and the Speaker tendered his resignation. English-speaking cabinet members urged that the resignation be accepted. French ministers and backbenchers insisted he must be spared such a humiliation. Much of Quebec's French press also rallied to his side, claiming that he was being used as a scapegoat by English parliamentarians. Eventually, Prime Minister St. Laurent issued a lame statement, in effect exonerating the Speaker and preserving him in his position. After 1956, the speakership regained dignity. In 1968, on the basis of a multiparty understanding, the highly respected incumbent Liberal Speaker stood for re-election in his riding unopposed; only an NDP candidate broke the pledge. It would appear that the partisan tradition of the Canadian speakership is dying out, with the result that parliamentarians of all parties will face fewer privations and inconveniences in exercising roles of criticism and review.

Parliamentary procedure can also affect private member contributions. It can be argued that the government's own convenience should usually determine parliamentary procedural ground rules, since it is the government whose responsibility it is to formulate and secure the enactment of public policies. Still, while governments are meant to govern, they cannot arrogantly assume a monopoly of wisdom, or be allowed to lose sight of their own party's, or for that matter the public, constituency. For parliamentary oppositions, of course, there is the partisan objective of probing weaknesses and inconsistencies, and hoping to alter the public image of who in fact is most fit to govern.

The lower houses in both nations provide spokesmanship roles for private members through debates and through questions which ministers answer orally and on the spot, or later in written form. Perhaps the House of Commons has been somewhat better able than the House of Representatives to serve as overseer, critic, and amender. The Commons has always been a much larger chamber, and there have therefore been more voices to fulfill such roles. This was particularly true when the Australian lower house numbered only 75 or so, and the absorption of numerous members into the cabinet left very few private members. However, Canada's cabinets draw their membership almost exclusively from the lower house;

Canadian ministries are slightly larger than the Australian; Trudeau took to appointing a very large number of parliamentary secretaries, from whom party orthodoxy is expected nearly as much as from ministers themselves. Furthermore, the Commons has regularly spent far more time in session than the House of Representatives. The Commons has averaged about 160 sitting days over a twelve-month period, but in recent years has gone as high as 250. The Australian House will ordinarily sit for 65–75 days annually in a nonelection year, and 50 days in election years. In 1970, pleading a heavy legislative agenda, the L-CP government won consent to reorder the schedule of sitting days; even so, the House managed to sit for only 73 days in that entire year. Taken by itself, this considerable disparity in time spent in session suggests that Canadian parliamentarians have more opportunities to carry out their roles.

The mood of parliamentary business in Australia has, if anything, become increasingly counterproductive for reasonable dialogue among reasonable men. Accusing the government of callousness, the Labor opposition in the early 1970's more and more resorted to urgency motions, divisions of the House, and raising elaborate questions on notice. Claiming the opposition to be obstructionist, the government more and more resorted to the imposition of closure, and to referring questioners to source materials, rather than itself producing answers.

The Canadian House has not been as acrimonious over procedures. The pipeline bill debate notwithstanding, when the government shut off debate amid anguished protests, closure has been rarely invoked. By the mid-1960's, the number of sittings had become considerable, and a portion of the time spent in floor deliberations was being wasted. The volume of business was heavy, debate proceeded at a leisurely pace, and challenges against speakers' rulings were frequent. A new set of parliamentary procedures for streamlining business was therefore adopted in the late 1960's. The new rules were a compromise, designed to accord opposition parties an adequate hearing, while expediting legislative business. For instance, 25 days per session were specially set aside for the opposition to discuss whatever it pleased. On the other hand, closure rules were tightened, and restrictions were imposed on appeals to the House on rules-of-order challenges.

The long-term results of the new Commons rules are not yet available. In the meantime, some observers are disturbed because absenteeism from Commons sessions has increased somewhat over the years, and averaged 38 per cent in the 1970–71 session. But the floor of a legislative chamber, whatever its internal procedures, is not necessarily the most promising site for the exercise of parliamentary initiatives of criticism, oversight, issue crystallization, and the refinement of government legislation. We still need to examine the role played by parliamentary committees, and the extent to which they have or might become a counterbalance to cabinet independence.

The position of parliamentary committees

Two basic types of parliamentary committees can be identified—select and standing. Both select and standing committees may be joint ventures, containing members from both houses or, far more frequently, confined to members of one house. Select committees are organized to examine a particular problem at a particular time, and are dissolved when the job is done. Standing committees are continuing bodies, regardless of the volume of business they transact. The standing committee structure in the two national parliaments has undergone considerable modification in the very recent past. Joint standing committees have remained few in number, and generally concerned with housekeeping functions or substantively minor subjects. The Australian Parliament does, however, include joint committees on foreign affairs, the Australian Capital Territory, public works, and public accounts, the last two having been established by statute as far back as 1913. Standing committees in the House of Representatives have been limited to housekeeping duties, such as the library, and standing orders. Likewise, apart from a committee on regulations and ordinances (statutory instruments), standing committees in the Australian Senate amounted to very little until fundamental changes occurred in 1970 and 1971. By 1971, the Senate had authorized the creation of standing committees representing the full spectrum of policy areas. The Canadian Senate has for a great many years housed standing committees responsible for a wide range of substantive topics. Commons standing committees are no novelty either, but the system underwent major reconstruction in the late 1960's in conjunction with changes in Commons procedures. The number of committees was increased to eighteen, and membership on each brought down to a manageable level, twenty in most cases.

So much for descriptive background. Our interest lies in examining the capabilities of the committee system for the exposition, review, criticism, and amendment of policy. In this regard, the attitudes of governments and of parliamentarians toward committee roles are central. Governments tend to harbor suspicions of powerful and independently minded committees, even when their parliamentary majorities are clear and secure. They do not wish to have their pre-eminence in policy-making usurped, or their legislative programs potentially diluted by inconvenient amendments, or to be subjected to embarrassingly searching criticism. They are wary of institutionalized committee forums through which serving government members might acquire excessively independent habits, or serving opposition members acquire publicity for their antigovernment expositions. On the other hand, a committee system whose powers are subject to prescribed limitations can be advantageous to governments. It can calm restless parliamentarians who otherwise feel isolated and neglected. It can help to obviate criticisms that governments are arbitrary and dictatorial. If properly organized, a functioning committee system can streamline the legislative process at large, relieving the legislature as such of tiresome and inefficient activity. Also, within limits, it can serve as a source of reasonable ideas which can improve legislation without actually emasculating it, and/or make legislation more palatable to the governing party, or certain organized interests, or whatever.

Parliamentarians themselves should not necessarily be expected to embrace the prospect of an elaborate committee network. Through party caucuses or informal means they may already enjoy adequate access to the parliamentary leadership. If of the government party, they may be fearful, like governments themselves, that committees can evolve into a sounding board for the opposition. Some parliamentarians may frankly be too lazy to relish committee service. Or, intraparty and leadership traditions may be such that parliamentarians are conditioned to follow instructions, rather than to insist on sharing influence. For example, although there have been several persistent Liberal champions of a meaningful committee system in the Australian House, the Liberal caucus in 1967 overwhelmingly expressed satisfaction with the status quo. Still, parliamentarians may wish to put their interests and talents to work through committee vehicles, and to have a hand in the policy process, be it for idealistic or partisan motives.

Reluctance to expand the standing-committee system has been stronger in Australia than in Canada. So far as the two lower houses are concerned, a partial explanation may lie in the fact that the small House of Representatives has been able to function without a committee system in a way that the much larger House of Commons has not. Recent alterations in Commons committees, and the promise of sending bills to committees as a matter of course, were made with an eye to unburdening and streamlining House business. Detailed estimates debates, previously concentrated in the committee of the whole (the entire chamber), were choking the House. Even so, all Commons committees have government party majorities, and all save the one on public accounts are chaired by a government member. The new committee on statutory instruments, which deals with sensitive matters of delegated legislation, operates under circumscribed terms of reference.

Australian-Canadian differences in attitude toward standing committee systems in lower chambers are also reflected in party-political terms. The ALP has not governed federally in Australia for many years. When it did govern, it did not choose to install an elaborate committee arrangement. In part, the explanation may be mechanical. When Labor last governed, the House of Representatives was much smaller than it is now, and the volume and complexity of legislative business was not as great. A somewhat more political explanation might be that on the last two occasions when it exercised power, during the Depression and during and immediately following the second World War, the party was too absorbed in high pressure concerns to toy with parliamentary reform. It can also be surmised that the ALP, with its paraphernalia of extraparliamentary decision-making authorities, collective caucus decisions, and attention to party discipline, regarded the fractionalization of policy-making inherent in strong committee arrangements as uncongenial. L-CP governments have not operated under constraints such as these. But their skepticisms toward allowing a meaningful committee system may also be understandable. There is a legacy of splits among the present Liberal party's loosely knit predecessor parties, which possibly raises caution about offering influence opportunities to present day parliamentarians. Also, L-CP antagonism toward Labor, and Labor doctrines, is more apparent than the intensity of feelings between and among Canada's parties, thus deterring the L-CP from "legitimizing" Labor by according it committee platforms.

Finally, while the CP, the PC, and the two Liberal parties all have traditions of deference to leaders, the tendency has become somewhat firmer among Australia's non-Labor parties. In Canada, Mackenzie King and St. Laurent were on top of their party, but essentially were accommodationists, as perhaps the most successful

Prime Ministers in a highly variegated Canadian political setting must be, and were hardly renowned for personal flair. Diefenbaker had flair aplenty, and earned the nickname of "the Chief." But his leadership manifested itself more in bluster and self-assuredness than in systematic party command. Pearson was, if anything, solicitous and permissive. Trudeau, who helped launch the reorganized Commons committee system, was cut from an unconventional bolt of political cloth. His career had been made outside of partisan, organized politics, and he became a Liberal in middle age. Even after becoming Prime Minister, he continued to be more captivated by ideas, style, and imaginative programs than by hard-nosed party manipulation and direction. His profession of commitment to participatory democracy may have spurred his acceptance of a strengthened committee system, though he simultaneously surrounded himself with a coterie of influential personal advisers. We have seen that Country party observance of leader direction has deep roots, and McEwen was an especially imposing leader. McMahon's three Liberal predecessors, Menzies, Holt, and Gorton, though markedly different stylistically, were assertive party leaders, and Prime Ministers.

All told, for a variety of reasons, Australian House standing committees barely developed. Only four joint standing committees with substantive responsibilities, one of which deals with the limited subject of Australian Capital Territory affairs, were formed. The existing joint standing committees have suffered from various structural frailties which have impeded their standing and effectiveness. For instance, the public works committee is concerned more with particular works projects than with departmental operations. The public accounts committee has not followed the British or Canadian assumption that a committee concerned with oversight of expeditures should have a nongovernment member as its chairman, and relies on outdated accounting procedures. For most of its existence, the joint committee on foreign affairs has been little more than a shell. For some time only ministers could refer subjects for committee consideration. They decided what materials to lay before the committee, they were judges of whether sessions could be made public, and members were sworn to secrecy about aspects of the unit's work. Until 1967, and then with some interruption, the ALP refused to serve, both for political reasons and because it found the committee tame if not irrelevant.

Impulses underlying the creation and reliance upon standing committees in the two federal senates require separate attention. Despite the openly partisan basis of their selection, Canadian senators are not subject to dictation by governments, and their behavior is only rarely tinctured by outright partisan considerations. The Senate is a more sedate place than the Commons, and considerable political experience is found among its membership. The Senate's committee system has existed for a very long time, and is the base from which much of the chamber's work in legislative review and revision has sprung. It is also the source for considering legislation introduced in the Senate before it proceeds to the House. Stated another way, governing parties have little control over what kind of standing committee system the Senate wishes to erect to facilitate its business. Governments occasionally, but ordinarily not, are at loggerheads with the Senate, but in the main find Senate amendments to government legislation to be useful and constructive, not mischievous; some 90 per cent of the Senate's recommended amendments are accepted, many with gratitude. With the Commons as burdened as it has been in recent years, there has been a growing practice to introduce some types of fresh government legislation directly in the Senate, where much of the detailed review and technical improvement, especially through systematic committee work, can be done at a saving to the House.

Australia's Senate is a party chamber, as much of its behavior testifies. Although historically there has been negligible government enthusiasm for building standing committees in the Senate, the matter eventually passed out of the government's hands. The scattered party situation in the Senate contributed to the 1970–71 reforms. ALP, DLP, and independent senators, all representing persuasions not included in the government of the day, were especially energetic in pressing for a major committee system, and the government lacked the numbers in the Senate to block such change. But senators of all parties helped to establish a viable committee system. Despite its party character, the Senate is a more relaxed and convivial place than the House, and less overawed and dominated by a ministerial phalanx. Some excellent inquiries by Senate select committees had also made it more apparent to senators that they had something important to offer through committees, if given the chance.

The influence of private members: An overview

We can now move toward an assessment of the public policy impact of rank and file parliamentarians, apart from what they might achieve through intraparty channels such as caucuses. Parliamentary influence, as we have seen, is almost never strong enough to compel a cabinet capitulation on matters of fundamental importance. Occasionally, the prodding efforts of persistent private members are rewarded. Such, for instance, was the case with the eventual adoption of uniform matrimonial legislation in Australia. Sometimes an opposition party can combine a passionate appeal with astute manipulation of parliamentary procedures to extract action from a government. This is what happened when the NDP filibustered the Commons some years ago, and was able to obtain reform in the handling of divorces. However, such instances are not only rare, but more often than not pertain to subject matter which has little partisan content. The more common situation, at least in the lower chambers, has been for oppositions to move numerous amendments, and for governments to rally their parliamentary troops to defeat such efforts. In 1971, for example, the ALP opposition in the Australian House moved 33 amendments to various bills of which only one passed; government backbenchers moved three amendments, of which two were accepted.

When the L-CP lost its Senate majority in the 1960's, the influence of nongovernment senators rose appreciably, in the successful moving of amendments, and otherwise. Although the DLP is hard on Communism and generally takes a law-and-order posture, its Senate leverage has not meant that it has persistently forced L-CP government legislation into a more conservative mold. Certainly no such accusation could be made in the area of social legislation. Despite their mutual political distaste, the DLP and the ALP have frequently combined to force amendments upon government legislative measures. Additionally, the Senate as a body has recently become something of a watchdog over the executive, pointing up acts of foolishness or impropriety, as with regard to the use of VIP aircraft at public expense. As a small and relatively relaxed body, the Senate wears such a role well, its influence as critic, overseer, and even refiner of policy having been enhanced by the absence of any single party or party group's absolute numerical majority.

Canada's Senate has become an important element in the policy review and improvement process because it too, through its own curiously anomalous and unrepresentative character, does not operate on a basis of government vs. opposition party line. Governments have come to recognize its work more as an asset than as an impertinence. More and more new government legislation is being introduced in the Senate before proceeding to the House. Occasionally, senators will rewrite a government bill. More often, when they do request changes, these are technical, or otherwise unsubstantial. As we have seen, an overwhelming number of Senate amendments are accepted by governments. Legislation is not, of course, value free. Its outcome tends to please some interests and to distress others. The Senate has not tried to pose as a stout defender of provincial rights, despite the regional/provincial basis of its representation. But senators from particular parts of the country, especially from the Maritimes and the west, have often spoken up for their "constituencies." Since the Senate hardly ever behaves on a party basis, such regional/provincial spokesmanship has usually been received as a genuine plea for equity, rather than for party interests, and has brought adjustments in the version of legislation produced by the Senate.

Outwardly, the Canadian Senate is a conservative body. Membership carries a property qualification, and there are many men of wealth and social connection in its ranks. Until the 1930's, the Senate as a whole, whether Liberals or Conservatives dominated, did demonstrate a decided preference for property, free enterprise, and stiff law-and-order measures. But its composition gradually shifted from business-world figures to lawyers, and above all to an appreciation of government as a distributor of social and economic resources. A close student of the Senate wrote in 1965 that

> the Senate as a parliamentary institution has made no articulate attempts in the last twenty-five or thirty years to erect a defence for certain economic and social principles in contradistinction with the express wishes of the elected representatives of the people. . . . The conservatism of the Senate became the common law and the idea of the supremacy of Parliament.

Its emphasis, in the high sense of being a house of review, has been

> First, to prevent the practice of government by decree, whenever it could be done without jeopardizing the underlying legislative policy. And second, to see to it that in the course of legislation the interests and the rights of the ordinary person were not brushed aside to any unreasonable degree.*

Many of the Canadian Senate's contributions have been made through its committee system. Illustration of how this has been accomplished also serves to lead us back to the question of how Canadian and Australian parliamentary committees generally have

* F. A. Kunz, *The Modern Senate of Canada 1925–1963. An Appraisal* (Toronto: University of Toronto Press, 1965), pp. 293, 294.

made it possible for private members to provide scrutiny, oversight, publicity, and refinement to public policy.

A good deal of the Canadian Senate's examination and redrafting of legislation is done in specialized standing committees which, like the Senate chamber at large, are generally free of strong partisan flavor. Also important has been the work of Senate select committees or, in a few instances, of committees jointly organized with the House. The main idea behind a select committee is that it can tackle a large or long-term problem with care and in detail, identifying problem areas and suggesting parameters of new or remedial legislation, should such be indicated. Being purely expository and recommendatory, a select committee report is not hampered by the committee members' misgivings about trenching on defined government policy. In recent years, Senate select committees have produced a number of elucidative reports, on the basis of which governments have then proceded to draft legislation. A report on land use resulted in fresh legislative approaches to forest utilization and the regional handling of agricultural problems. Another report, on manpower and employment, resulted in new approaches to industrial organization and assistance, and technical and vocational assistance programs. A joint committee report helped to persuade the government to establish a federal ministry of consumer affairs. Senate select committee reports on the media and on Canadian poverty have been first rate expositions.

We have already intimated that the flowering of Australian Senate select committee investigations has been a boon to that chamber's corporate self-confidence, and to its members personally. Despite being much more partisan than their Canadian counterparts, Australian senators have used the select committee vehicle to considerable public educative and even policy outgrowth purpose. Only seven Senate select committees sat before the second World War. There were a number after the war, including one in the early 1960's which prepared the first reasoned investigation of Australian television production. After a several-year pause, a chain of penetrating, select committee reports appeared. An investigation of water and air pollution helped to activate the environmental issue in the country, and the beginning of serious state and federal legislative action in the area. Following a major securities scandal, the inquiries of a select securities and exchange committee underlined the need for regulation. The House has also used select committees, sometimes in conjunction with the Senate—as it did when a study on constitutional reform was produced some years ago—but more sporadically, and generally to less advantage than the Senate alone has done.

The major contribution of Australian and Canadian standing committees, apart from those operating in the Canadian Senate, appears still to be made. The contributions of oversight committees have been mixed. The Commons committee on public accounts has enjoyed a good deal of autonomy, and the assistance of a large staff under the Auditor General, an official responsible to the House itself. It was this committee which uncovered widespread waste in the refitting of an aircraft carrier which not long afterward was decommissioned and sold for scrap. Australia's joint committee on public accounts, as we have seen, has operated under certain handicaps. But it has not by any means been purely ornamental, witness its sharp rebukes to inapposite practices of military equipment estimates and procurement practices. In both nations, as among modern governments generally, a great many parliamentary statutes entail delegated authority, that is, latitude for public officials to issue specific directives based on broad legislative authority. There is widespread feeling that the trend toward "government by decree" requires persistent oversight. Viewers are somewhat divided on the contributions of the Australian Senate's committee on statutory instruments. Its effectiveness in exposing shortcomings in statutory regulations, and having some disallowed, nonetheless has clearly been rising. In Canada, the House committee assigned to this task is of very recent origin, and operates under highly restricted terms of reference.

We have seen that in Australia standing committees responsible for examining the range of legislative subject matter are nearly nonexistent in the House, and the Senate has just recently organized itself for this purpose. Canadian House standing committees are not new, but have only recently undergone reorganization and the assignment of a genuinely serious role of reviewing and refining Commons legislation. Even after brief experience, the reconstituted committee system sparked up. Committee members have been able to draw on considerable research, have examined various officials, and have conducted on the spot investigations in Canada and abroad. Government party members of the reconstituted committees have assumed a keener interest than in the past, and have been emboldened to raise amendments. The government, sometimes with misgivings, has acceded to various suggested committee amendments, some of them manifestly important. In so doing, it has faced a dilemma, being

> confronted with either accepting the amendments to its basic policy or changing the bill back to its originally expressed policy before the vote on third [final] reading. To do the latter is to ignore its own party members in the committee; to do the former is to accept a bill which is not totally, even in its important features, an expression of the executive's policy. Either choice is difficult for any Cabinet.*

* Thomas A. Hockin, "The Prime Minister and Political Leadership: An Introduction to Some Restraints and Imperatives," in Hockin, ed., *Apex of Power: The Prime Minister and Political Leadership in Canada* (Scarborough, Ont.: Prentice-Hall of Canada, 1971), p. 11.

13

Nonauthoritative sources of influence on public policy

So far, we have concentrated on the way in which the shape and timing of public policy are determined by the interplay of roles within such authoritative decision-making structures as parliaments, cabinets, and the office of the head of government. Significant as this process is, it by no means subsumes the full range of structures and mechanisms which contribute to policy outcomes. Our focus in the present chapter will be on the investigative, public participatory, and bureaucratic channels which, while ostensibly only advisory to those who authoritatively govern, or which may even be entirely informal, carry policy influence.

Investigatory agencies and public policy

We have already seen that through the medium of parliamentary committees, significant public questions have been examined, and some impetus given to Canadian and Australian legislation. In both systems, both at the federal and the state/provincial levels, extra-parliamentary bodies have frequently been instituted by governments of the day to conduct searching inquiries. The most common vehicle has been the royal commission. Somewhat less stately but roughly similarly instructed bodies such as "committees of enquiry" in Australia and "task forces" in Canada have also appeared. Politicians have served on such bodies, but their membership is essentially not party-political, and reflects such qualities as professional expertise, identification with some relevant social or economic group, and public respect. Overall, impartiality has been a hallmark of such groups. Although sitting governments set frames of reference and nominate members, such bodies, and especially the royal commissions, are presumed to work in a reasonably detached atmosphere, and their findings to reflect a reasoned commentary.

Professed motives behind the creation of investigatory bodies such as royal commissions differ. For instance, they may spring from reactions to some scandal or calamity which demands an impartial assessment of cause or culpability. Such was the concern of the Australian royal commission which in the 1950's investigated Soviet espionage activity in Australia, and of a royal commission which in the 1960's investigated the disastrous collision between Australian naval vessels. Another motive for forming investigatory bodies may rest on a need to reset perspectives on some key problem area. Such was the task of the Australian committee of enquiry which probed a great range of economic issues following the economic downturn at the opening of the 1960's, while a Canadian task force on agriculture several years later addressed itself to the persistent difficulties affecting that sector of the nation's economy. Or such bodies may be organized to examine some foundational aspect of national life, as was done by Canada's Royal Commission on Bilingualism and Biculturalism.

Such investigatory bodies also have their political uses, explicit or not. They may be formed with an eye to damaging an opposition's reputation, as has sometimes been suggested of the Menzies government's creation of the royal commission on espionage. They may be formed in the reasonable expectation that their findings will supply the governing party with objectively derived evidence for pursuing a particular legislative program. This can be said for various Canadian royal commissions which have examined the permeation of the arts, media, and other facets of Canadian life by American influence. The Australian committee on economic enquiry may, in part, have been designed to buy time for a government in difficulty over the state of the economy. The creation of the B and B Commission was, in part, Ottawa's political gambit to calm Quebec's anxieties by proving that "something was being done" to re-examine from top to bottom the country's state of French-English relations. In both countries, investigatory bodies have often been designed as political decompression chambers, buffering controversies by at least for a time removing them from the active political realm. Over 300 royal commissions sat during the first hundred years of Canadian confederation. But, at least before the second World War, Australian activity in this area was far more widespread, with over 700 royal commissions being counted by 1939 federally and in the states. This high figure seems to sustain certain impressions about the Australian political system itself. It seems to point to its need for mechanisms through or into which particularistic interests can channel their views, the propensity to hedge partisan politics with nonpolitical buffers, such as the arbitration and conciliation machinery and the Tariff Board, and the taste for bureaucratizing politics generally—a theme to which we shall return a bit later.

In any event, the reports of royal commissions and related bodies have often spotlighted significant facts, identified problem areas, and recommended remedies which have affected official policy, political implications aside. In Canada, at least, the idea of large-scale investigations, sedulously researched by royal commissions, has acquired a rather special place in the policy-making process. Commission reports are given considerable publicity, and there is opportunity for various interested sectors of the public, as well as for political parties, to react to recommendations before the cabinet formulates a reasoned view of its own, and legislation is brought forward. An excellent illustration of this is the reform of the taxation system. A royal commission on taxation was in session from 1962–67. After its report had been produced and studied, the Liberal government issued a "white paper" on taxation—a general statement of its thinking. A great deal of discussion was generated. By 1971 a comprehensive tax bill was submitted, representing a variation on both the royal commission report and on the government's own white paper. Even then, the government took its time, gleaning parliamentary opinion, through committees and otherwise, testing out provincial reactions, and adjusting the bill's terms as it went along. Granted, only major subjects can be treated so thoroughly, and only some subjects can be dealt with at relative leisure; ten years is a long time from inception of study to passage of legislation. In the paradigm of amply scrutinized, publicized, and redrafted policy, the mapping role of royal commissions can be most constructive.

Public participatory roles and public policy

The example of the treatment of tax policy in Canada also brings to mind the role of private citizens, or groups, in the decision-making process, apart from their electorally related activity. There are several measures by which persons, acting on their own behalf or as interest-group delegates, may contribute to policy formation or implementation. Although with somewhat varying emphasis, such nonofficial inputs have become commonplace in both nations, often with official encouragement.

We have seen that political culture legacies left Australians more egalitarian-minded than Canadians, but also rather more complacent and insular. One consequence has been that Australians are less inclined to become agitated about the social and environmental problems around them, and less eager to mobilize themselves for citizen action. A perceptible change has, however, come about in Australia, especially among middle-class persons. When the Australian Consumers' Association was formed in 1961, many predicted modest success at best. But a decade later the organization enrolled 120,000 members, and was thriving federally and in most states. It was deeply involved in the drive toward metrication and decimalization, was agitating for a federal consumers' bureau, and was claiming credit for having persuaded the federal authorities to adopt a desirable amendment to its packaging legislation. A goodly number of persons involved in the new minor party movements, such as the Australia party and DOGS, first sharpened their political consciousness in various local-action groups in the outer suburbs of the large cities. Planners are finally beginning to tap the public resource. For instance, the "strategic plan" for the improvement of Sydney was drawn up by consultants who drew extensively on the submissions of local groups and individual citizens, and otherwise involved such persons in the urban planning process.

Australian voluntary organizations, of the civic action type and otherwise, have only recently, and quite meagerly, begun to be subsidized through public funds. Foremost is the Australian Conservation Federation, which conducts high caliber research and publicity on a subject which until lately attracted comparatively scant official attention. The Federation now enjoys the patronage of the Governor-General, and a $50,000 annual subvention from Canberra. The Canadian funding effort has been much more impressive. For instance, federal funds are distributed to a host of civic action organizations which are not in electoral politics as such —tenant groups, homeowners' associations, and the like—and a number of which are openly critical of established, official programs. This is additional to monies donated to community organizations to promote labor-intensive projects as an aid to economic revival; local governments receive separate funds for similar purposes. Then too, Canada has moved much farther than Australia in giving public money to volunteer workers in reconstruction and development projects. There has been no Australian equivalent of the Company of Young Canadians, a kind of Canadian domestic

Peace Corps. Nor has the Australian government been nearly as generous as the Canadian in underwriting volunteer workers in developing countries.

The incorporation of private persons into aspects of the political process has become common in both countries, and at most levels of governmental jurisdiction. Only in a very narrow sense, however, can this practice be equated with sizable "participatory democracy," or a handsome effort to "open government to the people." Governments at various levels have become large and complex organizations, subscribing to sets of norms and routines not easily amenable to reconstruction. "The people," on the contrary, are many, of disparate levels of social and political consciousness, and cross-sectioned along innumerable occupational, religious, social, and other cohort and loyalty lines.

When political officials consent to open channels for citizen participation in public affairs, they understandably stop short of depriving themselves of the right to choose priorities and to govern subject only to electoral review. The opening of outlets for citizen or associational group spokesmanship within government may be permitted because of sincere belief that the public is in principle entitled to greater access to what has become an impersonal and often unapproachable institution. It may also be done to persuade particular interests, some of them with substantial political leverage, that their views are welcomed and respected. Institutionalized participation by various nonofficial interests in government also alerts politicians and planners to what sorts of policies, or means of policy implementation, are apt to be acceptable. Such participation also serves as an important adjunct to the government's independent sources of facts and ideas, and in this sense can contribute to the actual form that public policy eventually assumes. In sum, fitting private persons or groups into the policy process may be inspired by variable doses of principle, astute politics, and practicality in the shaping and application of policy.

In Canada and Australia, the more direct avenues for public

political participation have taken several forms. The most traditional means have been in soliciting the opinions of various primary producing groups through referendums, by which governments have often felt obligated to stand. We encountered an example of this before, in dealing with the conflicts among Australian woolgrowers. Then too, many of the members of commodity marketing boards, which in both countries by statute enjoy considerable autonomy, are selected from among the constituent producing groups. In 1971, Canadian farm marketing legislation was amended so as to insure that an agency with power to regulate any farm product, except poultry and eggs, would only be created at the request of the producers themselves. Where essentially local community matters are not at stake, and/or where policy is likely to affect the citizenry quite intimately, certain innovations in participatory arrangements have begun to take shape in both nations. For instance, recent Victorian state land conservation legislation specifies that future utilization of Crown lands would be decided not simply by officials applying certain environmental protection and public interest formulas, but through maximum community participation in the decision process itself.

There is a truly staggering range of institutionalized bodies through which different kinds of interests can be heard. Only in fairly recent times, however, has attention been paid to the inclusion of views which may be said to represent general community, rather than specialized interests. Consider the treatment of social and public welfare questions generally. In Nova Scotia, agreement was reached to create a social planning council for the greater Halifax-Dartmouth region, with financial assistance from the provincial government. The council, which was to include provincial and local government, volunteer agency, and United Appeal representatives, was to handle subject matter crossing jurisdictional lines. Hence, its recommendations, based on study and research, were to be funneled to member voluntary associations and to provincial and local authorities alike. The nationwide Canadian Welfare Council, recently renamed the Canadian Council on Social Development, began as a private venture many years ago. It now receives a fair share of its funding from federal and provincial governments, and supplies considerable research and policy recommendations on a broad range of social and community issues of interest to federal officials, but with implications for the provinces as well. The Consumers Association of Canada considerably antedated its Australian counterpart. When in 1968 Ottawa created a Ministry of Consumer and Corporate Affairs, an advisory Canadian Consumer Council was authorized to stand alongside it, and by 1972 had an operating budget of $160,000. Administratively, the Canadian advisory councils often have provincial as well as federal and voluntary association representation. This enables the relevant federal ministry to foresee potential provincial reactions to future policies, as well as providing reasoned input from the private groups.

Both countries co-opt spokesmen with special connections into advisory bodies which deal with matters of broad public interest. Again, the motives, according to circumstances, are a mixture of political horse sense and a striving to construct policy based on advice from many sources. Australia's ambitious postwar migration program raised questions about the assimilation and education of newcomers, about national employment and economic growth, and so on. Hence, when the national Immigration Advisory Council was established, it included federal parliamentarians, local government representatives, and spokesmen for primary and manufacturing industries, employers, trade unions, chambers of commerce, and service clubs. In the aftermath of the 1970 Quebec disturbances the Canadian federal government concluded that it required more accurate and well-evaluated information on law enforcement. It therefore provided representation from among the police, military officers, lawyers, sociologists, and psychologists for its new Security Planning and Research Group.

Both national governments, and lower governmental units to

some degree, attach representatives of specialized interests to advisory groups which deal with specific matters such as agriculture, commerce and labor. At times, politics plays a conspicuous part in the formation or staffing of such bodies. When a Ministry of Labor Advisory Council was set up in Australia in 1954, both ACTU and employers' representatives were invited to participate. After several years, however, for essentially political reasons, the ACTU withdrew, and the council became defunct. Even so, non-Labor as well as Labor governments have consistently included trade-union delegates on a variety of advisory panels, and have consulted labor ad hoc on such subjects as automation and industrial safety. Despite its withdrawal from the Labor Advisory Council, organized labor did not boycott the numerous other contact points available to it. When the political climate had shifted somewhat, the ACTU in 1968 joined a newly constructed National Labor Advisory Council. As the result of the Australian business community's misgivings over the 1957 trade treaty with Japan, the Department of Trade arranged for continuing consultations between itself and industry groups. For the period they were in use, the "industrial panels" were sponsored by the ACMA itself, preparing briefs and delivering representations on purported damage to local business caused by the influx of Japanese goods. McEwen, in his position as Minister of Trade and Industry, occasionally took representatives of growers' and producers' organizations with him to overseas conferences, and made no secret of stepping out of negotiating sessions to confer with these figures.

Both in Australia and in Canada, criticism has been heard that the consultative machinery has become a platform for special interest groups to establish disproportionate influence in government. In particular, interlock between business and industrial spokesmen and governments is alleged to have overstated the conservative viewpoint, and to have induced conflict of interest respecting award of contracts, tax concessions, and the like. There is some merit in such accusations. But interest-group influence within government arises from an elaborate web of factors, not just the conspicuous presence of some persuasion on advisory agencies. In the 1960's the powerful Canadian Medical Association, despite vocal spokesmanship on advisory councils and a heavy lobbying effort otherwise, failed to divert the Liberal government from its commitment to medicare.

There are, of course, ways and means by which special interests can make their wishes heard in government circles apart from institutionalized advisory bodies. There is a ritual, annual in Canada and semi-annual in Australia, under which interest-group spokesmen meet with ranking federal officials, including ministers, to file submissions and discuss their concerns. There is some suspicion that this process is more a public relations gesture than anything else. Still, in access terms, some interests are somewhat more equal than others, assuming that a propitious political climate prevails. When Menzies campaigned on behalf of the Liberals in 1949, he promised the Returned Services League, Australia's foremost veterans' organization, a "special relationship" with Canberra. The RSL, with special concern in defense policy and veterans' affairs—"repatriation," as it is known in Australia—has indeed enjoyed special access to cabinet members, and has been accorded private briefings by the service departments. In the 1960's, under McEwen, the Department of Trade and Industry was exceptionally hospitable to lobbyists from secondary industry, a sector which was then being wooed by the Country party. But with McEwen's retirement, the access narrowed. The Canadian Manufacturers' Association has long had an advantage in its ability to submit reasoned briefs dealing with matters of ministerial discretion in the administering of various tax laws and tariff regulations.

The weight of nonofficial advice and demands for concessions is also affected by the receptiveness of the respective bureaucracies. An illustration of this relates to the status of advisory "superboards" in the two nations. Australia has not chosen to follow the

Canadian precedent of creating the equivalents of the Economic Council of Canada, the Science Council of Canada, or something on the pattern of the Institute for Public Policy Research. The institute's mission is to provide authoritative advice on long-range policy issues to all levels of government, with reliance on sophisticated techniques such as systems analysis. Australia's reluctance to proceed toward such superboards has, in part, been conditioned by bureaucratic apprehension about poaching and divided authority. Although the special Committee of Economic Enquiry which reported in the mid-1960's recommended a central economic planning agency, the Treasury was determined to preserve its dominant role in the field. Not until 1972, and then only to study federal-state financial relations, did the government authorize an independent economic research unit, to be housed at the Australian National University. Although an Economic Council of Canada was created, its image in Ottawa bureaucratic circles has been uneven. The council has on the one hand been accused of sacrificing economic rigor in order to placate its constituent groups, which include business, labor, agriculture, and consumer spokesmen, as well as academic economists. On the other hand, the council has been scolded in some federal bureaucratic quarters for co-opting too many Canadian economic experts for its own use, at the expense of the bureaucracy itself. The Canadian civil service establishment points to what happened in 1965, two years after the council's foundation. Council advice for a highly expansionary budget was accepted by the Pearson government, resulting in serious and long-term inflationary pressures with which professional administrators then had to live and cope. It might be noticed, however, that the Canadian federal bureaucracy is rather more receptive to soliciting the advice and counsel of academic experts than is true in Australia where, additionally, the academic community has until recently suffered from lack of high stature and public recognition. An example of the Canadian approach was the creation of an academic relations section within the Department of External Affairs in 1967, entailing stepped up seminar meetings, lectures to External Affairs officers, academic consultantships, and the posting of academics within the department for periods of time.

Bureaucracies and public policy

The Australian and Canadian bureaucratic establishments are themselves powerful influences in the shaping and application of public policy. Some of this influence derives from the various interest group importunings which, whether through formalized channels or not, are heard and assimilated by civil servants. Much of it is germinated within the bureaucracies themselves.

Bureaucratic influence within the two political systems should not be misread as the work of openly, politically partisan administrative empires. Merit, not patronage, has for some time characterized civil service recruiting, especially at the federal level, though somewhat more conspicuously in Australia than in Canada. Australia adopted the competitive principle for its federal service just a year after federation. Canada took a major step in this direction in 1908, and further tightened procedures a decade later, though coverage did not become quite as extensive as in Australia. At lower governmental echelons there were departures from the merit principle, notably in Quebec, where Premier Duplessis distributed patronage with a lavish hand. In New Brunswick, not until the early 1970's was an established practice of wholesale firings and hirings, associated with changes of government, discontinued. During Australian Labor's last tenure in federal office, there were some grumblings and resignations because of Dr. H. V. Evatt's highly personal involvement in External Affairs, but in general the Curtin and Chifley governments enjoyed the loyalty of their public servants. As the result of wartime and reconstruction activities, large numbers of persons were recruited into the Commonwealth public service by Labor, but no serious administrative-political tensions befell the transition to L-CP rule in 1949–50. Canada's federal bureaucrats enjoyed high standing and excellent rapport with the King and St. Laurent Liberal governments. The administrative establishment was skeptical about the PC government elected in 1957, and about Diefenbaker personally. Diefenbaker had his own doubts about the bureaucracy his government inherited after years of Liberal rule, witness the independent sources of advice his government sought through the proliferation of royal commissions which were formed during the early years of Conservative administration. While relations between the bureaucracy and the PC's were not as intimate as they had been under the Liberals, loyal service was given to the Conservatives.

There are various reasons why, despite conditions of merit recruitment and nonpartisan traditions, the bureaucracies have made their impact on policy. One factor, quite simply, is the sheer size of the civil service establishments. As governments have moved into fresh responsibilities, and increased their activities within more traditional fields, great numbers have been hired to fill the multitude of governmental tasks. As government has become more ponderous, bureaucracies have acquired more impressive responsibilities and wider vested interests of their own. The advice of higher echelon civil servants to political decision-makers has necessarily become more intensive and extensive, and reliance upon such advice more crucial. It is within government departments that many measures which are eventually approved by cabinets and are converted into legislation originate. It is there that professional expertise is found, and upon which nontechnically skilled ministers so often rely.

In 1901, the Australian federal government employed about 17,000 persons, and the Canadian federal government 12,000. By 1968, the Australian figure had moved to 315,000, and the Canadian to 371,000. Thus despite being considerably less populous than Canada, Australia now has a corps of federal employees almost as large as Canada's. It also has more state employees than all the Canadian provinces put together. By rough calculation, one in every twelve people who live in Australia works for government, while the Canadian figure is no more than one in twenty. As a reflection of recent expansion in services rendered by Canada's provinces compared to those of the Australian states, there has been a noticeable shift in the proportions of public employees working for different levels of government. While the postwar share of Australian federal employees vis-à-vis total public employment has been slowly rising, the Canadian federal employee proportion has declined. The fastest Canadian growth is occurring among local and provincial governments. Some further indication of the relatively greater national sway of the Australian federal government may be seen in the fact that the proportion of Canadian federal employees stationed in Ottawa is two and one-half times as great as the proportion of Commonwealth employees stationed in Canberra.

The overall ethos of the two federal civil service establishments is also worthy of mention. It has often been remarked that Australians have a talent for bureaucracy. In part, this touches on the life style of bureaucrats and their institutional norms. The very early federal adoption of a competitive recruitment system was an indication of what being a "bureaucrat" implied—enjoying a certain protected self-importance. While arbitration for Australian federal employees was adopted in 1920, their Canadian counterparts did not receive the right to bargain collectively until 1967. Although both the Canadian and Australian federal services undertook recruitment of university graduates in the 1930's, resistance within the Australian federal service was stronger. Appointments to high-level positions from outside the service have been far more frequent in Canada than in Australia where, in 1968, of 69 appointments made to the first and second divisions—the two highest—only one came from outside the public service; all others were promoted from within. In broadly distinguishing the two services, the Australian may be regarded as career oriented—that is, "working one's way up"—and the Canadian as job oriented. The archetypal image of the Australian service as self-protective, sheltered, and rule-bound has clearly undergone changes of late. Until 1962, for instance, only 200 university graduates were recruited annually; in 1970, the figure was over 1600, and there is an overall shift away from egalitarianism to merit for advancement, and more consciousness of the "job," in the Canadian sense.

Relatedly, the Australian bureaucratic penchant has historically manifested itself in officialdom's encouragement for bureaucracy and bureaucrats to multiply. One student of bureaucracy has taken special notice that in Canada the Depression gave rise to a network of self-help agencies staffed by elective officials, but that in Australia government agencies proliferated. For him,

> This enormously pervasive insistence upon authoritative action to deal with economic and social demands is one of the pillars of the bureaucratic ascendancy in Australian life. Instead of collective bargaining, public debate, or direct action the characteristic style of decision-making, firmly established in Australia since the turn of the twentieth century, rests on a broad public willingness to delegate the power to rule-making bodies of an administrative or quasi-judicial character.*

In neither country, of course, are the bureaucracies monolithic. Their separate parts, such as departments, contend for funds, for right of responsibility, and for having their particular views prevail with ministers. In the 1960's, for example, the Australian Department of Trade and Industry officials advocated high tariffs as a means toward generating employment, while the Treasury leaned toward less protection. The Treasury favored a fairly open policy for overseas investment, while Trade's view was more restrictive. In 1971, the two departments took very different views over the revaluation of the Australian dollar. Most Liberal ministers, including the Prime Minister, subscribed to the Treasury view, while Country party ministers turned to Trade's brief during passionate

* S. Encel, *Equality and Authority. A Study of Class, Status and Power in Australia* (Melbourne: F. W. Cheshire, 1970), p. 59.

cabinet sessions. In Australian government, considerable use is made of interdepartmental committees of officials, to resolve diverse and at times heated departmental differences. Likewise, cabinet committees are a partial counter to advice received by a particular minister from his official departmental advisers.

In Canada more than in Australia, as we have seen in several contexts, mechanisms have been developed which serve as adjuncts to what otherwise would be a near monopoly of information and reasoned advice to policy makers. Among these are parliamentary committees and the superboards, such as the Economic Council of Canada. The emergence of a cadre of closer personal advisers in the Prime Minister's Office is another such move, though it actually acquired some overtones of a counterbureaucracy, that is, a competing, second bureaucracy in miniature. To a degree, the reconstruction of the two departments directly responsible to the Australian Prime Minister is also a step toward independent sources of information. The Canadian government's recent drive to place a larger proportion of French speakers in the middle and upper reaches of the civil service, and the various material incentives which have been offered for unilingual administrators to become bilingual, have primarily been aimed at satisfying French Canada's yearning for recognition and equitable treatment. But there is an adjunct inherent in the Frenchification programs, with implications for the role and influence of the bureaucracy. Some call it disruption, others call it progress. The established, essentially Anglo, elite in the civil service will undergo some change. Styles of interpersonal and interagency relations will be affected. In the past, French Canadian ministers have often been at a disadvantage, dealing with senior departmental officials who were almost entirely English-speaking, and who had styles of behavior somewhat foreign and uncongenial to them.

All the same, Canadian and Australian bureaucracies, in an age of massive and pervasive government, are certain to retain a major role in the policy process, be it in filtering interest-group demands, tendering advice to political ministers, filling in particulars of delegated legislation, implementing policy in particular ways, and so on. The "quiet revolution" and the spate of social and economic reforms instituted in Quebec beginning in the 1960's were greatly advanced because the province was able to place more, not less, reliance on an expanded and highly competent bureaucratic apparatus.

Governments in Canada and in Australia are ultimately responsible to their respective publics. There has been, however, a growing recognition that much of what government stands for, what it legislates, and the services it makes available to the citizenry has become increasingly obscured by the sheer size and complexity of it, and by the power and influence of impersonal, publicly remote bureaucratic establishments. Although in both countries previously classified documents are now declassified after thirty years, rather than fifty as in the past, a mania for stamping nearly every internal document in sight with some classified grade remains very much in evidence. In this sense, official secrecy has become a style of political and administrative life. At another, more personal level, a Canadian task force reported in 1969 that public ignorance was especially acute among persons most in need of government help, such as the poor, the unemployed, and the undereducated. Public ignorance can undermine the effectiveness of public programs, and if sufficiently widespread can induce cynicism and even estrangement, with possible systemic-political repercussions.

One remedy with which governments in both systems have begun to experiment is public participation at various levels of the decision-formulating process, though such measures have other purposes as well. Ombudsman offices and related agencies help to restore public confidence in government by providing special mechanisms for redress of official abuse or negligence. Ottawa in particular has begun determined efforts to make government more accessible, and palatable, to the general public. At one level, it has greatly simplified and reduced the cost of appeal procedures for small taxpayers. At another and more general level, it has established "Information Canada," an agency for disseminating information and answering questions. The agency is national in scope, but regionally decentralized, and with local offices and ties. Such arrangements, even if they perform as intended, are not panaceas, but they are indicative of official concerns.

14

Public policy and the distribution of power

The profound importance of federalism for Canadian and Australian political life has already been discussed in various contexts. Now, having dealt with the authoritative and informal structures involved in policy formulation and decision-making, we need to make explicit what the distribution of power among national, state/provincial, and local and regional governments implies for policy outcomes. We will inquire into the consequences which proceed from jurisdictional fragmentation, the dynamics which govern substantive and financial relations among jurisdictional levels, and into some of the systemic implications of efforts which have been made to reorder the federal balance through constitutional amendment.

Documentary and judicial renderings of the distribution of power

The BNA Act and the constitution of the Commonwealth of Australia, together with the layers of judicial interpretation, custom, and usage which now surround them, are the frameworks which delineate authority over public policy. By the design of the framers, the language of the two basic law documents endows Can. a particularly strong central government, and Australia wi. much more mixed, or coordinate, form of governmental competence. Both documents enumerate various powers of federal government entitlement. The BNA Act makes the explicit point that the federal government's charge is to make laws for the "Peace, Order, and good Government of Canada." The specification of areas of federal competence was done in the interest of emphasis and certainty. Residual powers, those not explicitly donated to one governmental jurisdiction or another, were left with Ottawa. In other words, Ottawa was assumed to enjoy exclusive jurisdiction in all imaginable areas except those listed as belonging to the provinces. The two governmental levels were accorded concurrent rights to legislate in the fields of agriculture and immigration, but federal legislation took precedence. In 1940, an amendment to the BNA Act gave Ottawa control over unemployment insurance. In 1951 and 1964, amendments dealing with old-age pensions were added as a third concurrent power, though this time provincial legislation was to take precedence in case of conflict. With a few exceptions, powers enumerated as falling within the purview of the Australian federal government could also be legislated upon by the states, though federal legislation assumed primacy in case of conflict. Not only was the ambit of concurrent power made wider in Australia than in Canada, but residual powers were awarded to the Australian states, not to the Commonwealth. Indeed, the Australian constitution made very little mention of particular state powers. The states were, in effect, invested with exclusive jurisdiction except where the constitution specified areas of federal competence.

So much for the broad outlines of jurisdictional distribution contained in the two written constitutions. In both countries, the operation of judicial review has meant that what can or cannot be done by a particular level of governmental authority is determined by how the courts have chosen to interpret the two constitutions. In Australia, this has in effect meant what the High Court has had to say. By legislative enactment, the Commonwealth in 1907 precluded the carrying of appeals from the High Court to the Judicial Committee of the Privy Council in cases affecting the distribution of federal-state power without the High Court's own consent. The High Court has acceded to such an appeal only once, in 1912. Cases bearing on other features of the constitution, such as the consistency of federal and state laws, the distribution of jurisdiction among various Commonwealth instrumentalities, and matters arising out of the constitutional guarantee of freedom of interstate trade, could still be taken to the Privy Council without special leave of the High Court. Of over 600 constitutional cases adjudicated between 1903–65, only about 25 were decided by the Privy Council, and the remainder by the High Court. Although the few cases which were decided by the Privy Council were often highly significant, the Privy Council increasingly tended to be influenced by the High Court's own past legal reasoning, even in those instances when it overturned a High Court decision on appeal. In 1968, federal legislation removed these opportunities for appeal beyond Australia. Cases involving state law alone, and raising no constitutional issues, may still proceed to the Privy Council on appeal.

Since 1949, when Canadian appeals to the Privy Council were abolished entirely, the Supreme Court has been Canada's court of last instance. But until 1949, it was the Privy Council, not the Supreme Court, that set the tone of Canadian constitutional interpretation. In fact, of the 159 Canadian constitutional cases heard by the Privy Council, 77 had bypassed the Supreme Court completely. When the Privy Council's sway became established, it was the Supreme Court that came to rely on Privy Council reasoning, the opposite of Australian experience. One further feature of judicial review practice has distinguished Canada from Australia. By very long practice, the Supreme Court, and previously the Privy Council as well, has rendered advisory opinions on matters referred by the federal government. Ordinarily, this has been done to assess constitutionality of proposed bills. Provincial governments have also used references, via the provincial appeals courts. The constitutional dictums pronounced in advisory opinions have affected the fortunes of the particular Canadian legislation under consideration, and have also become precedents within the corpus of constitutional law generally.

Judicial explication of jurisdictional boundaries in the two countries has moved through phases, rather than following a single line of development, though there has been more consistency in Australia than in Canada. The courts have frequently chosen to emphasize and embellish portions of the two constitutions which would have greatly surprised the founders. The status of judge-declared constitutional law at various periods of Australian and Canadian history has, in turn, saddened and frustrated, or delighted, political contemporaries.

During the first two decades of nationhood, the courts sustained the BNA Act's tenor of wide federal authority, but in Australia a strict constructionist approach favoring "coordinate" federalism severely limited Commonwealth powers. Then, from the late nineteenth century until after the second World War, Privy Council interpretation of the BNA Act took a sharp turn on behalf of provincial authority. During the interwar period in Australia, the courts became more permissive toward federal competence. In postwar Australia, and in Canada since appeals to the Privy Council were stopped in 1949, a balance between the more pronounced positions of earlier times has been struck.

Despite certain discernible phases in their evolution, the Australian High Court's interpretations have inclined toward a conservative view of federal power, especially if taxation matters are excluded. The Court's most conspicuous judicial rationale has been its reading of Section 92 of the Commonwealth constitution, which states that "trade, commerce, and intercourse among the States . . . shall be absolutely free." This section was originally designed to avoid the creation of interstate economic obstacles. The High Court, however, has argued that the section's literal meaning deters the federal government from legislating comprehensively in a host of fields even when interstate activities are involved. To allow the Commonwealth to do so, the Court has reasoned, would emasculate the constitutional prescription of the "absolute freedom" of trade. Thus, the Commonwealth cannot assume widespread power over wage and price fixing, the production and marketing of goods, or monopolies and restrictive practices. Its authority to nationalize various industries is likewise strictly circumscribed, as was shown when efforts at bank and interstate airline nationalization were invalidated. Apart from the specifics of how it has parceled out powers, the High Court has adhered to a positivist view of the constitution. In other words, it has read the constitutional language on its face, avoiding judgments about the practical or social implications of its rulings.

For nearly a generation the Privy Council followed the intentions of the Canadian founders, allowing the central authorities considerable latitude. A generous definition was accorded to the BNA Act clause that invested Ottawa with responsibilities over the "Peace, Order, and good Government of Canada." Then the Privy Council shifted its attention to Section 92 of the BNA Act, in which "Property and Civil Rights in the Province" were listed as among the areas of exclusive provincial jurisdiction. It came to insist that the jurisdictional domain of any particular enactment be construed according to whether in "pith and substance" its actual effect was to trench on "property and civil rights." Thus "property and civil rights" were given very wide application, and generally superseded the "peace, order, and good government" entitlement of the federal government. Through a series of judicial rulings, Ottawa was barred from imposing agricultural marketing arrangements, controlling labor relations outside the narrow parameters of persons under some form of federal government employment, or adopting a system of compulsory unemployment insurance. With one possible exception, to be noted shortly, Canadian constitutional cases, like the Australian, were based on legal positivism, rather than drawing on principles of sociological jurisprudence.

There are some clues as to why Australian, Canadian, and Privy Council judges reasoned as they did. One area of explanation relates to the type of case load handled by these bodies. Their positivist approach may very well have been affected by the virtual absence of civil liberties cases, whose frequent adjudication in the United States has conditioned the Supreme Court to think about complex social and philosophical issues. Furthermore, unlike the United States Supreme Court, the preoccupation of the Canadian and Australian bodies has been with nonconstitutional cases being heard on appeal from inferior courts. Thus, "judicial constitution making" in Canada and Australia has been a part-time, more casual, less absorbing responsibility. Canadian constitutional law was also probably pushed toward positivisim by the large number of reference cases which appeared before the Supreme Court and the Privy Council. Since such cases do not deal with "real" issues and conventional adversary proceedings, they are judged in the abstract, and encourage legal absolutist reasoning.

The background of the judges themselves may also be considered as an influence upon the course of constitutional law; the noticeable dearth of academic lawyers on both national courts has probably reinforced legalistic thinking. The Australian High Court has tended to draw its justices from among prominent members of the bar, and the Canadian Supreme Court from among legally trained persons with prior judicial experience. Also, appointments to both courts have been very free of persons with the kinds of overt, ideological commitments which could be expected to color the nominee's judicial role. Most of the personnel of the two courts has been recruited from among persons of moderate to conservative inclination, and therefore not especially disposed to legal disputation on questions of social change. Over the entire period of the High Court's existence, only two ALP figures have been raised to that body. The following commentary on Australian selections is also pertinent to Canada:

> The non-Labor parties do not have to make deliberately "political" appointments to the Bench; they only have to choose from a small group of men whose professional eminence singles them out for judicial preferment, and those chosen will nearly all be as a matter of course supporters of non-Labor parties or apolitical men with middle-of-the-road or conservative temperaments, certainly not likely to be enthusiastic supporters of A.L.P. policies.*

There is also the matter of the judges' cultural and regional origins. Australian High Court judges have been very largely drawn from only two states, New South Wales and Victoria. But Australia is not culturally heterogeneous, and the several states represent a common strain of legal systems and training, and the presently seven members of the High Court reflect this uniformity. Not so in Canada, where Quebec has always enjoyed guaranteed representation on the Supreme Court; since the court's enlargement to nine in 1949, it has been accorded three seats. The French judges have been nurtured in the Continental European civil code tradition, while the other Supreme Court members, like Australian High Court judges, have been raised in the common law. Overall, though positivist thinking can flow from common law experience, the civil code tradition is especially susceptible to that result. Moreover, the Quebec judges were not only ruling from a civil code background, but were reacting in the context of the province of Quebec's own long-standing determination to deter the encroachment of federal power.

The last observation harks back to our earlier reservation about the proposition that judicial reasoning in the two nations has been almost entirely unconcerned with broader social and political ques-

* Geoffrey Sawer, *Australian Federalism in the Courts* (Melbourne: Melbourne University Press, 1967), p. 64.

tions. The Australian High Court has been quite consistent in its legalistic approach. In fact, the main phases of the court's history have generally not even coincided with the political mood of the times. The court has been quite steadfast in its objections to comprehensive federal ownership, and it is the ALP that has been forced to adjust its policies to this limitation, rather than the court adjusting to the ALP. During the first half of this century the Canadian Supreme Court became heavily dependent on Privy Council pronouncements. The Judicial Committee of the Privy Council consisted, and continues to consist, of extremely learned men of law, but who have largely been Britons. The Privy Council judges did in a sense pursue a legalistic approach to Canadian cases, insofar as they found and exploited a rich vein of constitutional ore in the "property and civil rights" clause of the BNA Act. They stuck to it even in the 1930's, when a number of federal actions, designed to alleviate economic troubles, were struck down. But what they also did, and the Supreme Court often echoed, was to recognize that after the initial 20 or 25 years of Canadian nation building, there was considerable provincial resistance to a continuation of centralizing trends. Provincial rights arguments perhaps most strenuously and consistently emanated from Quebec, but hardly from Quebec alone. Ontario, for one, has often stood with Quebec. Parties like the CCF/NDP and other critics have often been annoyed by judicial restrictions imposed on Ottawa. But the legalism of the Privy Council did seem to merge with and acknowledge that a strictly centralist constitution would cramp and perhaps even destroy the diverse Canadian state.

> The general congruence of Privy Council decisions with the cyclical trends in Canadian federalism not only provides a qualified sociological defence of the committee but also makes it clear that the accusation of literalism so frequently levelled at its decisions is absurd. [Law lords] Watson and Haldane in particular overtly and deliberately enhanced provincial powers in partial deference to the BNA Act itself.

> The Privy Council's solicitous regard for the provinces constituted a defensible response to trends in Canadian society.*

All the same, it would be inaccurate to assume that the weight of judicial review in Canada and Australia has in recent years handcuffed federal governments, and precluded the enactment of constructive, nationwide measures. In both countries, the courts have, under the patina of the defense power, awarded extraordinary latitude to central governments in time of war, and have stretched allowable peacetime federal powers during periods of postwar reconstruction. In the 1930's, the courts frustrated Canadian federal government attempts to acquire out of the ordinary power when Ottawa invoked obligations incurred under foreign treaties and agreements. High Court precedents seem to suggest that Australian federal governments could legitimately take the route tried by Ottawa in the 1930's, though for a variety of political circumstances they have chosen not to. Furthermore, although the High Court has preserved much of its infatuation with the constitution's "absolutely free" commerce stipulation, it has given the cause of national uniformity, and in a sense of centralization, at least two major assists. If the power to tax is the power to destroy, so can it be a power to create. As will be seen in more detail later, much of public policy in Australia, without any actual shift in substantive jurisdictional boundaries, has become closely geared to federal preferences. Canberra enjoys pre-eminent control over the collection and redistribution of revenues, and is able to enter and influence nearly any realm of policy by offering conditional grants to the states.

Since becoming the nation's final court of appeal, the Canadian Supreme Court has ushered in the third phase of Canada's judicial review history. It has clearly abandoned the restrictive, "property and civil rights" emphasis which had been dominant for over half a century, though it has not returned to the free-centralizing posi-

* Alan C. Cairns, "The Judicial Committee and Its Critics," *Canadian Journal of Political Science,* Vol. 4, September 1971, pp. 324–325.

tion of the first twenty years of confederation. Part of this may simply derive from having in practice been a *non*supreme court, existing in the shadow of the Privy Council. Part of it may possibly come from an increase in civil liberties cases, whose effect has been to force a broader line of thinking upon the court, though French Canadian judges continue to assume fairly restrictive civil libertarian positions when dealing with civil liberties cases. Part of it may come from the recognition that there has been a genuine ferment in the country about many things, including federal-provincial and intercultural relations, nationhood, and social policy, and which require sensible and sensitive attention from the court.

The tight Canadian constitutional compartments of earlier times are coming unsealed. More allowance is being made for Ottawa's power to regulate commerce, and to legislate for "peace, order, and good government." The Supreme Court is often willing to sanction a federal jurisdictional presence when it locates dominant national overtones in otherwise local matters, or if Ottawa steps into a field where the provinces have declined to act. The court has ruled that the BNA Act prohibits the interdelegation of powers between federal and provincial legislatures, but that interdelegation to an administrative instrumentality is permitted. This has been of help in an area such as commodity marketing arrangements which, once circumscribed by the Privy Council's reading of "property and civil rights," have been opened by the Supreme Court.

Public policy and federal dynamics

Written constitutions and judicial interpretations define the formal boundaries of Canadian and Australian public policy making. A great deal of the actual course of policy is, however, determined by the kinds of arrangements, conventions, and political constraints which regulate relations among the states/provinces, and between them and the central governments. Governments cannot operate in closed compartments. As public policy concerns become more numerous and complex, the effectiveness of intergovernmental consultation, cooperation and even codetermination of policy assumes major importance for the performance capabilities of the political systems at large.

One area of contact and cooperation lies between and among coequal jurisdictional units themselves, that is, the states and the provinces. In its simplest form, this may entail arrangements between neighboring or otherwise related states or provinces. For example, an agreement has been made for Quebec to acquire electric power from the Labrador region of Newfoundland. In another realm, Quebec makes donations to French groups in other provinces (and in New England and Louisiana), and has increased its cultural and educational ties with Ontario. Canada, unlike Australia, is definable according to particular economic regions. Practicality therefore dictated the formation of a Prairie Economic Council, and of a Council of Maritime Premiers. In 1971, the Maritime Premiers agreed to integrate various provincial functions in the interest of economy and efficiency. Agencies were to be created to coordinate control over higher education and over environmental affairs. There was to be a regional data bank, a statistical service, and a common police training center. Motor vehicle licenses and weight regulations were to be standardized.

Canadian and Australian political and administrative officials from all the provinces and states frequently meet to exchange views on a host of questions. There are meetings of education ministers, agricultural ministers, and so on. A Conference of Commissions on Uniformity of Legislation in Canada was formed as early as 1918, though Quebec did not participate until the second World War. Several types of results can and have come from these kinds of specialized gatherings. The federal nature of the two countries has allowed for state/provincial experimentation and innovation in assorted fields. The comparison of notes among expert persons on both successful and unsuccessful undertakings can stimulate interest and improvement among sister states and provinces. Thus, in 1970, the Australian state attorneys-general agreed to urge their respective governments to enact common share-market manipulation controls based on a model Victorian law. In some policy areas, uniformity of state/provincial legislation may be inherently desirable but can only be undertaken at the subfederal level because of constitutional restraints upon federal action. This is often a difficult and tedious process. Several units of government, governed by different political parties and holding separate legislative priorities, must be concerted, and the negotiations restarted as the need for amendments arises. Nevertheless, under the sway of an Australian High Court which has held a narrow interpretation of federal power, this has been the necessary price to pay for standardization in fields such as company law.

Contact points between the states/provinces and the two federal governments are even more complex, since they involve authorities enjoying distinctive jurisdictional entitlements, and often touch on profoundly important yet delicate policy areas. There has been a great deal of proliferation in the number and variety of federal-state/provincial committees and other consultative agencies. Some of these agencies are ministerial, others subministerial, still others technical in composition. Canada has moved farther in this area than Australia, partially because of the greater complexity of Canadian society, and the more elaborate terms on which the courts have defined jurisdictional terrain. The Prime Minister's Office and the Finance ministry in Ottawa both have federal-provincial relations divisions, and a special cabinet committee handles liaison vis-à-vis federal-provincial ministerial relations. In both countries, the institutionalization of intergovernmental contacts has become more than an exercise in promoting efficiency, sharing information, and supplying advice. It has also become a way of resolving various interjurisdictional questions without incessant resort to the courts, a significant arena for decision-making, and a political safety valve. Much of what is "federal" or "state/provincial" policy is now the product of joint effort.

Such relations may deal with concerns which are localized within one, two, or three states or provinces. For over half a century, the federal, New South Wales, Victorian, and South Australian governments have participated in the River Murray Commission, which regulates dams, locks, conservation, and other facilities and projects. The Queensland Sugar Board acquires the sugar produced in that state and, in agreement with New South Wales mill owners, also the small sugar crop grown in that state. The board then disposes of the crop in home and export markets, with the home market price being fixed under a Commonwealth-Queensland agreement. Localized arrangements can sometimes be inspired by political exigencies more than anything else. Several years ago Quebec was attempting to insinuate itself into international conferences and agreements virtually as if it were a sovereign state. This touched Ottawa to the quick, and at one point Canada suspended diplomatic relations with Gabon over that government's indulgent treatment of Quebec. Eventually, Quebec City and Ottawa agreed on a *modus vivendi* whose terms spelled out the rights of each party in international dealings.

The processes of intergovernmental relations highlight both the opportunities and the limitations conditioning the search for a working, cooperative federalism in the two nations. Canadian agriculture is concurrently in the federal and provincial domains. But this has not meant that Ottawa and the provinces have acted independently of one another. In 1971 Ottawa announced a new federal spending program for small farm development. The idea was first proposed some months earlier. Then followed consultations and agreement in principle among provincial and federal agricultural ministers. Once the plan was jointly approved, its details were to be worked over by a mixed federal-provincial technical committee. It was agreed that the actual application of the project would be through mixed teams of federal and provincial officials operating across Canada. But by early 1972 snags had developed. Ottawa announced that it would proceed with the small-farm development program alone, offering to meet with the several provinces individually to negotiate an expanded program. While preparing new income-security legislation in the early 1970's, Ottawa discussed the plan twice with provincial welfare ministers, on two occasions the federal Minister of National Health and Welfare and his advisers visited all the provinces, and the original draft legislation was, as a result, altered in several respects. Canadian pension-plan legislation was made to provide for three years' notice to provinces before changes in levels of benefits or contributions became effective; amendments had to be discussed with the provinces; substantial changes required the consent of two-thirds of the provinces, and containing two-thirds of the nation's population.

Although political wisdom may dictate attempts at universalizing state/provincial acquiescence in federal programs, the result of such efforts may be inordinate haggling and an uncomfortable delay in implementation, especially where conditional grants for federally promoted programs are concerned. Such programs are of long standing in both countries. They are designed to impose a minimum set of nationwide standards in subject matter areas where federal jurisdiction is either absent or partial. With the incentive of federal funds, the states/provinces make some financial contributions of their own and in some instances no contributions, and are able to proceed with programs otherwise too expensive for them to underwrite alone. When Canberra proposed a dairy reconstruction scheme, over two years expired before it could get under way. The states held out for more federal money in the shared costs of the program, and eventually Canberra indicated that, if necessary, it would resort to negotiating state-by-state agreements. In Canada, nine years elapsed before all provinces opted for the old-age pension program. For years after the second World War, Premier Duplessis refused to enter Quebec in various cost sharing plans such as civil defense and the Trans-Canada Highway project. In 1952, he forbade Quebec universities to accept federal per capita higher education funds. The actual application of shared cost programs can become so unnerving as to jeopardize their continuation. During the 1970 Quebec provincial election campaign, federal Liberal party authorities accused the incumbent Union Nationale of hoarding all the credit for certain joint federal-provincial projects. Politics as much as anything else inspired the UN's and the Liberals' complaints about one another. Federal minister Jean Marchand, himself a French Canadian, suspended contributions to technical school construction, because Quebec refused to abide by federal conditions on publicity, and he threatened further reprisals if Quebec failed to behave:

> If the Union Nationale wants a fight, just for the sake of fighting Ottawa, they will get one. . . . The federal Government has remained silent too long. . . . That kind of nonsense [of claiming full credit] will stop, or they will not get one damned penny.*

Sometimes, elaborate cooperation is stimulated as much by constitutional requirements as by criteria of common sense and efficiency. In Australia, for example, some arduous problems have arisen out of the need for the enactment of complementary federal and state legislation. Both constitutional and practical questions seem to affect Canberra's ability to legislate a reduction in the voting age for federal elections without the states proceeding likewise. At the time of writing, the federal and five of the six state attorneys-general had agreed to move toward an eighteen year voting age, but Queensland's misgivings had created an impasse. Commodity marketing and pricing arrangements are an integral feature of Australia's agricultural philosophy. The courts have ruled that, under Section 92 of the constitution, Canberra may engage in interstate trade, but not so as to enjoy a monopoly over the interstate movement of goods. Hence the Wheat Board's de

* *Globe and Mail* (Toronto), March 7, 1970.

facto monopoly is predicated on the sufferance of periodically amended, complementary federal and state legislation.

Apart from the various illustrations already noted, it is necessary to take a more systematic look at the meaning of intergovernmental bargaining for the policy process in contemporary Canada. During and immediately after the second World War, Ottawa initiated impressive reform programs in health, welfare and other fields. A number of the fields covered were actually within the sphere of provincial jurisdiction, but were constitutionally acceptable because they generally relied on the technique of conditional grants in aid. The provinces were tempted to accept these offers because they lacked the financial strength, or the will, to do the job through their own resources. General provincial participation was forthcoming, except for Quebec. Under Duplessis, many of the proffered opportunities were rejected on the grounds that they constituted an ensnarement of Quebec's provincial and cultural autonomy in a federal web. This position was taken at a price. Various Quebec social programs were starved for funds, and other programs were funded from scarce provincial money.

In the 1950's, however, discontent increased even among the English-speaking provinces. To be sure, the conditional grants system was resulting in more uniformity of national services than would otherwise have been possible. All the same, it was Ottawa, not the provinces, that was fixing provincial legislative priorities, yet the Canadian economy had not been made fully viable, witness the continuation of marked unemployment. By 1965, the Pearson Liberal government was prepared to offer the provinces an opportunity to opt out of shared cost programs, including important programs relating to pensions, disability and unemployment benefits, and medicare, and to reimburse the provinces for costs incurred in absorbing such programs. Quebec was the only province to accept the offer on some of the programs, including medicare, but remained in other programs. The other provinces did not follow suit.

They desired more province-by-province flexibility in the programs than Ottawa was sometimes allowing, that being an important reason why Ontario and some other provinces dragged their feet over entering the medicare program. But they were also uneasy that the entire structure of social services might cave in if they indiscriminately opted out. Also, they were not impelled by the kind of cultural preoccupations which were gripping Quebec. In 1969 the Trudeau government temporarily stopped further opting out opportunities pending the resolution of the tax-structure review then under way. In 1971, Trudeau said he was prepared to reopen opting-out discussions. But when at a federal-provincial conference later that year Ontario and Alberta indicated they might wish to drop out of some programs, Trudeau demurred.

The effects on public policy of the Canadian brand of intergovernmental negotiations have been widespread. Technically, by resorting to conditional grant programs, the federal authorities have not invaded forbidden areas of jurisdiction. New programs are ordinarily not legislated by Ottawa without prior, intensive consultation with the provinces. Once the programs are on the books, a province is technically free to join or not, and often bargains over the details of how a program will operate within its boundaries. For some time, the provinces have been free, and presumably will remain free, to disengage. In this sense, the standards of national services have been raised and made more equal, constitutional prohibitions have not been insulted, and the provinces enjoy a certain decision-making role, as well as a choice to withdraw. Quebec, which has always insisted it was a province "not like the others," has exercised its options substantially, somewhat calming French protestations that Ottawa is bent on domination. This notion of an enlightened, cooperative federalism has not, however, escaped cares and criticisms. Inherent in the approach is delay and spottiness in the nationwide application of programs. By allowing opting out for Quebec, Ottawa has abetted less attractive demands. Quebec itself has been building up demands for control over social programs such as family allowances—in which the federal government possesses constitutional entitlement it is unwilling to perjure, and wishes to retain because these represent the few remaining fields in which direct Ottawa-people contacts are still possible. Embarrassment has been caused by Ontario's and Alberta's interest in opting out of some shared cost programs, because of trepidation about the future of federally directed conditional grants, and because of the fiscal implications raised by the prospect of two of the most prosperous provinces demanding reimbursement.

Fiscal issues and federal dynamics

Fiscal issues are an indivisible part of federal-state/provincial relations. Our discussion of jurisdictional divisions, intergovernmental cooperation, and policy outputs characteristic of the Canadian and Australian political systems must now be averted to money—its sources, distribution and uses, and to the devices which these systems have invented to bargain over it.

Constitutionally, the states and provinces have been awarded substantial responsibilities. In Australia, basic but long underfinanced state controlled subjects, such as education, are receiving new and in some cases urgent attention. Quebec province has been exerting great efforts to modernize itself; from 1959, Duplessis' last year in office, to 1963, Quebec's education budget doubled, and doubled again by 1968. Both in Australia and in Canada, emphasis is now turning to environmental improvement and other costly programs. In Canada, not only do the provinces hold considerable constitutional privileges, but, as has been shown, Ottawa has instituted a number of extremely expensive social service programs in whose cost the provinces share, and Quebec has been assuming sole responsibility for some programs, including medicare. More and better paid civil servants have been needed by the states and provinces. In Canada, between 1946–66, federal employment doubled, but provincial employment more than quintupled.

At almost every turn, therefore, the states and provinces have been called upon to invest more, and in more ways, than before. In 1970–71, expenditures by Australian states rose 14 per cent, and among Canada's provinces by 15 per cent. Canadian spending patterns have been especially striking because of the steep rate at which provincial (and local government) proportions of all governmental expenditures have been rising. In 1952, the proportion spent by all subnational units was 35 per cent; in 1970, it was 58 per cent.

Are state and provincial financial resources sufficient to meet responsibilities? The question raises both constitutional and political issues. Constitutionally, no restrictions are laid on the ability of the two federal governments to tap whatever revenue sources they wish. However, the Australian states may not tax customs and excises, while the BNA Act confines the provinces to "direct" taxation. Not only are the states barred from lucrative fields such as sales and liquor taxes, but the High Court has chosen to apply a broad definition to "customs and excises," further constricting state access to taxation. For instance, in 1969 the Court denied to the states stamp-duty receipts for money paid as a price of goods sold interstate. The provinces, by comparison, have been given lenient judicial treatment. "Direct" taxes have been interpreted so broadly that the provincial tax base is nearly as comprehensive as Ottawa's. Moreover, while the provinces have retained their independence in borrowing, the states have not. As a result of an amendment to the Commonwealth constitution in 1928, the amounts of money borrowed by the states are contingent upon the approval of the Loan Council, a mixed federal-state body in which Commonwealth influence is decisive. Such considerations would appear to give the Canadian provinces substantial tax-raising superiority over their Australian state counterparts. Indeed, the share of all public authority revenue in Canada drawn from provincial sources alone is over two and a half times greater than the state share of the Australian public revenue total.

Calculations such as these can, however, mislead. Theoretically, at least, even with very sparse independent revenue, states and provinces could meet their obligations if sufficient funds were supplied on favorable terms from federal authorities. Federal largesse, or its absence, is what a great deal of the intergovernmental tax debate is all about. It not only exercises politicians, but affects the nature and quality of services at all levels of government. The two federal governments do provide the states and provinces with considerable sums of money. In fact, much of the federally dispensed money originated from sources, such as income taxes, from which the states and provinces are not constitutionally debarred.

Today, none of the Australian states and no Canadian provinces save one collect personal income taxes. The present system reaches back to World War II, when the collection of all personal and corporate income taxation was absorbed by the two federal authorities. There is no outward constitutional impediment to a return to a system of individually collected state/provincial, and federal, income taxes. Faced with challenges against Canberra's income tax monopoly, the High Court has upheld the practice as a justifiable exercise of Commonwealth authority, unrelated to the plenitude of power available in time of war, though it has told the states that they could set up their own income tax systems at their pleasure. This is easier said than done. The Commonwealth is constitutionally bound to impose an income tax which is uniform in all states. Thus, if some states started to impose their own income taxes, Canberra would be unable to reduce their share of the federal tax piecemeal. An end to the federal income tax monopoly partially depends on a tax schedule common to all the states, and commonly introduced, that is, by all states simultaneously. It also depends on the will of the federal government. After the second World War, Labor and L-CP governments alike invited the states to recommend a formula under which Canberra would surrender its income tax monopoly, but the states were unable to agree on the particulars. Eventually, the L-CP came to enjoy the influence which flowed from federal control over the income-tax purse strings. In the face of Canberra's present opposition to change, the states are pushed even farther away from reactivating their own income taxes.

There are two related reasons why present income tax arrangements have come to suit Canada's provinces rather more than they suit Australia's states. The Canadian system, in conjunction with other means of federal financial disbursements, has proved to be more generous to the provinces than Canberra has been toward the states. The Canadian system has also been more adjustable, period by period, and by its differentiation of provincial requirements. In 1970, in fact, the Australian state premiers petitioned Canberra—unsuccessfully—to incorporate much of the Canadian tax practice into Australian practice.

After the second World War, the provinces rejected a federal proposal that all income tax and succession taxes be transferred to Ottawa, which would have been done in exchange for per capita tax-rental payments and special equalization payments to needy provinces. Instead, Ottawa was compelled to negotiate with the provinces separately. During the first five-year arrangement which lasted from 1947 to 1952, Quebec did not participate because of its autonomist inclinations, and the wealthiest province, Ontario, did not participate because it felt its citizenry would be oversubsidizing the other provinces. Some adjustments finally persuaded Ontario to rent its personal, but not corporate, income tax, and only Quebec remained outside the plan entirely during the second tax rental period of 1952–57. During the next five-year tax plan, despite considerable improvement in the amounts of and terms on which provinces could rent their taxes, the need for a fundamental reconstruction of the system became evident. The provinces were insisting on the return of a larger and larger share of the revenues collected by Ottawa. Ottawa was distressed by the frequent adjustments in tax proportions being abated, by the opprobrium it faced as the sole tax extractor, and it foresaw that its own ability to control and finance large sectors of public policy could be subverted if provincial claims were not somehow subjected to a regularized arrangement. A fresh approach, begun in 1962, awarded to the provinces the right to set and to collect their own personal and corporate taxes. Ottawa gradually reduced its own tax rates to make room for the provinces. The amount to which such "tax room" was provided rose to 28 per cent by the late 1960's and, after vigorous provincial representations, a 30.5 per cent rate was promised in 1971. The federal government collects these taxes for the provinces *if they choose,* charging nothing for collection expenses. Most provinces have agreed to have their taxes collected for them by Ottawa, but Quebec collects all its own income taxes, and Ontario its own corporate levies. It must be stressed that the figure set for provincial "tax room" is optional. The provinces may, and some do, assess at higher than the standard rate, meaning that their residents pay higher income taxes than do persons living in other provinces. Similar arrangements were made for estate duties, though Ottawa promised to withdraw from this tax field entirely by early 1972.

To summarize: Canada's provinces are able to set income taxes at whatever level they choose. Ottawa has deliberately left a fair chunk of total income-tax receipts to the provinces, and therefore only if provincial assessments exceed the amount do taxpayers pay over and beyond the combined, standard rate. The provinces may collect their own taxes, in which case they receive an abatement equivalent to 30.5 per cent of what otherwise is the combined federal and provincial tax levy.

The Australian income tax system lacks these elements of flexibility. Formulas governing repatriation of funds from income and other tax sources operate on five-year cycles. The states argue for the best possible deal at premiers' conferences, attended by the state and federal heads of government. The formulas and sums arrived at are subject to Canberra's gift; states are unable to set variable rates. Money returned to the states is not, unlike under Canadian practice, simply predicated on a particular state's contributed share of its income tax payments. The formula used recognizes population, wages, and a so-called "betterment" factor for the needier states.

We have already indicated that both nations employ elaborate conditional grant programs. On the surface, the Australian states appear to have had rather more latitude in this area than Canadian provinces. In the mid-1960's, about 80 per cent of Australian conditional grant donations required no offsetting state contributions, while in Canada the proportion was only about half. Still, the states complain that those conditional grants which carry a cost sharing provision are a burden on them, and are often designed for purposes preferred by Canberra, but which do not necessarily command high priority among the states. The Canadian approach is not as burdensome on the provinces as might be imagined. There has recently been some shifting to unconditional federal grants, as for higher education, an area in which Canberra participates with the states on a conditional and cost-sharing basis. More significantly, as we noticed earlier, Ottawa has made it possible for the provinces to move out of various major cost sharing programs without financial loss to the provinces themselves. When Quebec took this option with medicare and other programs, it was reimbursed for the dollar amounts which otherwise would have been spent by Ottawa within Quebec for these purposes. Since Quebec has been adamant about assuming a prominent personal hold over social welfare programs, it followed that arrangements for rebating funds in the opted fields had to be made. It also explains why Quebec receives a larger slice of abatement on income taxes paid by its residents than does any other province. If Ontario and Alberta or other provinces were to opt out of some cost-sharing programs, their tax abatement would be increased accordingly.

Aside from general revenue and special/conditional program disbursements, both federal authorities provide funds whose basic purpose it is to assist less fortunate states or provinces, and to move toward a more equitable, nationwide distribution of resources.

Living standard disparities are wider among the provinces than among the states, suggesting need particularly for Canadian federal financial commitments of this type. Such a Canadian commitment is also necessary because provincial entitlement to income taxes, unlike in Australia, is not predicated on any factor of need of recipient provinces. The principal Canadian tool for softening interprovincial disparities is a system of equalization grants. The existing formula calculates all provincial revenues at average provincial rates, and makes up the difference between revenue scales in needy provinces and the national, all provincial average. In 1971, only Ontario, British Columbia, and Alberta were excluded from the group of provinces eligible for equalization grant assistance. In the same year, 7 per cent of the entire federal budget was devoted to equalization payments. Newfoundland, the most needy province according to this formula, required 65 per cent of its nationally averaged revenue figure to be met in this fashion. There also exists a related revenue stabilization project, under which net provincial revenues in any one year are insured against falling beneath 95 per cent of the preceding year's figure.

We have seen that correction for state "need" enters into the computation of funds allocated by Canberra to the states as general revenues. Money given under special purpose grants, whether containing a cost sharing proviso or not, does not carry an inherent "need" factor. Nor do capital construction grants, some of which are repayable. There is, however, occasional *ad hoc* assistance to the states, and money which is made available to claimant states via the Grants Commission. Lately, only Tasmania and South Australia have petitioned the Grants Commission for special assistance, but Queensland has recently entered its bid.

Compared to Canada, funds transferred from Canberra to the states have been modest. Between 1958/59 and 1968/69, the percentage of all income taxes collected in the states and then returned to them declined from 36.4 per cent to 29.4 per cent. In the decade of the 1960's Australian wages and salaries doubled and income-tax revenue more than tripled with no change in rates, yet the proportion of money redistributed to the states did not keep pace. Immense pressure for improved funding was exerted upon Canberra by state premiers in 1969 and 1970. Money transferred to the states had been rising at about a 10 per cent annual rate. The premiers were eventually able to extract a promise that by the mid-1970's their basic reimbursement would, over a five year period, have increased by 82 per cent. Clear comparisons among quite different types of funding arrangements in the two countries are elusive. Nevertheless, the above Australian figure of an 82 per cent rise over five years might be noticed vis-à-vis recent Canadian trends. Between the adjacent financial years 1969/70 and 1970/71, fiscal transfers from Ottawa to the provinces rose by nearly 32 per cent. In the late 1960's, Canberra was delivering about 26 per cent of federal revenues to the states. By 1971, Ottawa ran a budget of $14.3 billion, of which $4.4 billion was set aside for various provincial grants, and another $3 billion for tax abatements. The sums distributed by the respective federal authorities were therefore roughly proportionately twice as great in Canada as in Australia.

Some points about fiscal relations need to be re-emphasized. One is that interstate economic disparities are not as wide as they are interprovincially. The second is that a combination of constitutional and political factors has made Canadian federalism far more devolutionary than Australian federalism, requiring releases of substantial sums of money from Ottawa to the provinces. Nonetheless, Australia state responsibilities, and costs, are also considerable. Federal governments in Canberra have not been well disposed toward dispensing coin to the states generously. Constitutionally and otherwise, Australian federal governments have been better shielded from surrendering their income-tax monopoly than have governments in Ottawa. They have lately fallen under severe pressure from the states, including from their politically complementary Liberal and Country party state premiers. But the "states' rights" tradition is not as deeply rooted in Australia as in Canada, and there has been no Australian Quebec to act as pacemaker for a reconstituted and more devolutionary federalism. Although the states have recently been offered improved reimbursements, they continue to be very much dependent on Canberra's will, since their own, accessible tax bases are far narrower and more precarious than in Canada; for instance, no excises, and in practice no income taxes. Also, they are dependent on federally set priorities in devising borrowing programs. When states have submitted to borrowing schedules predicated on their personally defined needs, the Loan Council has not been averse to imposing cautionary limits in the interest of containing inflation, or for other reasons. The states are somewhat fearful that the presence of the new federal development corporation will make it harder, and more expensive, for them to borrow on the local loan market.

The states have tried to work around their problems through fresh approaches to taxation. They have fiddled with some taxes which seemed to bear as many counterproductive as promising revenue-bearing attributes. A Victorian surcharge on hotel and motel accommodations raised fears of driving away tourists. A Western Australian increase in rental rates on mineral claims and leases aroused fears that the state's mineral boom might be arrested. But there have been some successes in the states in areas of potentially lucrative "growth" taxes. For years Canberra had resisted state entry into the receipts-tax field. Gradually, in the late 1960's, the states began adopting such taxes, and Canberra relented —only to have the High Court invalidate these state efforts on constitutional grounds. In return, the federal authorities promised to collect such taxes on behalf of the states, and return the proceeds to them. Since the second World War, Canberra controlled payroll taxes, and had made the disbursement of income-tax money to the states conditional on its prerogative to maintain the payroll tax monopoly. The state of Victoria estimated that its lack of access to these "growth" payroll taxes had, in a thirty-year period, cost it $100 million. In 1971 the High Court rejected Victoria's legal challenge to the payroll tax practices. Later that year, however, Canberra yielded ground, and promised to abandon the payroll-tax field to the states. Part of the concession would be neutralized, however, since there was henceforth to be an appropriate deduction from funds awarded to the states under normal reimbursement grants. Only if the states raised the payroll-tax rate would they be able to realize a net revenue gain. In 1970, Gorton pledged that the federal government would progressively assume responsibility for the repayment of state debts, and as of this writing the process had started. Australian state financial problems remain sizable, but some remedies have been initiated, with the prospect that the quality of state services will improve.

15

Public policy in local and regional contexts

Constitutional theory in Canada and Australia identifies only two levels of authority, the federal and the provincial/state. While local governmental units are entirely subordinate to the states and provinces in which they are found, their existence raises important issues of policy determination in the two countries. An exploration of the dynamics of local governmental institutions, and of various experiments with political regionalism, provides further clues about the makeup of public policy, and about the political style and course of intergovernmental transactions which characterize the two nations.

Policy activity at the local level

The powers available to local institutions, compared to the state and provincial jurisdictions to which they are subordinate, are decidedly limited. As between the two nations, however, Canadian local governmental units enjoy more responsibilities than their Australian counterparts. Canadian local governmental bodies acquired major responsibilities in such areas as education, justice, welfare and transport quite early, often preceding the formal creation of what were to be their home provinces. In Australia, however, the colonies which later became states made an early appearance, wielding considerable powers and being expected by their residents to discharge them positively. It can also be argued that Australia's cultural propensity for egalitarianism and uniformity of standards was inimical to the emergence of disparate, semisovereign local bodies. Thus, as colonial/state governments jealously held to their prerogatives, little public outcry was heard for the widening of local powers. What impetus did exist for the award of some responsibilities to the local governmental level was more likely than not to have been inspired by colonial/state wishes to be rid of onerous local services. In recent times, it is instructive to notice that the 1971 defeat of the Alberta Social Credit government was partially due to urban voter resentment over the provincial government's *reduction* in local governmental authority. An equally strong reaction would be unlikely among Australians. There were no general and intense outcries over the emasculation of sacrosanct local government when, in 1967, claiming that the city had been run inefficiently, New South Wales dismissed the entire Sydney city council, and proceeded to reduce the size of the city of Sydney's political boundaries. In the 1930's and 1940's there was some shifting of responsibilities away from Canadian local institutions to the provinces, especially in health and welfare services, largely because of local financial distress. In 1967, New Brunswick embarked on a thorough overhaul of provincial-local government responsibilities and relations. The result was a transfer of more responsibility to the province itself. Under the old order, local government powers, which had been considerable, had brought about inefficiency and a decline in the standard of services. The point is that there have been meaningful powers for Canadian local bodies to wield, or to forgo, if they wished, but much less so in Australia.

Canadian local institutions hold jurisdictional privileges in such fields as police and education, but Australian bodies do not. Australian local bodies, in general contrast to the situation in North

America, are pretty much confined to such functions as food inspection, refuse disposal, the maintenance of city roads, libraries, and recreational facilities, sewerage and water supplies, and a few public health services. Australian housing commissions are state rather than locally constituted, and there is very little record of house construction by cities themselves. Of the principal Australian cities, only Brisbane has been granted general rather than specific powers, but the exercise of these powers is subject to the approval of the Queensland government. Expectedly, Australia has not undergone the kind of expansion in municipal employees which has developed in postwar Canada. Between 1946 and 1966, Canadian municipal employees rose from 56,000 to 224,000, almost reaching the numbers then employed by Ottawa, or by all the provincial governments combined.

The great majority of Australians and Canadians live in cities. Indeed, there are more people in Sydney alone than in all of rural Australia. Apart from differences in formal jurisdiction, the actual organization of local institutions in the two nations underscores the political weakness of Australian city government, and the relatively greater strength of Canada's cities. Among Australia's principal cities, only Brisbane operates under a unified form of local government. Elsewhere, there is a historical inheritance of small and ununified, or at least underunified, local government divisions. In 1966, for instance, Melbourne housed 43 local government units, and Sydney 35. Under such conditions, it is difficult to speak confidently of *a* "city government," or to expect much real authority and political muscle being exercised.

Although Canadian cities have not escaped fractionalization of political authority, such conditions have not been as pronounced as in Australia. Perhaps more importantly, a movement toward "greater metropolitan" political authorities is under way. The parent experiment was in Toronto. In 1953, thirteen municipalities federated into a "Metro Toronto"; in 1966, the number of constituent parts dropped to six. Essentially, the metro government covers overall planning and administration of the area, while the six member municipalities retain local, neighborhood responsibilities. Winnipeg's metro system began with constituent second tier governments, but these were eventually removed, leaving one centralized entity to govern greater Winnipeg. Some of the most interesting developments have been in Quebec. The province has undertaken local government reconstitution in earnest. With a peak of over 1100 separate municipalities, local government in the province had suffered from poor planning, widespread patronage, and simple incompetence. The Quebec government has prescribed new terms and salaries for local aldermen, has encouraged the standardization of tax rates, and above all has promoted reduction and consolidation among local governments. There is now a "Quebec [City] Urban Community," and a "Montreal Urban Community," both reflecting a form of two tier, metro-styled government. There is an assumption that the Canadian practice of pooling disparate municipalities under roof governments will promote efficiency and economies. There is also an intimation that the added strength and leverage which come from administrative consolidation may enhance the relative political bargaining position of Canada's cities.

Throughout Canadian and Australian urban centers, party politics have generally been subdued and even ineffectual. This has limited machine politics, and the sort of spokesmanship and pervasive political brokerage that have been found among American cities. Political weakness in Australian urban governments can be ascribed to the jurisdictional frailty and organizational fragmentation of city governments. Also, in a homogeneous and rapidly enfranchised society, politics in the Tammany style have lacked fertile soil. Since most Australian lord mayors carry more titular status than actual power, have little to "govern" over, and often are not even popularly elected, a magnetizing figure for party politics, or for the spoils of office is missing. Furthermore, perhaps because Australia is so heavily governed and compulsory voting is common, the usual practice of noncompulsory voting in local elections results in extremely low voter turnouts (30 per cent in Sydney in 1971), and an attendant public casualness about local politics generally. In Canada, the weakness of party politics in city government may have been contributed to by the survival of restricted franchise provisions. Also, the middle class, somewhat deferential aspects of Canadian culture have probably contributed to an acceptance of professionalism over partisanship, while the absence of a "corrupt" period in city politics—despite a few cases to the contrary—failed to generate a popular reformist movement. Relative apoliticism in urban Canada, at least in the country's west, may also have root in the early extension of mutual self-help notions inspired in an agrarian, frontier society.

Although it is the ALP and the CCF/NDP, among the major national political parties, which have made the strongest bids in city politics, even they have not been consistently involved, and their performance has often been less than eventful. For instance, the CCF/NDP has been out of Vancouver city politics since the 1930's. The NDP entered the 1971 Winnipeg election. It had been thrust into an active municipal role by a left faction of the party. The provincial NDP government remained aloof, and the party's municipal candidates fared very poorly. The ALP controlled Sydney's city council for twenty years after World War II. The party took relatively little interest in developing the city, and in most respects its record while in office was innocuous. Labor has governed Brisbane for some years. Its style of politics has been reminiscent of old line party politics, but its publicized achievements—such as extensions of sewerage and beautification of the city's center—can hardly be regarded as exceptional, distinctively Labor-inspired contributions.

Apart from the ALP and the CCF/NDP, city political movements in Australia and Canada have normally been collections of "civic" or "reform" groups. In Canada especially, these "semipartisan" groups have often enrolled supporters of both Liberal and Conservative persuasion. In the 1969 Toronto mayorality campaign, there was no Conservative candidate as such, and the Liberal candidate ran third. In Montreal, the highly successful Civic party functions with the tacit support of the Liberals, but is not an extension of the Liberal party as such. In Australia, the urban civic party movements have often been dominated by persons Liberal in their state and national allegiance, but have not operated simply as local emanations of the Liberal party organization. The entry of the Political Action Front (FRAP) into the 1970 Montreal city election was something of a novelty in urban politics by the standards of either nation. FRAP was a coalition of various citizens' groups interested in specialized causes such as housing and redevelopment, not a conventional "civic betterment" or left politics coalition. FRAP did, however, assume distinctively left-political overtones. It underwent accusation of extremism during the emotional period of FLQ activity in the city, and was crushed at the polls.

We have examined the standing of Canadian and Australian local government in terms of power, organization and political activity. Prior to attempting an overall assessment of local government contributions to the policy process, we will need perspective on local financing. In both countries, property taxes are the principal source of local revenue. All the same, the proportion of all governmental revenues raised by local authorities is decidedly higher in Canada than in Australia—about 19 per cent as opposed to 9 per cent. Canadian local government units are also rather more generously treated by their parent provinces than Australian local units are by their states, partially because of the heavier responsibilities borne by Canadian local government. Most of the state/provincial assistance extended to local bodies is for specific purposes, rather than as generally usable revenue. In principle, however, Canada's tax system allows more latitude for locally acquired revenue. Canadian provinces and their subordinate governmental units may impose excises, while in Australia only Canberra enjoys access to this taxation field. Hence, Quebec municipalities imposed sales taxes until 1964, at which time the province absorbed them and began to rebate a portion of them as unconditional grants to local governmental units.

Despite what appears to be a fiscal advantage for Canadian local bodies, local authorities in both systems have expressed their financial concerns in the strongest possible terms. Australian local authority indebtedness has been escalating at a devastating rate. Between 1950 and 1965, while Commonwealth indebtedness declined, state debts rose by 199 per cent, and local debts by 333 per cent. At the start of the 1970's, an estimated one of every three dollars received by local councils was being directed to service loan obligations. Over the period 1955–61, Canadian local units piled up debts of $2 billion. The cost of welfare services for Metro Toronto in 1971 was expected to reach $75 million, 50 per cent higher than in the preceding year and equal to Metro's total operating budget a decade earlier. In 1967, because of crushing costs and a decline in the standard of services offered, the local units in New Brunswick transferred a number of their substantive as well as financial responsibilities to the province. Four years later, Nova Scotia's municipalities petitioned their provincial government to assume funding of such basic functions as education, justice and welfare.

Despite the pressures felt by local authorities, the states and the provinces themselves—the natural sources of local financial assistance—have in both countries been severely pressed for funds, and have battered on federal government doors for larger allotments or opportunities to explore new channels of taxation. Recognition of state/provincial obligations to local, and especially urban, authorities has been a decided factor in the recent enlargement of federal concessions to the states and provinces. For instance, it was a factor which moved Canberra to reconstitute the formula governing petrol tax distribution between urban and non-urban road construction. The Canadian federal government has itself assumed a prominent role in assisting the nation's cities. This partially derives from its constitutional authority to become involved in particular "Local Works and Undertakings" by declaring them to be "for the general Advantage of Canada or for the Advantage of Two or more of the Provinces." Ottawa's activity also derives from an appreciation of the contribution of cities to national life, and of their fiscal requirements. In 1971, a Ministry of State for Urban Affairs was created in Ottawa. This is not a full-scale line department, since it lacks operational responsibilities as such, or a large store of funds at its personal disposal. Instead, it coordinates urban-related activities of the standard departments, and seeks to integrate federal and provincial ideas and funding in urban affairs. The actual funds brought into Canada's cities from federal sources have become impressive, certainly by the measure of Australia, where the federal authorities have had little direct association with local authorities. Moreover, a persuasive case can be made that Australian federal government priorities have reflected neglect of explicit urban needs. In 1968/69, for example, Canberra was estimated to have allotted about $20,000 for urban research, while the investment for tobacco industry research stood at $750,000. A large share of Ottawa's contribution has been aimed at urban housing and renewal, areas in which the federal government has become the principal donor. During the 1960's, Toronto alone received $352 million in federal money for urban renewal. Canadian local entities also benefit from other federal programs. In 1971, some $300 million was awarded to finance local-incentive programs, job-creating projects, and winter works. Apart from its social value, such funding has the effect of reducing local costs and strengthening the local tax base. Under regional improvement schemes, Ottawa has contributed to such local enterprises as historic site restoration in Quebec City and highway improvement in Hamilton, Ontario.

Overall, Canada's urban centers have performed more conspicuous roles than have their Australian counterparts. They have been more favorably placed in terms of responsibilities, organization, and revenue sources, and enjoy federal assistance which has no analog in Australia. Their sense of importance, and the participatory involvement of their citizens and voluntary associations, is being enhanced in ways other than through grants of money for basic projects. Ottawa now funds various civic-action groups, even those whose outlook conflicts with prevailing federal government opinion. There is federal money for fellowships and teaching grants to train specialists in local government administration, and Ottawa provides graduate fellowships in urban and regional studies, and subsidizes university research on urban affairs.

Australian urbanites, especially of middle-class backgrounds, have in the past several years begun to become seriously involved in various improvement causes, many of which relate to the ability and willingness of the cities, or the cities in concert with higher levels of government, to undertake planning and life-quality improvement projects. Most of the problems they and their allies in the political parties and in government positions face are at least partially structural. For example, except for Canberra and Brisbane, urban planning agencies are not entrusted with the actual spending of funds, and the result often is a lag in policy and a breakdown in authority. The postwar ALP federal government gave some encouragement to state urban planning. A Cumberland (Sydney area) council was formed in the 1940's for this purpose, and acquired a master plan. The Cumberland council was a kind of "parliament" or "metro" layer above the various independent councils. But the Liberal regime in Canberra failed to provide the necessary urban planning funds, the state Labor government in New South Wales was not a vigorous exponent of the idea, and the council was dissolved in 1963. In its place came the State Planning Authority, responsible to the New South Wales Minister of Local Government. Urban planning and environmental control in Australia's largest city are gaining momentum. The state and the city are cooperating on a major project to curb pollution on Sydney's famous beaches. In 1968, the State Planning Authority issued an outline plan for Sydney's development projected to the year 2000, and two years later the city itself appropriated $100,000—an admittedly slight sum by international standards—to develop a "strategic plan" for Sydney. Apart from an earlier and more modest endeavor in Perth, it was the first such broadly scaled project commissioned in Australia.

The fact remains that Australia spends a smaller proportion of rate (property tax) payer's money on planning than any other developed country. One summary, written in 1966, drew the depressing conclusion that

> Whatever may be said in favour of local councils in their role of housekeepers in their local areas, their performance in metropolitan planning and development in both Sydney and Melbourne has, on balance, been distinctively negative. It is difficult to see what contribution can be expected from local government as such, within the State Planning Authority, except as some kind of loyal opposition.*

In Australia and Canada, various recommendations have been sounded on behalf of upgrading the vitality and political role of the cities. In Canada, such recommendations build upon a number of existing precedents, while in Australia they emphasize the distance that still needs to be traversed. Ottawa's role in local affairs is not in dispute; there is a coordinating ministry, various programs, and considerable federal funding. The Australian Labor party, feeling that the states cannot or will not themselves render the necessary investments, has called for an Australian version of an urban affairs department. It has also proposed a far broader federal involvement in urban affairs. Constitutionally, such a role might not be as direct as applies in Canada, but even by indirection it could bring handsome payoff. For instance, Whitlam estimated that, one way or another, Canberra is able to regulate 90 per cent of housing

* Peter Harrison, "City Planning in Australia: What Went Wrong?" in John Wilkes, ed., *Australian Cities: Chaos or Planned Growth?* (Sydney, London, and Melbourne: Angus and Robertson for the Australian Institute of Political Science, 1966), p. 68.

finance, and astute policies could foster measurable town planning and housing improvements.

Both Australian and Canadian commentators are addressing themselves to problems of local authority involvement in decision-making which bears on the fortunes of the cities. Few pretend that such participation would be a panacea. Rather, they feel that contributions from those most directly affected—the cities and their populations—can only improve decisions, and that intergovernmental misunderstandings would be reduced. Especially in Australia, the rather moribund local governments and their citizen patrons, might become somewhat envigorated. The terms of the Canadian federal Water Act of 1970 suggest one level of cooperation. This is a federal measure to combat pollution. It envisages considerable federal-provincial coordination, and a cost-sharing plan. The legislation will depend upon agencies formed jointly by provinces and local bodies. There has also been some Canadian experience with local involvement in consultative roles. Representatives of municipalities have been included as advisers within province of Ontario delegations to federal-provincial constitutional conferences. In 1971, a committee representing the Canadian Federation of Mayors and Municipalities, and provincial local government associations, filed a brief which insisted on thorough consultations with local bodies in the course of federal and provincial programs affecting planning, building, and the governing of communities. In the same year, a PC study group urged the formation of a national urban council, with representatives from all three layers of government. The ALP's recipe for Australia is even more radical. It envisions an intimate, three-tier framework of consultation. It recommends local government representation on such key financial decision-making agencies as the Loan Council and the Australian Grants Commission, and even a new, national House of Representatives, an assembly of the dozen or so largest cities. Federally, the ALP, and the Canadian NDP as well, are now pledged to undertaking a fundamental reconstruction of local, and especially urban, government finance, despite the constitutional and political obstacles which such structural alterations portend.

Regional approaches to public policy formulation

Parallel to new approaches toward and ideas about local government is the theme of regionalism. As many in Canada and Australia see it, objectives of participation, efficiency, economy, and more respectable resource allocation can be better met if emphasis shifts away from conventional federal, state/provincial, and local government units. A real reconstruction of planning and investment functions can be undertaken at three levels—through the marking off of regions within a state or province, through interstate or interprovincial cooperation and/or amalgamation, and through national approaches to policy and investment on the basis of areas which cut across traditional state or provincial boundaries.

Intrastate/provincial regionalism has foundations in both countries, though to date the efforts have been rather tentative and experimental. A view is emerging that traditional and inelastic local government boundaries should, within a compatibly defined area, be remolded in the interest of efficient administration. On a small geographic scale, but embracing great numbers of people, this is what the metro arrangements in a number of Canadian cities were designed to achieve. In British Columbia, on the basis of local initiative, the government is encouraging regional groupings of various parts of the province, with responsibility being assumed by them for parks, environmental regulation, and so on. Regional and community planning in British Columbia is now consigned to districts by provincial statute. More ambitious is Ontario's regional master plan, not scheduled for completion at least until the close of the 1970's. Two regions have already been created, in Ottawa-Carleton, and in Niagara. They resemble Metro Toronto insofar as a higher governmental tier has been superimposed over existing local governmental units, but differ in that they incorporate a considerable rural-agricultural area. The Ontario regional plan has, however, had its share of critics from the beginning, and not just among entrenched local government units jealous of their prerogatives. After two years of its existence, there was an undercurrent of feeling that Ottawa-Carleton, the pilot region, had suffered setbacks, among them duplication of effort, high expense, administrative unwieldiness, and disgruntlement among the citizenry itself, especially in outlying, nonmetropolitan areas.

Decentralization as such has been another motive behind intrastate/provincial regionalization efforts. This has primarily been an Australian concern. The Australian capital cities overshadow the rural areas. There are few cities of even intermediate size in the interior of the states, and industry and residential settlement continue to gravitate toward the coastal capitals. The rural population is attached to its own interests and values, and in some respects resents the rule of the capitals, witness the "new states" movement. Four of the six states are territorially very large, and three of them are truly immense. Thus the outlying population is placed at a considerable geographical and even emotional distance from the capital cities where, in any event, there is a lengthy tradition of administrative centralization. On and off state efforts aimed at decentralization have generally miscarried. During the second World War, state premiers and the Labor government in Canberra agreed in principle on regional planning arrangements. Regions were marked off in some states, and regional committees were appointed. There were some accomplishments, particularly in the gathering of regional data. But, inexperienced at their work, the regional committees tended toward overambition and unrealism; state and even local government officials often kept their distance, fearful of depreciated power; postwar reconstruction activity overshadowed the regional experiment; once the Liberals assumed federal office, they reneged on their earlier promise of federal financial aid to the regionalization program. Following this brief experiment, regionalization lay dormant for some years; now there is momentum once again. The Labor party's platform promises special federal incentives for decentralization, and encouragement for literally scores of regional state assemblies, bodies which would enjoy more than purely research and advisory responsibilities. At the moment, federal Labor is out of office, and its programs cannot be put to the test. But Victoria has undertaken decentralization of planning in the education, public works and social welfare fields. In the 1971 New South Wales state electoral campaign all major parties stressed decentralization programs. The L-CP government was returned, and state cabinet formally announced plans for decentralizing New South Wales into nine regions. The project is a modest one, entailing the decentralization of state government departments and regional planning, and the formation of mixed advisory councils representing state and local government, industrial, and other spokesmen.

In Canada, regional cooperation has progressed beyond the borders of individual provinces. Here we are not simply speaking of the various cooperative measures outlined earlier. Essentially, we are dealing with the prospect of an actual union of the Canadian Maritimes. Their separate political traditions are among the oldest in all of Canada. Yet, Nova Scotia, New Brunswick, and Prince Edward Island have much in common, apart from physical propinquity. They are small, underdeveloped, and administratively and financially inefficient and overburdened. Per capita, there are two and a half times as many civil servants in the three provinces as there are in the rest of Canada. Prospects for union now seem more feasible than in memory. A Council of Maritime Premiers meets quarterly, and selected Maritime legislators belong to a standing, interprovincial, legislative committee. As we saw previously, all manners of functional pooling have been arranged. A 1970 opinion survey showed a surprising 64 per cent of the population in the three provinces approving of union, with only 25 per cent explicitly opposed. Francophone Maritimers are, however, relatively less enthusiastic about union than are Anglophones. New Brunswick is

40 per cent French, a ratio which would be cut back in an inclusive, Maritime province.

A final tangent of our subject lies in the application of regional criteria by federal governments for purposes of policy objective promotion. Ottawa has proceeded in this direction with considerable zeal, and Canberra hardly at all, apart from a general commitment toward fostering "northern development." Distinctive economic regions are more apparent in Canada than in Australia. Moreover, and perhaps more significantly, the level of living standards is more evenly distributed across Australia than Canada, spurring regionally defined Canadian remedies for regions beset by poverty, underdevelopment, structural economic frailty, and the like.

One indication of Ottawa's seriousness in attacking national economic problems on a regional basis has been the growth of machinery for program planning and execution. By the late 1960's, for instance, there was ARDA, the Area Development Agency, to promote incentives for industrial buildup in slow growth areas. There was FRED, the Fund for Rural Economic Development. There was the Atlantic Development Board, for planning economic development and distributing capital grants in the Atlantic region. In 1969, a federal Department of Regional Economic Expansion (DREE) was created, and a comprehensive Area Development Incentive Act was passed. For some purposes, entire provinces are defined within a regional program; at other times, portions of provinces. Programs are instituted only with the approval of the governments of the affected provinces, and in that respect the formal federal decision-making chain is preserved.

The scope and nature of Canada's regional improvement efforts have been impressive, though the actual effect has been more qualified. In less than three years after its foundation, DREE's budget nearly doubled, from \$219 million to \$407 million. A DREE staff of over 1500 was on hand in Ottawa and in the provinces, and there were more economists in its employment than were found in the entire province of New Brunswick. Where necessary, regional assistance programs are plotted over a period of years. Ottawa believes that lasting results require long-term investments, and that the provinces themselves must be able to foretell the extent of a federal role if they are to prepare complementary programs. In 1969, a fifteen-year program was arranged with Prince Edward Island. Much of the present rationale behind regional assistance thinking is that the programs mounted should construe "growth" and "development" in the widest possible terms, acknowledging the interdependence of town and country, agriculture and industry. To get at genuine "infrastructure" improvement, complete DREE funding can be provided for such normally local/provincial projects as water and sewerage systems, industrial parks, schools and roads, and community facilities.

Although DREE is well funded and well intentioned, Ottawa's regional development approach has not escaped criticism. In 1971, the Atlantic Provinces Economic Council, a private organization operating with provincial underwriting, complained of a lack of precise targets, of competition among the Maritime provinces for as much money as each could extract—causing excessive deference to DREE by the provinces—and of an excessive ministerial discretion within DREE which made the department overly susceptible to political manipulation.

Ottawa's regional approach, however imperfect, very amply illustrates our own broad analytic concern. Both in Canada and Australia, federalism has profoundly affected the nature and success of public policies. It has also directly contributed to shaping the process by which policies are initiated, bargained over, refined, and implemented. In both countries, a great deal of the stuff and process of policy is not perceivable from a reading of the written constitutions, or even from a perusal of court pronouncements. An extremely elaborate network of intergovernmental contact points has been established, some institutionalized and some not. Their operation, in the fullest sense of the word, has served a political brokerage function. This brokerage has been an important source of viability for the two federally constituted systems. It has also become a complementary form of politics, related to but not at all identical to the arena of political party and parliamentary intercourse. There has therefore been a significant increment to the widely diverse process of politics.

16

Systemic development and constitutional change

In a way, the de facto evolution of Canadian and Australian federal relations can be interpreted as demonstrating that necessity, as the mother of invention, has generated workable and adaptive methods of conflict resolution and overall systemic performance. Another view is that intergovernmental relations as now constituted, however necessary and in some respect desirable, cannot through informal tinkering clear away burdensome hurdles imposed by constitutions drafted generations ago, and by judicial review embellishments often formulated in politically rarefied atmospheres.

Constitutional perfection, like beauty, is found in the eye of the beholder. Different Canadian and Australian political parties and organized interests, at various stages of history, have held their own notions as to what if any constitutional reforms were required for the health of the polity. Our first concern lies in examining the extent to and means by which formal constitutional amendment has been an instrument for altering powers and procedures which bear on policy outputs. Secondly, we shall wish to assess some of the implications of the record of constitutional change for Canadian and Australian political life generally.

The two constitutional documents have not been subjected to

frequent amendment. Only five amendments have been appended to the Australian constitution, and some twenty to the BNA Act, exact identification of what has constituted genuine BNA Act "amendments" being open to argument. Additionally, only three of the Australian and the same number of Canadian constitutional alterations have explicitly redivided powers between federal and state/provincial authorities. Because of the amendment procedures followed, it is meaningful to ask how many constitutional amendment proposals have been defeated in Australia, but it is almost meaningless to raise the question with respect to Canada. In Australia, amendments require the concurrence of the two chambers of the federal Parliament, and ratification by public referendum, at which there must be popular majorities in over half of the states (four of six), and a nationwide majority. Of the proposals passed from Parliament to referendum, twenty-one have failed to meet the amending criteria. In Canada, formal amendment requires nothing, other than the formality of British concurrence on some aspects of the BNA Act, than the concurrence of both houses of the federal Parliament. There is no further check against which to measure a proposed amendment's success or failure although, as will presently be shown, many amendments are proceeded with only after an informal yet elaborate process of consultation and negotiation with provincial governments has been completed. Technically, therefore, apart from an instance when the Senate blocked an amendment sought by an incumbent government, there have been no Canadian constitutional amendment "failures." There have been instances when in fact a government has not proceeded with an amendment because provincial opposition was foreshadowed or plainly expressed, sometimes from many provinces, sometimes from only a few or even one. Thus the concept of constitutional amendment "failure" in Canada is most elusive, and no meaningful, arithmetic inventory of amendment fortunes can be drawn up.

In over 70 years of Australian experience, the realignment of constitutional power through constitutional amendment achieved the consolidation of borrowing activity under the aegis of the Loan Council, entitled the Commonwealth—under stipulated restrictions—to legislate in certain areas of social services, and strengthened Canberra's hand in dealing with Aborigines otherwise falling under state jurisdiction. The public has rejected various proposals calling for Commonwealth authority over commerce, industry, commodity marketing and social services. Some of the defeated amendment proposals were presented by Labor, and others by non-Labor governments.

There is no manageable way of sorting out and weighing the relative influence of factors responsible for the meager success of Australian constitutional amendments, apart from laying much of the responsibility on the doorstep of the stringencies imposed by the amending process itself. Beyond this mechanical factor lie tactical, political, and cultural factors whose relative importance has shifted over time and occasion. For instance, constitutional referendums have occasionally been presented in package form, with the result that unpopular measures have handicapped the passage of more popular ones. Some referendums have been staged in conjunction with federal elections. This has distracted public attention from the putative merits of the proposed amendments, or has meant that the competing parties have impregnated the amendment proposals with a strong partisan flavor, or both. Some proposed amendments have enjoyed the endorsement of both major party groups, but many have not. Even when no elections were at stake, the parties have employed referendum campaigns as, in effect, votes of confidence for themselves and their principles. A further complication has been that although one of the major federal parties may have supported an amendment, one or more of its sister state parties did not, thus crosspressuring the voter; his loyalty may have been equal to or greater to his state party than to the federal party of his choice. The inability of an Australian government to overcome partisan obstacles to amendment passage was underscored during the second World War. The incumbent ALP government wished for an increase in various Commonwealth powers in order to handle reconstruction problems. In a unique gesture of feeling out and assembling support for an informally arranged transfer of powers in 1942, it summoned federal parliamentary figures and state political leaders of both party groups to a conference. After much deliberation, an almost unanimously satisfactory compromise was achieved. Then came a change of heart in some states, problems with refractory legislative councils, and an about turn by the federal parliamentary opposition itself. The Labor government then felt it had no option but to go to the country with constitutional amendment proposals embodying what it had earlier sought informally. The referendum campaign was conducted on partisan lines, and the Labor proposals failed.

Australian political culture factors also seem to bear some responsibility for the poor record of amendment approval. The Australian habit of resentment toward unfettered authority would in this regard seem to be culpable. Although Australians expect their governments to "perform," their value system attunement has led them to prefer division and buffering within and among their political institutions. As recently as 1967, as we pointed out earlier, a seemingly innocuous constitutional amendment proposal to allow the enlargement of the House of Representatives without any increase in the Senate's size was defeated, despite its endorsement by the L-CP government and the ALP opposition. Some sense of avoiding "too many politicians," and preferring to insulate the Senate from any depreciation of its status as a parliamentary watchdog, appears to have flavored the vote. Coincidentally, it might be speculated that compulsion to vote at referendums, compounded by compulsion to vote at federal and state parliamentary elections, invites the referendum vote of disinterested, and possible perversely negative, people.

In a manner of speaking, it can be said that Canada's BNA

Act is amenable to amendment in one and one-half ways. The "one," straightforward, way is by the means already described. The "one-half" way actually has nothing to do with altering a single syllable of the BNA Act's language. It nonetheless has the potential, just as surely as if it were a formal amending method, to reshape and even to invert the entire course of the Canadian federal system. Its nature, and in particular its limitations as a viable tool for informal constitutional change, offer insights about the progress of the formal amending process itself.

Consistent with its strongly centralist spirit, the BNA Act empowered Ottawa to negate or "disallow" any provincial act within a year of its enactment. It also invested the federally appointed lieutenant governors, chief executive officers in the provinces, with power to set aside or to "reserve" provincial legislation for possible nullification by federal authorities. By the 1880's, it had become understood that lieutenant governors would employ reservations only upon Ottawa's own advice.

Disallowance and reservation were authorized in the BNA Act mostly to insure that general national interests would prevail when faced with incompatible provincial actions, and that minority, that is, cultural, rights would be sustained. In theory, however, there was—and is—no limitation on what can be disallowed or reserved, or for what reason. In this sense, when unsheathed, disallowance and reservation can be mighty weapons for emasculating provincial autonomy, and therefore the entire federal concept.

Over time, disallowance has been imposed against 112 measures, while of 70 provincial bills which have been reserved, only fourteen were allowed to come into effect. In a number of instances, offensive legislation was revised by the provinces to spare it from federal nullification. Disallowance and reservation were practiced quite freely in the nineteenth century, paralleling the early trend of judicial review which enriched federal authority. Even the Liberal Prime Minister Laurier, who in his time was on the decentralist side of politics, frequently resorted to disallowance, often directed at British Columbia's regulation of the status and employment of Asians. Disallowance and reservation began to fade in the twentieth century. The last instance of disallowance was in 1943, and of reservation in 1961, by a lieutenant governor of Saskatchewan who acted on his own authority. His action was repudiated by the Diefenbaker government in Ottawa. Reservation and disallowance have by now so much fallen into abeyance that they are very nearly dead issues.

The reasons for the discontinuation of disallowance and reservation reflect on the changing times, and on political realities. The early course of judicial review was reversed, and provincial rights acquired a hallowed constitutional stature. The original need for a firm, federal guiding hand in nation building expired. Provincial premiers and parties began to assert themselves forcefully opposite Ottawa. Federal manipulation of the federal system through disallowance and reservation then lost much of its *élan vital.* Shorn of much of its previously assumed power, Ottawa increasingly needed the solicitude and cooperation of the provinces, purposes to which the tightening of disallowance and reservation screws was counterproductive. Otherwise, as popular reforms such as franchise extension spread, reservation and disallowance fell into relative desuetude because they were essentially anachronistic, representing the power of an outside source to thwart the will of democratically elected provincial governments. Consensus now has it that if Ottawa believes a province to have acted imprudently, or even unconstitutionally, redress should be sought politically by the citizens of that province, or through judicial remedies.

The manner in which disallowance and reservation were applied during their closing period over the present century is in itself commentary on Canadian political realities. There was particular reluctance to apply these instruments against Ontario and Quebec, the two largest and most influential provinces, where electoral success is nearly a sine qua non for control of federal office.

Quebec's notorious padlock law was left standing by Ottawa, owing to that province's hypersensitivity about its dignity and autonomy. In any event, in 1935, at the federal election preceding the passage of the padlock law, the Liberals had taken 55 of Quebec's 65 seats, an investment well worth protecting. The law's demise, many years after its passage, was through constitutional invalidation by the Supreme Court. But in 1937, just months after the padlock law was inaugurated in Quebec, the Mackenzie King government in Ottawa came down very hard on a set of measures passed in Alberta. Some Alberta statutes were disallowed. Others were reserved and submitted to the Supreme Court on reference, where they were declared invalid for having trenched on federal prerogatives. The constitutionality of the Alberta statutes aside, it was politically not too difficult for Ottawa to cry out against them in moral indignation. The measures had been enacted by a new Social Credit government, derided by its detractors as a collection of funny-money cranks. Alberta was a modestly sized province, not approaching Ontario or Quebec. At all events, at the 1935 federal election, despite their victory nationwide, the Liberals had been massacred in Alberta, capturing only 21 per cent of the vote and but one of the province's seventeen seats; they had nowhere to go but up.

The record of disallowance and reservation is instructive for understanding the path of formal constitutional amendments to the BNA Act, pointing to the growth of provincial authority and political sensitivity. First, the decline of the application of these federal tools has coincided with a tendency on the part of Ottawa governments to limit amendments which would confer new powers on the federal authorities, and/or to avoid pre-empting provincial privileges in such areas. Privy Council decisions snipped off a great deal of what in the nineteenth century had been assumed to be federal prerogatives. But there has been only one substantive amendment, which in 1940 granted Ottawa authority over unemployment insurance, which has been explicitly used as a means for overcoming judicial opinion adverse to federal rights. A 1951 amendment, and a refining amendment in 1964, allowed Ottawa to enter the field of old-age insurance. However, not only was this to be a concurrent power shared with the provinces, but unlike the two concurrent powers engraved in the original BNA Act, this one gave precedence to existing or future provincial legislation in the field. These three, in fact, have been the only amendments which have clearly touched on a redistribution of jurisdictional authority. It can be argued that the emergence of an elaborate network of federal-provincial relations and agreements within the ambit of the existing constitution, together with a more flexible set of constitutional rulings by the Supreme Court, have rendered formal readjustment of power less vital. But these essentially are developments of the last quarter century or so, and anyway would not fully explain the absence of corrective amendments, apart from those pertaining to unemployment and old-age insurance, in the past several decades.

A corollary development in the Canadian amendment procedure, namely reliance upon the provinces for consultation and consent, also parallels the decline of disallowance and reservation. We are reminded that the BNA Act lays no obligation on Ottawa to follow any internal amendment procedure other than securing federal parliamentary approval. In the nineteenth century, although two amendments dealt with provincial representation in Parliament, the governments of the day did not bother with provincial consultation. A 1907 amendment, which revised the system of grants payable to provinces, was preceded by twenty years of intermittent federal-provincial consultation. The amendment's passage was not actually made conditional on provincial acceptance, though all provinces save British Columbia approved of it. In the years following, federal governments not only sought the advice of but in effect conferred a power of veto upon the provinces over those amendments which dealt with an adjustment of powers (1940, 1951, and 1964, plus a 1936 amendment which was defeated in the Senate after receiving provincial consent), and a 1960 amendment which covered the retirement ages of provincial judges. The federal-provincial amendment negotiations have by no means been routine, witness the three years of bargaining required before the 1940 unemployment insurance amendment was agreed upon intergovernmentally, and then passed to Parliament. Although the provincial consent which is sought for particular types of amendments has no formal basis, it has begun to assume the quality of a constitutional convention. Since Ottawa has delayed the submission of such amendments to Parliament until all provinces have been satisfied, constitutional amendment procedures in Canada have in actual practice become at least as difficult if not more so than in Australia.

Despite the various informal means that have been devised to manipulate powers and finances among federal and provincial authorities, sentiment for a thorough overhaul of the BNA Act has been obvious for some time. One particularly anomalous feature has been the British Parliament's authority to approve amendments to the BNA Act. Naturally enough, the British Parliament has for a great many years rubber stamped Canadian constitutional amendments. In 1949 the BNA Act was amended so as to remove all but the integral provincial and cultural protection clauses from future British consideration should amendment be undertaken by Canada. The underlying reason for excluding these clauses, and therefore for perpetuating the anomaly, was that Quebec, ever fearful of its autonomy, believed that should Ottawa try to force a distasteful amendment upon it, there at least was the outside possibility that the British Parliament could be appealed to, and persuaded to interpose itself.

Although British review of Canadian amendments is no longer desired by Quebec, the removal of this residual British authority has not in and of itself been sought by Canada. Rather, since the early 1960's, there has been a nationwide debate over revamping the entire constitution, with the removal of a British role in amendments assumed. These deliberations illuminate contemporary Canadian political life, both in the kinds of new constitutional provisions which have been adumbrated, and in the manner in which the dialogue itself has been conducted.

There have been two major efforts aimed at constructing a new Canadian constitution. The first effort began in 1960, during the Diefenbaker administration. Exhaustive federal-provincial discussions were put in train, first under a Conservative and then under its successor Liberal government. Four years were required to hammer out a draft mutually acceptable to Ottawa and the premiers. The draft constitution was then submitted to each of the provincial legislatures. Nine approved. In 1965, Diefenbaker, now out of office, had second thoughts about a constitution which his own government had earlier helped to shape, and he campaigned against it. Shortly thereafter, Premier Jean Lesage of Quebec withdrew his own earlier approval, and the entire constitutional plan was stillborn; it never reached the federal Parliament for formal amending action of the BNA Act. In 1968, the Trudeau administration launched another countrywide effort for an acceptable constitution. The federal-provincial conference which met that year organized itself into eight committees to study facets of a new constitution. In 1971, after considerable patching and revising, and seven federal-provincial conferences devoted to the subject, a fresh constitutional draft was presented to the premiers assembled in Victoria, British Columbia. Trudeau said that the bargaining was over; now the provinces had to reply, yes or no. The first returns were favorable. Then Premier Robert Bourassa of Quebec said "no," and the plan was dead for the foreseeable future. Canada's constitution remains the BNA Act of 1867, as amended, and significant amendments still must pass the ritual of British consent.

Although all provinces except Quebec agreed to the 1964 constitutional draft, and all save Quebec were on their way toward approving the 1971 Victoria version, in many Canadian quarters, and especially in the west, there was no sense of heavy drama.

Some premiers felt that the immense investment of time and energy poured into the architectural perfection of a new constitution, while not exactly wasted, could have been diverted to other priorities. The BNA Act was thought to be reasonably workable, and some premiers wanted to hear more about how they were going to realize more dollars from Ottawa, or how Quebec's seemingly insatiable appetite for preferential treatment was going to be checked. The 1964 constitutional formula had been laced together through the efforts of first a PC and then a Liberal government, and more particularly by the PC and Liberal Justice ministers, E. Davey Fulton and Guy Favreau. When Diefenbaker switched his thinking, he did so because he had concluded that the draft endowed Quebec with the status of a virtual associate state. When Lesage vetoed the plan, he did so for opposite reasons. Nationalist sentiment in the province was strong, and hostile to anything but the most permissive kind of new constitution; Lesage claimed there was not enough in the Fulton-Favreau draft to guarantee Quebec's control over its own affairs. In 1970, in a gust of bravado, a Union Nationale government in Quebec insisted that if no satisfactory constitution were produced by 1974, the province would stage a referendum on Quebec's independence. Quebec Liberal Premier Bourassa's trademark was that of a sensitive Quebec nationalist who was also a committed federalist. Yet he vetoed the 1971 plan. With an eye on his hypernationalist critics, and harboring some personal reservations about the plan, he charged that Quebec would not be receiving enough jurisdictional discretion over social services, though the draft plainly gave the provinces more responsibilities in this area than they already held.

More than that was lost through the scuttling of the Victoria formula. The provinces were henceforth to have had a voice in appointing Supreme Court judges. Quebec civil law appeals would have passed to a special Supreme Court panel dominated by Quebec judges. The national equality of English and French was to have been constitutionally insured for the first time, and a comprehensive bill of rights was to form part of the constitution. The amendment procedure was to take into account Canada's regional and cultural plurality, and to formalize the established practice of provincial concurrence. Consequential amendments were to become formally dependent upon approval of a majority of the provinces, including both Ontario and Quebec, and at least two Atlantic provinces and at least two western provinces. In this way Quebec, officially, would have enjoyed a personal veto over all major constitutional alterations. Amendments relating to one or more, but not all, provinces could be adopted if the provinces in question plus Ottawa agreed. Hence, the amending process was made strict for matters of general concern, and highly elastic in matters of specific provincial concern.

The double shock of the failure of the Fulton-Favreau and the Victoria formulas left its mark on Canadian opinion. Feeling spread that, despite the very wide areas of constitutional change to which even Quebec had submitted, root and branch constitutional reform was unattainable. On the other hand, with formal constitutional reconstruction now out of sight, some felt that perhaps fresh incentive now existed for further embellishment of give and take procedures and programs between Ottawa and the provinces.

Reaction in portions of English Canada to Quebec's repudiation of the 1971 formula was a mixture of sadness and anger. During eight of the eleven preceding years there had been interminable discussions and compromises among ten provincial governments and Ottawa to evolve a suitable constitutional package. English-speaking provinces had been lectured many times that their responsibilities to Canada included patience toward and accommodation with Quebec, which was changing socioeconomically, yet remained persistently nationalistic. Now it was Quebec that had ruined all the labor. Was it a case of hubris on Quebec's part? The evergreen question of "What does Quebec want?" was revived. English Canada pondered whether a mutually supportive, bicultural partnership was really possible. Lesage and Bourassa, by contemporary

French Quebec standards, were moderate and reasonable men, hardly the bombers, kidnappers, and murderers in the style of the FLQ, or prone to threaten secession referendums in the manner of the Union Nationale. But if English Canada could not do sensible business with them, then with whom? In other words, the failure of constitutional reform struck many as a bitter example of the gulf which had cut into Canadian politics and society. For some Canadians, it could all be summed up in the phrase "to hell with Quebec." For others, disappointed as they were, the 1971 failure was a signal to resume the work of getting on with the French, with or without a flossy new constitution. Too much—the very essence of Canadian unity itself—was at stake to tell Quebec that English Canada was fed up. This sentiment stressed the very extensive areas of agreement now apparent between Quebec and the English provinces, and pointed to how far, in province after province, by deed as well as by word, a recognition of the French fact had occurred.

The record of constitutional amendment in Canada and Australia is more than a record of what powers or procedures have been shifted about from time to time. It is also a telling illustration of how political styles, party life, understandings of the role of government, and cultural traits merge at one tier of the policy process. For instance, issues of constitutional amendment in Australia have largely been occupied with partisan political conflict—Labor against non-Labor—while ramifications of national unity have hardly appeared. The reverse has occurred in Canada, where national cultural unity and provincial assertiveness—not only in Quebec—have overshadowed party politics in a system where party politics are more diffused, the resemblance between a national party and its nominal provincial counterparts is tenuous, and public voting behavior lacks secure anchorage.

Many persons in both nations are disappointed that their particular preference for constitutional realignment has not been fulfilled. The ALP would prescribe more emphatic powers for Canberra, while most Quebeckers prescribe more autonomy for their province. All the same, an argument can be offered that the unamenability of the Australian and Canadian constitutions to swift and easy amendment may actually have steadied the political climate in both countries. For one, it may have contributed to a spirit of political incrementalism. Second, it may have encouraged, even demanded, a fair amount of tinkering in federal-state/provincial relations. Not all of this tinkering has by any means met the highest standards of efficiency, economy, or even political respect. But it has given each political system a reasonably workable dynamic of its own, and capable of being altered as time and circumstances might dictate. In both countries, there have been historically distinct phases when, for instance, the federal government or the states/provinces seemed dominant. Rushing into print with a new set of constitutional provisions during any particular phase might in retrospect have proved unnecessary, or overbinding, for future use. The inability of the two constitutions to undergo rapid formal change, and in particular to reverse judicial rulings which have tended to narrow federal jurisdiction, may very well have instilled a certain evenness into Australian and Canadian politics. It is not necessary to engage in normative judgments as to what is best for Australia and its people to concede that the difficulties inherent in overturning through amendment the High Court's prohibitions against federal nationalization schemes have tempered the Labor party. Some in the party would still prefer to nationalize the banks, or whatnot. Realizing that the High Court has demurred, appreciating the obstacles facing the enactment of corrective constitutional amendments, they have withdrawn such programmatic demands from the political marketplace. In so doing, the ALP has itself become more "tame," and more preoccupied with seeking feasible alternatives to government ownership, and has largely removed a divisive issue from the nation's politics. In Canada, neither ardent centralists nor ardent decentralists have been able to edit the constitution to their liking. Out of the endless, often exasperating, pushing and pulling inherent in Canadian federalism and in relations between the founding cultures has come an accommodation. To some, it simply is an accommodation which divides Canada least. True or not, it has kept a sprawling and diverse country together, secessionist slogans notwithstanding.

The Australian and Canadian constitutions, and the judicial readings given them, have had an indisputable effect on political life. Their actual operation, however, is result as well as cause of a multitude of systemic variables. The thrust of this book has been an exploration of how and why such constraints have shaped the political process in Canada and Australia, and in turn have affected these systems' capacity to react to and canalize the demands imposed upon them. For the author, the piecing together of these themes has been an absorbing task, and its own reward.

Select Bibliography

The following bibliography is designed to acquaint the reader with some of the sources through which further information may be pursued. No effort has been made at comprehensiveness. With few exceptions, official materials, and materials prepared for official use, have been excluded. The reader is alerted to the titles of some scholarly and more popular journals, and to digests of information relevant to Canadian and Australian politics. The bulk of the bibliography is divided into four sections. The first section deals with general literature on Canadian and Australian politics, such as texts and broad collections of essays and readings. The remaining three sections are arranged according to the subject-matter divisions of the present book, although a number of the titles contain material applicable to more than one section. Within each section, the included titles have been chosen to reflect thematic coverage, sound scholarship or provocative argument, and recency of publication.

PERIODICAL LITERATURE: CANADA

Canadian Journal of Political Science (formerly *Canadian Journal of Economics and Political Science*
Journal of Canadian Studies
Canadian Public Administration

Queen's Quarterly
Canadian Forum
Quarterly of Canadian Studies
International Journal (foreign policy)
Maclean's (magazine)
Saturday Night (magazine)
Canadian Dimension (magazine)

PERIODICAL LITERATURE: AUSTRALIA

Australian Journal of Politics and History
Politics
Australian Quarterly
Public Administration
Current Affairs Bulletin
Australian Outlook (foreign policy)
World Review (foreign policy)
Bulletin (magazine)
Nation (magazine)
Dissent (magazine)

Summaries of political events are available on both countries. On Canada, see the *Canadian Annual Review* series, edited by John T. Saywell and published by the University of Toronto Press. Canadian foreign policy developments are summarized in *International Canada,* compiled by the Canadian Institute of International Affairs, and in the External Affairs Department's publication *International Perspectives.* Reviews of Australian domestic politics and foreign policy appear in the *Australian Journal of Politics and History* and in the *Australian Quarterly.* Data on a variety of Australian subjects are available in *Australia in Facts and Figures,* prepared by the Department of the Interior, and on foreign affairs in *Current Notes on International Affairs,* prepared by the Department of Foreign Affairs. Canadian and Australian developments are regularly reviewed in the quarterly *Round Table* (London). A great wealth of factual material on political and other subjects is included in the annual *Canada Year Book* and in the *Year Book of the Commonwealth of Australia.* Survey research data are collected and published periodically by commercial organizations in both countries. These include the *Canadian Gallup Polls* (Canadian Institute of Public Opinion), the *Australian Gallup Polls* (Roy Morgan Research Centre), and the *Australian Nation-wide Opinion Polls.*

CANADIAN AND AUSTRALIAN POLITICS—GENERAL STUDIES

Canada

Dawson, R. MacGregor. *The Government of Canada* (Toronto: University of Toronto Press, 5th ed., revised by Norman Ward, 1970).

Fox, Paul, ed. *Politics: Canada. Culture and Process* (Toronto: McGraw-Hill, 3rd ed., 1970).

Kruhlak, Orest M., *et al,* eds. *The Canadian Political Process: A Reader* (Toronto: Holt, Rinehart and Winston, 1970).

Leach, Richard H., ed. *Contemporary Canada* (Durham: Duke University Press, 1967).

Lloyd, Trevor, and Jack McLeod, eds. *Agenda 1970: Proposals for a Creative Politics* (Toronto: University of Toronto Press, 1968).

Van Loon, Richard J., and Michael S. Whittington. *The Canadian Political System. Environment, Structure and Process* (Toronto: McGraw-Hill, 1971).

White, W. L., *et al. Introduction to Canadian Politics and Government* (Toronto: Holt, Rinehart and Winston, 1972).

Australia

Crisp, L. F. *Australian National Government* (Croydon, Vic.: Longmans, 1965 with 1967 corrections).

Davies, Alan F. *Australian Democracy. An Introduction to the Political System* (Croydon, Vic.: Longmans, 2nd ed., 1964, corrected 1966).

Hughes, Colin A., ed. *Readings in Australian Government* (St. Lucia, Qld.: University of Queensland Press, 1968).

Hughes, Colin A., and B. D. Graham. *A Handbook of Australian Government and Politics 1890–1964.* (Canberra: Australian National University Press, 1968).

Mayer, Henry, ed. *Australian Politics. A Second Reader* (Melbourne: Cheshire, 1969).

Miller, J. D. B., and Brian Jinks. *Australian Government and Politics* (London: Duckworth, 4th ed., 1971).

Preston, Richard A., ed. *Contemporary Australia* (Durham: Duke University Press, 1969).

Sawer, Geoffrey. *Australian Government Today* (Melbourne: Melbourne University Press, 10th ed., 1970).

SECTION 1. SOCIETAL CONDITIONS AND PUBLIC VALUES

Canada

Blishen, Bernard R., *et al,* eds. *Canadian Society. Sociological Perspectives* (Toronto: Macmillan, 3rd ed., 1968).

Boydell, Craig L., *et al,* eds. *Critical Issues in Canadian Society* (Toronto: Holt, Rinehart and Winston, 1971).

Canada. *Report of the Royal Commission on the Status of Women in Canada* (Ottawa: Information Canada, 1970).

Cardinal, Harold. *The Unjust Society* (Edmonton: Hurtig, 1969).

Clark, S. D. *The Developing Canadian Community* (Toronto: University of Toronto Press, 2nd ed., 1968).

Cook, Ramsey, ed. *French-Canadian Nationalism. An Anthology.* (Toronto: Macmillan, 1969).

Cook, Ramsey. *The Maple Leaf Forever. Essays on Nationalism and Politics in Canada* (Toronto: Macmillan, 1971).

Gallagher, James E., and Ronald D. Lambert, eds. *Social Process and Institution: The Canadian Case* (Toronto: Holt, Rinehart and Winston, 1971).

Godfrey, Dave, and Mel Watkins, eds. *Gordon to Watkins to You* (Toronto: New Press, 1970).

Grant, George. *Lament for a Nation. The Defeat of Canadian Nationalism* (Toronto: McClelland and Stewart, 1965).

Kilbourn, William, ed. *Religion in Canada. The Spiritual Development of a Nation* (Toronto: McClelland and Stewart, 1968).

Lieberson, Stanley. *Language and Ethnic Relations in Canada* (New York: Wiley, 1970).

Lumsden, Ian, ed. *Close the 49th Parallel Etc. The Americanization of Canada* (Toronto: University of Toronto Press, 1970).

Mann, William E. *Poverty and Social Problems in Canada* (Vancouver: Copp Clark, 1970).

Officer, Lawrence H., and Lawrence B. Smith, eds. *Canadian Economic Problems and Policies* (Toronto: McGraw-Hill, 1970).

Porter, John. *The Vertical Mosaic. An Analysis of Social Class and Power in Canada* (Toronto: University of Toronto Press, 1965).

Rioux, Marcel. *Quebec in Question,* trans. James Boake (Toronto: James Lewis and Samuel, 1971).

Russell, Peter, ed. *Nationalism in Canada* (Toronto: McGraw-Hill, 1966).

Schmeiser, D. A. *Civil Liberties in Canada* (London: Oxford University Press, 1964).

Schwartz, Mildred A. *Public Opinion and Canadian Identity* (Berkeley: University of California Press, 1967).

Wade, Mason, ed. *Regionalism in the Canadian Community 1867–1967* (Toronto: University of Toronto Press, 1969).

Wilson, J. Donald, *et al,* eds. *Canadian Education: A History* (Scarborough, Ont.: Prentice-Hall, 1970).

Winks, Robin W. *The Blacks in Canada: A History* (New Haven: Yale University Press, 1971).

Woodcock, George. *Canada and the Canadians* (Harrisburg, Pa.: Stackpole, 1970).

Australia

Anonymous. *Anatomy of Australia* (Melbourne: Sun Books, 1968).

Campbell, Enid, and Harry Whitmore. *Freedom in Australia* (Sydney: Sydney University Press, 1966).

Coleman, Peter, ed. *Australian Civilization* (Melbourne: Cheshire, 1962).

Davies, A. F., and S. Encel. *Australian Society. A Sociological Introduction* (Melbourne: Cheshire, 2nd ed., 1970).

Encel, S. *Equality and Authority. A Study of Class, Status and Power in Australia* (Melbourne: Cheshire, 1970).

Fensham, Peter, J., ed. *Rights and Inequality in Australian Education* (Melbourne: Cheshire, 1970).

Horne, Donald. *The Next Australia* (Sydney: Angus and Robertson, 1970).

Jupp, James. *Arrivals and Departures* (Melbourne: Cheshire-Lansdowne, 1966).

Karmel, P. H., and Maureen Brunt. *The Structure of the Australian Economy* (Melbourne: Cheshire, 3rd ed., 1966).

McGregor, Craig. *Profile of Australia* (Chicago: Regnery, 1967).

MacKenzie, Norman. *Women in Australia* (Melbourne: Cheshire, 1962).

McQueen, Humphrey. *A New Britannia. An Argument Concerning the Social Origins of Australian Radicalism and Nationalism* (Ringwood, Vic.: Penguin Books, 1970).

Masterman, G. G., ed. *Poverty in Australia* (Sydney: Angus and Robertson, 1969).

Mol, Hans. *Religion in Australia. A Sociological Investigation* (Melbourne: Nelson, 1971).

O'Farrell, Patrick. *The Catholic Church in Australia. A Short History: 1788–1967* (Melbourne: Nelson, 1968).

Palfreeman, A. C. *The Administration of the White Australia Policy* (Melbourne: Melbourne University Press, 1967).

Partridge, P. H. *Society, Schools and Progress in Australia* (London: Pergamon Press, 1968).

Rowley, Charles D. *Aboriginal Policy and Practice,* 3 Vols. (Canberra: Australian National University Press, 1970 and 1971).

Sawer, Geoffrey. *The Australian and the Law* (Ringwood, Vic.: Penguin Books, 1968).

Ward, Russell. *The Australian Legend* (Melbourne: Oxford University Press, 1958).

Wilkes, John, ed. *How Many Australians? Immigration and Growth* (Sydney: Angus and Robertson, 1971).

SECTION 2. THE MILIEU OF ORGANIZED POLITICS

Canada

Allen, Richard. *The Social Passion. Religion and Social Reform in Canada 1914–28* (Toronto: University of Toronto Press, 1971).

Beck, J. Murray. *Pendulum of Power: Canada's Federal Elections* (Scarborough, Ont.: Prentice-Hall, 1968).

Blishen, Bernard R. *Doctors and Doctrines: The Ideology of Medical Care in Canada* (Toronto: University of Toronto Press, 1969).

Brown, Craig, ed. *Minorities, Schools, and Politics* (Toronto: University of Toronto Press, 1969).

Courtney, John C., ed. *Voting in Canada* (Scarborough, Ont.: Prentice-Hall, 1967).

Engelmann, Frederick C., and Mildred A. Schwartz. *Political Parties and the Canadian Social Structure* (Scarborough, Ont.: Prentice-Hall, 1967).

Hockin, Thomas A. *Apex of Power: The Prime Minister and Political Leadership in Canada* (Scarborough, Ont.: Prentice-Hall, 1971).

Horowitz, Gad. *Canadian Labour in Politics* (Toronto: University of Toronto Press, 1968).

LeBlanc, Philip, and Arnold Edinborough, eds. *One Church. Two Nations?* (Don Mills, Ont.: Longmans, 1968).

Newman, Peter C. *The Distemper of Our Times. Canadian Politics in Transition: 1963–1968* (Toronto: McClelland and Stewart, 1968).

Pinard, Maurice. *The Rise of A Third Party. A Study in Crisis Politics* (Englewood Cliffs, N.J.: Prentice-Hall, 1971).

Qualter, Terence H. *The Election Process in Canada* (Toronto: McGraw-Hill, 1970).

Quinn, Herbert F. *The Union Nationale. A Study in Quebec Nationalism* (Toronto: University of Toronto Press, 1963).

Rea, K. J., and J. T. McLeod, eds. *Business and Government in Canada: Selected Readings* (Toronto: Methuen, 1969).

Regenstreif, Peter. *The Diefenbaker Interlude: Parties and Voting in Canada* (Don Mills, Ont.: Longmans, 1965).

Robin, Martin, ed. *Canadian Provincial Politics. The Party Systems of the Ten Provinces* (Scarborough, Ont.: Prentice-Hall, 1972).

Stewart, Walter. *Shrug. Trudeau in Power* (Toronto: New Press, 1971).

Taylor, Charles. *The Patterns of Politics* (Toronto: McClelland and Stewart, 1970).

Thorburn, Hugh G., ed. *Party Politics in Canada* (Toronto: Prentice-Hall, rev. ed., 1967).

Young, Walter D. *Democracy and Discontent. Progressivism, Socialism and Social Credit in the Canadian West* (Toronto: Ryerson, 1969).

Zakuta, Leo. *A Protest Movement Becalmed: A Study of Change in the C.C.F.* (Toronto: University of Toronto Press, 1969).

Australia

Albinski, Henry S. *Politics and Foreign Policy in Australia. The Impact of Vietnam and Conscription* (Durham: Duke University Press, 1970).

Davidson, Alastair. *The Communist Party of Australia. A Short History* (Stanford, Calif.: Hoover Institution Press, 1969).

Davies, Alan F. *Private Politics. A Study of Five Political Outlooks* (Melbourne: Melbourne University Press, 1966).

Ellis, Ulrich R. *A History of the Australian Country Party* (Melbourne: Melbourne University Press, 1963).

Jupp, James. *Australian Party Politics* (Melbourne: Melbourne University Press, 2nd. ed., 1968).

McFarlane, Bruce. *Economic Policy in Australia. The Case for Reform* (Melbourne: Cheshire, 1968).

Masterman, G. G., ed. *Big Business in Australia* (Sydney: Angus and Robertson, 1970).

Mathews, P. W. D., and G. W. Ford, eds. *Australian Trade Unions. Their Development, Structure and Horizons* (Melbourne: Sun Books, 1968).

May, A. L. *The Battle for the Banks* (Sydney: Sydney University Press, 1968).

Mayer, Henry, ed. *Catholics and the Free Society. An Australian Symposium* (Melbourne: Cheshire, 1961).

Murray, Robert. *The Split. Australian Labor in the Fifties* (Melbourne: Cheshire, 1970).

Overacker, Louise. *Australian Parties in a Changing Society 1945–67* (Melbourne: Cheshire, 1968).

Rawson, D. W. *Labor in Vain?* (Melbourne: Longmans, 1966).

Reid, Alan. *The Gorton Experiment* (Sydney: Shakespeare Head Press, 1971).

Reid, Alan. *The Power Struggle* (Sydney: Shakespeare Head Press, 1969).

Rorke, John, ed. *Politics at State Level—Australia* (Sydney: Department of Adult Education, University of Sydney, 1970).

Truman, Tom. *Catholic Action and Politics* (London: Merlin Press, 1960).

Webb, Leicester. *Communism and Democracy in Australia* (Melbourne: Cheshire, 1954).

West, Katherine. *Power in the Liberal Party. A Study in Australian Politics* (Melbourne: Cheshire, 1965).

SECTION 3. THE SOURCES AND PROCESSES OF PUBLIC POLICY

Canada

Cheffins, Ronald I. *The Constitutional Process in Canada* (Toronto: McGraw-Hill, 1969).

Cole, Taylor. *The Canadian Bureaucracy and Federalism, 1947–65* (Denver: Monograph Series in World Affairs, University of Denver, 1966).

Dawson, William F. *Procedure in the House of Commons* (Toronto: University of Toronto Press, 1962).

Doern, G. Bruce, and Peter Aucoin, eds. *The Structures of Policy-Making in Canada* (Toronto: Macmillan, 1971).

Feldman, Lionel D., and Michael D. Goldrick, eds. *Politics and Government of Urban Canada: Selected Readings* (Toronto: Methuen, 1969).

Gibson, Frederick W., ed. *Cabinet Formation and Bicultural Relations. Seven Case Studies* (Ottawa: Information Canada, Studies of the Royal Commission on Bilingualism and Biculturalism, no. 6, 1970).

Hoffman, David, and Norman Ward. *Bilingualism and Biculturalism in the Canadian House of Commons* (Ottawa: Queen's Printer, Documents of the Royal Commission on Bilingualism and Biculturalism, no. 3, 1970).

Hopkins, E. Russell. *Confederation at the Crossroads: The Canadian Constitution* (Toronto: McClelland and Stewart, 1968).

Kernaghan, W. D. K., ed. *Bureaucracy in Canadian Government* (Toronto: Methuen, 1969).

Kornberg, Allan. *Canadian Legislative Behavior. A Study of the 25th Parliament* (New York: Holt, Rinehart and Winston, 1967).

Kunz, F. A. *The Modern Senate of Canada 1925–1963. A Re-Appraisal* (Toronto: University of Toronto Press, 1965).

Lederman, W. R., ed. *The Courts and the Canadian Constitution* (Toronto: McClelland and Stewart, 1964).

Meekison, J. Peter, ed. *Canadian Federalism: Myth or Reality* (Toronto, Methuen, 1968).

Simeon, Richard. *Federal-Provincial Diplomacy. The Making of Re-*

cent Policy in Canada (Toronto: University of Toronto Press, 1972).

Smiley, Donald V. *The Canadian Political Nationality* (Toronto: Methuen, 1967).

Strayer, Barry L. *Judicial Review of Legislation in Canada* (Toronto: University of Toronto Press, 1968).

Trudeau, Pierre Elliott. *Federalism and the French Canadians* (Toronto: Macmillan, 1968).

Vaughan, Frederick, *et al. Contemporary Issues in Canadian Politics* (Scarborough, Ont.: Prentice-Hall, 1970).

Ward, Norman. *The Canadian House of Commons: Representation* (Toronto: University of Toronto Press, 1963).

Ward, Norman. *The Public Purse: A Study in Canadian Democracy* (Toronto: University of Toronto Press, 1962).

Willms, A. M., and W. D. K. Kernaghan, eds. *Public Administration in Canada: Selected Readings* (Toronto: Methuen, 1968).

Australia

Caiden, Gerald E. *The Commonwealth Bureaucracy* (Melbourne: Melbourne University Press, 1967).

Davis, S. R., ed. *The Government of the Australian States* (London: Longmans, 1960).

Encel, S. *Cabinet Government in Australia* (Melbourne: Melbourne University Press, 1962).

Leach, Richard H. *Interstate Relations in Australia* (Lexington: University of Kentucky Press, 1965).

Mackerass, Malcolm. *The Australian Senate 1965–67: Who Held Control?* (Sydney: Australasian Political Studies Association Monograph Series, 1968).

Maxwell, James A. *Commonwealth-State Financial Relations in Australia* (Melbourne: Melbourne University Press, 1967).

Menzies, Robert Gordon. *Central Power in the Australian Commonwealth. An Examination of the Growth of Commonwealth Power in the Australian Federation* (Charlottesville, Va.: University Press of Virginia, 1967).

Neumann, Eddy. *The High Court of Australia: A Collective Portrait, 1903–1970* (Sydney: Department of Government and Public Administration Monograph Series, University of Sydney, 1971).

Odgers, J. R. *Australian Senate Practice* (Canberra: Government Printer, 3rd. ed., 1967).

Parker, R. S. *The People and the Constitution* (Sydney: Australian Institute of Political Science Monograph, n.d.).

St. John, Edward. *A Time to Speak* (Melbourne: Sun Books, 1969).

Sawer, Geoffrey. *Australian Federalism in the Courts* (Melbourne: Melbourne University Press, 1967).

Schaffer, B. B., and D. C. Corbett, eds. *Decisions. Case Studies in Australian Administration* (Melbourne: Cheshire, 1965).

Spann, R. N., ed. *Public Administration in Australia* (Sydney: NSW Government Printer, 3rd ed., 1969).

Stretton, Hugh. *Ideas for Australian Cities* (Adelaide: Published by the Author, 1970).

Turner, Ken. *House of Review* (Sydney: Sydney University Press, 1969).

Wilkes, John, ed. *Australian Cities: Chaos or Planned Growth?* (Sydney: Angus and Robertson, 1966).

Index